Food
&Man

Food
&Man

SECOND EDITION

MIRIAM E. LOWENBERG
Professor Emerita
The Pennsylvania State University

E. NEIGE TODHUNTER
Visiting Professor
Division of Nutrition, School of Medicine
Vanderbuilt University

EVA D. WILSON
Professor of Food and Nutrition
Ohio State University

TX
354
F66
1974

JANE R. SAVAGE
Associate Professor of Nutrition
University of Tennessee

JAMES L. LUBAWSKI
Assistant Professor of Marketing
Department of Business
University of Northern Iowa

JOHN WILEY & SONS
New York London Sydney Toronto

Library of Congress Cataloging in Publication Data:
Main entry under title:

Food and man.

    1. Food.   2. Nutrition.   I.   Lowenberg, Miriam
Elizabeth. [DNLM: 1. Food.   2. Nutrition.   QU145
F686   1974]
TX354.F66   1974   641.1   73-15800
ISBN 0-471-54961-4

Printed in the United States of America

10 9 8 7 6 5 4 3

To all who share our thoughtful concern
for the importance of nutrition,
be they students, fellow staffmembers,
or friends, here and abroad,
this book is dedicated.

Preface

General courses in foods and nutrition now are offered in many universities and colleges to meet the needs of students in home economics as well as those in other areas of study. Such a general course may be the only course in foods and nutrition taken by students whose undergraduate major is in another specialty in home economics.

It is my opinion that the primary purpose of such courses should be to awaken the student's interest to the importance of food and human nutrition in his or her personal life as well as in the affairs of communities and nations. Once this interest is awakened, he or she may want to take courses in basic foods and nutrition, which this book makes no attempt to be. (See Appendix I for a list of books on basic foods and nutrition.) If this book stimulates the reader to begin to understand the vital importance of food and nutrition to everyone on earth, it will have fulfilled its purpose.

The topics covered in this text were chosen because they relate to the following main concerns of this book:

1. Problems in nutrition such as hunger and malnutrition.
2. Solutions currently being tried or projected. These include those of some national, international, and voluntary agencies whose primary purpose is to relieve hunger and malnutrition. In these programs, nations and people can and are working together for mutual benefit.
3. The background of these problems. An understanding of this background can lead to more effective solutions. We need to understand food customs and the influence of culture and religion, among other things, on food habits and foodways. The understanding of consumer behavior and problems is unusually necessary at present.

4. The history of how man has fed himself, and the knowledge of man's endeavor to understand the nutritive needs of his body.

Because this book is intended to be used by the college student who has no previous background in the physical or chemical sciences, the concepts are stated simply. This has been deliberate. It is believed that a textbook such as this should have depth, but it should be interesting to read if a student is to be intrigued with this subject. The simplicity of a statement, I believe, has little relationship with how profound it is. The authors have been encouraged when teachers have reported that students like this text.

Human behavior is influenced when a new idea is accepted and tried by an individual. The concepts are generously illustrated to bring the idea within the realm of thinking of the student.

The level of the difficulty of the material with which the student comes into contact is controlled by the teacher. This book has been used successfully in this way for students at different levels in their educational preparation up to those who were doctoral candidates.

There are three entirely new chapters in this revised edition. These are substituted for the former chapters two, three, and eight. Included in this new edition are two chapters written by the senior author: Food Patterns, Origin and Development from the advent of Homo sapiens (wise man) on earth through the nineteenth century. The latter includes especially the following:

1. A discussion of man's use of fire to cook his food.
2. The change from food gathering to food producing.
3. The development of domestication and breeding of animals.
4. The food patterns of the Egyptians, Greeks, and Romans.
5. The changes during medieval times, especially an in-depth discussion of British food patterns.
6. The development of American food patterns from colonial days through the nineteenth century. This includes the patterns of American Indians of different sections of the U.S.
7. The history of three foods important in many countries: corn, potatoes, and bread.

For all of these backgrounds, the food patterns are discussed.

Food, Man, and the Influence of Business, written by a specialist in the field of marketing, has been added.

All chapters have been brought up to date with the inclusion of new material made available since 1967, when the first edition was written. One new section on the diet of the Seventh-day Adventists has been added to Chapter 5. Chapter 9 has been thoroughly revised and re-written to explain new programs and policies of the agencies included. See footnote, page 351, for further description of how this was done.

The appendices have been greatly enlarged with a list of films which have been recommended by the teachers who have used *Food and Man*. A new listing of addresses for sources of reference materials has been added also. The list of books for the use of students has been thoroughly revised and includes many new titles.

The glossary at the end of the book may be used to look up unfamiliar terms.

The authors wish to thank John Charnow, Dr. D. B. Jelliffee, Dr. Arnold Schaefer, Dr. Katherine Bain, Dr. Ruth Leverton, and Dr. Bertyln Bosley, Mrs. Andromache Sismanides, Mrs. Amy Pound, Mrs. Mary Callahan, as well as others at UNICEF, FAO, AID, WHO, and other agencies for materials and criticisms so graciously furnished. Many other people have made helpful suggestions. I wish to thank the many teachers who used the first edition of this book for their helpful criticisms and suggestions. Special thanks are extended to five people who have been very helpful in the preparation of this manuscript. Mrs. Abbie Dale spent untold hours assisting in library work and tracking down materials for both editions. Mrs. Terry Schaeffer, whose baccalaureate degree is in Anthropology, and Mrs. Nancy Ashford have been invaluable as excellent and interested typists and friends of the book. To Mrs. Bernadette Taylor and Mrs. Evelyn Wells special gratitude is offered for their careful editing and proofing of the entire manuscript.

The authors, however, assume full responsibility for the contents of this book.

Seattle, Washington   Miriam E. Lowenberg

Contents

APPENDICES

1

Food Patterns—
Origins and Development

FROM EARLY TIMES
THROUGH ROMAN TIMES

Introduction

As modern man learns the extent of the interdependence among disciplines, he acquires knowledge of early man more rapidly, and his understandings of early man become more valid. Interested and informed botanists, biologists, agriculturists, cereal chemists, and geologists now accompany archeologists and anthropologists.

German archeologists were said to be especially interested in architecture, and French archeologists in art. But there has generally been disdain for man's foremost need—food and drink—in spite of such assertions as "The food supply has been the most important factor in the evolution of human society" (Orr and Lubbock); "The history of the world has

1

been the story of a struggle for daily bread" (Prentice); and "To this day few know that the history of mankind is also an agrarian history" (Jacobs). This chapter is concerned with discussing man's development in relation to what he ate and how through past centuries he got his food.

Digging for facts about what earliest man ate is extremely difficult, fraught with potential mistakes, and often unrewarding. The wonder is not that we do not know for certain what early man ate, but that we know as much as we do. Man's curiosity and eternal search for facts is in no other recorded history more commendable.

Many have pointed out that what distinguishes man from other animals are his brain and his hands. He has no claws, powerful teeth, or hooves, no horns for fatally wounding animals or mighty muscles to grasp his prey or even to defend himself. "Man's compensation for his relatively poor bodily endowment has been his possession of a large and complex brain, forming the center of an extensive and delicate nervous system. These permit a great variety of movements, being adjusted exactly to the impulses received by the keen organs of sense" (Childe, 1951). Man's brain furnishes him with his eternal curiosity and compels him to search for knowledge as well as giving him the power to use his accumulated knowledge to better his condition. Using his brain, he has devised tools and developed a technology which makes him able to cause the earth to yield for him a plentiful food supply.

Man has also been said to be the only one of all the animals who invites his own kind of animals into his lair or his home to share his food.

This section of the book will discuss some of the landmarks in man's efforts to control his environment as he progressed in his efforts to produce his food abundantly and efficiently. No attempt will be made to substantiate or refute theories held by individual archeologists or anthropologists, because this is not the book's major purpose and does not lie within the authors' competencies. Nor can the few pages of a book follow all of the stages of food-getting through which man has passed. Hoebel and Brace, as well as other anthropologists, give excellent charts of the geologic eras for the reader who wishes this information. Remington, in telling of the difficulty of studying the food patterns of ancient man, said that the study and evaluation of the social factors which have influenced the diet of man leads us back "to the very dawn of history, concerning which we must indulge in a certain amount of speculation which is more or less repugnant to the modern scientist."

Before men left their records in written language, we have only paintings on walls; most of these were in dwelling caves, so they were protected and have been fairly well preserved. Perhaps more important than the paintings are the more widely scattered and more abundant "kitchen middens"—the heaps of food refuse left by early man. In Denmark, middens 100 yards long and 50 feet wide have been found. There are, of course, hazards from using these kitchen middens. First of all, only a few unbroken objects hard enough to stand the ravages of time are found. Wood, for instance, cannot long survive weather and time, and pieces large enough to identify the original object are not found frequently. Since not all of a man's possessions are ever found, one can only conjecture what part of the total was found. Man probably only discarded the undesirable or inedible parts of his food. It therefore is easy to understand how uncertain are attempts to learn what man ate more than 300,000 years ago. Kluckhohn said, "Not without justification has anthropology been termed 'the science of left overs.'"

From what animal did certain bones come, and how did the man who ate it treat it before he ate it? Some of the important remnants are cereal pollens and bits of charred cereal grains; in later times in Egypt, yeast cells from the bread-making process have been discovered. Or were the yeast cells ones that escaped in making fermented beverages?

Modern carbon dating now makes possible a fairly accurate estimate of the age of these leavings. Pollen thrown out from a plant as early as 14,000 B.C. has been found (Flannery), as have remnants in caves in greater Mesopotamia of potentially domesticated sheep and goats from as early as 40,000 B.C. Many authorities, however, give later dates for what has been termed the preagricultural period. These differences of dates for periods in man's history only serve to illustrate that much is yet to be learned as new finds provide further evidence. Before the newly learned facts are published, they may be superseded; the student must hold an open mind and constantly seek newer and probably more accurate information. In addition to studying records left in caves and kitchen middens, archeologists also have had for study the stomach contents of mummies and bodies found in bogs as well as coprolites— the remnants of human feces.

There is no single type of food which was used by primitive people everywhere, and the type of food consumed was related to climatic and geographic conditions. There are and always were more herbivorous people, the next most prevalent being the carnivore, followed by the omnivore (Davenport). People in the tropics are mostly herbivore.

Carnivore are usually nomadic and often live in colder climates. Omnivore in temperate zones have usually advanced technologically more rapidly. "Civilization cannot exist without food production, but food production must be very efficient before civilization can begin" (Jensen).

The Beginnings

Agricultural cultivation and domestication of animals may have taken place gradually from 40,000 to 10,000 B.C. (Flannery). The origin of agriculture was not due to a chance discovery, as the sprouting of seeds thrown away after a meal; man probably experimented and developed the pattern of raising food over many thousands of years (White). Evidence which tends to refute the theory of the shock stimulus of the origins of agriculture has been produced during the past several decades. Early man did not merely make a blind choice of food as much as he observed and performed experiments to gain knowledge so that he could control his environment. Adolph suggests that these changes did not happen because of the survival of the fittest, but that early man deserves credit for using his head. There are other arguments against blind choice, such as the widespread use of rice, with its high-quality cereal protein, as a staple.

Learning to use fire was undoubtedly one of the most important discoveries. Man has been distinguished from other animals based on his general preference for *cooked* food. Hazlett thought that this preference is a more important difference between man and other animals than even man's prehensile hands. William Howells (quoted by Brown, 1963) believes that there is less difference between Buckingham Palace and a cave where man used fire, than between a cave where its occupants used fire and one where they did not. Charles Lamb's essay "Dissertation upon a Roast Pig" is probably pure fancy, but it has charmed readers for generations.

Man is thought to have used fire and to have fashioned rude tools which helped him survive among the wild beasts at least 340,000 years ago. The first tools were made from bits of stone, bone, or wood slightly sharpened probably with flint-like flakes of stone. There is evidence that man even fashioned these tools to fit his hands. Archeologists must of course determine whether human workmanship is evidenced in a specific find or not. Childe (1951) reported that "In quite early Pleistocene times there were certainly men manufacturing unmistakable implements of stone and also controlling fire." He also said that conclusive evidence has been obtained from a cave near Pekin. There were found with the fossilized remains of Pekin Man crudely fashioned flakes of quartzite and other stones and bones which had been subjected to fire. The exact use of such tools can only be a matter of conjecture; were they used in cutting up the flesh of animals, scraping the hide, or what?

Use of Fire and Tools

According to Childe (1951), "The control of fire was presumably the first great step in man's emancipation from the bondage of his environment." Not only could man now cook his food, but the warmth of the embers made it possible for him to warm his caves and rock shelters so that he could move into cooler areas in deep caves and also into cooler climates, allowing him to search throughout a wider area for his food. He may also have learned to use fire to drive large animals to places where he had a greater chance to master them.

At first, man probably discovered combustibles which had been ignited by lightning or other natural means. These fires were then kept constantly alive and alight. The tending and preserving of these fires undoubtedly extended to the carefully maintained fires of later times. The Vestal Virgins tending the sacred fires of Rome were symbolically carrying out an ancient practice.

Later man learned to produce fire from the spark of a flintstone against iron pyrites or hematite or by friction of two pieces of wood. Primitive peoples in different parts of the world still use variations of these methods to produce fire. *Man had truly created when he produced fire, and he was also asserting his power over nature.* We are reminded that here it is essential not to confuse historic progress and organic evolution. Childe (1951) said that "An invention is not an accidental mutation of the germ plasm, but a new synthesis of the accumulated experience to which the inventor is heir by tradition only."

Early Man and Homo Sapiens

These early, pre-Pleistocene or Pleistocene men, according to Childe (1951), belonged to several distinct species and were not our evolutionary ancestors. Rather, they were side branches of the main stem from which Homo sapiens (wise man) descended. Hoebel placed the first appearances of what he chooses to call *Homo sapiens sapiens* (modern man) at the time of the upper Paleolithic Age, or around 35,000 B.C. He also said that this age took shape quite suddenly in Iraq, Afghanistan, Israel, Cyrenaica, and North Africa. He reported that some prehistorians place the actual origin of the upper Paleolithic Age complex in Asia Minor, "followed by rapid diffusion westward via migrating." He questions the reliability of these data, but he does think the *homid* remains of modern man are always found in these assemblies. He lists *Homo sapiens neanderthalenis* and *Homo sapiens steinheimensis* as predecessors of *Homo sapiens sapiens*. Homo sapiens sapiens can interbreed freely, which sets him apart from the others. It is also said that early members of the family of man had the power of speech, so that they could tell others what they had learned to do.

The human infant is born with skull bones that are comparatively soft and loosely joined together, so that the brain can increase in size as the infant grows. The infant, during his growing period, is wholly dependent upon his parents. Man does not seem to have inherited the instinctual abilities of other animals; from infancy, he must learn from experience. Because of their power of speech, parents can transmit to the child the results of efforts to control his environment, including how to get and use food. When human beings speak to each other, they can also progress by pooling what they have learned individually.

Shapiro said "With the end of the last glaciation, Europe—indeed other parts of the world as well—were inhabited by populations that must be classified as Homo sapiens and as far as we know by no others. Thus we can say that beginning around 30–40,000 years ago modern man took over completely . . . ." However, he says that it is not yet certain "that this was the first appearance of Homo sapiens." He pointed out that, since this time, the human *physical* body has not changed much but that "progress in culture has indeed taken the place of further organic evolution in the human family."

Ages

The early stages of the culture of the past are divided into the Stone Ages (Old, Middle, and New, or Neo, Meso, and Paleo); the Bronze Age; and the Iron Age. These Ages did not occur as absolute periods of time in all places; but in all localities, the several Ages did follow one another in the same order. Of course, the several ages did not begin and end simultaneously all over the world, as Childe (1951) has reminded us.

It is thought that Homo sapiens appeared near the end of the Old

Stone Age. The men of the Old Stone Age had to rely on hunting animals, fishing, gathering wild berries and shellfish, or digging roots and slugs. Some believe that the first man ate only plants, but this statement seems to need further authenticating.

How early man captured and caused huge animals to die would be a fascinating story if we could unravel all of the details and therefore know with any degree of certainty. Did he wound the animal once he had tools and had learned to throw them, as modern Bushmen do? Did he, like some modern primitive Malaysians, build traps and pits into which the animal would fall and lie helpless? Or did he drive them off a cliff? These animals were so much larger than the men who sought them as food that killing them must have caused a great effort on the part of man. When we watch modern television programs about animal preservation where men struggle with modern equipment to capture a live elephant or rhinoceros, we can admire even more the intelligence and skill of these early men. The stories of how our American Plains Indians captured and manipulated the huge bodies of the American bison in order to use their bodies for food, clothing, and shelter can help us in these conjectures.

These primitive men truly must have been ready to gorge themselves after this effort and probable previous starvation.

The Beginnings of Agriculture

At the close of the Ice Ages, during what has often been called the "Neolithic Revolution," man began to produce his food rather than to rely on gathering it. We will discuss these great changes from *food gathering to food producing*. It must be noted here that, as Childe (1951) pointed out, the climatic changes after the end of the last Ice Age were followed by changes in plant and wild animal life. For instance, in the temperate zone of Europe, forests invaded the large tracts of tundra and steppes. Further south, the forests withered from drought, and prairies gradually turned into deserts. At about this time, some great rivers such as the Nile, the Tigris, the Euphrates, and the Indus began to overflow their banks in an established pattern. When man began to adjust himself to the new conditions, there was the creation of what archeologists call the Mesolithic Cultures. Mesolithic man appears to have "camped" more regularly than Ice Age man, and then he began the slow mastery of his environment to feed himself.

The last millennia of the preagricultural areas were, according to

Vayda, a time of "settling in" to one's area; interchange of resources among groups was now undoubtedly important. Vayda also speculated that during this time man probably removed certain key species of wild grasses from the niches where they were indigenous and put them in niches more convenient to him but foreign to the grasses. The term *niche* is used here to designate a habitat supplying the factors necessary for the existence of the species. In so doing, man had allowed these grasses to develop differently than they had previously. Vayda said that happily both wheat and barley grew well in the new environment. Archeological remnants of these grasses lead to the speculation that, when man used primitive cutting devices, he naturally selected those stalks which held their seed heads most tightly.

Man may well have learned other things during these transition years. He may have learned that roasting the husk-encapsulated grains enabled him to remove the tough outer *glumes* more easily. This heating also killed the germ so that the grain could be stored without sprouting. Mutations and genetic changes undoubtedly took place to alter the character of both plants and animals during the development of agriculture and animal husbandry.

Just how it all happened has been the subject of numerous theories and conjecturing. Some have written that wild grain stored in caves sprouted, and early man saw these growing plants. Others have thought that man observed the growth of wild cereal grasses where the alluvial soil waters had receded after spring flooding. One charming story written for young children tells of women throwing cereal seeds on the ground to thank the gods for food and then observing the growth of a patch of cereal grasses when they returned to this spot the next spring. This story may well have been originally true and subsequently preserved in the folk lore of the people. Jensen said that "during the later Magdalenian period, plants begin to appear along with animals on the walls of the art caves, indicating perhaps the importance of plants in the food quest and the dawn of agriculture." He is referring to the Altamira caves in Eastern Spain and to man living in Southern Europe during the late Ice Age. Wissler said that, where plants and wild animals were abundant, men also congregated. Of importance is not choosing the most likely story but seeking continuously for the facts.

The FAO Nutritional Study Number 23 (Aykroyd and Doughty) stated that "Whatever the uncertainties, there are reasonable grounds for supposing that, in the so-called Fertile Crescent of Western Asia, the cultivation of wheat and other wild plants indigenous to the area began during the years 8000 to 6000 B.C. and perhaps earlier." They also say that "the domestication of sheep and goats, common wild species of the area, took place simultaneously. How cultivation was initiated cannot be precisely known." The fact that nomads returned year after year to the places where wild food plants grew abundantly probably caused them to locate their permanent settlements there.

Childe (1951) has used the word "revolution" in connection with the practice of peoples keeping animals, but Braidwood (1952) thought the word misleading. He believed that man lived in villages and had a settled type of economy before he raised an appreciable amount of his food.

Emergence of Near Eastern civilizations is dated from such archeological sites as Jarmo, 6700 B.C. Peacock and Kirsch called the period 7000–6000 B.C. "primitive." They said that during this era the most advanced societies had undergone what has been called the Neolithic Revolution, passing from hunting and gathering food to raising and breeding stock while remaining socioculturally primitive.

Some believe that Africa was the site of the origin of agriculture; others choose the Trans-Caspian Steppe, Iran, and Anatolia (an ancient name for Asia Minor), as well as other Near Eastern places. Braidwood (1953) said that, following discoveries after World War II, it can be positively asserted that "Civilization in its most useful sense of the word . . . had at least two independent beginnings. One of these was certainly centered in ancient Mesopotamia which thus took preference over Egypt. One was certainly centered in the New World." He uses the word civilization to mean "a culture with fully efficient food production, cities and urbanization, a formal political state, a new sense of moral order, formal projects and works, classes and hierarchies, writing, and momentuality in art."

Mesopotamia in the *Fertile Crescent* is regarded by most authorities as one of the first if not *the* first center for the development of cultivation of plants and breeding of animals. This Crescent is usually defined as an area which begins in a small portion in Northern Egypt and extends through Palestine, Syria, and Mesopotamia and eastward across the oasis and mountain slopes to the Indus River and the Punjab of India. It had four environmental zones from the standpoint of agriculture and grazing potential: (1) the alluvial plain of Mesopotamia proper; (2) the steppe land of Assyria; (3) the woodland belt of the Zangros mountains; and (4) the edge of the high central plateau of Iran.

Braidwood believed that the culture of Mesopotamia spread to Egypt, but he said that whether centers arose also in Indo-Malaysia and China is "still highly speculative." Jensen agreed that the cultures of Meso-potamia and Egypt were the first to arise from the primitive existence but thinks that the transition from primitive to civilized life happened more than once. Flannery said that Mesopotamia is probably one of the few areas where agriculture and animal husbandry seem to have origi-nated autonomously. Aykroyd and Doughty said that cultivated wheat had a position of importance in the simple and widespread village and semi-urban economy which developed between 7000 and 6000 B.C. over this extensive area of Western Asia.

Many archeologists agree that women were responsible for the first agriculture; the men hunted. Later, when oxen and plows were used, the men of the family began to cultivate the fields and the women stayed home to prepare food and perform the many household tasks.

When seeds were planted, primitive people regarded the earth as "the great mother." Around this idea and the prayers and religious rites for inducing fertility grew many practices. Women and fertility were, of course, associated; so they are associated today in the rites of many primitive people. It is also easily understood how, when the bodies of the dead were buried in the ground, men's prayers to their ancestors were for good crops.

Flannery held the idea of preagricultural use of cereal grains because cereal pollens dating back to 14,000 B.C. have been found in caves. He also said that the remnants of "potential animal domesticates" (sheep and goats) have been found in cave debris dating back to 40,000 B.C. He believed that "From 40,000 to 10,000 B.C. man worked out a pattern for exploiting the natural resources of this part of the world." He also supported the idea that "The cultivation of plants required no new facts or knowledge but was simply a new kind of relationship between man and the plants with which he was familiar."

It has been conjectured that Adam was a food gatherer before his fall in the Garden of Eden and that he became a food-producer after he fell from tasting the fruit of the tree of knowledge. Genesis (iii—18:19) is quoted in support of this assumption: "Thou shalt eat the herb of thy field; in the sweat of thy face shalt thou eat bread." The term "herb" is often

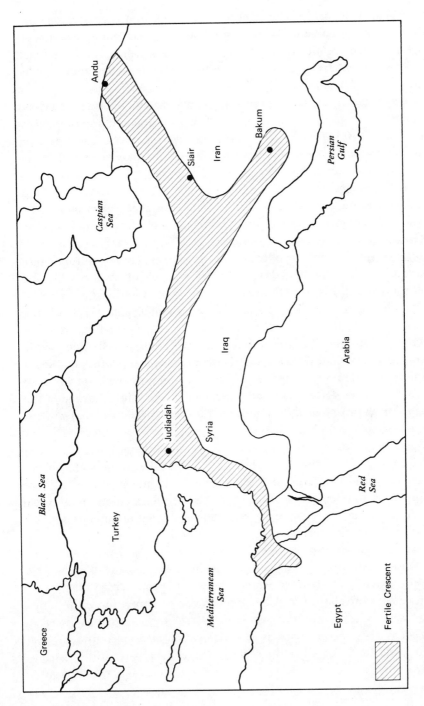

The fertile crescent.

used in ancient literature to refer to wild plants or grasses. It is said that the strife between Cain and Abel symbolizes the strife and jealousy between the food producers and the food gatherers. Cain was the producer, and his descendants are supposed to have been the ones who founded cities.

We are discussing these divergent points of view because we believe that this change in man's mode of getting his food was perhaps, *next to the use of fire in food getting and preparing, the most important occurrence in the development of man's food patterns.* Perhaps the word *revolution* is applicable in this light.

There is suggestive evidence that by 4000 B.C. specialization of occupations had begun and that regional-temple-market towns produced a symbiotic network of agriculturists who engaged in extensive irrigation. Here traders even dealt in obsidian, copper, salt, asphalt, fish, and regional fruits. Migration of those who engaged in garden culture would partially explain the rapid diffusion of this idea of cultivation, which has led some to call it a "revolution."

In what directions did the idea of food producing spread? Braidwood (1948) thought that these ideas were carried into Europe in two directions: (1) through Turkey and Greece into South Russia and up the Danube Valley; and (2) along North Africa or by the sea to Italy, Spain, France, and then on to Britain and north. Much evidence of the early introduction of agriculture and animal husbandry into Europe is furnished in the artifacts of the culture of the Lake Dwellers of Switzerland, whose records date back to 6000 B.C. These peoples are among the best known of any early village assemblages because they dwelt where they could throw their refuse into the water of the lake; these water-logged remnants were better preserved than the middens on dry land. Stone tools set in wooden and antler hafts have been found along with pieces of cloth and remnants of grain, fruits, and vegetables. Braidwood doubted that these people were more clever than others but thought that their remains were better preserved.

Jensen also described a culture which existed on the shores of the Baltic, when it was a fresh water lake where people lived on pine-log rafts moored to the shore. Their kitchen refuse, thrown into the water, is now revealed in layers of peat which have been exposed as the water receded. These people used as food fish, wild game, pigs, ducks, geese, and water fowl as well as the seeds of the yellow water lily.

Wheat and Grain Culture

Wheat had a central place in the cultivation of cereal grains; barley played a secondary role. The use of millet, rye, and rice followed. Wheat and barley had the same position in Egypt. These two cereals offer the advantages of being highly nutritious and easily stored, and the return in usable food is relatively high in relation to the effort man expends on raising them. The elastic gluten formed from two proteins of wheat when mixed in the presence of water makes risen bread possible, as is described more in detail on page 102. In addition to the abundance of its yield, its usefulness in bread-making probably explains the early and continuous use of wheat. Rye has some of these proteins, but less than wheat. Other cereals lack them entirely.

Dinkels and *wild emmers*, grasses ancestral to wheat, are known to grow wild, the former in the Crimea and Asia Minor and the latter in Palestine and perhaps in Iran. The ancestors of barley are mountain grasses growing over a wide area of Palestine, the Caucus, Iran, and Asia Minor as well as Afghanistan and Turkistan. It is not known exactly when cultivation began in different parts of the Near East, but it is thought that wheat and barley were grown in Mesopotamia as early as anywhere. Probably cultivated wheat and barley seeds were taken into Egypt.

Wheat grows best in broad, well-watered valleys. In many places, the potential fields were former forests cleared by slashing and burning. The first cultivation was evidently done on small plots or gardens and was therefore termed garden culture by those who found evidences of it. The Egyptians, according to Wissler, put the seed in the soft alluvial mud and used animals to tramp it down. At that time, man probably did not know about the use of fertilizer or about allowing land to lie fallow; therefore, it was necessary for him to seek new plots every few years, and settlements were temporary. More permanent settlements were apparently situated to take advantage of the alluvial soils produced by the intermittent torrents flowing from the hills to the plains and of the soils along rivers which regularly overflowed their banks.

Anthropologists and archeologists have pointed out that one reason why we know more of the details of the Egyptian use of grains is that their *mummified* grains have been better preserved than grains in other cultures. Helbalk told of the grain which has been found in the galleries beneath the pyramids as well as in storage pits in the open desert—grain almost as fresh, he says, as when it was put there 5–6000 years ago. The myth that some of it has been sprouted and grown into a plant has been refuted. Some of this grain belongs to a species which has not been grown since Roman times.

Much of our other evidence about these grains grown in early times comes from carbonized seeds. Perhaps the men roasting them discarded them because they were burned, as we discard charred popcorn kernels.

Concomitant Innovations

Another innovation was necessitated when man began to cultivate food and breed animals; man observed the close relationship of the growth of plants and the breeding of animals to the seasons and he made a calendar for himself. The early Egyptians devised a clever calendar which is really the forerunner of our own. About this time, they also developed astronomy and mathematics, which helped them in predicting seasons. This was, of course, of prime importance in countries which were dependent on seasonal rains like the monsoons or the flooding of the Nile.

Planning for irrigation and water storage systems led to the development of the science of engineering. The planning for the storing of food brought into being the art of planning and administration.

In areas along streams and lakes where there were some primitive settlements, fishing was profitable; fresh as well as dried fish were probably used. Childe (1951) told of fishing nets weighted with perforated lumps of clay or "waisted" stones (weighted).

Many have believed, as did Brogger, that the wealth of the sea was not well used by primitive man because he had not developed sufficient technology to make this use profitable. Consider the extensive efforts of today's FAO to help developing nations to use the sea as a source of food.

Animal Husbandry Begins

Neolithic men around 10,000 B.C. were known to have had pets or sacred animals. We will probably never know, however, just when man first domesticated animals to raise them for food. As has been said, the taming and the domesticating of animals are very different processes. Domestication means continuous breeding.

Why did man want to domesticate animals? He probably did not at first realize what he was doing, but gradually domestication occurred as his association with his dogs and other young wild animals became stronger. Man and the animals derived mutual benefits when he began to protect these animals from predators and to provide them with food. Those animals which were tamed first were probably the ones most socially and psychologically adaptable to this association with man. Of course it was necessary that reproductive ability not be interfered with. Undoubtedly men, women, and children made pets of young wild animals. Man probably also used them as decoys when he went hunting.

Some people believe that cultivation of plants is older than the domestication of animals, but many believe that they occurred at approximately the same time. Perhaps they occurred at the same time but in different groups of people. Only a few authorities believe that man bred animals before he cultivated plants.

Wissler wondered why it took man so long to undertake the raising of plants and the domestication of animals, when "instead of persistent killing of game animals, thus making them scarce and wild . . . he could have lived in friendly cooperation with them, protecting, conserving them and living in luxury on their increase by the simple device of saving the females and sacrificing the males. . . . Within a generation he could have come into control of his animal supplies." He also thought that it was less obvious what to do with the grasses and that it took man 400,000 years to learn what to do with seeds.

How did man learn to domesticate animals? We can report on only a few theories which have been advanced. One is that his pet dogs helped him corral several animals at once and that these were often the younger and less powerful animals. He learned to pen these up and to watch them develop before he used them as food. Northern European man is known to have tamed the dog to help him in hunting and to have used it as a scavenger and as a companion as early as 6000 B.C. Jensen postulated that pigs, like dogs, were "attracted to man's communities by waste food," which would be another opening wedge for taming and domestication. Wild boars are known to have been adopted by villagers of prehistoric China and Egypt. Ames and Wyler credited the success and widespread use of the pig as a domestic animal to the fact that they have an appetite for all kinds of food and they raise large litters. The fact that the pig is not adapted to "pastoral nomadism," Vayda believed, explains why it was not domesticated in certain places in the Near East. He favored this reason to that which says that religious or dietary laws caused its disappearance from these sections.

There is evidence of the very early domestication of sheep in three cities of France as well as in the Near East. Sheep are known to have been domesticated and used by Neolithic and Mesolithic people in Southwestern Asia and Asia Minor. The Neolithic emigrants to Europe brought their sheep with them. Early Neolithic Egyptian sheep were of the hairy type, but around 1500 B.C. these were replaced in the Nile Delta and Upper Egypt with a fleecy sheep which had fat tails like the modern Afghan sheep.

Indications of the domestication of deer in Northern Europe have been found, as has evidence of domestication of horses in several great mountain ranges, particularly the steppes and mountains of Southern Russia. The Kassites, who invaded the Persian plateau in the middle of the eighteenth century B.C., are thought by some to have domesticated the horse. In many countries where early horses appeared, they were eaten as food, as is true in many countries today. Satisfactory evidence (according to Childe, 1951) of the use of horses for milking and riding is not available before 1000 B.C. There are, however, stories of earlier use of horses in different parts of the ancient world.

Cattle are the most important domestic animals in all history, according to Forde. Zeuner said, "It is no exaggeration that the domestication of cattle was the most important step ever taken by man in the exploration of the animal world after the domestication of the dog." The wild ox was widely distributed in Southwest Asia in the late glacial period, and it has survived in Eastern Europe until recent times. *Aurocks,* the ancestor of the domesticated European ox, were common in early Europe and in the Fertile Crescent, being widely distributed in both areas. The bulls of this species came out of the primeval forests and interbred with domestic cows. Egyptians in early dynastic times are known to have raised shorthorn and polled cattle as well as a type of longhorn cattle. Chickens were probably domesticated after cattle, sheep, goats, and pigs, and probably in India.

When man had to seek grasslands for grazing his animals, he began to prefer plains rather than the forests in which he had found it previously profitable to live when he lived by hunting alone. Large areas of grasslands were prerequisite for the domestication and breeding of animals. Domestication probably flourished during the time that grasses were spreading to their present area of growth over one-fifth of the earth's surface.

In the process of domestication of animals, man learned to exercise restraint not to kill the youngest and the tamest and not to frighten the beasts in which he was interested. Once he had inadvertently spared the shyest and most amenable bulls, he had begun selective breeding. He had now to learn to find out about their reproduction as well as their needs for food, salt, and water.

The domestication of animals is evidently a deliberate exploitation by man of his environment even though the practice is rooted deeply in man's natural contacts with the beasts. *As a deliberate exploitation of the environment, it is another important stage in the development of man's food patterns.*

The Beginning of the Use of Milk and Other Uses of Animals

Once man began using animals for meat, he must have had herds and he would have observed that he, as well as young animals, could use the milk of these animals as food. He would also have found their hides useful to keep him warm or to protect him from insects or other pests. He later learned to use animals as beasts of burden to help him with cultivation. He probably observed that where animal dung had lain and rotted, the young grass was greener, and so he perhaps gained his first idea of the use of fertilizer to increase crop yields.

It is not known why some primitive peoples used milk whereas others did not. Adolph pointed out that even in dim history the "bean" (soybean) was the "Milk of China." Coming down to recorded history, we find statements in the writings of Homer and others that milk was scorned as repulsive. We doubt, however, that this explains differences in the use of milk among primitive groups. Many old wives' tales and primitive practices which have survived the test of time have grains of truth in them. The Sumerians are known to have had a well-developed dairy industry over 5000 years ago.

In different parts of the world, man has milked cows, goats, mares, asses, reindeer, buffaloes, camels, and zebra. Early Persians used camel's milk; Asians and Africans used water and cape buffalo's milk; Europeans used the milk of the cow, ewe, goat, and ass; while the Tartars and Mongols used mare's milk. Northern European people used the milk of the reindeer. The milk of the yak has long been used in Pamirs (Tadzhikskaya, a U.S.S.R. province in Central Asia) and Tibet, whereas Peruvians have used the milk of the llama and vicuna for many centuries. In many of these areas, the same animals are used for milk today.

Other Inventions Useful in Food Getting

Domestic plants and animals probably appeared 8000–6000 B.C. The rest of the complex of pottery making; the use of the plow, the sickle, and the wheel; metallurgy; and the use of the sailing ship appeared later in North Mesopotamia, Syria, Palestine, Iran, and Egypt.

Generally the earliest established dates for domestication of animals are around 5000 B.C.; for metallurgy, 4000 B.C.; and for sailing ships, 4000–3000 B.C. The wheel probably appeared somewhat earlier than 3000 B.C.; more accurate dating, however, must await more definitive evidence.

Some have thought that incipient agriculture began around 9000 B.C. locally in what has been called "the natural habitat zone" in Southeastern Asia.

Possible Native Habitats of Different Plants

Vavilov of Leningrad has postulated that there were seven centers of the development of cultivation. While his premise is not supported by many other archeologists, his classification of where plants came from is interesting and, according to other authorities, probably fairly accurate.

Rice was grown in North India 3000 years ago and probably in China 5000 years ago, according to Pirie. Because Southeast Asia is now the source of 95% of the world's rice, he thinks it originated there. He speculated that Africa may have been an independent center of its beginnings.

He also pointed out that, with the exception of rice, every plant now is grown more extensively in some countries to which it has been taken than in its native home. This is true certainly of maize in the U.S., which was brought from its native habitat of Mexico. Another example is the banana, which is thought to have originated in Southeast Asia; the peanut, in tropical America; the potato, in Peru, Bolivia, and Chile; as well as the soybean, in Northeast Asia; and sugar, in India.

Most vegetables which are used today came to us before written records were kept. Prehistoric people took their vegetable and fruit seeds with them along with those of their cereals. Boswell thought that

TABLE 1   Native Habitats of Plants (Vavilov)

Country or area	Native plants
1. S.W. Asia: 　　Asia Minor 　　Persia 　　Afghanistan 　　Turkistan 　　Northwest India	Soft wheat, rye, flax, apple, pear, sweet cherry, grape, bean, pea, carrot
2. India: Valley of Ganges	Rice, "naked" oats, "naked" barley, millet, soya, sugar cane, tropical fruit
3. Great river valleys of East and Central China (These plants are supposed to have spread from here to Japan and Malaysia)	Radish, citrus fruit, peach, tea, mulberry
4. Mediterranean Basin: 　　Iberia, Italy, Coast of Asia 　　Minor, Syria, Palestine, 　　Egypt, Tunisia, Algeria, 　　Morocco	Olive, fig, oats, pea, barley, wheat
5. Mountains of East Africa and Abyssinia	Sorghum, coffee
6. Northern Mexico	Maize, cacao
7. Peru, Bolivia	Potato

the best way to determine where a plant originated was to determine where it is still found growing wild. This is not always a reliable guide, however, as evidenced by the carrot, which is not native to North America but does grow wild here. Probably we need to seek the place where the greatest number of varieties grow wild. Boswell in his lengthy article gave a history of practically all commonly known vegetables. The reader is referred to this excellent article for further details on the origin of vegetables.

In Southeast Asia, plants other than wheat and barley were available to the primitive cultivator. These were rye grass, wild flax, and large-seeded wild legumes like lentils, vetch, vetchlings, and chick peas. The lowland areas had dates; the foothills, acorns and almonds; and the northern mountains, grapes, apples, and pears.

Development of Use of Metals Affects Man's Farming Practices

Brew said "Toward the end of the era of prehistory known as the Neolithic or New Stone Age, man became aware of special properties in some hard metals of the earth's surface." Man "learned how to mine these metallic ores, and how to work the metals when they had been extracted. The effect of this new knowledge was tremendous and far reaching." It would be an interesting study to compare food producing, storage, and preparation before and after metals were known and used.

Copper was the first metal used. It was probably obtained from the rugged mountains of Iran and was traded at around 6500 B.C. with people living as far away as in the Assyrian Steppes. Later, man learned to smelt it with tin to make the harder and more useful bronze. The use of bronze always involved specialized industries and organized trade. In order to make bronze tools, according to Childe (1951), a "community must produce a surplus of foodstuffs to support bodies of specialists— miners, smelters, and smiths." Some men had to withdraw from direct food production to become workers in metals.

Copper appears first in Mesopotamia and Egypt between 4000–3500 B.C.; smelting of it came about 500 years later. The making of bronze possibly began in the mountainous regions of Asia Minor and Armenia. Brew, however, said that this is far from proven to everyone's satisfaction. Experimental alloys appeared in Egypt around 3000 B.C. Brew also said that this metal was probably used 500 years later in India, 1000 years later in Northern Europe, and possibly 1500 years later in China. It is thought that the practice of the use of bronze was taken north and west as peoples moved out of Mesopotamia, and it has been conjectured that the Neolithic peoples of Europe traded their valuables, such as Danish amber for bronze knives, swords, and pots and pans. Around 1500 B.C., the amber of Jutland was traded for gold and bronze. The first Bronze Age men in Britain came from Spain.

Although gold and silver were known to have been used in Neolithic times, they were too soft to be used in food getting or preparation, and man had to wait for copper and bronze to make great difference in his daily life. Iron came into use later because of its advantages as a material for tools and weapons, as well as the fact that it could be found almost anywhere. The time of the introduction of iron is not known; according to Brew, it is said to have been "invented" in Asia Minor at "an unknown date." It was apparently known in the Near East as early as bronze (about 3000 B.C.), but many centuries passed before it was in general use. Iron was used, according to Linton, in the Near East in 4500 B.C. and reached Britain by 2500 B.C., although he thought that there is evidence of its use in the western plateau of Turkey by 1800–1600 B.C.

This discussion of the use of metals is presented here because it affected man's farming practices, food getting, food storage, and food preparation.

Man Makes Tools and Devises New Methods as He Has Needs

Once man began to cultivate plants, he had new needs for tools—to sharpen his digging stick, to make a hoe, and later to make a sickle and a plow. Man also had need for vessels for storage of his grains. The archeologist finds only a part of man's tool when he excavates a site, making it difficult to know what the original tool was really like.

Early Digging Tools and the Plow

In the development of agriculture, the plow was a comparatively late invention. The digging stick, weighted with a stone, was the first digging tool; from this stick, the spade and garden fork were developed. The plow and the horse were both used in the Bronze Age in Europe (Linton); according to Wissler, the Spanish took the plow to Mexico.

As soon as man made the wheel, he found many uses for it. After its invention, oxen were drafted to help man do the heavy work of cultivating plots.

Early Cooking Utensils

It is thought that man first roasted his grains on hot stones. Later these grains may have been ground in a kind of mortar and pestle; possibly the earliest method of grinding was the use of sticks against stones. In 1959, Senegalese women were still using huge stone containers for grinding cereal grains and dried roots. Against these stone surfaces they used large wooden pestles with handles long enough to allow them to stand upright.

Different kinds of mortars and pestles have been found in the remnants of successive cultures. In the early twentieth century, children in

California were still digging up mortars and pestles with which the early Indian women had ground their acorns.

Ground-up grains were probably first used for porridge, in which grain must be cooked. It is probable that early man used leather vessels by placing hot stones in them for some of his cooking. Northwest American Indians are known to have used tightly woven baskets for this type of cooking.

Pottery-making was another innovation. One story says that women first put wet clay inside baskets woven of reeds to make them hold water. As these were used on fires, the clay was hardened by the heat into a form of pottery.

As soon as women had pottery, they may have used it for boiling as well as for roasting meats. Roasting over an open fire was undoubtedly the first form of cooking meat. In modern times the terms roasting and baking are sometimes used less accurately than they probably were originally. Were the Polynesians the first to use pits filled with hot stones to roast an entire pig? This is not known.

Other Advances

Between 6000 and 3000 B.C. man learned to use oxen, and he invented and learned to use the plow, the wheeled cart, and the sailboat. He also devised and used the solar calendar.

The creation of canals for irrigation called for disciplined group work; some claim that this was the time when man became self-disciplined. The large-scale canal irrigation in Mesopotamia around 3600 B.C. has been credited by some for the spectacular rise in population and the creation of cities in Mesopotamia.

Jensen said that, whereas the discovery of agriculture gave people earthroom to spare for hundreds of years, "climatic changes and growth of towns ushered in man's everlasting productivity and warfare." He also believed "that a cycle of interplay of planned labor, which increased food supply, with increasing population of workers, resulted in increased complexity of organization, until we now have our industrial and social-political wheels creaking and rolling at great speed—no man knows whither."

Childe (1951) gives 2000 B.C. as the approximate time that merchandise was carried on donkeys back and forth between Babylonia and Asia

Minor. It is thought that the donkey, a native of Northeast Africa, was domesticated there long before 3000 B.C.

Migrations into Europe

Montague in *Man: His First Two Million Years* (1969) told of the 1965 announcement of the discovery of the earliest-known village site in Europe—a site in the Macedonian plain of Northern Greece. Radiocarbon dating places the probable date for existence of this village at 6220 B.C. In this village, farmer-herdsmen raised wheat, barley, and lentils and tended sheep, goats, and almost certainly cattle and pigs— the earliest dated occurrence of cattle anywhere in the world. These people also hunted birds and wild animals and fished.

Waterbalk said that the first farmers probably migrated into Greece from Anatolia. These farmers slashed and burned the forests after the change from nondeciduous to deciduous species of trees. He believed that the seacoast peoples who had lived in that area by hunting and fishing were receptive to new ideas of food production so that, when the migrating farmers arrived, the seacoast people probably followed the ideas of their new neighbors.

The Swiss Lake Dwellers

The lake dwellers of Switzerland and elsewhere are the first peoples of Western Neolithic culture for which there are reliable records. It is thought that theirs was a mixture of Neolithic and Mesolithic North African cultures with a trace of Danubian element. The farmers in these communities lived together in rectangular wooden houses raised on wooden piles and strung out along the lake shore. Their houses were first probably built along the shore; later, when flooding occurred, they were surrounded entirely by water.

They cultivated emmer wheat, barley, linseed, caraway, poppy seeds, beans, lentils, carrots, plums, and apples, and they are thought to have brewed cider. They raised pigs, sheep, goats, and horned cattle, stalled their cattle, and used cow manure as a fertilizer. They also speared and netted fish. Leather and pottery cooking and storage vessels were used.

The remnants of their bread show that the dough was not fermented, but they knew about fermentation because they made wine from raspberries, cherries, and mulberries. They used wheat, barley, and rye and apparently emphasized cereal raising. They used the ox-drawn plows. Cattle, pigs, sheep, game, fish, and shellfish were used as food, as were seasonal fruits and nuts.

About 3000 B.C., all the plains south of the Scandinavian Mountains were inhabited by peoples who lived in more or less permanent villages. They cut deciduous forests with stone axes, cultivated a variety of crops, and raised cattle, sheep, goats, and pigs. Hunting was of little importance. Pottery of varied shapes and with various ornamentation has been found everywhere in this region.

As peoples migrated, they went into a broad zone between the Alps and the west coast of the North Sea, as well as across the European continent to the Danube (Waterbalk). The diffusion of culture, however, was slow during the Neolithic ages in Northern Britain, Northern Norway, and Sweden due to isolation.

Present-Day Primitive Man

Even today there are many groups on earth who are using methods credited to Early Man. Anthropologists often conjecture about Early Man by studying Modern Primitive Man, although this approach is undoubtedly misleading because the influences of highly developed peoples must touch these primitive peoples. One of the best illustrations is a drawing of Australian aborigines used in an anthropology textbook. These primitive men are shown tearing down a telephone line in order to obtain the materials they need for hunting and other primitive pursuits.

Consider the many current illustrations of the remnants of primitive food patterns. Women of the Bushmen of Africa gather roots, fruits, and seeds while the men hunt. Some Tanzanian tribes use the digging stick in planting. The Hunzas of Northern India are hardy, possessed of superior strength and endurance, and enjoy buoyant health. Their workmen and artisans are skilled, and they are generally regarded as having superior intelligence. These people have interested nutritionists since 1921, when McCarrison first studied them. He found that their diet consisted of cereal grains, vegetables, fruits (especially apricots), milk and butter daily, and goat's meat on feast days only. They eat the same diet today and still eat sparingly. Their agricultural practices are traditional; they terrace and irrigate their fields and renew the soil by bringing down "glacial milk" from the near-by mountains. They also return to the soil all human, animal, and vegetable refuse.

Many combinations of food have been found in different ethnic groups of people to furnish nutrients needed for good health.

EGYPT

The early Egyptians left us better records of what they ate than some ancient peoples because they believed that food must be placed in tombs for the use of the dead in the afterlife. The Pharoahs were well supplied with food for their afterlife. The poor, however, who could afford only a coarse cloth for a coffin and who had to be buried in communal graves, were provided with only a few scraps of food. The dead who had been wealthy were offered food daily, whereas those of moderate means were offered food only on festivals.

The Egyptians believed in "eat, drink, and be merry" in this life because they were perhaps not really sure of an afterlife. Even the poor were said to have been gay and to have loved life, according to those who have made a study of these people.

Foods Used

The Nile left fertile silt along its banks after the seasonal floods. In these lush bottom lands were grown vast fields of grain, mostly wheat. After the Egyptians learned to make leavened bread, the use of barley decreased.

Beans, parsley, radishes, and especially onions, leeks, and garlic were grown and used. Some say that the Greek historian Herodotus was the first to report that onions and garlic were the main foods of builders of the great pyramid of Cheops at Gizeh, 2900 B.C. This assertion is probably not true, although the Egyptians liked onions and garlic and still grow them for export. Melons and grapes flourished in the Nile Delta, and olive oil was probably used as early as 3000 B.C. They developed a less-bitter table olive. Fish was preserved both by salting and by drying; grapes were dried for raisins.

Hunting was a favorite pastime of the wealthy, and wild fowl were prized. As many as 1000 geese were consumed in one day at opulent public feasts. Some fish were considered sacred and there was a proscription against the use of these fish, but the poor paid little attention to such regulations.

Egyptian priests were able to predict the flooding of the Nile; these early scientists thus gained power, becoming some of the first rulers to demand food as tribute. Thus, some of the farmers' harvest had to be used as payment for taxes. Much grain was stored and saved for use in years of famine, but the priests also used some for themselves.

Grain was reaped with a sickle, carried in rope baskets, and threshed by oxen treading on the grain; finally it was winnowed by allowing the wind to blow out the chaff. These processes are well depicted in their tomb murals; in one of these, four scribes are recording yields. Records were also kept of yield per acre.

Ancient Egypt is best known of all ancient cultures for developing the art of bread-making. Grain was crushed between heavy grindstones; water was added to make dough. At first, flat cakes of bread were baked in clay-lined ovens hollowed out of the ground; the ovens were heated by burning coals. Some people placed earthen jars outside their houses; these were heated much like the hearth ovens used by our ancestors and still used in some bakeries in our country today.

Meals and Banquets

The first course at an Egyptian banquet often consisted of appetizers such as green cabbage (supposed to delay drunkenness), pickled onions, and sesame, anise, and cumin seeds. The main course usually consisted of roast goose, legs of small calves and gazelles adorned with lamb frills, wild duck or quail, fish served raw or grilled, or a combination of these. Vegetables such as lettuce, endive, dried peas, cardoons (forerunners of artichokes), onions, leeks, beans, parsley, and radishes might also be served with this course. Beer was usually served with this course but wine was sometimes served. Sweets such as fruits, cakes, and melons were served as dessert.

GREECE

The food patterns of all ancient civilizations or even all periods of one culture cannot be discussed here. We have chosen, therefore, to discuss a few in depth.

In early Greece, many of the poor were on the very edge of starvation; they demanded land and power from the rich.

Athens, which during the fifth century B.C. was already a democracy, was able to resist the armies of Persia, as was Sparta, where the idea of the ancient monarchy persisted. Athens and Sparta became the important centers of this part of the ancient world. Thessaly, which had an agrarian society, was also important in the Greek food economy.

The Greeks firmly believed in the worth of the individual man, an attitude which distinguished them from all previous civilizations. This philosophy may have developed due to the geographical isolation of the different areas of Greece, effectively preventing one ruler from subduing the entire country. Thus, each local group became deeply aware of their own being; within his group, each person was aware of his own responsibility. The Greeks prized liberty and respected law. They also had a sense of personal achievement and of each man's obligation to make the most of his own natural endowments. They therefore had high standards for their work.

The Grecian food patterns after the rise of Athens and Sparta and their cities and colonies are interesting. Attica included Athens, the port of Pireaus, and numerous villages; all the people in this vicinity were called Athenians. Pireaus at one time was the busiest port of the world.

The city, or polis, was a political and geographical center. A rich civic life emerged in the polis to distinguish the Greeks from their neighbors. Even long after the aristocracy lost power, the polis remained the focus of Greek life.

When these cities became overpopulated, colonists were sent north to the Aegean littoral, to the Sea of Marmara, and finally to the Crimea. These colonies provided new sources of foods which were scarce at home.

In science as in medicine, the Greeks were good observers. In contrast to the modern scientist, "The Greek philosopher began with little data, developed his theories by the application of logic, and then stopped . . . . The influence of this attitude was reflected in Greek technology. Until well into the Hellenistic period, it was characterized by an increasing perfection of manual dexterity and an almost complete lack of new basic inventions or even of borrowings which might have fundamentally altered the existing technical patterns" (Linton). He was speaking here especially of architecture, but this influence was no doubt also relevant to agricultural practices.

The Greeks apparently knew nothing about crop rotation (they used little fertilizer), but they probably, by necessity, allowed their fields to lie fallow one season. They reaped their grains with a sickle and had no scythes. They threshed grain by driving cattle over the stalks, as was done by others in ancient times and can still be observed as a practice among some primitive peoples today. The Greeks, however, drained the swamps and terraced their hillsides to use all available land efficiently. It is said that, during the fourth century B.C., agricultural experts began to study crop rotation and means of soil improvement; they also began to use manure as a fertilizer. Their first attempts toward research in the production of food concerned arbor culture of olives, grapes, and figs.

The Greek farmers were never able to feed all the population. They did, however, produce olive oil, wine, and wool, which could be used in addition to their pottery and jewelry to trade with the peoples around the Mediterranean and the Baltic Seas for foods which they needed. The Greeks evidently journeyed as far as the Crimea in the East and to France and even to Ireland in the West, so they knew what foods other peoples produced. There are records of their journeys to Sicily and southern Italy as early as 750 B.C., and they traveled up the coast of Italy as far as the Bay of Naples. These travelers are said to have brought back cheese and pork from Sicily.

One of the Greek inventions that greatly facilitated foreign trade was their production of coins, which were much more convenient for barter than were food and wine. It is said that the earliest merchants traded their barley, but it often went moldy before they could use it for barter. Some of the earliest Greek coins were stamped with an ear of wheat, a reminder that one of the world's first forms of money was food. Greek civilization arose because their farmers could produce more of certain foods (primarily olives and olive oil and wine) than they needed, so they could trade these for other foods which they did need (Orr).

The ancient Greek farmer's life was one of hard labor and want. They had, except for some water power, no mechanical source of power to supplement their own labors; animals were probably infrequently used. One author mentions a farmer using mules to draw a plow but finishing by hand with a hoe. "The civilization which hand labor supports is a simple civilization. This is the secret of the 2300 years of what seems to us a stagnation, if so we may call it, which lasted from early history to the beginning of the nineteenth century" (Prentice).

The Grecian supply of a variety of foods was influenced by their love of travel; their invention of coinage, which enabled them to buy foods from other lands; their overcoming the difficulties of an inhospitable land; and their using readily available seafood.

Boetia (cow land), from Homer's time to the classical period, had pasture lands lush enough to graze cattle. Boetians also bred cattle and pigs, and mules and donkeys were used for farm labor. The fact that the lushness of Boetia is mentioned often in discussing agriculture and food in Greece leads us to the supposition that other portions of Greece, except perhaps Thessaly, did not grow lush grass. It is said that the Boetians were gluttons who made their probably hungry, frugal neighbors jealous. Some Athenians are said to have called them "pigs."

At best, the Greek diet was not lavish. But the Greeks apparently enjoyed living frugally; their ability to do physical exercise regularly is well known, as in their excellence in physical pursuits. "It is interesting to note that the Greeks said they must never forget the body in training the mind" (Jensen). They believed that they must train the whole man by gymnasia and diet. Jensen believed that their good diets and frugality influenced greatly the success of the Greek civilization. He also said that the decline of Athens after 350 B.C. was "closely connected with shortage of foodstuffs" and that the reduction of their marketable goods resulted in their not being able to import the needed foods.

Foods Used

The simple Greek diet consisted mostly of olive oil, fish, goat's milk, cheese, wine, and bread. Occasionally, probably mostly at festivals, they had goats and sheep for meat, but these animals usually served as a source of milk to make cheese. Honey from the mountains of Hymeltus near Athens was said to be famous throughout Ancient Greece. This area was also famous for its olives.

Greek pigs were allowed to forage for "mast," which consisted of nuts, such as acorns or beechnuts, found on the forest floor. The pork was not eaten fresh but rather as salted meat. Beef was a rarity because the land was not suitable for grazing cattle.

They had a variety of fish during the seasons when fishing was possible. In fact, the Greeks came to know the sea well. They caught and used tunny, mullet, anchovies, and sardines. Dried fish was imported from the Bosporus. They also caught fresh water fish. Whenever the price of sardines and anchovies rose, the man in the street became alarmed. Shellfish, mollusks, squid, and octopus were available. Often fish was smoked or preserved in brine; the winter seas were too rough for fishing. In Homer's time, fish was despised as poor man's food. Was this the same attitude that made a New England Puritan family hide the shad (then costing less than 10¢ a pound) when during a meal an unexpected knock was heard on the door? Three hundred years later, however, fish was considered a gourmet food in Greece. Homer considered roasted or boiled meat the only meat for a gentleman's meals. He thought that it should be served with bread, cheese, and salad, which was a food for the gods. Milk was drunk only in the rural areas sometimes as soured milk, but it was used for making the cheese eaten by all ancient Greeks. Cheese was also imported from Bithynia. It is said that garlic with cheese was eaten in large quantities.

In Homer's day the people were called "grain eaters," and porridge made from wheat and barley was called *sitos*. This term was probably used for their yeastless bread, which was baked in thin cakes. The porridge, made from grain ground in a mortar, was served with salt and honey.

Wheat was difficult to grow on the Greek barren soil without summer rains. Barley grew better on these soils. The yield of all grains was low; a farmer could expect to get only 9 to 10 bushels per acre from 2 bushels of seed (Prentice). Yet porridge kept the early world alive. No wonder the Greeks looked to the full granaries of their neighbors and early became good traders, importing wheat and barley from Sicily, Thrace, Egypt, Cyprus, and Southern Russia.

Bread was sometimes made from wheat but more often from barley. Because their barley cakes were "stodgy and rather flavorless" (Perl), they were often dipped in honey and vinegar to make them taste better. These cakes or scones were said to have been served on straw or clean leaves. Barley was also made into flat griddle cakes, or *maza*, which was a staple in the diet of many people. One of Solon's ordinances decreed that "wheaten bread proper (*artos*) baked in round loaves should be served only on feast days." Bread and cakes were inspected for weight and contents by market police. In Pericles' time, both maza and artos were obtainable from bakers daily. Xenophon mentions leavened bread, but it is not known when it was first made. Olive oil and wine were used to supplement the porridge diet, but butter was not used.

Vegetables were mostly eaten fresh, but they were also pickled in brine. The Greeks grew grapes and olive trees in the narrow fertile valleys between the mountains. Here they could also grow some grain. Within the walls of a great villa, the family might grow apricots, peaches, plums, figs, and almonds. One author called oranges "golden apples of Hesperides," while another said the Greeks had no citrus fruit. Lemons, which are now much used in Greek cookery,. were brought from India after the invasion of Alexander the Great in 326 B.C.; rice was also acquired at this time. Apples, pears, and quince were grown at home, but plums and currants were imported. Nuts were imported from Babylonia, prunes from Damascus, and raisins from Bertytus. The importation of much of their foodstuffs kept Greeks well fed in the frugal way they apparently enjoyed.

The old Greeks were fond of a little roll of spicy chopped meats wrapped in grape leaves such as the dish they now call dolmas. The recipe for fava, a thick stew of dried split peas seasoned with onion, garlic, parsley, and oregano (the favorite Greek herb), has changed little over 2500 years.

Beverages

A popular beverage of the Spartans was a famous black broth, which was a thick stew made of pork, blood, and vinegar. Another cross between liquid and solid food which was popular with the Greek peasants was made with barley meal and water. The most popular drink was water, but country people also drank milk. Sometimes for drinking, honey was mixed with water.

Wine was not aged, so it had to be preserved with salt to keep it. It was usually drunk mixed with water. Hippocrates is said to have drunk wine made from honey and herbs, probably later known as *mead*, later a favorite drink of Europeans. Hundreds of years later mead could still be purchased in modern U.S.

Seasonings

The Greeks used the word *aroma* for all spices. These were used judiciously and with respect. In addition to adding flavor, parsley was supposed to improve brain power and it was believed to be a cure for intoxication, so men wore garlands of parsley when embarking on a drinking bout. Dill seeds were chewed because the Greeks believed this kept them awake and was also a brain stimulant.

The Markets

In ancient Athens, life centered around the marketplace, or *agora*. Portable booths, probably one for each kind of food, were set up each morning in a long, covered promenade supported by a row of columns. These markets were conveniently located near the government buildings and meeting places. There were no fixed prices; purchasers bargained for wares. The poor carried their coins in their mouths and baskets for their purchases; the rich had purses and servants to carry their goods. Some middlemen also sold to the public.

People came to the market from single-story homes along narrow, crowded, and refuse-strewn lanes; they had no sewer system as did the later Romans. Even wealthy Greeks had no water supply in their homes.

Poor Athenians ate their porridge of wheat and barley (flavored with salt and honey), barley cakes, beans, peas, lentils, cabbage, onions, figs, and other fruits, and olives. Beans and lentils, which were the cheapest food they had, were usually eaten in stews. People were fond of sausages and black pudding, which probably was like modern European blood pudding. Even for those of moderate means, the diet was largely vegetarian; when possible, however, they had mutton, pork, dog, and dairy foods. Fish and eels, served mostly at festivals, were popular. The well-to-do ate more than the poor of eels, fowl, lamb, pork, wheat bread, fruits, and vegetables. The vegetables were dressed heavily with olive oil, vinegar, sauces, and honey. It took 14 years to mature an olive tree, and a man had to be wealthy to wait for his own trees to mature.

Imported vegetables were considered a luxury but were highly appreciated, as were the home-grown Attican vegetables—cabbage, lentils, peas, onions, and garlic. Mushrooms, lettuce, asparagus, cabbage, beans, radishes, and varieties of leek, onions, turnips, and lentils were eaten in large quantities by all Greeks. Walnuts and almonds came from Persia and Mesopotamia, and beets, citrons, melon, apricots, sesame, geese, and pickled pork were introduced from the East. In the country, the farm people had a regular diet of mutton, goat meat, and fowl.

Sauces for fish, meat, and game were made from vinegar and wine, seasoned with salt, mustard, garlic and onions, pennyroyal, and marjoram. No pepper was available, and their only sweetener was honey.

A family might have a stew simmered in a pot put over the fire on a tripod; the cauldron containing the stew would be brought to the table like modern cook-and-serve ware. The author is also reminded of seeing, some 15 years ago, cooks for a school lunch in Accra, Ghana cooking in a kettle over a very simple clay stove made of three clay legs under which a small fire was built on the ground. Even now Africans such as the Zulus successfully use such primitive stoves out-of-doors.

Meals

Spartans and Athenians ate lightly; the warm weather and scanty supplies were probably partial explanations for this frugality.

Breakfasts were composed mostly of bread dipped in wine with a few olives and figs. The Athenian businessman came home and ate a light lunch, often of fresh or salted fish, ham, or sausage. He usually spent his evenings at home, sometimes with guests coming to dinner around sunset. The Athenian dinner is said to have been for social enjoyment to be eaten without gluttony; to eat alone was feeding and not dining. They wanted only a little of all good foods; it is said that in Homer's day, all meals in aristocratic homes were served daintily. Such was Greek hospitality that even male strangers off the street were invited in to dine.

Utensils for Eating

Foods were eaten with the fingers and gravies and sauces were sopped with bread. Spoons were used only for soups or purees. No forks or knives were used at first, but later knives were used to cut meat. Greeks had no napkins, so they used bread to wipe their fingers. Wooden bowls and flat scones of maza served as plates, but they did have some terra cotta and metal platters and wooden or metal goblets.

Place of Women

Some have said that women, especially slave-women in wealthy homes, did the cooking. In early ancient Grecian times, women baked their own bread; but later it was baked in bakeries, as were fancy cakes and pastries. However, women ground the cereal in a mortar and probably baked bread and made porridge and soups, but men did the "serious" cooking (Jensen).

Women lived by themselves even in a villa, where there were often as many as 50 women including slave girls. Men ate alone in the dining room. Grecian women were expected to run their households and to stay out of sight, enjoying their husband's company only when there were no guests (Bowra). There seems to be disagreement, however, among some writers about whether the women were present at family meals and banquets. Some reports state that women had their own banquets separate from the men. During the Periclean Age, however, women were present only at the male banquets to amuse the men with music, dancing, and seductive charms.

Cooks and Chefs

When in the fourth century pastry cooks began to appear, all professional cooks were highly respected as artisans and were paid better than many other working men. Some were educated, and a cook was often invited to drink with the guests when he had produced a masterpiece. Greeks considered a new dish as important as a new poem. In Sybaris, cooks were said to be respected more than in Attica, and there the cook who served the best dish at a banquet was crowned on a dais before the crowd.

Tracts on the culinary arts were produced beginning in the fourth century, and twenty cookbooks are said to have been produced in the time of Pericles. Archestratus produced his masterpiece, *Gastrology*, in 350 B.C. after he had traveled widely to gather the recipes, many of which are still in use. Others besides epicurean aristocrats collected recipes, and historians tell us that a law was passed by which a cook could copyright an outstanding recipe so that he got all the profits from its sale for a year during which no one could copy it. In how many modern plays do cooks give out recipes over the footlights, as they did in the old Greek plays?

Banquets

Banquets, which were popular with all Greeks except the Spartans, were given by those who could afford them. These were lavish even though other home meals of the same people were simple. A Greek is supposed to have said "Tomorrow I go back to barley meal and cheese" as we might say "I'll go back to bread and water."

Men ate in reclining positions propped on cushions on couches. It was customary to offer guests basins of water to wash their hands before eating. They probably needed to wash their hands also during the meals because they had no napkins; guests wiped their hands on pieces of bread, which were then thrown on the floor for the dogs.

A cup of herbally-infused wine was often served as an aperitif. The main course usually contained meat. One historian said that, at a wedding feast for 20 guests, a huge platter was presented to each guest. Each platter contained a roast boar stuffed with thrushes and garnished with egg yolks and oysters or periwinkles. Hippocluchus told of an Athenian friend who presented each guest with a platter containing a whole roast kid.

The dessert course was fresh fruit and salted nuts, often almonds and sweet meats. Salted cheese might also be served at this course. They used sweet meats and cheese cakes, which were deep-fried pastries holding a soft cheese mixture; other pastries, molded and chilled in snow, might be served in a box. Some so-called cheese cakes had no cheese in them but were made of nuts, fruits, oil, and honey; some were made with sour wine blended with soft cheese, or with a mixture of grated or sieved cheese and mead.

Drinking was controversial in Greece. Plato, whom some called a prig, was not the only one to plead for temperance. In Sparta, a fine was exacted from anyone found drunk even at festivals for Bacchus; drunkenness was forbidden by law, and the Greeks were proud of their fashion of sobriety.

Epicurus, an idol of Athenians, is quoted as saying, "The fountain and root of every good is the pleasure of the stomach." He also said that boys should not taste wine until they were 18 years of age, and then they should drink moderately. After 40, they should relax and enjoy themselves invoking the gods, especially Bacchus.

At the end of a meal, wine was drunk. Then a chairman of the symposium was elected. The word symposium originally meant a drinking party session. This chairman decided how much water would be added to the wine; he probably also decided how much the guests should drink, and he always chose the topic of conversation.

It is said that a wedding feast might last for days. At a Macedonian wedding feast in 310 B.C., each guest brought a servant to carry home the gifts. The first course of wine was served in silver drinking bowls, which were given as a gift to each guest. The brazen Corinthian platters on which were served poultry, ducks, pigeon, or goose were also given to the guests. No one was expected to eat everything, so servants wrapped up the leftovers and carried them home along with the gifts of silverware.

After the poultry course there might be a course at which were served hares, kids, doves, turtle doves, partridge, and every imaginable kind of bird.

In one elegant picnic in which each guest contributed his share of food and wine (Wason), the food was carried to the picnic in baskets like food for a modern pot luck dinner. The Greek picnic guests ate more elegantly than modern picnickers do, however, using alabaster dishes and silver bowls. For dessert, they nibbled cheese cakes served in gaily decorated boxes.

After the Golden Age

The downfall of Athens and other Greek cities was probably a time when exports fell off so that money was no longer available for imported food. "The adequacy of the food supply depends upon the relation between possible production and necessary consumption and the nature of the government reflects the adequacy or inadequacy of the food supply" (Prentice). Wechsberg says, in *The Best Things in Life*, "The Greeks had more than a word for the art of cooking" and "The Greeks were the first Europeans to have a literature of gastronomy. . . ." He remarked, however, that modern French critics doubt that "the Athenians ever knew great cooking in the French term of the word."

ROMAN FOOD PATTERNS

What the Romans ate was influenced by previous discoveries and the stage of agriculture and animal husbandry.

About 1500 B.C. invaders, who are thought to have come from Central Europe probably through Hungary, knew and used bronze before they established themselves in the Po Valley. This theory is supported by reports that they almost certainly spoke an Indo-European language. They were able to establish villages and to dominate and to absorb the older Neolithic peoples. Archeology was in its infancy in the 1880's when these villages were unearthed and the sites were not dug with the care employed today (Linton). However, Middle-European-type bronze objects and pottery from early Italian cultures of traders and farmers were found.

By 750 B.C., there was a fortified marketplace settlement made up of traders and farmers on the left bank of the Tiber River about 15 miles from its mouth. By 338 B.C., Romans had made themselves masters of the area of Latinum. By 270 B.C., they had conquered the Greek cities in Italy and Sicily and welded the whole southern peninsula into a single confederacy. One group of invaders, the Etruscans, were able to stay, leaving their influence on Roman culture. Scholars believe that the Etruscans came from Asia Minor around 900 to 800 B.C., probably in search of copper and tin to make their bronze, bringing a civilization with them. The Etruscans, who copied the artistic forms of the Syrians, Egyptians, and Greeks with whom they traded and who lived north of the Tiber, had a society with marked upper and lower classes. Each city was ruled by priest-kings.

The Roman Republican system provided an inadequate structure for new conditions (Linton); there was no educated or leisure class among the poor, hard-working peasants. The loyal, disciplined Roman army with superior military techniques was the one institution able to survive after the fall of the Republican system. After the wars of Marius and Sylla, the Roman Empire under Augustus was created. The organization of the Empire called for a creation of an honest and devoted civil service of professional people. The spread of Roman influence after this is well known.

When governmental control was lacking, following the collapse of Rome and the resulting chaos, there arose the Western European feudal system. The control which powerful landowners wielded over the peasants and owners of small farms created the world of feudal lords, serfs, and fiefs.

Food Patterns

During the Republic, which lasted almost through the second century B.C., the Romans are said to have cared little for the pleasures of the table. They ate frugally; many were vegetarians and ate their food cold. At this time, food was served and eaten in common crockery and iron, but a silver salt cellar was a prized possession. To be seated above the salt at the table was to be honored, as it was in later times. Table knives and forks were not known, but spoons like those of today were used.

At this time, there was little distinction among different classes in what foods were eaten. In the last two centuries of the Republic, these simple ways gave way to luxurious living for the rich, but the poor still lived frugally. This luxury followed successful wars in which fertile lands were conquered and acquired; thus, more food was furnished for all. After imported foods came from Mesopotamia and North Africa, meat became more common; among the upper classes a vegetarian diet came to be despised.

There are better records of what the wealthy ate in the luxury-loving periods than what the poor ate. We do, however, have some records for the diet of the poor, and this diet will be discussed before the Lucullan feasts are described. It is said that the principal food of the poor Roman was a thick soup; undoubtedly the thickness varied with the availability of food. With this soup the common person had coarse bread and water. Some say, however, that even the poorest had common wine at least to flavor his drinking water; often this wine was diluted eight to one. These people might also have had turnips, olives, beans, figs, and cheese, which were evidently cheap and abundant. During these times, pork was said to have been the only meat; one author said a suckling pig was made to last three days. The people who lived close to the sea also had fish. An ordinary dinner of the poor may have been a meal of salt fish or goat's milk, bread, olive oil, and wine mixed with water (Perl). The more prosperous in Rome had eel and pike from the Tiber and fish brought by runners the 17 miles from the sea.

The bread of the poor people, called common, army, or dark, contained much of the husks of the grains and sometimes was probably made entirely of husks. It differed greatly from the fine white bread or even the second grade white bread of the wealthy.

What the Roman soldiers ate is difficult to learn in detail. The modern cereal advertisement that the Roman soldiers lived and marched on grain probably has some basis in fact. Caesar remarked during the Gallic campaigns that Roman soldiers regretted it when they had to eat meat instead of grain. Perhaps the meat was often tainted and putrid by the time it could be distributed to the units engaged in warfare (Jensen). Tales of Medieval Europe and the "bully beef" of the Boer war let us know that before mechanical refrigeration and rapid transportation, this was often true. Therefore, cattle on the hoof were often taken along by Roman armies.

On the Roman farm, the main meal of the day was eaten at noon. An early light supper of food left over from noon was served with some raw vegetables or fruits raised on the farm. This may sound familiar to American farm folk.

Cereals and Bread

In addition to wheat, the Romans had barley, oats, and rye. Probably they found the latter growing on the farms of the middle or northern European barbarians, whom they met in their efforts to extend their Empire. Rye and barley, however, were not much used. They also learned from these barbarians to cultivate new kinds of wheat and oats.

In earliest times, the cereals were pounded in a mortar with a pestle, the resulting meal being mixed with water and cooked into a porridge called *puls*. This dish was long remembered as a national dish, as is the oatmeal porridge of Scotland.

Mills for grinding the grain gradually developed. An excavated Pompeian bakery shows several hand-turned mills; these were probably used by the baker to prepare his own flour. Later the wheat and water mixture was made into flat loaves of bread baked in front of a fire. The exact date of the first use of ovens, either in the home or in a bakery, is not known, but there were in 171 B.C. professional bakers who were organized into a guild with a president. Before 164 B.C., the mother baked the family's bread at home; only later did they have bakeries. Only the very wealthy families who had servants used their own ovens, but the farm housewife was said to have baked her own bread.

There are records of bread instead of grain being doled out to the poor as early as the later part of the first century and during the early part of the second century A.D.

The fine wheat flour for the best bread was produced by the use of fine sieves in the milling process. "People preferred fine white bread though then as now they considered whole wheat bread more nutritious" (Johnston). Some say that it was not, however, the fine-grained white bread as we know it.

Bread was so basic in the Roman diet that the word became synonymous with the word food, as it is in the Bible. It is reported that at one time as many as 62 kinds of bread were baked by the Romans. In the "latter days of the Empire, Rome was weaker and the supply of grain could no longer be depended upon" (Prentice), but it was still true that grain was the staff of life.

Much of the grain came from Egypt and North Africa. Nearly 1.5 million bushels were imported from Africa and Egypt in a year.

Cakes, pastry, cookies, and confectionery also were made and sold by the bakers. Specimens of buns with crosses on them as well as charred loaves of bread of a variety probably dating back to 1800 B.C. have been found in the ruins of Pompeii.

Use of Other Foods

The Romans used dairy products such as milk, cream, curds, whey, and cheese freely. They drank and made cheese from the milk of the cow, sheep, and goat. They occasionally used butter as salve, but olive oil was their chief edible fat; later they learned to use butter as food from the Northern Europeans, who salted their butter to keep it fresh. In the colder climates, it also, of course, remained fresh longer, and salting was not so necessary.

It is said that the Roman meat shops, which closely resembled many in Europe today, were sanitary and that police patrolled to watch over the sale of meat, exacting fines and ordering the spoiled meat thrown into the Tiber. These butchers and meat chefs (Jensen) prepared and used cracklings, bacon, tenderloins, oxtails, pigs feet, salt pork bellies, loins, kidneys, shoulders, liver, and lungs. They had fig-fed hogs from which they made many varieties of pork sausages, as well as meat balls. They used steaks, chops, and roasts. They knew the technique of boning beef, lamb, veal, and pork. The meat dealers traded in wholesale and retail cuts much like those of today. Because the meat dealers lacked refrigeration, poultry was easier to dispense than beef or pork.

Johnston and others have said that honey as well as sweet fruits such as dates were used as sweetening and that sugar was unknown. This point has been, however, disputed by some writers. Jensen said that they did get sugar from India and that their word "saccharum" refers to sugar. Aykroyd said that there are some vague references to sugar in the literature of classical Greece and Rome. He also said that "Pliny, the Elder, had heard of 'honey from reeds' which is not surprising since Rome was in contact with India and Indian sugar had reached markets on the coast of the Red Sea as an article of commerce." However, he considered Pliny "not well informed" about sugar because he said it was used only in medicine. Galen commented that "it" was not as sweet as honey so he must have tasted sugar. Apparently not until the sixth century A.D. did much sugar move westward from India into the Mediterranean area and Rome.

The Romans had many of our common vegetables; among them were lettuce, cucumbers, beets, cabbage, turnips, and radishes; asparagus is said to have been a favorite vegetable. Apples, pears, peaches, grapes, mulberries, and raspberries were used.

Roman beverages consisted of water, milk, and wine, which was drunk by all classes. It was considered by some people as uncivilized to drink wine neat. Only the most dissipated were reputed to do so. Often wine was diluted 8 to 1 with water. Ordinary wines sold for a few cents a quart, but choice wines were expensive.

Wine was made primarily from grapes. A drink called mulsum was made of four parts of wine and one of honey. When it was fermented, it was called mulsa. Cider was made from apples. Tea, coffee, and cocoa were unknown.

Salt first was obtained by evaporating sea water but was later mined. The government maintained a monopoly on this industry, so the price was kept low. When more was made than was needed, it was exported, and some fortunes are said to have been founded on this trade. Our word *salt* comes from the Latin word for salary, *salarium*; Roman soldiers for a time were paid in salt.

Sources of Foods

Fine wheat is said to have come from Etruria as well as from Egypt; milk and cheese, from Tuscany; wine, from Campania; game, from the Laurentine forests; olive oil, rabbits, pickles, and more wine, from Spain; apricots, from Armenia. Peaches and apples came from Persia; pears and dates, from Chios; pomegranates, from Libya; plums, from Damascus; quince, from Sidon; cherries, from Pontius. Pheasants were brought in from Greece; guinea fowl, from Africa; and from Gaul came pork sausage and vension. Scotland, China, India, Africa, the Near East, and Arabia also traded and furnished the Romans with food.

The Roman Kitchen and Equipment

Liversidge, writing in Rosenbaum's 1958 revision of *Apicius Cookbook,* said that we know most about the kitchens of Pompeii, several of which have been unearthed from under the lava thrown out by the 79 A.D. eruption of Mount Vesuvius. She described the hearth as the most recognizable feature; the raised masonry platform was faced on top with tiles. Much of the cooking in one Pompeian home which has been excavated and studied was evidently done in the hearth on small iron tripods and gridirons over burning charcoal. In the hearth, the cooking pots were found still standing on the tripods. Ovens, constructed of rubble and tile, shaped like low beehives, and provided with a flue in front furnishing a draught, have been found. As in hearth ovens of later times, the stony interior was heated with an active fire which was scraped out before the food was put in to be baked. Charred loaves of bread almost 1900 years old were preserved in the volcanic ash and only relatively recently excavated.

Possibly wood was burned on the raised hearth, the smoke escaping through a vent in the kitchen wall. The sausages or suckling pig were hung on a well-placed hook over the fire to smoke, according to Apicius. A stove was discovered also in which a low iron frame with a cement hearth could have been used for either wood or charcoal.

Collections of kitchen equipment from various military sites as well as in Pompeii include gridirons and cooking vessels of various shapes and sizes; all of these show evidence of hard usage and of having been burned (Liversidge). Roman utensils were amazingly modern in appearance (Wason). For mincing herbs, meat, or vegetables, they had a crescent shape blade attached to a wooden handle. They also had strainers and colanders of many sizes and shapes, a device to deshell shrimps, and a small spoon to remove snails from their shells.

When the food was dished up, it was put on a circular plate or dish. Large platters and shallow bowls of silver, bronze, and pottery have been found, but it is also thought that some fine pottery was used in the Roman dining rooms.

Food Patterns of the Leisure Class

The food patterns of the wealthy differed greatly from those of the poor. There were probably not more than 200 great houses that could afford the luxurious diet (Root). These people were not the patricians but the newly rich, who won attention because their feasting was astonishing, extraordinary, and excessive.

During the Republic—that is, almost to the end of the second century B.C.—the Romans apparently cared little for the pleasures of the table; people ate small amounts of food and lived frugally. Many were vegetarians and ate their food cold. "So long as the Romans were a race fighting for independence, or to win the mastery over neighbors as poor as themselves, good cheer was unknown among them; their very generals were plough men and lived on vegetables, etc." (Brillat-Savarin, 1960).

In the last two centuries of the Republic, simple ways, at least for those who could afford it, were replaced by luxurious living. Yet the poor still lived frugally. The ostentatious waste of food in a world of want apparently resulted when, with the abolition of the old Roman Republic and the establishment of the Empire, citizens found their sphere of activity very much restricted (Prentice). It was no longer wise to spend money on the "pleasures of properties," and other outlets were denied to them. So there was practically nothing on which they could spend their money except costly dwellings and expensive food.

There were servants to do the cooking, serving, and all household duties. During the second century A.D., it was a pauper's household in which the same person had to do the cooking, dusting, and bed-making. Wealthy households had large kitchen staffs. Cooking was considered an art, and good cooks were ranked with artists. The chefs were said to be one of a wealthy family's prized possessions; a chef cost as much as a horse or, as one author says, even three horses.

During the Empire, Vulgarians (as Seneca called them) were fascinated mostly by gourmandism and boasted about the expense and origins of the dishes they served guests. Some of the emperors, such as Tiberius Caesar, who wrote a cookbook in which he discussed 17 ways to cook suckling pig, were evidently gourmets; some even called Tiberius a "wealthy glutton." He is said to have committed suicide after spending 100 million sesterces on food and having only 10 million left. One wealthy Roman spent 10 million sesterces for one dinner party. Historians say, however, that the cost of a dinner party also included gifts for the guests. One sad note about the dinner parties was that the guests sometimes fought over their gifts even frightening the women, because the gifts often were *the women*. Atticus, who spent only 3,000 sesterces per month on household expense, is reported to have spent 200,000 on one meal at which Pompey and Cicero were entertained. Rare and very expensive fish, one of which Cato said cost as much as a cow, were used at these feasts in the second century A.D. Peacocks costing as much as $10 apiece and wild boars were some of the rare foods served. The peacocks were often garnished with their own feathers after they had been cooked.

The Roman fondness for food is an historical fact. Balsdon (1969) said "Fortunes were squandered on food by men who lived for their palates whom Seneca regarded as the most deplorable spendthrifts." In extreme cases, eating led to bankruptcy. It is said that the Romans tried to ape the Greeks, whom they met in travels and wars, but the rich in the Roman Empire became gluttons rather than gourmets, as the Greeks were.

Most historians say that almost all Romans ate a modest breakfast, sometimes only water, or bread dipped in wine, or bread and honey, and these sometimes with cheese and a few olives and raisins. Lunch, called *pranduim,* was a light meal of cold meats or eggs, cheese, and fruit with or without wine. The workmen as well as the rich ate the meal around noon; the latter then took a siesta and the workmen went back to work. The poor are said to have bought lunch at cookshops where cauldrons of stew, lentils, peas, or beans steamed over the charcoal fires. This food, dipped into little cups by the seller, was eaten on the spot by the workers standing up. One is reminded of lunchtime for workers in modern Hong Kong.

Concerning Banquets and Dinner Parties

Balsdon (1963) said that a dinner party often consisted of three courses: the appetizers, the main course, and the dessert course. Some writers also tell of a fish course which was separate from the meat course and of another course of savories served after the dessert, as may still be found today in Great Britain.

The appetizer course, called *gustus* or *gustatio,* was made up of vegetables and herbs such as lettuce, leek, and mint. With these might be served sliced cooked eggs, snails, or shellfish such as sea urchins or oysters.

The second course was called *cena* and might have three parts, *cena firstus, cena secunda,* and *cena tertia.* Some called this course *mensol.* At this course, young kid, fowl (chickens, ducks, pheasant, geese, or pigeons) were popular. Guinea fowls were expensive but valued. Ham cutlets, hare, or fish might be served if the latter was not used as a separate course. Sow's udders and wild boar were sometimes served. Fresh fish, some rare and very expensive, was used, as were oysters, which were as popular then as now. A cheaper salt fish was used also, perhaps more by the poor. Elaborate and rich sauces covered the dishes; some say that the Romans had counterparts of many of our modern sauces. For dessert, called *secunda mensa,* apples, pears, grapes, nuts, and figs might be served, followed by savories. It is told that many guests had a hard time making a choice among the foods offered and that not everyone tasted everything. A dinner menu of 100 A.D. was said to go from "eggs to apples" as we now say from "soup to nuts."

Stories of men eating to excess and then going out to vomit so they could eat more are common. We read of vomitoria. Seneca wrote "men eat to vomit and vomit to eat." He said that, even though foods were brought from every corner of the earth, guests did not "deign to digest them." It is said that doctors prescribed emetics and that abstentious people also took them. Gross overeating and vomiting is said not to have been typical in daily life but was indulged in by wealthy dilettantes.

The dining room was an important room in wealthy homes, since the dinner party was the main event in Roman social life. Guests half reclined on couches beside the table. Position on the couches denoted the rank and importance of a guest. When the guests were ushered into the dining room (Johnston), the gods were invoked, a custom much like our saying grace. After the guest had been seated, an attendant removed his shoes; then water and a towel were passed around for the guests to wash their hands. Johnston also wrote that each guest brought his own napkin, which seems strange to us. Trays were used to carry in each course and also to remove dishes. Between courses, the table was wiped with a cloth or sponge after it had been cleared, so tablecloths must not have been used. Guests threw shells of sea food, cherry stones, and apple cores on the floor, and servants cleaned them up.

Wine was used sparingly during the meal, but drinks were served afterwards to accompany the entertainment of poetry, music, or conversation. Some guests had drunk heavily before they arrived. It is said that toasts were offered after the banquet, rather than before, as was true in later times. Romans were interested in good wines, and the art of wine making is said to have developed rapidly once it became of serious interest; 121 B.C. during the last century of the Republic was the first vintage year of which we know.

The men in power were alarmed by the excesses in food, and from time to time laws intended to curb these excesses were passed. These laws included how much could be spent on food; in one law, the number of guests was limited to five at a dinner party and three for a family meal. Such laws were difficult to enforce; however, soldiers are said to have had the right to enter private houses while a meal was in progress.

Cook Books

Apicius, who is sometimes called the Fannie Farmer of Rome and was referred to by his countrymen as the uncrowned king of the culinary world, wrote what has remained probably the most famous of Roman cookbooks. It is called *Romanae Artis Coquinariae Leber* (The Roman Cookery Book); it was translated into English and printed again in London in 1958 by two authors who meant it to be a real cookbook and not just another history of Roman foods. They tested the recipes and tried to write them for modern usage. Apicius was a rich merchant who gathered information about food wherever he traveled. He also is said to have invented new ways to handle food, such as spraying his lettuce with mead the night before he picked it, so he thought it tasted like "green cheese cakes." He is also credited with having invented a way to store oysters in pitch or in vinegar to keep them fresh. He knew how to keep certain fresh vegetables green by cooking them in copper pans with soda added. He sweetened salt meat or fish by boiling it in milk and even used sour vinegar dressing to keep vegetable foods "safe" from causing food poisoning.

Restaurants and Inns

"There were no public dining places in Rome that came anywhere near meeting the lavish standards of the aristocracy," according to Perl. She said that the better restaurants did, however, send vendors to the public baths with trays of sausages, eggs, and sweet cakes for sale "to the people who frequented the special rooms for recreation and relaxation." She also said that "the inns and restaurants were crude and dirty."

Was Food a Cause of the Decline of the Empire?

Jensen credited the failure of the great cities and their trade after 250 A.D. to the poverty which descended on city dwellers and countrymen alike. He believed, as some others also have written, that decline in fecundity due to the lack of proper food was not the main cause of the failure of the Roman economy. Rather, the Germanic and Gothic hordes, when they invaded the classical world, precipitated the Dark Ages because of the break-up of political unity.

It has been said that the food supply of Ancient Rome was often critically low. Because people were crowded at the foot of the capitol, feeding them was often one of the most critical problems faced by the magistrates. As is frequently seen in modern poverty areas in great cities, the maintenance of order was closely connected with the food supply. Hordes of poverty-stricken freedmen, former farmers, were in trouble because imported foods sold below the prices they could match when they raised these foods, which sounds like a modern problem.

STUDY QUESTIONS

1. How different are the findings from archeological expeditions when botanists, cereal chemists, and geologists accompany the French or German-oriented archeologists?

2. What conditions were necessary for the beginnings of agriculture?

3. What events led man to have time or desire to develop the arts which included more attention to his choice among foods?

4. How did the Greek and Roman diets differ in general? What were the underlying reasons for this?

5. What are the principal foods which are important in the U.S. which came from Mesopotamia? India? China?

TOPICS FOR INDIVIDUAL INVESTIGATION

1. Compare the diets of the peasant in Egypt and in Greece.

2. Trace the development of the culture of modern U.S. wheat and show how important changes took place.

3. Investigate the growth of the cultivation of rice as a major world's cereal.

4. The efforts of man to assure a safe food supply were crucial to his survival. How did he guard his food supply in preChristian times?

5. Compare the productivity of man's early gardens and fields with modern U.S. yields. Give proof of the efficacy of his efforts in this area to control his environment.

For references, see page 109 after Chapter II.

2

Food Patterns-
Origins and Development from Medieval Times through the 19th Century

MEDIEVAL TIMES IN EUROPE

Early Middle Ages

After the last western Roman emperor left his throne in 476 A.D., many northern peoples came south and took control, bringing in an immense new vitality. The entire Mediterranean world underwent a profound transformation at this time. Once vigorous Roman-controlled cities became ghost cities from which the population had fled. As the powerful landowners resisted the nomadic Germanic hordes, they withdrew behind high walls where, with their newly assembled armies and attendants, they resisted tax collectors. For about 300 years, the invading hordes lived their nomadic life while a self-sufficiency necessarily developed within the walled fortresses.

Charlemagne became the King of the Franks and the Lombards in 774 A.D. The new creative upsurge which had been at work during previous centuries was apparent also in agricultural technology. Food production increased beyond the levels of the Romans and was the result of some important inventions and new technology. The Slavs used a new plow with wheels, a colter, a plowshare, and a mold board which cut deeply into the soil, turning it into ridges and furrows. This plow was a great improvement over the old scratch plow of the Romans. Because few individual farmers could afford one of these plows and the oxen to pull one, villagers shared their equipment.

Between 476 and the eleventh century A.D., the peasants throughout Europe became firmly attached to the soil, even though they had infinitely diverse agrarian practices. Councils were necessary to make their systems work. At this time, from a dozen to several hundred families, later each with separate farms, clustered together in villages for their mutual benefit. There were only a few separate farms outside of these villages. In twentieth-century Germany, there still exist many such villages.

At about this time, the three-field system, one for autumn planting, one for spring planting, and one for fallow, replaced the Roman two-field system, which had included only one for planting and one for fallow. With increased productions of food, new prosperity came. The new technology, however, was more adapted to use in Northern fields than it was in the Mediterranean food-producing areas.

Along with these innovations came greater use of water-driven mills to grind grains. The pagan Nordic peoples who worshipped Odin credited poor farm production to supernatural forces and resisted man's use of water power in milling grains. The Christian priests persisted at length in their efforts to Christianize these peoples and to persuade them that "The mill makes your bread and bread is Christ." In due time, the lords of the manors succeeded in making a regulation that all grain must be ground at the mill and not at home, thus claiming one-third of the flour as their due. This practice was one cause of the peasants' wars.

Around 1000 A.D. the horse shoe and the horse collar, invented in Siberia and Central Asia, came to Europe; the more energetic horse replaced the slower ox as the draft animal.

In the twelfth century, the Dutch windmill provided additional energy for the farmer. During the High Middle Ages, 1050–1300 A.D. (a classification of man's devising to aid historians), the economies in many places were improving, and human labor was augmented by mechanical devices and animal power. Of course, many peasants still remained on the subsistence level; one year of bad weather could ruin a farmer.

During the previous ninth and tenth centuries, when the Vikings were invading Europe, feudalism began in France as the loyal warriors clustered about their kings, counts, bishops, or abbots. Here as elsewhere in Europe, the manors became political, legal, and economic units; one lord might rule from his manor over one or several villages. Some villagers were bound as slaves to the lord of the manor.

At first, the fields were open and unfenced and farmed in common. Each peasant, however, usually had his own garden, orchard, and place for fowls as well as a field for pasturing work animals; wooded areas were also kept as a source of fuel and building materials. One stream for fishing, a water mill for grinding grain, and a bakery to bake bread were used in common by all the villagers.

By the eleventh century, most village communities were organized as parishes with a village church and a priest from the peasant class. This village community formed a closed system which did not provide much contact with the outside world, nor did it promote the development of a vigorous commercial life or lay the foundation for a significant urban population. The only markets were those which handled the surplus grain of the farmers. At this time, peasants were also beginning to have fields of their own.

High Middle Ages

During the High Middle Ages with the expanding markets, improved agriculture, and therefore an increase in surplus grain, the village system eroded; the uneventful, tradition-bound, circumscribed, and narrow horizons gave way to a different kind of life. The holdings of the lords known as *demesne* comprised one-fourth to one-third of the available land. The rest belonged to peasants whose holdings, really intermixed with those of the lord, were known as *tenements*. The lords by strong custom were prevented from exploiting the peasants; the latter were not chattel slaves. Expansion of arable land occurred when primeval forests were reduced to isolated patches. Swamps and marshes were drained, and many new areas were opened for cultivation.

A new age dawned rather gradually and unevenly, with a great cultural awakening and new creative energy, during the eleventh, twelfth, and thirteenth centuries. Innovations of this time—the three-field system, the new plow, the use of the horse alone and in tandem, and the water mills and windmills—caused increased production of food and a great commercial revival. With these changes, there was a general awakening of urban life; towns became the foci of this re-invigorated culture. Commerce also thrived along some seacoasts. The population, however, as far as numbers were concerned, remained mainly agrarian because the surplus grain was still the wealth to be traded for foreign goods.

The tillers of the land were chiefly freemen, and even the serfs, though legally under the lords, were not slaves. The lords on the continent, who now did not have enough dependent laborers, leased their lands.

By 1050, England and Germany were well organized into compara-tively stable kingdoms. The French monarchy, still weak, took another century to dominate France. Normandy, Flanders, and Anjou were moving toward coherence. Hungary, Poland, and the Scandinavian world had become Christianized. In 1095, Pope Urban II summoned the European nobility to take up the cross and rescue the Holy Land from the Moslems. So the Crusades, prompted by religious fervor and also probably by greed and stubborn wills, were launched. Their cause was greatly promoted in the summer of 1099 by the successful siege of Jerusalem under the knights of the First Crusade. No further crusade enjoyed such success, and in 1157 Jerusalem again fell to the Moslems. The impact of the returning crusaders on the people's food patterns is described latter.

Late Middle Ages

About the year 1300, at the end of the High Middle Ages, Europe suffered a depression resulting from debilitating wars which had brought about a decline in population among the rebellious peasants. These following few centuries are known as the Late Middle Ages. The economic boom had ended. The Black Death (the Plague), 1348–1349, which caused a death toll of one-fourth to one-third of the people of Europe during the mid-fourteenth century, certainly accounted for much of the decline in the population, which in turn caused contracting markets, economic slump, and deepening social antagonisms. Northern Italy suffered less than other parts of Europe, thus accounting for the agricultural period of prosperity in Lombardy and Tuscany. Some people remained wealthy and some nobles were able to hold their land, but serfdom had almost disappeared. Fields were abandoned; landless people wandered about. Eastern European peasants suffered even more than those in the West. Western monarchies began to curb the powers of the landed aristocracy. The Tudor monarchy of England initiated the giving of favor to the mercantile class. By 1789, France had not yet passed beyond the stage of tenth-century agriculture. It had had eight famines and a short crop in 1788, which was one cause of the revolution. Heavy taxation in France was also a cause of the misery of the common people.

Food Patterns

In Italy, which remained more affluent than most European countries, Italian cooks had gained fame; Catherine de Medici took her Italian cook to France with her when she left Italy. Splendid banquets and gargantuan feasts staggered the imagination (Wason).

During the thirteenth century, cloth tablecloths came into use; it was then acceptable to wipe one's fingers on the edges. The tablecloth had to be changed several times during a feast. At the time of Louis VII of France and as late as the fifteenth century, rushes were strewn thickly on the floor to absorb grease.

It became fashionable for knights and ladies to eat together; previously they had been seated on separate sides of the room. They now drank from the same cup and ate from the same trencher, which was sometimes a piece of hollowed-out bread. Some pewter trenchers were used. There were no forks or spoons at the time. A knight wishing to place a piece of meat in his lady's mouth might pick it up with his fingers, his pocket knife, or a short dagger.

During the late fifteenth century, there was a general economic upsurge following the long depression, during which technical progress had not ceased. Advances in ship design and navigation made possible longer Atlantic sea voyages. In 1500, Europe experienced the full impact of the introduction of printing. It was then possible to publish the maps needed for exploring new regions. Cookbooks and Bibles were the first books printed. Ideas about food subsequently spread.

Because commerce again thrived, the population of Europe grew, although somewhat slowly. England, France, and Spain now had stabilized governments. European ships had reached America and India. There were probably no great increases in population in Europe over the long period of the Middle Ages until around 1650. Famines and the great pandemic bubonic plague, as well as wars of conquest and intertribal wars, kept the population in check. Death rates were high, and infanticide and abortion were probably common in some groups. Low birth rates probably were also now a basic cause of the stabilization of the population.

Later, advances in medicine and sanitation came into being, along with systems of law and order. Per capita income increased; and as production increased, there was greater interdependence; one family no longer had to sustain itself alone. All of these were basic reasons for the later increasing rate of population growth.

In 1000 A.D. when the population was widely scattered, transportation was underdeveloped, difficult, and expensive. People ate only what was produced in their immediate neighborhood. At this time, diets probably differed from region to region. In eleventh-century London, there was said to be little food on the table which was not produced in England, most of it coming from a few miles away. At this time, 90% of the food was consumed by the family which produced it.

Age of Explorations

No other age in history has seen such an increase in knowledge as the age of explorations. This knowledge greatly affected the food patterns of peoples over the period from 1420–1620. Europeans, interested for various reasons, now learned that all seas were one, a fact fundamental to undertaking long sea voyages. They also gained confidence in sailing the oceans when they realized that seamen, given adequate ships and stores, skill, and outstanding courage, could reach any country in the world that had a seacoast and that at least some of the seamen could return home. On some of these voyages, the return of 50% of the seamen was counted as a successful voyage. With all of this unprecedented increase in knowledge of the planet, much was yet to be learned about how to deal with and conquer illness and malnutrition (often scurvy on the long voyages), tempests, unmarked shoals in unmarked seas, cannibals, and constant uncertainties. Travel was not new to the world, but the systematic organization of the knowledge of it and the rapid improvement of maritime techniques were.

Why did men undertake these voyages? First of all, there was the desire for wealth and a desire to acquire rich new lands. In addition, life at home was hard and uncertain; life expectancy was only 30 years. In some cases, more farmers died of plague than sailors died of scurvy. The pay for the seaman on the government-financed voyages was frequently higher than pay at home. The captains often had a great crusading zeal and a desire for glory. They did not, however, become rich. Great profits were realized only by administrators and the later conquistadores. These captains endured many hazards, one of which was mutiny.

Why did Europeans become explorers? There were probably a number of reasons. First, there were available ambitious captains and skilled, adventuresome crewmen, both of whom felt the pressure of material needs. Europe possessed the needed technology; the people were psychologically distinguished by an individualism that promoted action. European living standards were higher now than in much of the then-known world, and Europeans aspired to become rich. "Institutionally, Europe was a densely packed mosaic of thriving, thrusting, independent states, jealous of one another and determined not to be left behind in any race for power and wealth. Where Portugal led, Spain was bound to follow, France to envy, England to intervene" (Hale). In addition, European Christians had "a militant and expansionist religion that in practice allowed as much scope for profit as for the prophets."

Two distinct traditions of European shipbuilding gave these explorers a distinct advantage. The stout, broad, square-sailed trader of the North Sea and Atlantic Coast was combined with the oared galleys and lanteen-rigged, coast-going vessels of the Mediterranean. Increased trade by the Europeans led them to know about both kinds of ships and use them to advantage. These ships were more adapted to long strenuous voyages than, for instance, the open boats of the Norsemen or the Polynesian boats which depended on wind and currents. In addition, European ships were armed with guns firing fore and aft and others which could fire from the ports cut in the side of their ships.

At this time, Southern Europe was in need of metal to make coins, since their own sources were insufficient to keep up with the demands. Furthermore, the unappetizing European food was another strong motivation for these people to risk so much and for governments to put forth finances for the explorations to find spices to cover the flavor of the food. The meat available during the long winter months was spoiled and generally unpalatable. Spices were the only substances which could cover the foul flavor. Some people, as for instance the English, used onions, garlic, and native herbs, but pepper covered the flavor more effectively. After Constantinople fell to the Turks in 1453, the Turks, Moors, and Arabs were exacting impossible tribute from the overland caravans which had been bringing spices from India and Southeast Asia. So the finding of a sea route as short as possible was necessary.

The less advanced tribes of the West Indies and of Brazil offered the least resistance to European domination. Even though the Iroquois Indians in North America were good hunters and strong in their political organization, they could not cope with the quick-thinking and clever invaders. The weapons of the Yucatan and Guatemalan Mayan were far inferior to their advanced agriculture, their organization, and urbanization; the people of these countries had also been weakened by civil wars. The Aztecs and Incas also proved vulnerable to the invading Spaniards. So what the Europeans decided to do, they were able to accomplish.

Scurvy on the long voyages was one of the greatest deterrents to success in these early explorations. This is discussed on pages 177–181. Various nations have throughout history learned to use different foods to prevent scurvy. Citrus fruits were used in England and other countries. The Saracens taught the crusaders to use a brew of the leaf of a tree, Norwegians used sauerkraut, Eskimos used a brew of the newly emerged leaves of trees, especially the willow, which has been and is now used by other groups. A brew of pine needles has been used for centuries by Laplanders.

The explorations had a marked effect on agriculture all over the world because of the exchange of plants from one country to another. Thus, more crops were made available to be raised in a given locality.

Aftermath of the Explorations

Several factors caused a great upsurge in the world's population after the explorations (Bennett). They were:

1. Dispersion of plants and animals.
2. Inventions and innovations in every line of economic effort.
3. Savings and investment of capital.
4. Division of labor or economic specialization.
5. Growth of exchange which accompanied this division of labor and specialization.

6. Expansion of facilities for transport more efficient than the backs of men and animals and crude carts.
7. Widening use of crop rotation.

This economic advancement was most readily apparent after 1750, though more than one aspect of it emerged earlier.

Because it is obviously impossible to discuss in detail diets of different European peoples, only those of Britain will be discussed here.

Sweets

Honey was the basic sweetening for centuries in Europe, as it had been in Egyptian, Grecian, and Roman times. Until the sixteenth century, sugar was a luxury in France as well as in England. Although sugar had been imported, possibly from India, into the Middle East around 300 B.C., it reached Europe much later. It is said that colonists took the European honeybee to America in the seventeenth century.

Spices and Herbs

Undoubtedly the search for strong flavorings to make spoiled meat palatable sent men searching for wild herbs and led to man's domestication of herbs. Angelica, basil, bay, chervil, chives, dill, fennel, juniper berries, marjoram, and mint were known to have been used. Black and white mustard seeds, pennyroyal, winter and summer savory, sorrel, tansy, tarragon, parsley, sage, rosemary, and thyme extended the list of medieval herbs. The spices of the East had been found to be better than native herbs for covering the flavor of spoiled meat. As has been said, pepper was especially effective for this purpose, but cloves, ginger root, nutmeg, mace, cinnamon, turmeric, cardamon, and coriander also were used. So the Eastern spices became desirable and were often more precious than gold or gemstones.

As is well known, Columbus was looking for the Spice Islands when he landed in the New World. Perhaps less well known is the fact that Vasco de Gama's spice cargo on his return around the Cape of Good Hope from his second trip to the lands of spices was worth 60 times what it cost to outfit his 13 vessels.

Of course Columbus could not know that the American food, maize, would be worth more as a crop someday than the gold and spices he sought.

Marco Polo had, over a period of 20 years, told of fortunes which could be had in Java by obtaining their peppercorns, nutmegs, and cloves. Ever since the Crusades, Europe had received only a trickle of spices from the Orient. By the time it got to Europe, pepper reached 40 times its original purchase price, and one pound of cloves was worth as much as one cow.

The contrast of the medieval search for and use of spices is interesting in comparison with what we now use. In 1968, according to the statistics put out by the International Trade Center in Geneva, Switzerland, 178,560 metric tons of spices were imported by the U.S., Canada, West Germany, France, Italy, Netherlands, Belgium, Great Britain, Switzerland, and Japan. These countries import more spices than other countries. Presently the world trade in spices is worth $156 million.

When it is remembered that the flavor of spoiled meat was basic to the desire for spices, it is of interest that, in 1968, the World Spice Trade Report said that the largest user of spices was the meat industry. Even with adequate methods of preservation of meat, modern man apparently likes his meat spicy.

Foods of Spain

When the Moslems from Arabia, Asia Minor, Persia, Syria, and Egypt invaded the Iberian peninsula during the seventh and eighth centuries, they brought in many new foods. Also, a diffusion into Europe of foods from China, India, and Western Asia resulted from the emigration of these people to other countries. Sugar cane and rice were two of the principal foods, but they also brought figs, dates, almonds, mulberries, pomegranates, lemons, citron, and bitter oranges. The sweet oranges came from China in the late 1400's. When the Phoenecians had sailed to Spain in the twelfth century B.C., they brought garbanzo beans, which became a staple of the Spanish diet. The Spanish conquistadores took these beans to Florida and New Mexico. Olives and olive oil also were taken from the Mediterranean. From the Greek colonists and the Roman conquerors, the Spanish had learned to make wine, from the Germanic tribes, they learned to keep this wine in wooden kegs.

The Moslems had green thumbs; they knew about irrigation, crop rotation, and fertilizing the soil. They had skill in grafting fruit trees, and they loved gardens and orchards.

Columbus brought chocolate, vanilla, tomatoes, pimentos, pineapples, white and sweet potatoes, maize, varieties of squash, turkey, and tobacco back with him from America. The Spanish in turn took sheep, pigs, chickens, wheat, sugar cane, citrus fruits, apricots, peaches, grapes, olives, and other fruits and vegetables to America.

Eating Utensils

In 1662, when Catherine Braganzo became the bride of Charles Stuart, King of England, bowls and trenchers were still used to hold mounds of food, and thick liquids were drunk from mugs or tankards. These utensils used by the common man were made from porous earthenware. Burlwood or stitched leather, pewter, silver, or very rarely fragile china was used by the wealthy. Forks were still scarce and a curiosity in England so that each guest had to bring his own when he came to eat.

The Rich and the Poor

There was always a vast difference between what the poor and the wealthy people ate. Mush, flat cakes, or leavened bread for the poor were always made from coarse grains, often with additions of the ubiquitous peas and beans. The grain for the rich was always whiter and finer. The poor thus probably profited by having bread from which less nutrients had been removed. Great contrasts between the monotonous and meager diet of the poor and the unbelievable extravagances in food and drink of the wealthy may be traced through all times, probably even more so before modern times.

Famines

A famine differs from a period of scarcity of food in several ways. A famine is usually agreed to be a general, acute, and extreme shortage of food within a region, which is not relieved by supplies of food being sent in because of inadequate distribution. Famines cause deaths from starvation and diseases which follow the extreme shortage of food, calories, and nutrients. Infections readily take their toll under these circumstances.

Bennett said that famines, which were always localized, usually lasted a year; only occasionally were they longer. They were most frequently caused by the vagaries of weather, by insects such as locusts, or by plant diseases such as the fungus which caused the 1845 potato famine in Ireland. Devastating wars were also contributing causes of famines.

The European famine of 1315 stretched over an unusually wide geographic range from the British Isles to the North Pyrenees and the Alps and eastward to the Russian border. In upper Flanders, the burials rose by 33% in one month and 60% in three months, falling by 85% during the first week after the new crop was harvested. During the eleventh and twelfth centuries in England, a famine was recorded on the average every 14 years.

Such famines should not and do not usually occur now because the seas, open to traffic, permit food to be shipped; most governments now permit the passage of food. We cannot, however, forget the recent Biafra disaster. The network of other means of transportation also is another way in which the medieval-type of famine has, in recent years, been prevented. Western Europe is no longer dependent on local food products; heavy industrialization, economic reserves, and credits are now also deterrents to medieval-type famines in Europe.

Medieval attempts to prevent famines were inadequate, but they must have prevented some hunger. For example, farmers planted rye and wheat in the same field because wheat grows better than rye in wet weather and rye grows better than wheat in dry weather. Also, monasteries kept stores of food and fed the people in the area as much as they could and as long as their food lasted.

The Potato Famine (1845) in Ireland

In 1845 and 1846, Ireland had a universal failure of their potato crop. The potato disease attacked the growing and thriving green plants without warning. Before the tubers could be harvested, they had begun to rot. Even the potatoes which had been gathered previously rotted before use. The consequences are well known and cannot be detailed here. For those seeking more information, Salaman (1970) gives a detailed description of this famine. Also well known is the fact that the Irish came to America in large numbers as a result of this disaster, and by 1850 Ireland had replaced England as the chief source of settlers. The

Irish came to be 44% of the foreign-born in the U.S. between 1820 and 1920, when 4.25 million people left Ireland to come to the U.S.

Britain, Backgrounds for Food Patterns

In medieval times, there were two kinds of cultivated lands in England. One kind were the lands belonging to the great manors. These lands were the first ones to be cultivated by the serfs; they then farmed their own plots. These serfs lived in villages under a primitive communal system. A century later, the villagers had common fields, which proved disadvantageous because the individual farmer had less incentive to farm efficiently than when the land belonged to him alone.

The manors had their own gardens, orchards, and vineyards. Considerable numbers of draft animals, cows, sheep, pigs, and poultry were kept at the manor. But the villagers usually had an ox, a cow, pigs, a few sheep, and poultry of their own.

Britain is even now a young country compared with many others. Osborne said that "4000 years before Britain's inhabitants emerged from tribal chaos, the Egyptians had reared an empire along the Nile." He also reminds us that "When Christ died for a world already surfeited with vanished civilizations, head hunting was still a practice among the island's [England's] tribesmen," and "Fifteen centuries of the Christian era had passed before England fully acquired the qualities of a nation and began to reach for world power." Yet the British character began to take shape long before Britain as a nation existed.

The first Stone Age tribesmen who had come from Europe were adept at farming and animal husbandry and knew how to use copper and bronze. Later, the Celts who came from east of the Rhine River brought fine metal crafts as well as their proclivity to war with other tribes. Imperial Rome as ruler of Britain for three and one-half centuries left little except the site of London and fine roads. The invading Norsemen and Normans in turn gave names and essential characteristics to the people. The Angles, Saxons, and the less numerous Jutes from Germany and Denmark, who are usually grouped together as Anglo-Saxons, gave England its name. They had, before they came, been noted for their farming, their loyalties to rural life, and their tender regard for women while the men were still savage warriors. These later people who had first raided the coast of England came in to settle after Rome collapsed around 450 B.C.

During the sixteenth century, a depression occurred (Drummond). There were several causes: Many farmers had taken up raising sheep for wool at the expense of raising food crops; coinage was debased, raising the price of food and resulting in unemployment; and the government was unstable. Progressive Tudor landowners began paying more attention to manuring for the main crops of wheat, barley, rye, beans, and vetch. In the gardens, the greatest change occurred when the 1568–1572 terror drove the Flemish to England to resettle. These excellent gardeners brought their knowledge and skill with them. The productivity of modern English gardens for vegetables and flowers is said to have dated from this time. Also about this time, with the dispersal of the monasteries, the vineyards disappeared. Now the lords drank ale, cider, and every kind of mead. Some had the wines of France and the Rhineland. Both the villagers and those in the manors brewed beer and ale from barley, wheat, and oats.

The government began protecting the consumer as early as 1319, when the mayors and their officers visited meat shops to watch for abuses. When prices of grain (called corn in England) rose about 1390, the civil authorities bought quantities of grain for the poor and held large reserves in granaries. Rules were also made to assure equitable distribution and to prevent waste. The famous Corn Laws of 1815 were passed to placate the farmers who protested that cheap corn (grain) would ruin them. This of course made the price rise and this caused severe hardship among the poor, whose condition went from bad to worse until the repeal of these laws in 1846.

Famines are known to have occurred in Britain in 1371, 1383, 1437, and 1439. The Plague sometimes followed hunger.

During the seventeenth century, great country estates were founded by those who had made fortunes from trading ventures; the rural areas in some instances came under the control of these landlords, who were receptive to new ideas and had the money to indulge them. The big landowners are said to have lived extravagantly in gluttony and overeating. French and Italian cooking became popular in their homes. There was now a steady increase in the acreage of wheat. Many new books on agriculture and gardening were published due to the influence of the Flemish and the Dutch. The improved vegetables became more popular as articles of the diet. Also, a new growth of market gardening occurred following the influence of the Dutch and Flemish immigrants.

Only a few farmers, the progressive ones, paid attention to the quality of their farm animals and tried to improve them by better breeding practices. The approach of winter still meant little food for the animals until the late seventeenth century, when turnips were used as stock food. Their use increased during the eighteenth century. Lord (Turnip) Townsend discovered what was an almost obvious fact—crop rotation preserved the nutritive elements in the soil. He rotated turnips and clover with wheat and provided the former as forage for livestock. Another discovery which Dutch farmers made was that cattle would eat and thrive on the mealy residues after the crushing of the rape seed for rape seed oil, which was used then in Holland for lighting.

During the nineteenth century, scientific agriculture came to England largely due to Liebig, whose work helped the farmers begin to understand what nutrients were needed by plants. John Lawes, who had considerable estates, decided to use his fields to test the manuring process. This laid the foundations for the Rothamsted Experiment Station. Progress was made in winter feeding of livestock by the use of the by-products of the crushing of cottonseed and linseed for oil.

English Fairs: To Buy and Sell Food and Other Things

The English fairs, of which there were two or three dozen by 1400, each lasting one to seven days, provided a place for the selling of some foods as well as a place to buy other needed products. In the fourteenth century, the St. Giles Fair at Winchester, and in the fifteenth century St. Lukes at Huntingdon, the Stourbridge Fair at Cambridge, and St. Bartholomew at Smithfield in London were the most important. The fairs were suited to the times, because there were not enough goods available for permanent shops to be open all of the time.

Retailers

During the time of Elizabeth I, retail merchandising came into being. *Corn chandlers* or *meal men* were retail dealers who found their customers multiplying as London grew because the poor and those who lived in small rented apartments needed to buy small quantities of grain. The chandlers broke the old laws which would have prevented their trade, and despite persecution, they flourished. Middlemen were needed; during the 100 years between the ascension of Elizabeth I and the restoration of the Stuarts, the middlemen came to be important in the business of the sale of food. They were fruiterers, butchers, poulterers, fishmongers, cheese, and dairy-produce sellers. So in the seventeenth century, London was able to turn its back on the local markets and fairs as the chief places to buy foods. Thus, food buying became, during the eighteenth century, shopping and not marketing.

Food Patterns in Particular

According to Drummond in *The Englishman's Food*, there were at different times in English history four classes of meals: (1) those of the village laborer, (2) those of the lords of the country manors, (3) those of artisans, and (4) those of the wealthy merchants and noblemen of the towns. In general, the English were better fed than the equivalent classes on the continent; during the good years, even the English peasant was better nourished than his equal on the continent.

During times of a depressed economy, the peasant might eat only coarse black bread made from maslam (wheat and rye) or from barley, rye, and bean flour, as well as cheese and eggs; sometimes milk and occasionally fowl and bacon were added to his fare.

The general character of the peasants' diet improved during the greater part of the fifteenth century, but there was a sharp turn for the worse following a later period of deep depression when food prices rose sharply. During these latter times, soups were popular. After the people began using potatoes, they were used in hearty stew pots. Gruels and pease and bean potages were also used, with fennel often added as flavor. When the peasant could get bacon, he had bacon and eggs—eggs were cheap. Drummond thought that the traditional bacon and eggs probably came from this time. Prosperous yeomen ate beef and mutton, which gave rise to the story that the British were a meat-eating people. The beef, beer, and bread diet of England became famous at that time.

During the Early Middle Ages, the pattern of eating mostly what one grows was the same in England as elsewhere. The vast majority of the people were peasants, although some peasants were richer than others. Churchmen and nobility were very powerful but few in number. Peasants had to use money for taxes and anything they wanted to buy.

The extravagance of the wealthy was illustrated by the fact that they might be served three different meats and three different kinds of fish at each meal. After each of these six courses, they might have some kind of pastry, sweetmeat, or a jelly of gooseberries or cherries. The gargantuan meals were largely for special occasions, but the ordinary meals were always extravagant both at the tables of the lords of the church and of the state.

The size of towns and markets grew as the economy prospered. Markets were usually held once a week; some small markets were held outside churches on Sunday for country folk to buy and sell. We have better records of the legal and administrative matters than of those concerning food—that is, lacking are the homely details of what the vast numbers of the poor ate. Probably they bought food infrequently and in as large amounts as they could afford. Only barrel goods were sold in containers. The wealthy bought foods in large quantities. The diet of the poor was no doubt very monotonous.

Town people bought bread, meat, and ale as well as cooked foods, firewood, candles, articles of leather, wood, or metals, and linens and cloth. Some merchants tried to buy for later retail selling, but at first this was frowned on and rules were set up against such selling. At one time, a London fishmonger could sell only a fish already exposed for three days by the man who caught it.

There were always quarrels over weights and measures. One of the problems in English markets was that England had no small coins, and small French and Scottish coins had to be used. Prices varied, and one of the early attempts to stabilize and control prices and weights was an ordinance called the Assize of Bread of 1266.

Bread

Bread was considered the staff of life, and the quality and sale early became the concern of governmental authorities. The Assizes of Bread lasted until 1822, when the first so-called Bread Act replaced them.

Breads of three kinds were used: white or wheaten, labeled with a *W* by the baker; brown or whole wheat; and black rye; the latter two were labeled with an *H* for Household bread. The bakery also used an identifying initial which was registered at the halls of the two bakery companies, so bread could be traced to its source, if necessary, when it was inspected. Whole wheat bread was thought to be more nutritious, but white bread was preferred. Hot, unleavened coarse breads were considered indigestible. Alum was used as an adulterant when whiteness of bread became prized.

The poor still took their dough to the bakery for baking. In summer before the grains had been harvested, poor people used horse bread, a bread made of peas and beans ordinarily used to feed horses when hay was scarce.

Davis said in *Fairs, Shops and Markets—A History of English Shopping*, "nothing can recall for us the taste and texture of seventh century bread; one deeply suspects that it was pretty poor stuff."

Bread had been made at home for a long time except where it was baked in the manorial bakeries. The baker baked the owner's bread, meat, meat pies, and pease pudding. It was common for the baker to stay open on Sunday even when by law other businesses were forced to close because many people depended on the baker to cook their Sunday dinner—they did not have their own cooking facilities.

Drummond says that it has been impossible to trace any ergotism in England, except for one eighteenth century outbreak in Suffolk, where rye was mixed with other grains. He believes that this was because at no time were the English wholly dependent on rye.

Meat, Fish, and Dairy Products

The peasant ate little meat, except what he poached or was given by his lord. Most animals used for meat were raised at home, but even so quite a lot of meat was sold by the butchers. These butchers sold the fat for candles and the hide for leather; the by-products were almost as valuable as the meat. The rules said that the meat must be fit to eat (Davis) and that the animal must not have died by itself. A rule was made that meat could not be sold by candlelight; all left-over meat not sold within a specified time had to be salted. There were also recipes in the cookbooks of that period which recommended the use of garlic, as well as hot spices, to make tainted meat palatable. Large amounts of onions for flavoring meat were imported from Flanders. Because of the demand for imported pepper, the "Peppers" who sold it were first organized in the eleventh century. These Peppers became known as Grossari (from which the word *grocer* came) because they were allowed to use the great beam which had 15 ounces in one pound. This was the origin of our avoirdupois system.

Under Henry VI, the Freemen of Mistry of Grocers sifted spices; they were empowered to confiscate poor and adulterated spices. It was said that Edward I spent 1600 pounds on spices in one year. Sugar was also sold by these grocers, although at first it was used mostly for medicines. Later, it was used for marzipan and other sweetmeats.

Next to bread, meat was the most important food. The very poor often had only tripe, offal, trotters, and "hoggs" pudding made by country women. The more affluent ate beef, mutton, pork, veal, and hens, the latter raised in some Londoner's backyard. Choice poultry and wild fowl were a luxury enjoyed only by the rich.

Slaughtering took place in any convenient shed or backyard in certain areas of London. Much of the meat was tough and stringy flesh from runts or oxen too old to work. In order to get good meat at a reasonable price, a housewife had to go to market early. Fat flesh sold at a premium. Butchers were said by some to be a deceitful race who often did not take out as much blood from an animal as they should have. They also cheated on weights.

Fish was a good substitute for meat; shipbuilding and the training of mariners was encouraged; and everyone urged to eat fish on Friday and on Lenten fast days. Fish, however, except salt herring, was expensive, so anyone who could caught his own fish. Salt herring was a staple of European diet by the twelfth century (Brown). Two of the fatty herring giving 200 calories and two and one-half ounces of protein per serving could contribute much to a limited diet.

Scandinavians had trouble salting fish; the water from their "sweet" Baltic seas and their sunless west shores made obtaining salt from evaporation of sea water difficult. The Germans thus found it profitable to export salt to Scandinavia, bringing about the Hanseatic League. In England, oysters and mussels were popular; the latter inexpensive, as was salmon. In the fifteenth and sixteenth centuries, apprentices protested too frequent servings of these seafoods.

Eggs were plentiful and cheap all during the Middle Ages and were used liberally, as was butter, cheese, and sometimes milk, although milk and cheese were often scarce in the spring and summer, and milk could not be kept fresh. Butter was salted to keep it fresh.

In the fifteenth and sixteenth centuries, the price of milk was low during most of the year. Dairy products, known for a long time as white meat, were eaten mostly by peasants. The milk production of a cow was low; sometimes it took one week's milk from a cow to produce one pound of butter. Butter was also used to oil cartwheels because other oils were almost unknown. During early Tudor times, however, the wealthy used olive oil, imported from Spain, for cooking.

Pigeons poached from the landowner's own stock by the less fortunate were used often. Pigeon lofts were found on all the lands of the rich.

Meals

Englishmen usually ate three meals a day, the heaviest at midday. A working man might take a meal of roast meat or meat pies at the tavern. Stews or soups might also be bought at the cookshop and taken home to be eaten with bread, cheese, and ale or beer. The 5 pm supper usually consisted of cold meats, cheese, bread, and ale or wine. Vegetables apparently fell into disuse in the thirteenth and fourteenth centuries. There is much more written about Middle Medieval gardens on the continent than about those of England. The earliest work, published in 1440, on English plants, lists 78 as suitable for cultivation, but many of these were savoury herbs; the only ones mentioned in this list which were used as vegetables are radishes, spinach, cabbage, lettuce, onions, garlic, and leeks. Apples, plums, and cherries were said to be plentiful. Only the wealthy in town could have their own gardens inside their own walls; however, some less wealthy people in the suburbs did have gardens and orchards.

During the seventeenth century, the Jerusalem artichoke, sometimes later called the Canadian potato, and the sweet potato, called the Spanish potato, came into use. White potatoes, which had been rare until this time, were now used as a substitute for grain products even in making of bread and cakes. Around the middle of the sixteenth century, the sale of fruit increased, but it was sold in the public markets because hawking fruit on the street was prohibited. Improved quality of apples, cherries, strawberries, and gooseberries now appeared. New strains of raspberries and walnuts came from America, and later currants and apples were available from there. Oranges, lemons, plums, apricots, peaches, and quince were more plentiful, but supplies were erratic and prices were high. The price of fruit was still beyond the purse of most people. The only vegetables commonly eaten before the Flemish gardeners brought better methods for home gardening to England during the late sixteenth century were onions and cabbage, which were used to cook with meats and in soups. Vegetables were considered "windy" and unfit for use as food except in soups, in broths, or occasionally with oil in salads, which were made largely of onions and herbs.

Beverages and Their Service

Coffee houses became popular in seventeenth-century England, and many of them were opened. In 1688, there were said to be 100 coffee houses in London; in Queen Anne's time in the early eighteenth century, there were 500.

The use of tea, made in the Chinese manner as a weak infusion, by all classes expanded enormously after 1700, replacing coffee as national beverage because it was cheaper and because one pound of tea made more cups than did a pound of coffee. It was then drunk without milk, but later it became popular to use milk in it. After sugar became cheaper, it was also used more commonly in tea. Sugar was at that time one of the most important imported items, although the first sugar which came from India and Arabia was expensive. After it was imported from the Caribbean Islands, the price fell. Around 1680, the use of sugar also made fruit a more popular item in the English diet.

The passion for fine china grew along with that for tea, and the quality of English-made china improved very rapidly to meet the demand. Chelsea, Worchester, and Derby china appeared along with the more common and cheaper Staffordshire ware, with which Josiah Wedgwood made his fortune. He was a clever salesman who sold china and tea together. In Victoria's reign, all tea came from China. For the poor, tea was a warm drink in a cold climate, and the boiled water was safe to drink.

Other Foods

In the nineteenth century when the English people bought most of their food, the diet of the rural areas, towns, and cities became more uniform. The building and rapid increase in the use of railroads promoted the distribution of food.

Milk was first pasteurized in 1890. The first powdered or dried milk came after an 1855 patent. Borden's patent for condensing milk in 1856 also brought that form of milk into use. After 1850, the conditions under which animals were slaughtered and meat was produced improved. Food preservation both by canning and drying improved. Captain Cook is said to have taken, in 1772, portable soups (dried) for his round-the-world voyage. The staple food was still bread, but more vegetables and meat were eaten even by laborers, the latter always at least for Sunday.

After 1722, the west end of London was known for its good class of

Early victorian milk shop in Golden Lane, London. (Courtesy British Museum.)

butcher and fruiterer shops which catered to the well-to-do. Food generally was cheaper, more plentiful, and of better quality than it had been. Fresh fruits and vegetables, however, still often needed to be bought from farmers if one wanted them fresh. Butter and cheese were cheap, but the former often was not good. There was plenty of milk, but methods of distribution were not adequate. It is said that, "milch-asses" were driven from door to door to furnish fresh milk for infants and invalids who needed it.

One hundred years ago, 50% of the shops in England were food shops. Peddlers with their packs of food as well as other items on their backs were common in the fourteenth century, but only after 1872, when Thomas Lipton opened his first grocery store in Glasgow, did one-man grocery stores come into being. Twenty-six years later, he had 245 grocery stores all over England.

AMERICA

The food patterns of early North Americans were greatly influenced by East Coast and Florida Indians. Later, American Indians in the Southwest used some foods adopted from the Mexicans. Both the food patterns of the American Indians and of the colonists who came from Europe during the early seventeenth century were dependent on a staple food not previously known to Europe and Asia. This food, called *corn* in America, is more properly called *maize*.

Food Patterns of Early North American Natives

Although most authorities agree that some Asian people driven by hunger probably came across the Bering land bridge, what other groups came in prehistoric times is still not entirely clear, and detailed discussion of their food patterns will not be attempted here.

Apparently the first North American natives hunted only easy-to-kill game. They led furtive lives, were afraid of large animals, and probably only rarely were able to obtain their flesh for food. They gathered wild fruits, nuts, and roots. Around 12,000 years ago, a dramatic change took place—these early people learned to make tools for killing. Beautifully made spear heads dating to 10,000 B.C., have been found at Clovis, New Mexico. These artifacts were found among the bones of mammoths, American camels, and hairy elephants. Men may have stalked a mammoth, wounded it with a spear, and then followed and harassed it until it was weak enough to kill with the same spear by stabbing at a vital organ. Modern day Pygmies do this. The early Americans may have driven these animals also into bogs or ponds or over cliffs. It is thought that they ate the flesh of smaller animals as well as vegetable food. About 7000 B.C. the glaciers retreated and the climate of what is now the Western U.S. became hot and arid; therefore, the large animals disappeared.

Foods of Indians of the Later Periods

After the end of the Ice Age, the southwest Indians developed into seed-eating agricultural people and began to live communally in villages. The remnants of domesticated red and yellow beans have been found. Around 2500 B.C., a variety of maize with a tiny ear made its appearance; by 2000 B.C., maize was a well-established crop.

It is understandably difficult to compare the food eaten by peoples living under such different geographic and climatic districts as did all the American Indians. Most American Indians were and still are, however, semi-agriculturists. They also were and are clever and industrious in gathering the bounty of forest, field, rivers, and sea: wild huckleberries and cranberries; wild plums and cherries; and lobster, salmon, and other fish. They gathered wild rice in Minnesota, acorns in California, and the bulb of the camus and of the sego lily in the meadows of the Rocky Mountains. They killed and used the bison of the Great Plains. They learned to dry fruits and meats and taught the white man how to make jerky and pemmican. They extracted and used the oil of chestnuts and walnuts and learned to boil down, in birch-bark vessels, the sap of the maple tree to use in sweetening food.

Many of the foods we have on our tables today were known and used by the Indians when the white man first came to our shores. Indians had pumpkins, squash, melons, various kinds of beans including lima beans, wild turkey, walnuts, hickory, and butternuts. Most important of all, however, almost all of the Indians grew corn and used it in many ways. They roasted the unripe ears, soaked the dry corn in the lye of wood ashes to make hominy and grits, soaked and ground it into meal for kinds of bread which the white man came to call cornpone, hoe cakes, and Johnny cake. The Indians also had a kind of popcorn. An Indian is said to have produced a bushel of popped corn as a surprise after-meal treat at the first Thanksgiving feast in Plymouth in 1621. From the beans which the Indians planted among the rows of corn, they made and taught the white man how to make succotash.

These Indians have been called rudimentary, sedentary cultivators by Bennett, who suggested that they were in a "transitional position emphasizing cultivation of the soil but not excluding hunting and gathering." Had they not known and taught the Pilgrims how to fertilize each hill of corn with a dead fish, the rocky barren soil around New England would probably not have supported life for those early colonists who were neither agriculturists, hunters, or fishermen but were ex-tradespeople and craftsmen. The Indians taught them to plant four seeds of corn in a circle in a hill and to form a row of these hills, and they taught them the ingenious method of planting beans, peas, pumpkins, squash, and melons between the rows of corn which allowed these plants to form a symbiotic relationship.

The Indians in Central America are said to have made beer from corn, but North American Indians did not make or use fermented drinks from corn or wild grapes. The first alcoholic drinks apparently came to these Indians from the white man.

The Indians dried wild berries, plums, cherries, beans, peas, pumpkins, squash, meat, and fish.

Some of the now classic dishes which the Indians gave us are roast turkey, barbecued meats, steamed lobsters, spoon bread, and cranberry sauce. Verrill said that, when we gather for a Thanksgiving feast, we enjoy an almost all-American meal: pumpkin pies, cranberry sauce, turkey, white and sweet potatoes, the vanilla in the cake and ice cream are from North, South, and Central America. The tomatoes in the salad and some of the nuts of the last course also originated in the Americas.

For further discussion, it will be necessary to divide the food of American Indians into regional patterns. Kimball said that there are five distinct areas represented by typical tribes, as follows:

1. Southwest: Pueblos, Papago, and Hopi (Navajos might also be added here)
2. Northwest Coast: Tlingit, Kwakiutl, Salish
3. Vast Plains: Nomadic Dakotas, Cheyennes
4. Warm South: Powhatan, Cherokees, Creeks
5. New England: Narragansett, Penobscot, Iroquois, and other woodsmen

Southwest Indians

As has already been mentioned, after the Glacial Age, the inhabitants of our Southwest were forced by the different climate to change from hunters to semi-agriculturists. Corn became their primary crop. From Mexican Indians, the Southwest Indians learned to soak the corn kernels in lye and to make a paste which they later baked in flat cakes on hot stones, as present-day Mexicans and Indians make tortillas.

Beans were also one of their important foods; some of these were used as Mexicans use frijoles. Prickly pears and the fruit of other cacti were eaten. Mesquite furnished a yellow starchy substance between the seeds which the Indians used to make a cake. This was said by Newberry to have a little of the appearance and taste of yellow cornmeal. Buffalo berries were much used and esteemed by Indians in Montana, Colorado, and New Mexico. The California Indians used acorns in their somewhat different diet. They made a meal from these which, when mixed into a paste with water, was baked or steamed. During this process, the bitterness of the acorn was lost and the bread was reputed to be well flavored and wholesome. As much as 100 bushels of acorns were reported by archeologists to have been found in one wigwam.

The Northwest Coast Indians

Salmon, giant clams, crab, mussels, barnacles, cod, whale, halibut, flounder, herring, sturgeon, smelt, seal, and sea otter were the principal foods of these people, who lived richly from the sea. In some of the Pacific Northwest Indian languages, the word for salmon is the same as the word for fish, which suggests their high regard for salmon. These fish are even now treated with great respect by these Indians. They early believed that salmon were "spirit people," and there was a ceremony for the first salmon caught. Waterfowl, ducks, geese, and gulls were also used, as were kelp and seaweed; sea water furnished the salt in soups and stews. Small cranberries were found in the bogs of Oregon, although they were not as abundant as they were in Maine. Service and salmon berries, huckleberries, blackberries, raspberries, and salalberries were used fresh and in dried pastes. The Klamath Indians also used the seeds of the yellow water lily. For Indians in Utah, the bulbous root of the sego lily was an important food, as was the bulb of the blue-flowered (not the poisonous white-flowered), onion-like camas for the Nez Perce of Idaho. The latter Indians fought wars with the white man over the preservation of their camas meadows. The land also furnished deer, elk, bear, and wild goats as well as small game birds, acorns, hazelnuts, and wild carrots.

Feasting occurred frequently. One of the most colossal of their feasts was the *potlatch*, to which a chief invited both friends and enemies to show how powerful he and his tribe were. The practice became very competitive because each guest strove to provide a bigger and better potlatch.

Food was easy to get; therefore, there was much leisure time, and the civilizations were able to develop to a high degree. The arts of basket and rug weaving and wood carving were advanced or even more advanced than similar arts of other American Indian tribes.

The Great Plains and Other Western Indians

The Plains Indians were great hunters of bison, antelope, deer, and some small game. Those who have tried to study the habits of these meat-eating Indians have had to look at the bones outside the remains of a camp. Apparently the large dead animals could not be brought home intact, so the women brought home small parts or stripped off the meat to carry home either to eat fresh or to dry for later meals. The small limbs of antelope and deer, however, have been found in the remains of an old campsite in the Angostura Basin, once occupied by South Dakota Indians.

In arid regions of the West where pine trees grew, pine nuts were gathered regularly and were a principal food. Farther East, water chinquapins (filbert-like nuts), found in a few places around Lake Erie, were a prized food.

The diet of the Indians of the Midwest, especially in Minnesota, was different because they had thousands of acres of wild rice, found in the shallows of their chain of lakes. Women working in boats beat off the seeds with sticks.

Indians in Florida and the Warm South

The Creeks and Seminoles taught the Spanish colonists of Florida how to make a sweet milk to use in enriching soups by pounding the hickory nut (Kimball & Anderson). These Indians also taught their new neighbors how to wrap a fish in grape leaves and steam it. The Spanish brought the orange to these Indians, who then used it to cook with fish as well as with honey for dessert.

Venison was used with corn cakes; it was either barbecued or stewed with bear's oil. Cherokee women used green beans from the field in making delicate stews from venison, squirrel, or rabbit; they also prepared puddings of wild persimmons and a bread of dried beans and corn meal. They used many kinds of wild berries and fruits. Contributions of these cooks were recipes for succotash, Brunswick stew, corn pone, hominy and hominy grits, roasted peanuts, fried green tomatoes, and a stew of fresh shrimp and okra.

New England and North Eastern Indians

The Iroquois are said to have known about and used 40 methods of cooking corn, including soups and broths from ripe and unripe corn, succotash, and different kinds of unleavened breads which were boiled or baked in ashes; they also used hominy made from corn by cooking it in lye.

A visitor to a feast of the Iroquois in 1743 described the meal as consisting of an Indian corn soup in which eels were boiled, a dish of squash and its flowers, and Indian dumplings made of new soft corn scraped from the ear, mixed with boiled beans and wrapped before cooking in corn leaves.

Feasts and ceremonies around planting and harvesting time were common among the woodsmen Indians of the East. They were mostly "solemn religious affairs" and "seasonal thanksgiving"; the land was good to them, and they appreciated it. These Indians gave us what now are considered New England classics, such as codfish balls, clam chowder, Boston brown bread (probably sweetened with boiled-down maple syrup), cranberry puddings, satin-smooth pumpkin soups, and wild beach plum jam.

Cornfields were limited to eastern Connecticut, Rhode Island, central and eastern Massachusetts, and a fringe not more than 50 to 75 miles inland from the coasts of New Hampshire and Maine (Bennett). Evidence indicates that corn raising was risky in the Northeast because of the climate. All of the seacoast Indians relied heavily on fish and sea foods and wild game from their forests and probably did not use nearly as much corn as did Indians living farther south.

The Northeast Indians cooked in pits dug in the ground and heated with hot stones as well as in kettles; they also broiled or roasted meat over open fires and baked it over hot ashes. Food was sometimes rolled in a cover of fresh leaves or ingeniously baked on hot stones under an inverted kettle covered with coals. They also stored their supplies in pits dug for that purpose.

It seems probable that these Indians used maple sap boiled down as a sweetener until later, when wild honey became available to them. It is thought that the tame European honeybees brought by the white man escaped and became wild, therefore making wild honey available to the Indians.

These Indians knew and used the Jerusalem artichoke, which grew wild; it may possibly have been cultivated by them (Bennett). Bennett summarized his extensive article by saying that "Indians—even the Christianized ones—took to domesticated animals and European crops only in a small way, continuing to prefer their traditional hoe-culture of corn, beans, squash, and pumpkins, and their activities in hunting and fishing."

Corn—Beginnings and Widespread Use

The word "corn" outside America means "grain," especially wheat and barley. Columbus and his men, landing on the shores of North America, expected to find rice because they had known for years that rice was grown on the Spice Islands. They instead found a grain which they had never seen before, and it was very different from rice. Jacobs quoted from the diary of Columbus, dated November 5, 1492: "It (corn) is good tasting and all of the people of this land live on it." The seeds of this "tall grass," which they found American Indians growing and using, were new to them. The American Indians called it *zea mays*, from which we get the word 'maize,' a more precise term for world use. Maize came from a larger plant than other known grains; the grains grew on huge ears which were protected by husks, and the plant had huge green leaves.

The Spaniards must have been astonished when the Indians said it grew in 90 days, wondering probably whether one could see it grow. (In the latter part of the twentieth century, the sounds of corn growing rapidly have been recorded by scientists! Walden told of seven scientists who went with wire recorders, microphones, and wind gauges deep into a 100-acre Wisconsin cornfield "to hear corn grow." If some were skeptical when they went in, they later believed that "occasional cracklings were identified as the sound of corn growing.") Hariot, after a 1588 voyage from England to Roanoke, Virginia, wrote about maize, which he called "West Indies guinney wheate." He noted in his journal that it increased greatly, yielding 2000 grains for every grain planted.

All American Indians have surrounded corn with mysticism, legends, and religious ceremonies. They knew it did not grow wild. Even the Incas of Peru had lost or forgotten all history of corn. Because they did not know where corn came from, all tribes had fanciful tales about it. Verrill said that the Indian tribes living in other parts of the Americas who had never heard of the Incas or even those who dwelled in Mexico, where corn probably originated, never dreamed that it had made its way step by step, mile by mile, from hand to hand, thousands of miles from lands unknown to them. American Indian fables credit the crow with bringing them corn. They believed that corn was always a gift of the gods.

Scientists have puzzled over where corn really came from, and though they believe that it was a native of the Americas, the wild corn ancestor was not found for years. Corn in its present form or even in the earliest known form cannot seed itself, which is of course necessary for any plant to grow in the wild. The husk of corn completely covers the grain, preventing autonomous reproduction.

The first important contribution to the archeological solution of this problem was the finding of prehistoric vegetable material in Bat Cave in New Mexico in excavations by Herbert Dick in 1950 and 1968. Cobs and other parts of corn were found here in the layers of accumulated trash, garbage, and excrement. The cobs of this corn showed a distinct evolutionary sequence from the lower to the upper levels; the lowest ones (both pop corn and pod corn), dated at 3600 B.C., were approximately one inch in length.

Mangelsdorf later was able to produce a genetic reconstruction of the ancestral form of corn by crossing pod corn and pop corn. This ancestral form had seeds borne on the fragile branches of the tassel, as well as seeds on the ears, which were not entirely enclosed by husks. After these discoveries, the scientists knew what to look for in wild corn. In 1949, MacNeish found corn in similar evolutionary sequence in some caves in northeast Mexico; others found similar remains near Mexico City. The cobs found in these places are the oldest (from 5200–3400 B.C.) available for botanical analysis and are thought to be those of wild maize. It has been conjectured that perhaps only a small amount of wild maize grew in á sheltered and favored spot, and that as soon as it was cultivated, the wild corn was crossed by natural forces with the cultivated and thus the wild grain was lost. Walden said that pollen grains found by Sears and Clisby 200 feet below Mexico City were assigned to the last interglacial period and thus were 80,000 years old. Mangelsdorf believes that there may be two or more geographical races of wild corn.

The pollen grains buried for 80,000 years are now accepted as evidence that corn is a native American plant. Some of it may have been taken from Brazil to Africa, which would account for the reports of maize having been grown in Africa from the beginning of the sixteenth century or perhaps even earlier on the Guinea Coast. There are also stories of maize having been used as payment of tribute in South China in 1575. It is thought that perhaps the Portugese took it to India and it spread overland to the north. Flint maizes, which have harder kernels and contain a higher percentage of hard or flinty starch than flour corn, were grown in Europe soon after Columbus returned. These are said to have spread to Egypt within a few years.

The Inca civilization was founded on corn; without their stores of corn, the armies of the Incas could never have traversed the Andes Mountains or the deserts and subjugated distant tribes to extend their domains and develop one of the most advanced civilizations in their world.

The later developments of scientific breeding, hybridization, and introduction of modern machinery have written the later history of corn in North America.

Food of the Colonists

When the Pilgrims landed at Plymouth Rock in 1620, they were hungry and tired of what had been their fare—hardtack, salt horse (salted beef), dried fish, cheese, and beer. They came ashore ravenous; after prowling along the shore looking for shellfish, they found soft-shelled clams, young quahogs, and large fat mussels. The latter are said to have made them sick.

It is said that the Pilgrims landed at the wrong time of year, December 23, 1620, at the wrong place, and with the wrong amount of food. They were expecting to land on the James River, where they hoped they would be fed by their countrymen who had preceded them. For the 63-day sea journey, they carried 15,000 brown biscuits, 5000 white hard bread (crackers) and were rationed to only three pieces of bread and biscuits per person per day. With this bread stuff they had smoked or half-cooked bacon, salted and dried codfish, and smoked herring. They also had parsnips, turnips, onions, and cabbage for boiled dinners with their pease pudding, boiled mush, and beer. But instead of fertile and warm Virginia, they landed on the rocky, forbidding Northeast coast.

In the Pilgrims' first searching for food, it is reported that they found buried in the ground a large number of Indian baskets filled with corn. This was a welcome sight; although they had never seen corn before, they used it. One wonders how they cooked it. This corn was the winter's food supply and seed for spring of a group of local Pamet Indians. The Pilgrims did replace the corn as they promised their consciences they would, but meantime the Pamets starved. Because they did not have proper gear or technical skills, the Pilgrims were not at first successful in fishing.

The Indians in the immediate vicinity mostly had been wiped out by a smallpox epidemic. Squanto, who was said to be the sole survivor, taught the Pilgrims how to plant corn and other crops. He probably also furnished directions for cooking these foods. A peace treaty with Chief Massasoit and his strong confederacy of followers allowed the Indians and Pilgrims to live in peace for half a century.

The celebration of the first Thanksgiving feast, to which Massasoit brought 90 brightly-painted braves, was symbolic of the good relationship. The Indians also provided wild game and taught their newfound friends how to hunt for game and wild foods. This Thanksgiving holiday, first proclaimed as a national holiday in 1863 by President Lincoln, had for years been celebrated religiously in New England.

Colonists in the South

On June 2, 1607, nine ships carrying 800 passengers and a crew set sail from England for Virginia. To last them for the journey and until the first harvest, they carried cheese; dried salted fish; cured beef, pork, and bacon; oatmeal; biscuits; and bread and butter; the butter probably spoiled before the journey was one-fourth over. They also carried pease, onions, raisins, prunes, and dates, barrels of cider, beer, and sack (a dry white wine), as well as drinking water. For future planting, they had seeds of mustard, cabbage, turnips, lettuce, onions, and garlic. When they landed, the 650 survivors joined the 80 people already in the James River settlement. They scooped up oysters, which were plentiful, and learned how to hunt deer and wild fowl, how to fish, and how to use the corn meal which the Indians gave them. They also found wild turkey nests with eggs in them, wild grapes, strawberries, raspberries, and mulberries. There was plenty of fish, especially sturgeon, and there were large meadows for pasturing the animals which they had brought with them.

These British settlers were not accustomed to agricultural work, and the expected supplies from England failed to arrive on time. Of necessity, they made friends with local Indians and from them learned how to steep maize for two hours, to pound the softened corn in a mortar, and finally to form it into molded balls or cakes. These were then baked in ashes, which were washed off while the bread was hot. Sometimes the bread was boiled in water. The Indians taught them how to make *suppawn*, a kind of porridge, and *samp*, a porridge from parched corn; they also learned how to make succotash with beans, how to roast green corn ears, and how to pop corn. The Indians also shared their knowledge of how to prepare and use acorn flour for making bread. They helped the British find walnuts, chestnuts, wild plums, cherries, and crab apples. They also instructed them in ways of hunting and fishing. In the areas where food supplies did not last until the next crop of corn was harvested, the tender young shoots of wild plants—what we probably would call weeds—were used as food.

In 1608, Captain John Smith asked two Indians to show him how to plant corn, and the 40 acres he planted yielded a good crop. At first, the fields were communal, but when the results of this arrangement proved disastrous, each farmer took his own lands, where his incentive to grow a good crop was greater.

Corn is said to have been taken for taxes once a governing body was set up. It was legal tender along with the scarce gold and silver coins. Corn was used even in balloting; a grain of corn signified a positive vote and a bean signified a negative vote.

Native pumpkins, squash, beans, and sweet potatoes were used; the latter probably came from farther south after the Spanish had brought them to Florida.

Food Patterns of Colonists

It will be easier to discuss the food patterns by separating those of the North from those of the South. The topography, the weather, the kind of settlers, and the potentials for future crops made a great difference in the kinds of foods grown and used. The Southern colonists soon began raising crops for money, which led to a need for cheap labor; so slavery came into being. Tobacco proved to be a valuable crop for exporting to England; the owners of large tracts of tobacco lands became wealthy. Living was easier and for the rich became luxurious. In contrast, the puritanical, religious Pilgrims of the North had a forbidding soil and climate, and their general motivation was fundamentally different. However, some who built fishing ships and others who undertook to build commerce with England and Europe became wealthy. These differences should not be oversimplified, because other peoples—Dutch, Germans, Swedes, and Irish—soon came to America, bringing their own motivations, ideals, skills, native abilities, and foods. They intermingled and became a part of the total Northeast coastal settlement. Any divisions are, therefore, artificial ones used here only to clarify points in this brief discussion.

Food Patterns of the Northern Colonists

Once the colonists learned what food was available and how to get and cook it, the supply was plentiful. Deer were so numerous in the forests that by 1695 they were frequently killed only for their hides. Wild turkeys weighing 30 to 40 pounds apiece came in flocks of 100 and could be captured by placing corn in pens. Pigeons, pheasants, partridge, woodcocks, and quail were abundant, as were water birds—plovers, snipe, and curlew—in the swamps.

There were said to be as many as 100 kinds of fish available. Lobsters were plentiful; some caught around Salem weighed up to 25 pounds. Patriarchial lobsters caught in New York Bay were five to six feet long. Governor William Bradford is reported to have been ashamed that, when 67 new colonists arrived, he had only lobster to serve to them. By the mid-nineteenth century, this lack of respect for lobster had been overcome. When we now pay a very high price for lobster, we should remember its early history.

Codfish of the first grade was exported to Europe and sold to Roman Catholic Europeans and to the English for their high church fasts. The second class codfish was used at home, and the third class was sent to the West Indies as ballast on ships sent for molasses and rum. Salt codfish even today is a main article of diet in Puerto Rico and the Virgin Islands, which surprises some people visiting the Caribbean area for the first time.

Woodward said that, during the seventeenth century in Boston, money was scarce, two shillings a day being a wage for a skilled workman; but it had as much purchasing power as $3 did in 1945 or $6.90 in 1972. A 12-pound fresh codfish sold for two pence (pennies to us), and a quarter of venison, enough for a large family, was only nine pence. Beer was one penny a quart. Everyone had a garden in which to grow their own vegetables. Candles were often too expensive to use, so splinters of pine and rushes soaked in oil were used for lights.

Salmon was then held in low regard and sold for one penny per pound. Shad was profoundly despised; it was thought to be disreputable to eat it. There is a now familiar story of the family, when a knock was heard at their door during a meal, who first hid the platter of shad before opening the door. As has been described elsewhere, on page 72, corn was used in many ways. It was mixed also with huckleberries and sweetened to make a fruit cake called Indian pudding. This was evidently very different from what is now called Indian pudding in New England. Potatoes were brought from Ireland to New Hampshire in 1719 by a man named Derry.

Wheat did not ripen well in New England, so white bread was rarely eaten. If a family had any white bread, it was saved for the minister's visit, because brown bread was supposed to give him heartburn and inhibit his preaching. Rye-and-Injun bread was made of one-half rye and one-half corn meal. Later even bakeries made this bread, but it was so dry that those eating it were forced to drink water to get it down. Later, milk was drunk when available, and breakfasts and suppers of bread and milk became common. In Salem in 1630, milk cost one penny per quart. In 1836, milk was delivered in cities by wagons carrying it in wooden barrels; housewives and serving girls came out and dipped their pitchers into the barrels.

The Indians did not have wheat and oats until the white man brought them. A small bag of rice is said to have been brought from Madagascar in 1671 by Henry Woodward, a sea captain, but it did not become a staple food until the 1800's, when it was first raised in South Carolina.

The settlers had wild grapes, but no apples, peaches, or pears. Cider was diluted with water; bread and Johnny cake were soaked in diluted cider much as the Greeks and Romans soaked their breakfast bread in wine. Bread was said to be buttered only by the wealthy because butter was three to six pence a pound. Cheese was plentiful and good, especially on the East Coast after the Dutch and Germans introduced their excellent cheeses. Scrambled eggs, called battered eggs, were used.

There was no way of preserving meat by refrigeration, so as in medieval Europe, spices were used to cover off-flavors. Even perfumes are said by Earle to have been used with meats in Colonial America.

The colonial housewife made pickles, spiced fruits, preserves, and candied fruits and marmalades, putting the very sweet, nonspoiling food in large, unsealed jars. These people knew and used herbs to improve the flavor of food. Most families had only maple sugar or maple syrup as sweetening until the importation of the honeybee. Honey had become an important sweetening agent by 1638–1648. Housewives of dignity and elegance, said Earle, had loaf sugar—great loaves or cones weighing nine to ten pounds, which had to last a thrifty family for one year.

Later, around 1650, ships began to bring sugar in from the West Indies; but not much came until the 1700's, and even then it was expensive. Molasses and tropical dried fruits were also brought back from the merchants' voyages to the West Indies. Spices, a luxury to English housewives, now became more common in North America. Spice trees grew well after they were introduced into those islands by early explorers. Nutmegs and other spices were obtained whole and ground in the home with a mortar and pestle. Mills similar to modern pepper mills were also used for grinding spices.

For drinking, perry was made from pears, cider from apples, and peachy from peaches; all were very popular drinks during the seventeenth and eighteenth centuries. Mead and methegalin, drinks from the days of the Druids, were made from honey, yeast, and water, with locust beans added to make methegalin. Mead (honey wine), discussed on page 31, is the oldest of alcoholic beverages. In olden times, it was called the nectar of the gods and was used as a festive drink, a drink of courage, and a love potion. The Druids, Greeks, Romans, Hindus, and Norsemen all drank it. The word honeymoon, some say, comes from the practice of Viking newlyweds drinking mead for the first 30 (a lunar month or the full cycle of moon) days of marriage, probably to encourage fertility.

Light drinks were made from persimmons, elderberries, juniper berries, pumpkins, cornstalks (for their sugar), hickory nuts (a form of milk also used by the American Indians), sassafrass bark, and birch bark. The leaves and roots from other plants were also used. Chocolate and coffee were used later as drinks. In 1670, a Boston woman who was licensed to sell coffee and chocolate opened the first coffee house in New England. Two dealers who were probably apothecaries were licensed to sell tea in 1712 in Boston. An almost unbelievable story is told that at first the colonists boiled their tea in water a long time, threw the water away, and ate the leaves. In Salem, this tea was considered unappetizing, and butter and salt were added. When Bostonians learned to brew tea correctly, it became as popular there as in England. For those who could not have tea or coffee, substitutes were used, such as dried raspberry leaves for tea and caramelized grain for coffee. The afternoon snack called "Tea" probably originated on the American Continent in New York City where, in wealthy homes, coffee and chocolate and later tea were served with small meat pies, cheese, delicate sugar cakes, and confections.

Carson said "Perhaps only a sturdy race of fishermen, farmers, and freeholders could have subdued the glaciated, rock-strewn Yankee land and flourished in the robust climate. Yet they formed there a pattern of civilization which has been dominant in the social development of the northern parts of the U.S., determining not only how we think and feel but also what we eat."

Agricultural Practices and Equipment

In 1797, Newbold invented an all-iron plow, cast in one piece, which could be operated by one man driving a yoke of oxen attached to it. The farmers at first would have nothing to do with this plow, saying that iron poisoned the soil. Jethro Wood, a New York farmer, improved Newbold's plow by using several parts of iron attached to each other, so when the plow hit a rock and broke, only a part of it needed to be replaced. His plow was accepted because by this time the farmers began to think iron was good for the soil. Newbold's plow was ahead of its time, but Wood's was invented at the right time. The Puritans then plowed a furrow for their corn, an improvement over the Indian way of digging holes.

Meals and Utensils

The early New England housewife had no servants, so she probably was forced to use the slow methods of cooking meats and fish stews and baking beans in open fireplaces, because these needed little constant attention while cooking. She used a Dutch oven to bake bread or potatoes but was too busy to fry much food. It is said that kidney beans and salt venison was one standard dish in simple meals; pumpkin was often served for dessert. The seeds were taken out of the opened pumpkin, which was then cooked; afterwards milk was poured into it so it could be eaten as a pudding. Mince meat for pies was made of bear's meat, dried fruits, and cider or wine added. Hasty pudding was made of cornmeal mush, maple sugar, and cream.

The housewife made apple butter; dried corn, fruits, and vegetables; made cheese and butter, soap and candles; and brewed wine and beer. To make cheese, she obtained the rennet to curd the milk by soaking dried stomachs of unweaned calves.

Colonial women brought their cooking vessels and recipes with them from the old country. The ancestral saltbox for storing cooking salt hung beside the fireplace. It was often made of black cherry wood and was the colonial symbol of good cooking and provident domestic management.

Families ate from wooden plates, called trenchers—one for every two people. From this the word "trencherman" is derived. These plates might be carved out of a plank of wood in rows and the board containing the trenchers set on trestles for a table. Thus, the trencher could be removed and washed. Sometimes one side of a plate-like trencher was used for the main course and the other side for pie. When a maid and man ate from the same trencher, they were known to be engaged to marry. During the seventeenth and early eighteenth century, wooden, pewter, and silverware spoons were used. Knives and forks came later. The first fork, which had white steel tines, reportedly belonged to Governor Winthrop of Boston; it was imported from England in 1633 encased in a leather pitkin.

Midway down the length of the family table a polished silver bowl standing on three legs held the precious salt. This so-called standing salt cellar was a prized family possession. It was coated with a lining of gold to prevent corrosion by the salt. As in Roman times, there was a rigid custom of who should sit above and below the salt. Servants and children were always below it, but the chief of an Indian tribe who was a dinner guest would always be seated above it. Anyone who sat below the salt was not supposed to start conversation, only to follow.

The Puritans carved and whittled many thousands of household items. One of these special tools was used to crack and pound the cones of sugar for use. Copper kettles were used for making apple butter because iron turned the butter black. Jacks were used to turn meat on the spit on the fireplace. Dutch ovens were later used for cooking fowl and meat.

Pewter made in Holland and England was expensive. After 1750, when pewter was made in America by Paul Revere and others, it became cheaper. Before this time, tankards were made of wood and stitched leather.

In 1770, Baron von Stiegel brought expert glassmakers to America, and glass was made for the first time in the New World. A little imported Chinese pottery and porcelain was used.

Wedding feasts included a great variety of dishes and prodigious quantities of food. At even a simple ceremony, roast venison, roast turkey, fricasse of chicken, beef hash, boiled fish, stuffed cod, pigeons, boiled eels, roast goose stuffed with chestnuts, succotash, many kinds of other vegetables, pumpkin pies, and apple tarts might be served.

All the food was put on the table as a single course, so each person could eat any food at anytime according to his own fancy. Beer, cider, claret flip, syllabub, brandy, ale, and a heavy sherry called sack might also be served.

Most New England colonists were thrifty. In 1787, one colonist is said to have spent only $10 for nails and salt in one year; these were probably most of the supplies he found it necessary to buy.

During 1789–1840, there was no lack of food, but travelers complained about the quality and the monotony. They claimed that they had salted meat three times a day, although the lack of other methods of preservation, particularly in certain seasons of the year, should have made the reason obvious. Brillat-Savarin, in *Physiology of Taste* (1960), praised a dinner he said he enjoyed at a Connecticut farmhouse. The colonists probably had more meat than they had enjoyed in Europe. But perhaps the women who gathered wild greens like dandelion, pigweed, and cowslip were discouraged when their men called green vegetables "fodder."

Food Patterns of the Southern Colonists

The foods of the Southern colonies differed from those of the Northern ones. Yams and sweet potatoes, the latter known as Spanish potatoes, pecans, and wheat did not grow well in the North but were important foods in the South. Opposum, turtle, and terrapin for stew and green turtle for soup were favored foods. Negro cooks whose main job was preparing food had much more time for cooking than did the Northern housewife, so they made such time-consuming foods as beaten biscuits. Rice cultivated after 1694 became a favorite food. It is believed that oranges for marmalade were used as early as 1770 in South Carolina.

In the waters off the Virginia Coast, lobster and huge crabs (the latter said to be a foot in length and six inches broad) were often caught. These crabs, described as having "many a long tail and many legs," were each said by Earle to have been sufficient for one meal for four men. In these waters, oysters which measured 13 inches in length were found. The fish were so abundant in the brooks that they could be killed by hitting them with a stick.

Negroes lived on grits, black-eyed peas, sweet potatoes, and pork; on prosperous plantations, they also had molasses. In winter, they ate salt fish and sometimes even fresh beef. One white women noticed that

Negro children were healthier than her children. She accredited this to the "pot liquor" from vegetables which she observed the Negro children drank, so she gave it to her children and thought that their health improved as a result.

Large plantation-manor houses had detached kitchens. They also had their own mills for pounding grain. Other buildings were used for grading and polishing rice and other grains.

Farther west, the Southern settlers were influenced by Mexican food and copied their chili con carne and out-of-door barbecues. They learned from these neighbors to grow avocados, olives, citrus fruits, white walnuts, almonds, and grapes. Because they had food fresh all year around, they did less preserving than settlers in colder climates. Lye hominy was used as in New England, but here the water was often thrown on the lye-soaked corn so that it could be mashed, forming a *masa*, a paste from which the spanish tortillas were made.

As more money became available to spend on food, meal service became more elaborate. French influence, beginning in the mid-seventeenth century, probably stemmed both from the French in New Orleans and from Thomas Jefferson's influence when he returned from France after the French Alliance of 1778. George Washington had a French steward during his stay in the White House and Jefferson had a French cook during his life there.

In Williamsburg, Virginia, in 1742, William Parks published a cookbook written by E. Smith called the *Compleat Housewife*, the first work on the art of cookery adapted to American needs. He had published an earlier edition of this book in 1727 in England.

Food Patterns of Other Colonies

New Orleans.   After French explorers came to Louisiana and Florida, the French influence was added to the Spanish, especially in New Orleans. This Creole cooking combined the delicate foods of the French with the highly-flavored Spanish foods. The Negro cooks also contributed their skills in cooking, and the Indian contributed his herbs and wild game. The French use of onions and the *roux* combined well with the hot piquant foods introduced by travelers returning from Mexico.

Cacao beans were used sometimes as a medium of exchange. The tribute paid to one great Indian chief is listed as maize, cacao beans, and 2000 pounds of fine salt. Taxes and church contributions sometimes were paid in agricultural products.

In Florida, fruit was the principal crop from the beginning. Guavas, peaches, grapes, pineapple, figs, limes, oranges, and lemons, along with sugar cane and molasses, were products. Both corn and rice were grown and eaten.

The Settlers in New York.   In 1623, thirteen families of *Walloons*— Celts from Southern and Southeastern Belgium and France—set up a trading post on Manhattan Island. They had brought with them farm equipment and livestock, which they cared for well. The Patroons, who were the owners of manorial estates, especially those under the original Dutch grants, took up large estates along the Hudson River, and other settlers rented from them. On these estates, good rye, wheat, and corn were grown. They planted and meticulously tended their orchards. Food supplies were carefully stored. Fish and game were plentiful and were well used.

The Dutch also settled in New York. Dutch housewives contributed doughnuts, pancakes, crullers, and waffles to the American diet, as well as cakes using honey and ginger. From their meats, they made beef and pork sausages and pasties, or meat-filled pastries. Early writers called the Dutch settlers milk-and-cheese men because of their abundant use of dairy products. Butter, cheese, and dark breads were some of their principal foods. The father drank beer, the mother tea, and the children milk.

Their hearty meals lacked green vegetables and had too much pastry by modern nutritional standards. Extensive baking was a part of the celebration of Christmas, Easter, May Day, and St. Valentine's Day. As mentioned on page 84, they were the first to make a social occasion of tea drinking. The early records of the use of tea are few, but one report says that, when tea was first imported from Java, it cost as much as $100 per pound.

The Dutch had come to America better prepared than other ethnic groups. Instead of wooden trenchers they had brought Delft pottery ware, silverware, good china, kitchen crockery, and glazed earthenware.

The Settlers of Delaware.   The Swedish settlers also came well supplied with domestic animals and settled mostly on small farms, where they had fruit orchards and garden plots. They started the fruit and garden vegetable truck industry in New England and Delaware. They also cured and salted meat and fish, but most of their food except for rye crisp was different from that of their native Sweden. When food was scarce, they are said to have lived on oysters and cornbread. Wine and beer were approved beverages. They did not have forks, but they did use wooden spoons and metal knives.

The English and Scottish Peoples of New Jersey and Pennsylvania. The Quaker settlers, many of whom had been well-to-do in England but who had lost their possessions, built wooden houses at first. Later they learned how to glaze bricks and to use them to build houses with glass windows. Most of the landed gentry lived along the rivers, but there was really little social distinction among economic classes of the Quakers. They were not hunters, but they did fish and gather native blueberries and cranberries, which they later cultivated. They took up grazing of sheep in the hills, whereas most other colonists did not raise sheep.

Some of the early Dutch and Swedish settlers had slaves, but the Quakers were opposed to slavery and did not own slaves.

The Pennsylvania Germans. During the seventeenth century and the early and mid-eighteenth century, German settlers from the Palatinate came seeking religious freedom and were welcomed into Pennsylvania by William Penn. The first of these settlers came in 1683, two years after Philadelphia was founded. They formed the sturdy backbone of a prosperous state after they chose and cultivated their fertile farmlands. They built big red barns and plain homes and were noted for ample meals of home-produced foods. They also gathered wild foods, such as berries. They were heavy users of milk and other dairy products. They were good millers and became known for their excellent baked goods and they contributed the idea of the round pie. Muskmelons, watermelons, asparagus, and cauliflower were introduced by them. They used little tea and coffee.

In contrast to the Netherlands Dutch, these Pennsylvania Dutch (from *Deutsch,* or German) used quantities of many kinds of vegetables, quantities of which were stored during the winter. Sauerbraten, "Philadelphia scrapple," "schnitz and knepp," and Lebanese sausage were some of their contributions to the American cuisine.

Thomas credited the mixture of Pennsylvania Germans, English, Swedes, Finns, Scottish, Welsh, French, and Irish settlers with making Philadelphia a culinary capital. She says that even the simplicity-loving Quakers prized good food and extended hospitality graciously.

Pennsylvania had several sects of "Plain People" to whom food became a religious symbol. The Dunkers held love feasts after church worship services, suppers in which the main dish was a lamb stew symbolizing the "Paschal Lamb." The Moravians, who lived largely in Bethlehem, Pennsylvania, held love feasts in their churches, especially on Christmas Eve; they served warm, fragrant buns and steaming hot coffee. The House Amish, probably to keep members from backsliding, held (and still hold) church services in their homes. The custom of following the service with a sumptuous meal persists to the present day.

Cookies baked at Christmas times were symbols of the season even before the Christmas tree was used. Original cookie cutters are now prized possessions of antique collectors. The eating of animal cookies was probably a remnant of pre-Christian and early Christian religious sacrifice of animals.

The modern Amish farm differs less from the old ones than do farms of other cultural groups. It was and even now is a food factory, where the surplus food brings a good price when sold to "the fancy" (non-Amish) at a farmer's market.

Diets of Frontiersmen.   Early explorers and travelers found deer and wild birds plentiful in forest, fields, and swamps. French woodsmen and mountainmen pushed west for various reasons; some wanted to live as the Indians did. On their journeys, most of them carried hard biscuits and depended on the land for the rest of their food. Because they had to travel light, they usually carried a kettle and sometimes a skillet as their only cooking equipment. Flavorful stews were their mainstay. It is said that travelers on the Old Northwest Trail carried salt-cured pork for making stews with dried peas, so on the "fur frontier" they were known as "pork eaters."

Frontiersmen considered beaver tail a great delicacy. They were prodigious eaters, especially of buffalo meat; it is said that thirsty travelers even drank the contents of the buffalo paunch. They learned from the Indians how to make and use jerky and pemmican, although they preferred fresh meat. Cannibalism was not unknown among them when they were driven to it. Mountain men are said to have bled their horses and drank the blood when they were starving.

Some of these men were not fortunate enough to have meat on the new lands they explored, but many of them caught and cooked fish. Bread was mixed from the eggs of wild birds, flour, and water and baked before the fire on a frying pan. They used lumps of dough saved from each bread-making to make their sourdough bread, as did the men in the Alaskan Klondike.

Prices for such beverages as alcohol, often used raw and unmixed, and coffee were high when these items were bought at trading posts. Flour is said to have cost the gold-seeking California 49'ers, $40 a barrel.

From the tales of prodigious appetites and the lusty traveling frontiersmen grew the tales of Paul Bunyan told all the way from Minnesota to the Far West.

John Chapman, known as Johnny Appleseed, planted his way west from the Alleghenies to the Mississippi River. An old apple tree in Vancouver, Washington, is said to be the product of British seeds: a young woman, a guest at a farewell London dinner party for a departing seafarer, put seed from the apples served as dessert into the traveler's pocket to wish him luck. Seeds of grape, pear, peach, and plum were also put in the pockets of some of these adventurers. An old diary and the letters of the first white woman who went overland to Fort Vancouver verify the origin of this apple tree, which was discovered and reported by Lucille Palmer. This woman is said to have been surprised to be served apple pie and other unusual foods at Dr. John McLoughlin's Fort Vancouver.

Corn was still the most important food in newly settled areas because it could be planted even before all the stumps were out of a field. But salt was almost more important than food to the frontier people. It was essential for farm animals as well as for meat preservation; in the beginning, salt cost four times as much as beef. (The term "packer" refers to packing meat in barrels of salt.) Daniel Boone was noted for his ability to find salt licks where his animals could find their needed salt; his last land grant on the Missouri River is known as Boone's Lick.

The coming of railroads made it possible to ship fresh produce, meat, eggs, and milk into cities like New York and Boston. The preference for white eggs in New York City and for brown eggs in Boston has been accounted for because the chickens raised around each city produced that color of eggs. When eggs of the other color were seen, it was known that they had been shipped in and would not be as fresh as local eggs.

Gustavus Franklin Swift, a Yankee from Cape Cod, went to Chicago in the 1870's to set up a packing plant. He is credited with true Yankee thrift because he used all parts of the animal and with being the first one to use and promote the use of refrigerator cars in which to ship meat. He had the vision to see that excellent dressed and well-fattened beef could bring a high price in the Eastern cities. The large meat-packing firm he founded is testimony that he was right. P. D. Armour founded his meat packing firm in the same year—1875.

In 1890, cattle drives of 60–90 days' duration brought over 10 million cattle from San Antonio, Texas, to Kansas. The blue stem grass around Abilene and Manhattan had a reputation as excellent cattle feed.

The process of making artificial ice was patented in 1846 by John Dutton, who lived in Pennsylvania; four years later, Alexander Twining patented an ice-making machine, which was a great boon to the meat distribution industry and furnished cleaner and more sanitary ice to be used around food. It also made possible the shipment of tropical fruits for long distances.

After Nicolas Appert showed the way to can foods in 1819, William Underwood and Thomas Kensett landed in New York City and founded a firm to preserve foods by canning. The need for canned foods to feed the armies during the Civil War gave a great stimulus to this industry.

Few inventions for the home have ever affected life as much as the invention in Europe by Massachusetts-born Benjamin Thompson, later called Count Rumford. During the late eighteenth century, in a workhouse in Munich, he invented and built the cooking range. He worked assiduously for a long time on different models and pans to use on this range. In 1840–1850, old fireplaces were beginning to be boarded up, but even in Eliza Leslie's *Cook Book*, published in 1870, it was taken for granted that cooking was still being done in the fireplace. Marian Harland, in 1872, noted that some housekeepers still used a spit. Some thought that the food cooked on a range did not taste as good as that cooked in a fireplace, an attitude with which modern barbecue fans would probably concur. But the task of cooking was certainly made easier as gas and electric ranges later replaced wood- and coal-burning ranges.

Transporting and Selling Food

The rivers were the highways before the days of roads, and goods were transported on rafts. A "raft of pins" meant just that. After roads were opened, the Conestoga wagon, usually 16 feet long by 4–5 feet wide and 6–7 feet high, afforded a cargo space of 500–600 cubic feet; a raft 60–100 feet long could easily carry ten times what the wagon could.

Peddlers with packs on their back could walk through fields and unopened brushlands. It was more efficient and less tiring, however, to use a horse or mule and a wagon as soon as paths or roads were opened up and made this possible. Sometimes a peddler, tired of traveling, settled down in a likely place, usually at a crossroads, and opened a general store.

"Shake hands?" Kitchen ⌐ the mid-nineteenth century (Courtesy Library of Congress.)

Electric stove. First patented 1895 in U.S. (Courtesy Seattle City Light.)

Gas range, 1930. *(Courtesy Brooklyn Union Gas Company and Washington Natural Gas Company.)*

An electric kitchen of the 1970's. *(Courtesy Seattle City Light.)*

These merchants carried food, household items, and farm supplies and equipment. The first specialty stores in America and England were bakeries. Some of these stores used barter, exchanging feathers for molasses, potatoes for salt, cherry boards for tropical dyes, or hemlock bark for tea and coffee.

In 1789, when George Washington was on a tour, he stayed at a tavern in Milford, Pennsylvania. He criticized the tavern for the poor food and the fact that they had no silver spoons. Not much relishing his supper of meat and potatoes, he called for a bowl of bread and milk. When a pewter spoon with a proper handle was served with this and he complained, he was told the house could afford no silver spoons. He gave the serving maid a two shilling piece and told her to go and borrow a silver spoon, which she acquired from the minister.

In 1825, John Delmonico, a Swiss captain of a trading ship going to the West Indies, wished to sell European wines; he opened near a bakery in New York City what has often been and still is called "a hole in the wall." This was the small beginning of Delmonico's Restaurant.

G. H. Hartford and his partner, G. Gilman, watched tea being unloaded from ships and decided to devise ways to sell it more cheaply. They bought tea wholesale and brought the cost down to $.30 per pound. Thus, they founded the great American Tea Company, which later was called the Great Atlantic and Pacific Tea Company.

The day book of a midwestern grocer in 1862 is said to have shown the entire list of imported articles of food to be coffee, tea, figs, mustard, pepper, cloves, allspice, nutmeg, ginger, cinnamon, lemons, oranges, sago, prunes, raisins, and almonds.

Farm Machinery

The plows used by early settlers were discussed on page 85. John Deere, a blacksmith in Vermont, peddled the first 3 plows, which he had invented, in 1837. They were designed so that they would slide smoothly over the sticky prairie earth and come out clean. In 1839, he made and sold 10 plows; in 1842, he sold 100. Cyrus McCormick invented the reaper in 1832. Later a binder and the J. J. Case threshing machine were developed. Modern mechanized farming followed.

Food preparation on the nineteenth- and twentieth-century farm was influenced when more men were needed to run the huge machines. The farm wife then had to cook in a much larger quantity. The large threshers dinners became neighborhood affairs. The farm wife and her helpful neighbor housewives prepared the big dinner. Often the woman of the house and her daughters worked for days in advance preparing the food.

Large-Scale Farming Begins

Oliver Dalrymple of the Northern Pacific Railroad began what was then called "bonanza" farming on the 75,000 acre holdings of that railroad in the Eastern North Dakota Red River Valley. In 1880, Dr. Hugh Glenn harvested a crop of 1 million bushels of wheat on his Sacramento Valley, California, ranch; this was one of the largest wheat farms of the times. These were the forerunners of the large-scale farm food production of today.

Improving the Quality of Food

An expert on the household, Lillian W. Betts, complained in the late nineteenth century that cookbooks were not scientific; "they not only contradicted each other, they contradicted themselves." She encouraged a young woman, Fannie Farmer, who was interested in preparing good food, to write a scientific book. By the time Miss Farmer was 39 years old and had suffered two paralytic strokes, she had distinguished herself as a teacher of cooking. She had attended the Boston Cooking School and graduated when she was 32. After graduation, she was asked to be assistant director of the school; two years later, she became its director. Fannie Farmer's *Boston Cooking School Cookbook*, said to be the first scientific cookbook, was first published at her own expense in 1896. The page of copyrights in new editions of this book gives an interesting history. In 1965, the eleventh edition, called *Fannie Farmer Cookbook*, came out. At that time, over 3 million copies had been printed. Miss Farmer saw this book through 2 revisions and 18 reprintings herself before others took over. In these first 18 printings, 291,000 copies were produced. A paperback, first published in 1957, was in its thirty-first printing in 1973. Because the Preface to the first edition (1896) is historic in itself, it is quoted here:

> With progress of knowledge the needs of the human body have not been forgotten. During the last decade much time has been given by scientists to the study of foods and their dietetic value, and it is a subject which rightfully should demand much consideration from all.

It is my wish that it may not only be looked upon as a compilation of tried and tested recipes, but that it may awaken an interest through its condensed scientific knowledge which will lead to deeper thought and broader study of what to eat.

So nutrition and food preparation were jointly promoted. The work of Ellen H. Richards and Mary Hinman Abel in the New England Kitchen in Boston forms another interesting chapter which can be found in other books.

Legal attempts to improve food are illustrated by Massachusetts' passing of a law in 1850 prohibiting the adulteration of milk. Milk was sold in bottles in the late 1850's in Brooklyn; bottling and the concept of certified milk, for which the medical milk commission set up standards, were further efforts to produce and sell safe milk. Dr. Harvey Wiley, who was the prime mover in the enactment of federal pure food and drug legislation, became chief of the Chemical Division of the Department of Agriculture in 1883.

These are only a few of the early efforts which have developed into the present system of safeguarding our food supply. Others can be found in other source books.

The Land Grant College Movement

In 1862, President Lincoln signed the famous Morrill Act which granted the proceeds from federally owned lands for perpetual endowment of what would be colleges for the sons and daughters of the industrial and working classes. These colleges were directed to offer instruction in agriculture and the mechanical arts; the latter included home economics. These colleges, most of which later became universities, were directed to teach, to do research, and to take knowledge to the people. The Iowa legislature had passed a bill in 1858 to establish an agricultural college, so they promptly took advantage of the proferred aid, becoming the first state to accept the provisions and responsibilities of the Land Grant College Act. Other states used the money which came to them in different ways, making it difficult to state which was the first Land Grant college.

The Iowa Agricultural Experiment Station, established in 1888, has a long history of research designed to help farmers. Many people credit the bounty of our food supply to the increase in production made possible by the Agricultural Research Stations and Land Grant Universities in every state in the union.

America is said to have given the world 11 botanical beverage plants, 5 cereal grains, 145 fruits, 24 nuts, 34 root plants, and 27 miscellaneous plants.

Important Foods

Space does not permit extensive discussion of the many foods especially important in man's diet; therefore, we have chosen to tell in depth only a few of these stories. Potatoes and bread as widely used staple foods around the world will be discussed separately here.

The Potato: Number One Vegetable of the World. *Papata, Murphy, mickey, spud, and Irish potato* all refer to the vegetable we commonly call the white potato. Yet the uncles, aunts, cousins, and grandparents of this potato have skins of white, pink, red, yellow, brown, green, purple, orange, black and spots of many colors. Their meat may be yellow, lavender, pink, or white. No one quite knows how many varieties of this useful vegetable grow in its native home, the Andes Mountains of Peru, Bolivia, and Chile.

When the potato was first found in Peru, it was observed that the natives in the high country—10,000 feet altitude or more—had a method of freeze-drying their potatoes in the sun. They used the frozen potato cooked whole or pounded into a flour, which they dried in the sun. Frozen potatoes could be kept from one season to another. Prehistoric stories of dried potatoes have been found, showing that potatoes were as much in demand in the days of the Incas as they are today. The skins of the frozen dried potatoes were rubbed off by walking over them with bare feet, which must have been a hard task. These potatoes turned black and were as hard as stones, so they had to be soaked three to four days before they could be cooked.

Salaman said that the natives of Peru and Bolivia, having been frightened by the terrors of the jungle which spread over the plateau to the coast, migrated out to the eastern slopes of the mountains. They found secluded valleys and fertile portions of the high tablelands around the great inland sea of Lake Titicaca, where the altitudes vary from 12,500 to 15,000 feet above sea level. Because their usual plants, such as manioc and maize, would not grow at such altitudes, they had to look for hardier plants. They also had to protect their food supply by using a vegetable which would be edible after it was frozen. Salaman commented on this: "Perhaps one of the most remarkable of man's conquests of nature gave him the key to success." It is for this reason that the potato is discussed separately. On the Andean highlands from Columbia on the north to Chile on the south, these early men found the different species of the tuber of the parent stock of our domestic potato, the species named *Solanum*. It is thought, that the hybrids were not produced by these men but were found as wild varieties. On these highlands, the use of the potato made life possible, giving the people a way to survive in this environment.

The frost-resistant varieties now grown around the highest levels are said to be tasteless and insipid and are reserved to make *chuno* (the sun-dried potato). Other varieties were probably grown by the Incas to use fresh, as they are today. A recent observer says that she counted 89 varieties of these potatoes at the Potato Fair in La Paz, Bolivia.

History has recorded that the potato has made more trans-Atlantic voyages between Europe and America during the past 300 years than any other vegetable. During the latter half of the nineteenth century, research by the eminent Russian scientist, Vavilov, proved that the European potato had come from Peru. Others believe these primitive potatoes also grew in Chile and Bolivia. From available records, it has been concluded that the potato reached Spain between 1564 and 1576, where for a time its cultivation was local and insignificant. It probably left South America around 1569 and arrived in Seville in 1570. It is said to have been brought to New England in 1719 by Irish immigrants from Londonderry.

Some credit Sir Walter Raleigh with first growing potatoes in England in 1585, and others say Sir John Hawkins introduced them into Ireland in 1565. Others believe that Hawkins' potato was the *batatas,* or Caribbean sweet potato. In some of the early records, the Jerusalem artichoke and the sweet potato have been confused with the white potato. Salaman, who has studied extensively the history of the potato, supports the belief that Sir Walter Raleigh introduced it into Ireland. Salaman also says that it possibly may have reached there accidently when, at the dispersion of the Armada, some ships were wrecked on the west coast of Ireland, the hulks were plundered, and potatoes were found in the cook's stores. These may have been planted on the coast of Kerry and Cork; Whichever way they came, Salaman fixes their date of entry into Ireland at between 1586 and 1588. He says of the potato that "One can only suppose that it won the confidence of the people because it fitted readily into the economic structure of their life. . . ."

The people in the rich, semi-industralized western part of Europe took 100 years to begin to appreciate the merits of the potato. It took 250 years for the potato to gain acceptance in England and only 50 years for the Irish to adopt it as their own because the latter appear not to have developed prejudices against it originally.

There are numerous stories, not all of which can be recounted here; the reader is referred to Salaman for a fuller description. The stories detail the difference between the autocratic methods of the Prussians trying to force people to grow potatoes and the clever method of the French, carefully guarding potato plots during the daytime and purposefully leaving them unguarded at night so people could steal the plants. Louis XVI is said to have worn a potato blossom in his buttonhole and Marie Antoinette to have worn one in her hair. The nobility also planted potatoes in their gardens and were careful to be observed by the peasants as they ate the potatoes. Parmentier, a French military pharmacist, is credited with having learned to eat potatoes as a prisoner of war in Germany, and in 1780 he encouraged the French people to grow and eat potatoes.

By the middle of the nineteenth century, the potato was a staple of the British Isles, Northern Europe, and North America. Although the potato has been known in Japan for 200 years, according to Boswell, the Oriental people have never cared for it. Even after World War II, the state of culture of the potato in Japan was below that of other foods.

Brogger said that the potato, introduced into Norway about 1750, contributed slowly to the transformation of agriculture there. He describes the resistance it encountered during the generation which was required to introduce it. The Presbyterian clergy in Scotland also are said to have opposed the use of potatoes as food, because they were not mentioned in the Bible and therefore were not safe to eat. At one time, Europeans believed that potatoes caused leprosy, fevers, and other maladies. As late as 1771, the French government asked the medical faculty of Paris about the ill-reputed potato, and they replied that the potato was a good food of great use and not injurious to health.

The potato produces more food per acre than most other crops and can be raised in a variety of climates. It grows farther north and at higher altitudes than cereals. It is easy to cultivate and pleasant to eat.

It furnishes great protection in times of want and has spread extensively over widely scattered populations and territories. The Irish found the potato easy to grow; it was not necessary to plow before planting; all that they needed to do was to spade and to dig trenches. The word *spud* is said to have come from the word *spade*.

Although potatoes are credited with having saved people from famine after the 30 Years War, the one-crop potato economy brought about disaster in Ireland in 1845–47. See page 60.

Bread. Our word *cereal* comes from *Ceres*, the Roman goddess of agriculture and the harvest. When men first began to cultivate grains or used wild grains as food, they first parched them to make them edible. To be able to remove the tough glume (outer husk covering the grain), they had to parch the emmer wheats. They then learned to grind the grains to make a porridge. The next step was to make a flat loaf of bread from the heavy cereal paste and to bake this in front of the fire, as did the marching Roman soldiers even after ovens were in use back home.

The earliest records of the use of wheat are said to come from the "finds" of the archeologists at Jarmo, 6700 B.C. It is said that the seeds of wheat are the seeds of civilization. During the thousands of years which followed its domestication, wheat was grown in ever-increasing amounts in the Fertile Crescent, see page 9.

Wheat is the only cereal grain which contains sufficient gliadin and glutenin, two proteins which, when mixed with water, form the elastic protein gluten, making possible the rising and elasticity needed for bread. Rye contains some gliadin and glutenin and can be used to make bread, but for a more highly risen bread, some wheat flour is mixed with the rye flour. Barley, the other cereal used by early man, does not have the proteins to form gluten and therefore makes heavy loaves. Barley was, through the centuries, the cereal of the poor. It is said that as soon as wheat became plentiful the Egyptians abandoned the use of barley. Naked wheats became important during the Middle Ages. These wheats have glumes less coarse and less difficult to remove than the earlier varieties of wheat, hence their threshing is easier. Rye grows more easily and—abundantly on the soils of Northern Europe, which probably explains why the people of this region have for centuries used much rye bread.

The next development in bread making was fermentation. There are various theories of how man discovered that this process could be used to make his heavy cakes lighter and more palatable. Perhaps he forgot to bake some cakes, the dough fermented, and he discovered the air bubbles in the cakes. The Egyptians were probably the first people to use fermentation in their bread, although the peoples of Mesopotamia may have done so; the former often are called the "fathers of bread" and the "bread eaters." The Greeks and the Romans both recognized the hard and soft wheats and the use of the former in bread-making. The Egyptians undoubtedly advanced bread-making more rapidly than any other ancient peoples. Dough found in a 4500-year-old Egyptian tomb showed, when examined microscopically, 100 million yeast cells per grain of dough. When did the art of cultivating yeast begin? This is not certain, but we do know that the Egyptians brewed beer and probably would not have used a piece of dough as the source of that yeast; so they must have cultivated yeast. It should be pointed out that each stage in the use of cereals and in bread-making can be found today, beginning with porridge, flat cakes and other flat breads, and sour dough starters.

The whiteness of bread has been prized from Egyptian times through Grecian, Roman, and Medieval times, as it is today. The Romans recognized the higher nutritive value of whole wheat (brown) bread. See page 39. The theater-going public, if they could afford it, as well as other wealthy people in Athens, are said to have demanded and eaten white bread. The Greeks, however, called the whole-wheat cakes "health cakes," probably because they considered the bulkier stools produced when whole wheat bread was eaten as healthier. White bread is said to have been given by the Greeks when an individual had diarrhea.

Throughout history, there are records of the adulteration of flour; in Medieval England, for instance, flour was adulterated with alum and ammonium carbonate to make the bread whiter. Barley meal and cooked potatoes were used also for this purpose. The weight of the loaf of bread and the adulteration of flour have been the subject of laws since Grecian and Roman times. See page 30. Market police watched the weight closely. The description of these ordinances is discussed on page 65.

It is easy to understand how the development of a civilization is often a story of bread-making. First of all, men had to settle in a permanent village before they could grow grain efficiently and make bread. The kind of ovens which man learned to use rather early in the process were not portable. In order to improve methods of grinding and milling, the wheat demanded man's best efforts; baking of large numbers of varieties of bread was considered worthy of praise and reward. The Egyptians

Kitchen bakery thought to be from Wayfarers' Lodge in 1890's. (Courtesy Library of Congress. Photo by C. H. Currier.)

Commercial baking today is one of the largest industries in the U.S. food field.

In Tunisia, bread is precious. (Courtesy CARE.)

Kurdish woman baking bread. (Courtesy FAO, Rome, Italy. Photo by Jamal Hammad.)

are said to have prepared and baked 50 kinds of bread and cakes, muffin-shaped long rolls, spiced breads, and breads sprinkled with seeds, like today's caraway rolls.

Improved agricultural methods made more abundant crops of wheat available, giving a nation such as Egypt money and power. So it was said in Roman times "who controls Egypt will be Emperor of Rome." Under Augustus, at the beginning of the Imperial Period, 144,345,000 bushels of wheat, enough to feed 2 million people for one year, were imported into Rome from Egypt and Africa.

Grain cutting progressed from the sickle to a scythe to the great modern combines. Threshing was first done by men stomping on the grain and later by the use of animals to tromp on it. The Romans are said to have had a water mill in 100 B.C. From the use of the first primitive mortars and pestles to modern rolling mills is a story of man's struggle to produce food with less human effort. Aykroyd and Doughty said that, today in North America, it takes 3 man hours of work to harvest an acre of wheat, whereas it took 50 hours 100 years ago.

The prestige of the miller and the baker was great during Egyptian, Grecian, and Roman times but fell drastically when the barbarians took over Europe. However, Christians considered bread holy because of Christ's prayer "give us this day our daily bread" and because he said "This is My Body"; and as Christianization took place, the barbarians' respect for bread changed. Early Christians put three crosses on each loaf of bread. The word bread occurs 264 times in the Bible, and it probably always refers to wheaten bread. Israelites are thought to have learned to make bread from the Egyptians.

In 100 A.D., Roman miller-bakers were well organized into a college, (guild) the members of which were represented in the Senate and were forbidden to associate with comedians and gladiators. They were classed as artisans along with tailors. Every year, these bakers' guilds celebrated a festival on June 9th, when baking tools and ovens were wreathed in flowers.

Around 1000 A.D., the situation of bread bakers worsened. The hatred of millers and bakers by the populace arose probably because some millers stole grain when they were hard pressed. These millers were, however, the only knowledgeable engineers among the technically ignorant people of the Middle Ages, so they did acquire some power, even police powers—rights of local jurisdiction. They began to interfere in peasant's affairs, which was one cause of some of the peasants' wars.

The bread of the Middle Ages is said to have been of lower quality than that of Classical times. When grain became moldy or cultivation was interrupted because of war, the terrible famines of the twelfth and thirteenth centuries resulted.

During the days of the luxury-loving kings and queens of France, poor people were starving for lack of bread or other food while the tables of the court had heaping baskets of bread on them. Trenchers were made of bread and were usually 6 inches wide and about 3 inches high. The table cloth was also often made of bread. Paupers waited at the doors in the courtyards to get this food-soaked bread after the royal meal.

In these terrible times, tenderness toward bread was especially evident. In the Medieval German provinces, all bakers always faced and avoided turning their backs on ovens to show respect to bread.

In early societies, the housewife baked the bread, but as populations became more concentrated and artisans came to be specialists, bread was made in bakeries. In Jerusalem, the bakers took their bread to a bakery-factory for baking. Aykroyd and Doughty said that commercial bakeries have existed in towns and cities for 4000–5000 years.

In ancient Egypt, bread was the coinage of the realm; for hundreds of years, workers were paid in bread; for the servant, the daily average wage was three loaves of bread and two jugs of beer. Old Anglo-Saxon landowners, called halfords, believed that in order to do good work a man must be well fed. The title lord came from this old word and it came to mean "Man who gives out bread." In the middle of the eighteenth century, alms bread was made of five parts of wheat, four of rye, and three of peas (Ashley).

It is said that, if the Egyptians had not developed the art of bread making, the French would have because they are alike in their worship of bread. Bread has been held to be precious by many peoples throughout all history. In modern Romania, if a person drops a piece of bread, he kisses it after picking it up. Every Greek who had any part of the souring or making of bread was held to be performing a priestly service as a religious apprentice to Mother Earth (Jacobs).

Hot-cross buns, which Christians use on Good Friday, actually originated in pagan times (Spicer). The early Egyptians offered to their moon goddess cakes marked with horns said to have been symbolic of their horned ox, used as a sacrifice. Early Greeks presented horn-imprinted cakes to Astarte and other deities. Later, the horn became a cross. This cross was supposed to have represented the quarters of the moon. The Romans ate hot-cross buns at sacrificial feasts. The Saxons inscribed loaves with crosses in honor of Eostre, the Teutonic Goddess of the Dawn, who was associated with the vernal equinox. Our word Easter came from Eostre. The early Christian fathers adopted making crosses on bread, and the eucharistic wafers were imprinted with the Greek cross as an emblem of the Host. The English have made hot-cross buns for centuries: the original Royal Bun House in Chelsea made buns which became famous. Everywhere pastry cooks and bakers competed. Hawkers peddled buns on the streets from 6 am to 6 pm. One cry of the sellers went like this:

> Hot cross buns
> If you have no daughters,
> Give them to your sons;
> But if you have none of these merry little elves,
> Then you may keep them all for yourselves.

In 943 A.D. a plague struck the Franks around Limoges. They ate a bread which was wet and had a black, sticky substance inside. Today this illness is known as ergotism, caused by a fungus which grows on rye. Insects visited the "sweat drops" on the blackened grain and spread the spores in wet weather. No Roman farmer would have used this grain, nor would a Roman miller have milled it or a baker have baked it; Columella had instructed the Roman farmers how to fight the disease. Romans also knew that cleanliness was necessary in bread-making. This tenth-century plague in France was the only mass disaster from ergotism (occurring because knowledge of technical procedures in the art of milling and baking had declined). The church had banned medical research as magic, so not until the late Renaisance did two physicians, one in 1582 and one in 1600, discover the cause of ergotism.

Bread for the poor has been made throughout the ages from many foods other than our common cereals. Prentice told of the use of acorns, fine sawdust and bark of young pear or cherry trees, or the twigs of young chestnut or oak trees. He also recounted the use of a number of vegetables and their roots, as well as beechnuts and chestnuts.

In Auvergne, France, loaves of bread weighing 20 to 30 pounds were kept for a month in winter. In an Austrian country home museum in the Tyrol, huge doughnut-shaped loaves of bread can still be seen strung on the original wires. Because it was scarce, this bread was used dry as crumbs on soups and stews so less would be eaten.

STUDY QUESTIONS

1. Why do we have more information about the eating habits of some early Europeans than about similar habits of other groups?

2. How did early food production and distribution in England lay the foundations for our great modern food industry?

3. In what ways are we in debt to the entire world from medieval times until the nineteenth century for our abundant food supply?

4. Describe how the foods and food preparation of a seventeenth- or eighteenth-century American Thanksgiving dinner compares with such a meal in the late twentieth century?

5. How is the potato connected with American politics of this century?

TOPICS FOR INDIVIDUAL INVESTIGATION

1. Trace the development of agriculture and animal husbandry for one of the following cultures: China; one section of Africa; the Mayan or Aztec; one group in Northern Europe.

2. Trace Medieval agriculture through its major stages with illustrations of the following:
a. Development of efficiency of tools;
b. Attempts to deal with weather conditions;
c. Interchange of foods with groups who lived great distances away.

3. Show how the European backgrounds of early colonists affect our modern-day foods.

4. Discuss in detail the contributions of one group of American Indians to our modern-day food.

5. Trace one major food industry through its development during the last 150 years.

REFERENCES AND SUGGESTED READING

Early Man

Adolph, William H. What Early Man Discovered about Food. *Harper's Magazine*, 212: 67–70, May, 1956.

Brace, C. J. *The Stage of Human Evolution.* Prentice-Hall, Englewood Cliffs, New Jersey, 1967.

Braidwood, R. J. *Prehistoric Men*. Chicago Natural History Museum Press, Chicago, Ill., 1948.

Braidwood, R. J. Did Man Once Live by Beer Alone? *Amer. Anthropology*, 55:515–516, 1953.

Brew, J. A. The Metal Ages. Copper, Bronze and Iron. Chapter V, pp. 111–138. *Man, Culture, and Society*, Ed. H. L. Shapiro. Oxford University Press, New York, 1960.

Brogger, A. W. From the Stone Age to the Motor Age. *Antiquity*, 14: 163–181, 1940.

Caldwell, J. R. *New Roads to Yesterday*. Basic Books, New York, 1966.

Childe, V. Gordon. *Man Makes Himself*. Mentor Books, New American Library, New York, 1951.

Childe, V. Gordon. *New Light on the Most Ancient East. The Oriental Prelude to European Prehistory*. D. Appleton-Century Co., Inc., New York, 1934.

Childe, V. Gordon. *What Happened in History*. Penquin Books, London, 1946.

Curwen, E. Cecil. *Plow and Pasture (Present and Past Studies in History of Civilization)*. Cattell Press, London, England, 1946.

Davenport, C. B. The Dietaries of Primitive People. *Amer. Antiquity*, 47: 60–82, 1945.

Flannery, Kent V. The Ecology of Early Food Production in Mesopotamia. *Science*, 147: 1247–1256, 1965.

Harris, David R. The Origins of Agriculture in the Tropics. *Science*, 60: 180–193, March/April, 1972.

Helback, Hans. Studying the Diet of Ancient Man. *Archeology*, 14: 95–101, 1961.

Hoebel, E. A. *Anthropology. The Study of Man*. 3rd Edition. McGraw-Hill Co., New York, 1966.

Keesing, R. M. and F. M. Keesing. *New Perspectives in Cultural Anthropology*. Holt, Rinehart and Winston, New York, 1971.

Kluckhohn, Clyde. *Mirror for Man*. McGraw-Hill Co., New York, 1964.

Kroeber, A. L. *The Nature of Culture*. University of Chicago Press, Chicago, Ill., 1952.

Lamb, Charles. *The Essays of Elia*. Malcolm Elwin, Ed. Macdonald and Co., London, England, 1952.

Linton, Ralph. *The Tree of Culture*. Vintage Books, Random House, New York, 1955.

Montagu, Ashley. *Man: His First Two Million Years—A Brief Introduction to Anthropology*. Dell Publishing, New York, 1969.

Moore, Alma Chestnut. *The Grasses. Earth's Green Wealth*. The Macmillan Company, New York, 1960.

Orr, John Boyd. *The Wonderful World of Food. The Substance of Life*. Garden City Books, Garden City, N.Y., 1958.

Quennel, M. and C. H. B. Quennell. *Everyday Life—Early Iron Ages*. G. P. Putnam and Sons, New York, 1955.

Quennell, M. and C. H. B. Quennell. *Everyday Life in Prehistoric Times*. G. P. Putnam and Sons, New York, 1959.

Reed, Charles. Animal Domestication. *Science*, 130: 1629–1638, 1959.

Waterbalk, H. T. Food Production in Prehistoric Europe. *Science*, 162: 1093–1101, Dec. 1968.

White, Leslie. *The Evolution of Culture*. McGraw-Hill, New York, 1959.

General

Ames, G. and R. Wyler. *Food and Life.* Creative Education Society, Inc., Mankato, Minnesota, 1966.

Aykroyd, W. R. and Joyce Doughty. *Wheat in Human Nutrition.* FAO Nutritional Studies #23, FAO, Rome, Italy, 1970.

Bennett, M. K. *The World's Food.* Harper and Brothers, New York. 1954.

Boswell, V. R. Our Vegetable Travelers. *National Geographic Magazine*, 46 No. 2: 145–217, August, 1949.

Brillat-Savarin, J. A. *The Physiology of Taste.* Dover Publications, New York, 1960.

Brogger, A. W. From the Stone Age to the Motor Age. A Sketch of Norwegian Cultural History. *Antiquities* 13: 163–181, 1940.

Brothwell, Don and Patricia Brothwell. *Food in Antiquity.* Fredrick A. Praeger, New York, 1969.

Brown, Ina Corrine. *Understanding Other Cultures.* Prentice-Hall Inc., Englewood Cliffs, New Jersey, 1963.

Brown, Lester R. and G. W. Finisterbusch. *Man and His Environment — Food.* Harper-Row, New York, 1972.

Butzer, Karl W. *Environment and Archeology.* 2nd Ed. Aldine and Atherton, Chicago, 1971.

Cottrell, Leonard. *The Anvils of Civilization.* A Mentor Book, New American Library, New York, 1957.

Crissey, Forrest. *The Story of Foods.* Rand McNally and Co., Chicago, Ill., 1971.

Cuppy, Will. *The Decline and Fall of Practically Everybody—Some Royal Stomachs.* Ed. by F. Feldkamp. Holt Publishing Co., New York, 1950.

de Kruif, Paul. *Hunger Fighters.* Harcourt, Brace and Company. New York, 1928.

Hazlett, W. Carew. *Old Cookery Books and Ancient Cuisine,* Elliottstock, London, England, 1902.

Howell, William, *Mankind in the Making.* Doubleday and Co., Garden City, New York, 1967.

Jacobs, H. E. *Six Thousand Years of Bread—Its Holy and Unholy History.* Doubleday and Co., Garden City, N.Y., 1944.

Jensen, Lloyd B. *Man's Food.* Garrard Press, Champaign, Ill., 1953.

League for International Food Education Newsletter. February 1972.

Lee, Norman E. *Harvests and Harvesting.* Cambridge University Press, London, England, 1960.

McCarrison, R. *Studies in Deficiency Diseases.* Oxford University Press, New York, 1921.

Milikian, C. and L. K. Rudd. *The Wonder of Food.* Appleton-Century-Crofts, Inc., New York, 1961.

Orr, John Boyd. *The Wonderful World of Food. The Substance of Life.* Garden City Books, Garden City, N.Y., 1958.

Orr, John Boyd and David Lubbock. *The White Man's Dilemma.* Barnes and Noble Inc., New York, 1964.

Peacock, J. L. and A. T. Kirsch. *The Human Direction.* Appleton-Century- Crofts, New York, 1970.

Perl, Lila. *Rice, Spice and Bitter Oranges. Mediterranean Foods and Festivals.* World Publishing Co., New York, 1967.

Pirie, N. W. *Food Resources. Conventional and Novel.* Penguin Books, Baltimore, Md., 1969.

Prentice, E. Parmalee. *Hunger and History.* Caxton Printers, Caldwell, Idaho, 1951.

Remington, Roe E. The Social Origins of Dietary Habits. *Science Monthly* 43: 193–204, 1936.

Ritchie, Jean A. S. *Learning Better Nutrition.* FAO Nutritional Studies #20, FAO, Rome, Italy, 1967.

Sauer, Carl O. *Agricultural Origins and Dispersal.* M.I.T. Press, Cambridge, Md., 1969.

Shapiro, Harry L. (Ed.). *Man, Culture, and Society.* A Galaxy Book, Oxford University Press, New York, 1956.

Smallzried, Kathleen Ann. *The Everlasting Pleasure.* Appleton-Century-Crofts, New York, 1956.

Tartan, Beth. *The Good Old Days Cookbook.* Westover Publishing Co., Richmond, Va., 1971.

Traeger, James. *Foodbook.* Grossman, New York, 1970.

Vayda, A. P. *Environment and Cultural Behavior.* American Museum of Natural History, The Natural History Press, Garden City, N.Y., 1969.

Wason, Betty. *Cooks, Gluttons and Gourmets. A History of Cooking.* Doubleday and Co., Inc., Garden City, N.Y., 1962.

Wecksberg, Joseph. *The Best Things in Life.* Little, Brown and Co., Boston, Mass., 1965.

Wissler, Clark. Wheat and Civilization. *Natural History,* 52: 172, 1951.

Zeuner, Frederick E. *A History of Domesticated Animals.* Harper & Row, New York, 1963.

Medieval

Bailey, Adrian. *The Cooking of British Isles.* Time-Life Foods of World Series, Time-Life Books, New York, 1969.

Brown, Dale. *The Cooking of Scandinavia.* Time-Life Foods of World Series, Time-Life Books, New York, 1968.

Davis, Dorothy. *Fairs, Shops, and Supermarkets.* University of Toronto Press, Toronto, Canada, 1966.

Drummond, J. C. and Anne Wilbraham. *The Englishman's Diet. Five Centuries of English Diet.* Jonathan Cape, London, England, 1969.

Erlanger, Philippe. *The Age of Courts and Kings. Manners and Morals 1558–1715.* Harper-Row, New York, 1967.

Hale, John R. *Age of Exploration. Great Ages of Man.* Time-Life Inc., New York, 1966.

Hazlitt, W. Carew. *Old Cookery Books and Ancient Cuisines.* Elliott, London, 1902.

Hollister, C. Warren. *Medieval Europe—A Short History.* 2nd Edition, John Wiley and Sons, New York, 1968.

International Trade Center, UNCTAD/GATT, Geneva, Switzerland. Markets for Spices in North America, Western Europe and Japan, 1970.

LaFay, H. *The Vikings.* National Geographic Society, Washington, D.C., 1972.

Merrill, E. D. *The Botany of Cook's Voyages and Its Unexpected Significance in Relation to Anthropology, Biogeography and History.* Chronica Botanica Company, Waltham, Mass., 1954.

Osborne, John. *Britain-Life World Library.* Time, Inc., New York, 1967.

Penrose, Boies. *Travel and Discovery in the Renaissance 1420–1620.* Harvard University Press, Cambridge, Mass., 1960.

Perl, Lila. *Rice, Spice and Bitter Oranges—Mediterranean Foods and Festivals.* World Publishing Co., New York, 1967.

Prentice, E. Parmalee. *Hunger and History.* Caxton Printers, Inc., Caldwell, Idaho, 1951.

Quennell, Marjorie and C. H. B. Quennell. *A History of Everyday Things in England 1815–1914.* G. P. Putnam and Sons, New York, 1965.

Stewart, C. P. (Ed.) and D. Gutherie. *Lind's The Treatise of Scurvy.* University Press, Edinburgh, Scotland, 1953.

Tannebaum, Edward R. *European Civilization Since the Middle Ages,* 2nd Edition. John Wiley and Sons, New York, 1971.

Thomas, G. Z. *Richer than Spices.* Alfred A. Knopf, New York, 1965.

Trevelyan, G. M. *Illustrated English Social History.* 4 volumes. Penguin Books, London, 1964.

America

American Heritage Editors, *American Heritage Cook Book.* Simon and Schuster, Inc., New York, 1964.

Bennett, M. K. Good Economy of the New England Indians, 1605–75. *Journal Political Economy* 43: 369–397, 1955.

Carson, Gerald. *The Yankee Kitchen from American Heritage Cookbook.* American Heritage Publishing Co., Simon and Schuster, New York, 1964, Chapter 3.

Crawford, Mary Caroline. *Among Old New England Inns.* L. C. Page and Co., Boston, Mass., 1907.

Crawford, Mary Caroline. *Romantic Days in Old Boston.* Little, Brown and Co., Boston, Mass., 1910.

Cummings, R. O. The American and His Food, Revised Ed. Arno Press, New York, 1970.

Dolan, J. R. *The Yankee Peddler of Early America.* Brownhall House, New York, 1964.

Drucker, Philip. *Cultures of the North Pacific Coast.* Chandler Publishing Co., San Francisco, Calif., 1965.

Earle, Alice Morse. Abridged and edited by Shirley Glubok. *Home and Child Life in Colonial Days.* The Macmillan Company, New York, 1969.

Farb, Peter. *Man's Rise to Civilization—As Shown by the Indians of North America from Primeval Times to the Coming of the Industrial Stage.* E. P. Dutton and Co., New York, 1968.

Farmer, Fannie M. (Ed. by Wilma Lord Perkins). *The Boston Cooking School Cook Book.* Little, Brown and Co., Boston, Mass., 1965.

Kennedy, John F. *A Nation of Immigrants.* Harper and Row, New York, 1964.

Kimball, Yeffe and Jean Anderson. *The Art of American Indian Cookery.* Doubleday and Co., Garden City, New York, 1965.

Kluckholm, Clyde and D. Leighton. *The Navaho.* Harvard University Press, Cambridge, Mass., 1956.

Langdon, William Chauncey. *Everyday Things in American Life 1607–1776.* Charles Scribner's Sons, New York, 1937.

Langdon, William Chauncey. *Everyday Things in American Life 1776–1876*. Charles Scribner's Sons, New York, 1941.

Leonard, Jonathan N. *Ancient America. Great Ages of Man*. Time Inc., New York, 1967.

McMillen, Wheeler. *Land of Plenty. The American Farm Story*. Holt, Rinehart, Winston, New York, 1961.

Newberry, J. S. Food and Fiber. Plants of the North American Indians. *Popular Science Monthly*, 32: 31–46, 1887.

O'Meara, Walter. *The Last Portage*. Houghton-Mifflin Co., Boston, Mass., 1962.

Palmer, Lucille. The Pacific Northwest's Oldest Apple Tree. Magazine Section, Seattle *Times*, March 19, 1972.

Renaud, E. B. Influence of Food on Indian Culture. University of Denver *Social Forces*, 10: 97–101, 1931–32.

Scully, Virginia. *A Treasury of American Indian Herbs. Their Lore and Their Use for Food, Drugs, and Medicine*. Crown Publishers, Inc., New York, 1970.

Thomas, Gertrude I. *Foods of Our Forefathers*. F. A. Davis and Co. Philadelphia, Pa., 1941.

Verrill, A. Hyatt. *Foods America Gave the World*. L. C. Page and Co., Boston, Mass., 1937.

White, Theodore E. Observations of Butchering Technics of Some Aboriginal Peoples. *American Antiquities*, 17: 357–8, 1952.

A Winnebago Family Dries Food. *Christian Science Monitor*, April 19, 1962.

Woodward, William. *The Way Our People Lived*. Washington Square Press, New York, 1965.

Yearbook of Agriculture, 1962. *After A Hundred Years*. Superintendent of Documents, Washington, D.C.

Bread

Ashley, William. *The Bread of Our Forefathers*. Oxford at Clarendon Press, Oxford, England, 1928.

Aykroyd, W. R. and Joyce Doughty. *Wheat in Human Nutrition*. FAO Nutritional Studies #23, FAO, Rome, Italy, 1970.

Furnass, C. A. and S. M. Furnass. *Man, Bread and Destiny*. Williams and Wilkins, New York, 1937.

Graubard, Mark. *Man's Food—Its Rhyme or Reason*. The Macmillan Company, New York, 1943.

Jacobs, H. E. *Six Thousand Years of Bread*. Doubleday-Doran, Garden City, New York, 1944.

McCance, R. A. and E. M. Widdowson. *Breads, White and Brown*. J. B. Lippincott and Co., Philadelphia, Pa., no date given (about 1956).

Moore, Alma Chesnut. *The Grasses—Earth's Green Wealth*. The Macmillan Company, New York, 1960.

Spicer, Dorothy Gladys. *Feast-Day Cakes'* Holt, Rinehart and Winston, New York, 1960.

Potato

Salaman, Redcliffe. *The History and Social Influence of the Potato*. Cambridge University Press, Cambridge, England, 1949, reprinted in 1970.
See *General*.

Egyptian

Casson, Lionel, *Ancient Egypt*. *Great Ages of Man*. Time-Life Books, Time Inc., New York, 1965, 1957.
See *General*.

Greek

Bowra, C. M. *Classical Greece*. *Great Ages of Man*. Time-Life Books, Time, Inc., New York, 1965.
Flaceliere, Robert. *Daily Life in Greece at the Time of Pericles*. The Macmillan Company, New York, 1965.
See *General*.

Roman

Aykroyd, W. R. *Sweet Malefactor, Sugar, Slavery and Human Society*. Heinemann, London, England, 1967.
Balsdon, J. P. V. D. *Roman Women—Their History and Habits*. John Day and Co., New York, 1963.
Blasdon, J. P. V. D. *Life and Leisure in Ancient Rome*. McGraw-Hill Book Company, New York, 1969.
Hadas, Moses. *Imperial Rome*. *Great Ages of Man*. Time-Life Books, Time, Inc., New York, 1965.
Johnston, Mary. *Roman Life*. Scott, Foresman and Company, Chicago, Ill., 1957.
Root, Waverly. *The Cooking of Italy*. Time-Life Books, Time, Inc., New York, 1968.
Rosenbaum, Elizabeth and Barbara Flower, Translators. *Apicius, The Roman Cookery Book*. Peter Nevill Limited, London and New York, 1958.

Corn

Mangelsdorf, Paul C., Richard S. MacNeish and Walton C. Galinut. Domestication of Corn. *Science*, 143: 538–545, 1964.
Mason, Gregory. Native American Food. *Natural History*, 37: 309–318, 1936.
Reports Arizona's Oldest Cornfield. *Science*, 132:33, 1960.
Walden, Howard T. *Native Inheritance. The Story of Corn in America*. 2nd Edition. Harper-Row, New York, 1966.
Willett, Frank. The Introduction of Maize into West Africa—An Assessment of Recent Evidence. *Africa*, 32 (No. 1): 1–13, Jan. 1962.

3

Food Habits and Foodways

In some parts of the world, grasshoppers and grubs are food delicacies; in others, aged beef brings a high price. Food habits and foodways differ from group to group. The term *food habits* may have different meanings. Cussler and De Give used the term to refer to individual food habits and the term *foodways* "to apply to all those parallel elements of the food pattern which have considerably more than 'individual application.' "

These authors also pointed out that "*in general*, foodways do determine what the individual food habits are, and often they may exert a negative as well as a positive influence on him." The term food habits is used here "in reference to habits of a group that reflect the way a culture standardizes behavior of the individuals in the group in relation to food, so that the group comes to have a common pattern of eating." No effort is made to distinguish between these two terms in these discussions.

As travel increases both in the U.S. and in foreign countries, people become aware of likenesses and are less bothered by differences. It is apparent that many more Americans are now appreciating, as Perl has said, "The vivid patterns of a nation's customs and folkways, holiday and religious festivals, cooking methods and dining habits. . . ." She believed that, because the U.S. has been a "gathering-in place of a wide sampling of the world's peoples in modern times," our people should be especially "attuned to the diverse flavors of other lands." She said that this, however, does not keep some Americans from shuddering at the mention of boiled octopus, fried squid, or goat's milk cheese.

By way of illustrating what is meant by a food pattern or food habits of a group, some things which characterize the pattern and use of food in the U.S. today will be examined. One is the ever-increasing use of convenience foods, which require a minimum of preparation; the other is the value placed on gourmet foods, which are expensive and take great care and effort to prepare. Two extremes are represented in this American pattern.

In affluent nations such as ours where the majority of people are well nourished, foods usually are not eaten just to appease hunger but because they appeal to the appetite. For the upward socially mobile parts of the population, status is attained by the foods which are purchased, served, or eaten at the restaurants at which these people entertain. Once an individual in this group is secure in his social position, he may go "slumming" for his food, seeking the alien and exotic.

Adults in America, in general, prize variety in their food and consider a monotonous diet undesirable. Nursery school children usually prefer familiar foods and do not react against a sameness in the way adults do (Lowenberg). Dorothy Lee pointed out that, in contrast to our preferences, some cultures value sameness of diet and monotony is "good and sought."

In American supermarkets, the display of foods is elaborate, giving evidence of great abundance. The display of seven thousand or more separate items is not unusual. The display of exotic foods shipped from distant places varies with the affluence of the district in which the supermarket is located.

It has been said that, in addition to the foods people have available, food habits depend on a combination of psychological and biochemical factors. Within limits, people eat what they like and what they think is good for them. Food patterns are based on food lore and in part (at

In America, foods usually are eaten because they appeal to the appetite. (Courtesy of Central Soya Co., Inc.)

least in a modern, highly technically developed country) on commercial advertising and sound knowledge of nutritional needs. Jacques May said: "The factors governing human diets can be listed as follows: (1) men eat what they can get from the environment, (2) given a choice they eat what their ancestors have eaten before them." It must be pointed out, however, that what is eaten must be related to the physiological needs of the body or the group of individuals do not survive.

Choices among foods are made only when food is plentiful enough to permit choices. It is common knowledge that food taboos and restrictions are relaxed during starvation. In fact, hidden in the annals of our own history are examples of cannibalism among starving pioneer migrants. When there is sufficient food so that choices can be made, there develops a set of food habits and foodways with their attendant taboos and prejudices.

CULTURAL BACKGROUNDS

Food habits vary from one cultural group to another because each group, in its own evolution, sets up a complex pattern of standardized behaviors. Individuals within a culture respond to the approved behavioral pressures by selecting, consuming, and using those foods which are available. It is true, therefore, that the food habits of a group are, as May said, the product of the groups' present environment and past history. Those food habits and customs which have become meaningful to the group are carefully held and not quickly changed. It follows, therefore, that anyone who would change a food habit must first understand the deep meanings of the particular habit to the people. Those food habits which do not have deep meaning may be changed rather easily.

Except for people who live apart from other groups, as do the aborigines of Australia and the bushmen of Africa, it must be expected that outside influences affect the environment, resulting in changes in food habits as well as in other patterns of living. Such changes have been seen when white flour and white sugar as well as American canned goods have been shipped into developing countries. When a group is subjected to outside influences, it often has been observed that the older people in the group change less quickly than the younger individuals.

Two excellent examples of the initial retention of native food habits by several cultural groups living within a confined area and the consequent blending of these habits into a new cuisine are seen in Viennese and Hawaiian foods. Poles, Bohemians, Hungarians, Yugoslavians, and Moravians kept their native food patterns when they first migrated to Vienna and for many generations thereafter. Finally, all of their foods were blended into a new cuisine, the now famous Viennese food. Hawaiian food shows the same blending: the sweet potato, the pit-roasted pig, and the many products from the coconut came from the Polynesians; vegetable and meat cookery, from the Chinese; soups, raw fish dishes, and rice and seaweed combinations, from the Japanese; curries, from India; pickled vegetables, from Korea; and sweets and pastries, soft drinks, hot breads, hot dogs, and expensive steaks, from U.S. mainlanders. Thus, Hawaii has become a paradise for those who are interested in intercultural foods. The food markets, especially the ones with many stalls, are fascinating to poke around in to see unusual fish, vegetables, and fruits.

The mark of the immigrant is left on the food habits in every one of the fifty U.S. states. Kolachies from Bohemia are found in parts of Iowa; limpa, lutefish, and lefse, as well as lingonberries (especially at Christmastime) from Scandinavia are common in Minnesota; chili con carne from

Mexico is found in Texas; the French bouillabaisse is found in New Orleans; and German sausages are served in Pennsylvania. Some of these foods now are considered almost native to these regions.

Stability of Patterns

Each ethnic group carefully passes on its foodways through the training of the children so that each child knows what is considered to be food and what is not. The primitive African child learns early to prize grasshoppers and grubs as food, as the American child learns to drink milk. Children also are taught socially acceptable behavior in relation to food. Thus, they come to know what the limits for food refusals are, so the original impulses of children toward the satisfaction of hunger are transformed into socially acceptable appetites.

The mother's direct control exerts an important influence on the eating habits of her children. She may pass on her own dislikes or force herself to eat disliked foods in order to set a good example. Usually she attempts to get her children to eat what she believes is good for them. If she buys the food for the family, she truly "controls" most of the food which comes into the home.

Not everyone in a cultural or ethnic group eats exactly alike. Small and large subgroups form. Differences in food habits arise due to differences in environment such as climate or growing conditions or differences in religious beliefs. One of the best examples of this division into subgroups is shown in the variety of food patterns in Italy, in part due to differences in growing conditions from north to south.

CHANGING FOOD HABITS

The profound and complex effects of culture on human behavior must not be underestimated; nor is there an easy way to circumvent culture. At the same time, however, it is not wise to stereotype all the people in a cultural group as being exactly alike. Human behavior is always multiply motivated, and every human being is endowed from birth with physical, intellectual, and emotional characteristics, all of which have the capacity for change. We also know that, when individuals are confronted with a need for change in their food habits, especially for health reasons or during periods of privation, they react differently.

It has been said that man is distinguished by the very wide range of foods he can eat because of his teeth; his incisors are similar to the ones of a rodent, his molars resemble those of plant eaters, and his canines are like those of carnivore.

There are many blocks to the changing of food habits, some of which may represent inertia or even resistance to change. People have been categorized as: (1) those who seek to lead groups to change; (2) those who accept change easily; and (3) those who resist change.

Certain factors that relate to the reaction to change in food patterns must be understood and considered by those who wish to make a change. The primary deterrent to this change may be fear of the loss of a familiar food which has been basic to the invididual's security. Here there is a conflict of choice between the old and the new. Lack of understanding of what is needed and why may also block a change. E. E. Patrice Jelliffe pointed out that "many nutrition education programs flounder on the rocks of sophistication, as mothers from humble home circumstances cannot translate what they have seen at demonstrations at the clinic or home economics center into practical reality in their own environment."

Rebellion against authority and the insult of being deprived of personal choice likewise can be basic deterrents. Resistance to change also may be traced to treating the *effect* of a food habit, such as obesity, instead of recognizing, understanding, and effectively treating *underlying* or *accompanying* psychological factors.

Graubard, in his discussion of food taboos, said:

> A taboo may become established because the animal is a totem, or because it resembles some other animal already in ill repute, or because its name may inspire some evil association, or it may symbolize an undesirable quality. Often animals become tabooed simply because they are not eaten.

He speaks of shellfish not being eaten in places far from the source of supply. Margaret Mead, in *Cultural Pattern and Technical Change*, said that changes which concern a program aimed at control of the social processes are more effective than changes directed to individuals.

The Committee on Food Habits, in Bulletin lll , pointed to some basic reasons why some foods are eaten:

> Whenever food becomes a part of the celebration of a holiday, the observance of a religious feast, the mark of some life crisis such as a funeral feast, the setting for some business transaction or for the maintenance of social position, a great many reinforcing factors enter in to make certain foods valued and others disapproved or reserved for special occasions.

It is also suggested that resistance to a series of suggested dietary changes may be traced to fear of losing the food in its "culturally oriented significance." So even the inclusion of one favorite dish into a menu for mass feeding may weaken the resistance to change. This has been experienced often by nutritionists and dietitians in school and hospital feeding. Burgess and Dean, in *Malnutrition and Food Habits,* pointed out that in self-sufficient, peasant-type cultures, where even a meager diet has proven adequate for survival, planting, harvesting, storage, and consumption, are closely interwoven. Survival in such a situation demands transmitting the whole pattern to each succeeding generation; a single change in this pattern may bring disaster. Margaret Mead, contrary to some other writers, warned that food habits are not always harder to change than other personal habits. She believes that the resistance to changing food habits may be related to patterns of rearing children. Thus, she postulates that where children "are fed lovingly and food is a great source of pleasure and delight" there is resistance to change. She also said that the difference in how immigrants change their food patterns is related to whether they like the foods of their native lands. It is known that immigrants first change the kind or manner of wearing clothes and their language because they do not wish to be conspicuous. But eating is a private affair; therefore, food habits are changed last. Others have postulated that immigrants to a new country, especially if they eat out at their place of work, change their weekday meals but cling to the Sunday dinners of their native land.

Some believe that food habits are resistant to change because they are a form of self-expression, but it is hard to understand why this is more true of food than of clothing.

Many studies have shown that it is easier to change food habits in the young than in the old; therefore, a delay in attempting to make a change is unwarranted.

The mere possession of knowledge does not guarantee a change, though probably too often professional people whose business it is to give out knowledge behave as if this were not true. Charlotte Young's studies have shown that nutritional knowledge is greatest in the younger, better-educated homemakers from the upper-income brackets. She found, when she studied what the homemaker knows about nutrition, that the number of years of formal education, even when nutrition *per se* was not studied, was highly related to the knowledge of nutrition. Many of us agree with her that merely studying what to eat does change food patterns, at least in some people.

Frederick C. Fliegel, in a study of food habits and national backgrounds, also found that educational level was a potent factor in the adequacy of the diet served in the families he studied. He pointed out that occupation reflects income as well as status. He also believed that such factors as the Italian background of liking fruit fresh and the milk-drinking habits in their homelands also may have affected his findings.

In a study of changing food habits of rural children in Dakota County, Minnesota, it was reported that the children improved their food practices when they discovered what changes they needed to make and were "strongly motivated to learn about foods and to apply what they learned to their own diets—that is, if they had access to these foods in needed amounts." These investigators point to the fact that the best teaching is done where the teachers are well informed and highly motivated to teach the subject and where the facts are put into practice within the environment, as in the school lunchroom. Projects under the poverty program, such as Head Start, also makes food available to children for the purpose of trying to improve their food habits. Therefore, these programs require that parents be educated simultaneously with their children.

Martha Hollinger and Lydia J. Roberts, in their 1929 study of "Overcoming Food Dislikes: A Study with Evaporated Milk," pointed out that favorable attitudes are contagious, that repetition itself is not enough, but that "repeated tastings together with the right mental attitude are essential to learning to like a new or disliked food." Many studies during the last 45 years have reinforced these ideas. Increased income and improved standards of living bring a simultaneous change in food habits, especially in the use of the more expensive animal foods.

The entire philosophy of community development programs around the world should be emphasized here. The first prerequisite of those programs, especially where outside food aid is given, is to find out what the people themselves want. Roberts and her co-workers, in their reports of the Puerto Rican Dona Elena Project, said that changes in nutrition must first be preceded by general changes in ways of living which follow the desires of the people. Burgess and Dean confirm that this first step may have little to do with nutrition, but it must be founded on what the people want and can take part in accomplishing. Thus, from the first, successful achievement, hope, and confidence are engendered, and horizons of needs and motives are widened.

It also has been recognized that the majority of the peoples of the world, especially those in the developing countries, now live in societies which are in a state of rapid change and where old patterns are being replaced quickly by new ones. Masuoka said, concerning the change of food habits of Japanese living in Hawaii, "The introduction of a new mode of eating and production of food, as well as an impact of commercialized foodstuff and new modes of cultural life, all function to modify man's pre-established food habits." He cites, "external and impersonal forces as trade, rise in income, and the availability of different kinds of food and such subjective and personal forces as changes in food tastes and in conceptions of social status" as causal factors. He also says that "disorganization of traditional institutions" is probably the most important force to be reckoned with. This unfastens the traditional and customary control over what man eats and how he eats." In most of these groups, there are desires to improve the standard of living and to give the children a better chance for survival. Often, however, it must be demonstrated to these people that there is a connection between health and food. Those who work in international programs believe that the task of changing food habits in many places is one in which the nutritionist, the agriculturist, the economist, and the anthropologist must work together to change present nutritional patterns to more desirable ones. Jean A. S. Ritchie warned that:

With the rapid spread of modern civilization during the present century, many peoples are in a transitional stage between old and new cultures. Too rapid an advance can create grave difficulties.

She also said that to teach people to drink milk and eat raw salads may be disastrous when the available supply of these foods may carry organisms of dangerous diseases. The UNESCO book on *Cultural Patterns and Technical Change* gave reasons why "the introduction of change, however limited and harmless, can be very disruptive":

To introduce adequate nutrition, it is most important to bring about changes that are in keeping with the established food habits of the people, and are acceptable within the framework of their value system.

It is known that it is better to improve than to change a food habit because every diet has its good as well as bad points. Often, increasing the use of a highly nutritious food, such as certain varieties of beans in Latin American countries, is wiser than upsetting a familiar, trusted, food pattern. Roberts, for instance, in Puerto Rico, promoted the use of calabaza, an already acceptable yellow squash.

National influences are described by Todhunter in a talk which she gave at the Plenary Session of the Third International Congress of Dietetics in London (1961). She summed up changes in the American dietary history during the last 350 years by dividing this history into three periods. The first was the colonial period (1600–1800); the second was the period of westward exploration, development, and industrialization (1800–1900). In describing the third period, the twentieth century, she discussed the new influences which have been brought to bear on the food pattern:

> . . . [the] twentieth century, brought new influences to bear on the basic food pattern. The young science of nutrition grew rapidly, food values received attention and the knowledge was spread throughout the land by the schools of home economics, the experiment stations, and the extension service home agents who worked with rural families in every state. Tomatoes ceased to be regarded as a luxury and were recognized as sources of vitamin C as were citrus fruits; fruits, vegetables, and salads received new dietary emphasis. Regional food patterns, such as the fried chicken, corn bread, grits, and greens of the South; chile beans and barbecued beef and corn cakes of the Southwest; and German-type foods of Pennsylvania, which had been maintained in early isolation continued to be used and still are but they were quickly shared by others as highways and automobiles linked every hamlet of the country.
>
> Today is the age of technology with new means of preservation and packaging and endless new products, such as packaged mixes, cooked frozen meals, minute preparation foods, and fast transportation' These make all food products available the year around to everyone. More food is purchased at the supermarkets and more people eat away from home. Three meals a day is the pattern with a coffee break, mid-morning and afternoon.
>
> Today's food pattern retains a dominance of the early foods of the new land but these have been modified and have blended with the patterns of scores of nationalities that came as immigrants. There have been shifts in the amounts of various foods used, as nutrition science spread and all this has given rise to a more universal pattern accepted because of advertising and the mass media and because of the remnants of the pioneer spirit which leaves people still willing to try something new, especially in food and recipes.
>
> The country that has been called the melting pot of all nationalities also has become the melting pot of all nations' food patterns.
>
> Over the last fifty years there has been little change in the consumption of meat, fish and poultry; an increase in the use of dairy products especially

over the last twenty years; slight increase in fats and oils; increase in sugars and syrups; a steady decrease in grains and potatoes; and a marked increase in the use of citrus and tomatoes and also in green and yellow vegetables.

This excerpt describes a national pattern made by many individuals and forming the background for the individual food patterns of millions of Americans. Perhaps this, best of all, illustrates what Margaret Mead and Jean Ritchie mean—that to change fundamental food habits, a whole culture must change.

We have numerous other proofs of the changes of food habits from countries all over the world and throughout all history. It is said that man probably gave up the use of acorns as one of his staple foods after a devastating blight of oak trees, when he found other foods he preferred. Wheat bread is said to have been first prepared in Egypt when the use of barley declined. Oats have been either stoutly defended or rejected as food, and the idea of rejection probably spread from pre-dynastic Mesopotamia into Greece and Rome. It is said that the Scythians scorned the Gauls for using a cattle feed for human food, as the English later scorned the Scots. At the present time, the Japanese are reported to drink 20 times more milk than they did 20 years ago. Kluckholm pointed out that, under present-day conditions of communication, only a small percentage of the material objects used by any people represent its own inventions. As an example, he cited a menu for a week in an American home, which, may include "chicken, which was domesticated in Southeast Asia; olives, which originated in the Mediterranean region; cornbread, from the meal of an American Indian plant, baked in an aboriginal fashion; rice and tea from the Far East." Coffee "was probably domesticated in Ethiopia"; and "citrus fruit, which were first cultivated in Southeast Asia . . . reached Europe by way of the Middle East. . . ." Four steps have been shown to be desirable in a deliberate attempt to bring about a change.

1. Those who possess the knowledge must want to bring about a change.
2. The group whose practices need changing must be helped to know that they need to change.
3. This group must be motivated to make the change.
4. It must be possible for the group to make the change; in other words, in the case of changing food habits, the food must be available.

Discussion-Decision Method

Ben Willerman, working under Kurt Lewin in 1942 in Iowa City, investigated the relative effectiveness of two methods of changing food habits. He used the so-called *group decision method,* in which the group decided for itself whether it wanted to change and to what degree it wished to change. The second method, with which the first was compared, was the *request method,* in which a group was asked to make a change, and the goals were set by others outside the group. Willerman's 1942 experiment concerned the increase in consumption of whole-wheat bread as compared with white bread. It must be remembered that white bread, which was not then enriched, contained less of the needed nutrients than did whole-wheat bread.

Men from eight cooperative dormitories at the University of Iowa were used. The eight groups, containing from 20 to 44 men each, were arranged in four pairs of groups, matched on similar consumption of whole-wheat bread. One of each of these group pairs was to make a group decision, and the other was presented with a request.

For the week before and during the experiment, no breadstuff except white and whole-wheat bread was served. Waiters counted the slices of bread eaten during both periods and made certain that as much bread as was wanted was available. The student proctor in each dormitory read a letter by an authority to the decision group, urging the students to eat whole-wheat bread. Then he called for a discussion. At that time, if the group agreed to cooperate, they set their own goals of how much they would increase the consumption of a whole-wheat bread. In the request groups, the proctor merely read the request letter and asked for comments. The amount of change for the *request group* was set at the same level as the amount which had been chosen voluntarily by the *decision group* with which it was paired. The results were obtained from a questionnaire filled in by each student at the end of the experiment.

From their previous levels of 50% consumption of whole-wheat bread, one group voted to go to 66%, another to 90%, and two to 100% —the group designated as the D group being one of the latter. In the *request groups,* 48% reacted favorably, whereas 78% in the *decision groups* were favorable to the proposal as read. Although the majority (8% for *request groups* and 86% for *decision groups*) considered the request reasonable, only 22% of Group D considered it so. It must be pointed out that, in Group D, a *decision group,* the 100% level of change was arrived at after a bitter fight in which a small vocal minority swayed the decision.

The results showed that with the *group decision* method:

1. A more favorable attitude was created.
2. Individuals were more eager to succeed.
3. The wish to cooperate was more independent of personal likes and dislikes.
4. There was a "kickback" in the groups where the decision was based on too small a majority. This made the outcome less favorable than with the *request method.*

Others later working under Lewin (housewives who were asked to consider changing their food habits for the war effort) obtained similar results in trying to introduce a new vegetable, escarole, and organ meats such as kidney, brains, and heart.

Marian Radke and Dorothy Klurisch, in 1947, used the methods described by Willerman in trying to change infant-feeding practices and later in increasing milk consumption in families of low socio-economic status. They say, "The group decision method was significantly more effective in leading mothers and housewives to action than were either individual instruction or lectures." Lewin's explanation of why the group decision method works better is worth reviewing here. He states that he believes the effectiveness of the method is due to:

1. The higher degree of individual involvement required in the discussion method.
2. The existence of resistance to change, perhaps due to a disinclination to deviate from a social norm or from standard group values. The discussion method offered the individuals the chance to see how others felt on the question, thus making their own decisions easier.
3. The group decision method placing full weight behind one of the two conflicting alternatives so that one choice completely displaces the other. .

He also says that, when change is facilitated, resistance is lowered and vacillation ceases. He says, further, that the process of social change is a three-step procedure: (1) unfreezing the old level, (2) moving to the new level, and then (3) freezing at the new level of performance. Marian Radke and Elizabeth Caso, in 1948, tried a similar method, which they called the lecture and discussion-decision method, with junior high school students in Newton, Massachusetts. They used the improvement of poor lunch habits as their goal. Again the discussion-decision method proved superior, and improvement proved more lasting with this method.

Perhaps some of our ineffectiveness to bring about changes in food habits should lead us to pay more attention to these theories and researches of Dr. Lewin and others.

Public Health Needs for Change

D. B. Jelliffe and F. J. Bennett, working in Uganda, pointed out that it is helpful to divide the food practices in a cultural group into categories based on public health needs for change. They suggest that, before any attempt is made to change practices, they be divided into:

1. Beneficial practices such as breast feeding. These should be supported and promoted in local health teaching.
2. Neutral practices such as massaging the limbs with oil to make the bones strong. These seem to have no significant value nor to be harmful and should be let alone.
3. Unclassifiable practices such as the mother's pre-chewing of foods for her infant. These need further observation and consideration in special groups.
4. Harmful practices such as failure to give young children fish in Malaya where it is the main source of protein but is said by the people to produce worms. This fourth category should be the basis for "friendly persuasion and convincing demonstration."

Whether the food habits be those of a group in Uganda or a group in the U.S., it would probably be wise to make a decision, after careful study, of what particular habits are most in need of change.

In 1948, the Philadelphia Child Health Society prepared, for use by public health workers, an exceptionally useful chart. For each of the major cultural groups in the city, they listed typical daily meals with food preferences. They also listed good points about the diet as well as points to emphasize or discuss and to consider in need of changing.

Making Food Available

Many examples of changes in dietary patterns because a food becomes available in a convenient form have already been cited in the quotation from Todhunter on pages 126–127. The extensive use of frozen orange juice today is one illustration. Many of the older generation no doubt still remember the one orange a year in their Christmas stocking. The frozen-food industry has made locally produced foods available all over the U.S. and, in fact, in many other countries of the world. When production costs, as with frozen foods, decrease so that the average consumer can afford the item, the use of that food often increases.

The story of the Aarey Dairy Project, located some twenty miles from Bombay, India, is worth telling here. One of the startling sights to a stranger in this part of the world was the filthy open sheds for water buffalo which were then used in dairies in this region. It was not difficult for the observer to understand why these animals gave a low yield of milk; they were really pitiful looking creatures. Neither was it difficult to understand why, in 1916, Dr. Lamuel Joshi, who was then the municipal analyst for the city of Bombay, found that samples of Bombay milk contained more bacteria than the sewage water of London. He found many causes, including adulteration, antiquated methods, bad sanitation, ignorance, and greed. So the name "dirty milk" lingered for some decades. For years apparently little was done to clean up this deplorable situation. In 1940, however, a special campaign to feature the "dirty milk" of Bombay was undertaken when D. N. Khurody reproduced the 1916 statistics in his report on "Marketing Milk in Bombay."

In 1914, there were 5000–6000 water buffalo which furnished milk for Bombay. By 1944, this number had increased to 35,000; but with inadequate care and food, these animals became useless after their first lactation. In 1941, World War II conditions further increased the troubles encountered in the milk industry of India. The price of milk also increased sharply. With the bombing of Calcutta, evacuation from the large cities, including Bombay, took place. Food rationing included food for cattle, and the ban on exporting animals from other provinces to consuming centers such as Bombay made the milk problem more than a municipal one.

Although public milk schemes were then unknown in India, the Civil Supplies Department of the Bombay state government took a great step forward. On August 17, 1944, they introduced the Bombay Subsidized Milk Distribution Scheme. It soon became evident that this subsidy was not the total answer, so in 1945 a group of interested officials created a separate milk department headed by a commissioner. This group acquired 1100 acres of land near the village of Aarey and built a dairy plant on it. Milk from the surrounding area was brought into the new dairy. Because obviously so few buffalo could do little to supply the milk needed in Bombay, a bold plan was made for housing all the milk-producing water buffalo of the area owned by the farmers in one colony. In 1948, the government of Bombay also took action to remove water buffalo from the streets of Bombay City. They also decided that the processing and distribution should be done by modern methods. Very soon the number of animals increased to 12,000, then 15,000, and later 17,000. In 1959, there were, on about 3500 acres, 15,000 water buffalo housed and milked in clean sheds, 1000 to a shed. A modern plant was pasteurizing whole milk and also producing "toned" milk. The fat content of water buffalo milk is around 7.5%. For toned milk, powdered nonfat milk and water are added to the water buffalo milk. This milk can be sold for about one-half the price of the whole milk, with its natural fat content. In 1962, the imported skim milk powder used for toning milk reached 5500 tons.

The project combined the efforts of the municipality of Bombay and the state of Bombay with the efforts of international organizations. UNICEF, in 1958, put a large sum of money into the equipment and building for the pasteurization and processing plant. The nonfat powdered milk was being donated by the U.S. and New Zealand. For what UNICEF contributed, the government of Bombay agreed to distribute one and one-half times the original investment in free milk to mothers and children.

Technical assistance from veterinarians and others in animal husbandry was, from the beginning, also partly supplied by outside agencies such as the U.S. agency now called AID. Early in the formulation of the scheme, it was decided to donate to the farmers veterinary aid and to provide for artificial insemination free of charge. Also from the first, feed was purchased in large quantities and sold to the farmers at cost.

The farmers who now own the water buffalo care for, feed, and milk them. They sell the milk to the city of Bombay in the pasteurization plant just after the water buffalo is milked. At this point, the Milk Commission of the city of Bombay controls the handling of the milk and is responsible for its pasteurization and bottling as well as distribution.

The bottled milk is trucked into the city and sold twice daily between 5 and 6 am and around 4 pm from nearly 1000 small stations located throughout the city. Getting on the list to buy this milk was a privilege not usually sacrificed by failure to live up to the regulations. Each customer was required to present a clean bottle each time and was not allowed to miss calling for the milk more than twice.

Within a relatively few years after this Aarey Project Dairy was built, with the additional milk brought in from the surrounding district and processed at this dairy, it was supplying at least some milk daily for approximately one-half the people of Bombay. Another plant was then built, with the hope that the other 50% of the people, if they so desired, could be supplied with this clean milk. This new plant (Worli), located just outside of the city of Bombay, was opened in November 1961; during its first year, it processed 53 million quarts of milk; in 1963, the hourly capacity was doubled. It is reported that from 1959–1964 (when the program for low-fat milk had to be suspended because of the shortage of the skim milk powder), there were 36 million beneficiaries of this scheme.

The success of this remarkable project resulted from the cooperative efforts of government (the city and state of Bombay), the farmers, and international agencies. It was said in 1959 that the water buffalo came from four states in India, feed from six, operators from all over the country, the pasteurization machinery from the United Kingdom, the milk clarifiers from Sweden, the refrigeration machinery from the U.S., and the milk-testing machinery from Switzerland, adapting a process which had originated in the brain of the French genius Pasteur.

Because the entire district around this dairy has become more prosperous and because of the demonstration, the surrounding villages improved all kinds of sanitation. Clean water supplies were installed; housing and food are better; more and better schools are in operation. The grounds around the processing plant and the milk bar are so attractive that people spend a holiday there and learn firsthand how to produce clean milk and what it and the ice cream made from it can taste like.

A report from UNICEF, date September 1966, said:

> . . . the full nutritional value of India's large production of milk has not been utilized because of lack of facilities for collection, processing, and distribution of fluid milk and its products. It has been recognized at the highest levels in India that one of the most valuable forms of international assistance for the improvement of nutrition is help in the development of greater milk production, proper collection, processing, and distribution of low cost milk.

The objectives of all these milk projects were to provide safe milk to mothers and children free or at subsidized prices lower than the regular market price and also to stimulate milk production.

The Worli and Aarey Dairy Projects in Bombay produced 320,000 liters of milk in December 1966; in December 1972, 535,000 liters were produced; and it is anticipated that by 1974, over 600,000 liters will be produced under the World Food Program. Three foreign agencies, UNICEF, an agency from Sweden, and one from Denmark, furnished dried powdered milk and anhydrous milk fat.

In the report by UNICEF, *Children of the Developing Countries,* it is said:

> The rapid growth of dairying and industrial milk processing in Europe, North America, Australia, and New Zealand in the first third of the present century probably did more to improve the nutritional status of children and mothers in these countries than any other single development in the field of food and nutrition.

There are probably few stories as thrilling as this, where making a needed food available has benefited so many people. It must be pointed out that most of the people of India like and drink milk when it is available. Furthermore, it represents almost the only source of animal protein in the diets of some Indian families.

Group Influences

Sociologists and anthropologists have pointed out that, in primitive cultures, with the exception of the most simple societies, the raising and harvesting of foods are often group activities. Rice harvesting in Bali, where the small fields of rice are full of people working, would remind tourists of this point.

Pride and satisfaction in food production become forces that cement the group together. Individuals cooperate and yield to mutual preferences which are culturally acceptable; in many of these groups, eating together is also intimately associated with the family group. The cooperative efforts and this eating together come to imply a kind of kinship even outside of the family of true blood relatives. Cussler and DeGive very well pointed out that "securing food and eating together entails an intensifying of communication and an increase of the rate of interaction to a degree found in no other act repeated so constantly."

Some types of food production which are basic to the group's economy, such as the production of grapes for wine, are long-lasting, whereas others may be temporary in formation.

The tendency of a society to have pockets of culture with groups of individuals who keep their own food habits is greater perhaps in societies where communication across a country is not highly developed. In larger cities, groups which move in from totally different cultures may exert potent influences for change and, therefore, cause a change in food patterns. Wherever travel to outside places becomes common, suspicion of strange foods breaks down. The more secure individuals in any group dare to try new foods; in this type of people, there is less rigid demarcation in what is considered a proper food.

In many cultures, eating is considered a private affair to be enjoyed within the confines of a family group. There are reports of places where individuals eat away from all others, even family members. For instance, in some parts of Melanesia and Polynesia, men and their wives lead separate lives; they have separate lodgings, meals, work, and property. There the rule is that men and women should never see each other eat. Among the old Semites, it was not the custom for a man to eat with his wife and children. Sumner in *Folkways* (1960) reported that, in northern Arabia, "no woman will eat before men" and "there is a widespread notion that one should not be seen to eat by anybody." In the Sudan, it is said that the practices of eating and drinking in private and covering the mouth when eating and drinking were to prevent the evil eye from affecting the individual. It is thought that this belief originated from the watching of others eating by hungry people who might be envious. Others believe that the homeless evil spirit could wander into their open mouths and cause trouble. In some countries, workers as well as schoolchildren are given long noon hours so that they may go home to eat with their families. In the U.S., family members make great efforts to be together for dinner on Thanksgiving or Christmas. There is the now oft-told tale of the Greeks, after the World War II occupation of their country, who preferred to take hot soup given to them by the Red Cross to their cold homes to eat with their families rather than eat it in the warm Red Cross canteens. It is said that in the early middle ages in Germany, after the formal marriage ceremony, the spouses ate together as a part of the total procedure of marrying. So the origin of the American custom of the bride feeding her new husband the first piece of wedding cake she has just cut may be very old.

Jensen said that with primal man the "sharing of food and drink between man and woman universally defines the legal relationship

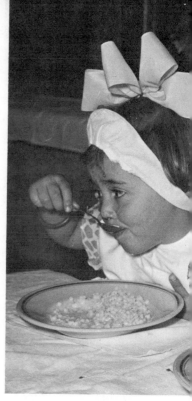

A child eating in India. (Courtesy the Rockefeller Foundation.)

A nutritious school lunch in Bulgaria. (Courtesy World Health Organization.)

Methods of eating differ—these children live in India. (Courtesy Food and Agriculture Organization.)

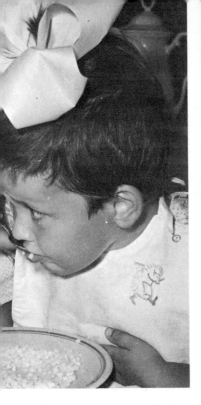

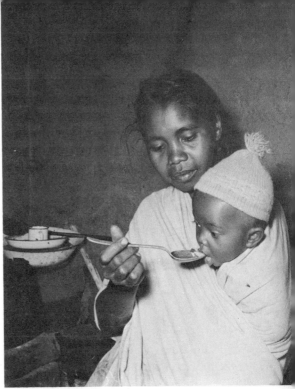

*Feeding an infant in Madagascar.
(Courtesy Food and Agriculture
Organization.)*

*Facilities help determine the kinds of food eaten. Foodways are
affected by technological and economic factors. (Courtesy the
Upjohn Company.)*

between the two." He also says that "The offering of cooked food and sometimes ale (bride-ale of the Vikings hence 'bridal') figures largely in early day marital ties."

Ethnic Influences

In the UNESCO book, *Cultural Patterns and Technical Change*, it is pointed out that "where food practices reflect cultural structuring and values, any change introduced into the society may produce imbalance." For instance, knowing the structuring and meaning of meals among the working classes in Japan following World War II, their nutritionists, also knowing the importance of miso soup for the first meal of the day, introduced the idea of adding the extra fat needed in their diet to that food.

Families also tend to develop their own food habits. The attitudes toward food vary in different families, from indifference to excessive preoccupation with food. One of the best illustrations of differences in food practices among families in the United States of America is the bread stuffing with which the family thinks it is proper to stuff the Thanksgiving turkey. Some of us know of women who put one kind of dressing in the front part of the bird and another in the back part to satisfy the firmly held opinions of her husband and herself. In fact, our feasts often become unnecessarily elaborate because each partner wants a special kind of food that was used in his childhood home, such as mashed white potatoes for northerners and sweet potatoes for southerners.

In diverse ethnic groups, food has different prestige and emotionally satisfying properties. The French, for instance, hold food in high regard and are justly famous for their cuisine; the Italians take great pleasure in eating and in family meals. In some cultural groups and families, eating is a matter of duty and is lacking in emotional satisfaction.

In other groups, thrift may be uppermost in the minds of people, even going beyond the requirements of income restrictions. For some people, the nutritive value or even supposed value may dictate food patterns. One is reminded of the old story of the daughter whose mother was trained in nutrition. When asked what she wanted to eat, she surprised her hostess in a restaurant by replying "Anything but healthful food. I get so much of that at home."

In some ethnic groups more than others, the women are said to be kitchen-bound or neighborhood-bound. When migrating to a new home, these people tend to settle in neighborhoods where they find former emigrants of like ethnic backgrounds. They spend their lives near where they live and even shop in grocery stores carrying only foods of their nationality. In some of these groups, of course, change comes about as children go to school and bring home new ideas. Often, though, the group-imposed ideas of marrying one of like nationality tends to preserve the group patterns.

It has been said that cooking reveals the culture of a country and that a country's soul is reflected in its food. For instance, Felix Martin-Ibanez suggests (though some others disagree) that the tendency of the Spaniard for violence and his love of bright color are reflected in the sharp-flavored polychrome *paellas,* that the food of the Japanese reflects their love of order and cleanliness as shown by the array of beautifully cleaned and cut foods for *sukiyaki.* He also believes that the national foods of Britian reflect their aseptic robustness and reserve, while the Gaelic subtlety of expression is shown in their delicate sauces. And the earthiness of the Italians is demonstrated in their *pastas.*

Cussler and DeGive, from a study they did in the southern U.S., believe that of all group influences on food patterns, the family exerts the greatest effect. With Renner, they wonder why any food habits change since, as he says, "there is a circle. What one eats when young, that one likes and hands on to one's offspring which should rotate forever."

The Committee on Food Habits of the National Research Council, in their 1945 Bulletin III, summed up the subject when they said,

> Another aspect of the way in which edible materials are classified as inedible, edible by animals, edible by human beings, but not my kind of human being, edible by human beings such as self, and finally edible by self. These classifications are further reinforced by various sorts of attitudes— that materials which are not eaten are defiling, wicked to eat, coarsening, would alter one's status, etc.

We are at once reminded of the derision of Samuel Johnson that the Scotsman eats oats which should really be fed only to horses. We remember that the Irish rejected corn (maize) as inedible by human beings during the mid-nineteenth-century potato famine, as did the hungry Germans in the mid-nineteen forties, when they said it was only feed for chickens. Pirie said that "irrational food prejudice is extraordinarily widespread." He points out that "in Britain a chicken would be rejected long before it has putrified to the extent considered proper with pheasant, raw oysters are eaten but snails are not eaten even when cooked, and the pig is accepted but not the horse."

What food is considered edible by a group is an important consideration, as was illustrated when a new kind of hybrid corn was introduced into a Spanish-American group. Although this corn gave a yield three times that of the one commonly used, within half a decade these people ceased to grow the new corn because the wives objected to the texture in the tortillas and no one liked the flavor. Edibility or acceptability was foremost when the hungry rice-eating people in India rejected wheat because it was not white like their rice. In the U. S., many complaints were registered about the gray color of the bread made from the more nutritious and economical high extractions of wheat flour used during wartime conservation of wheat. Large numbers of people the world over feel that the lighter the color of a food, the more desirable it is.

It should be pointed out that individual food dislikes and reactions fall between the classes of edible by individuals like myself and edible by self. One person may eat liver, but another finds it inedible. This may be partly because two people as individuals taste its flavor differently and react differently to its texture.

Pirie pointed out that some people have rational reasons for rejecting foods, but these rejections are regarded as prejudices by those who do not understand them. He cited rejection by mountain dwellers of cereals and beans, which require an intolerable amount of time to boil at the lower boiling temperatures at 10,000 foot altitudes.

Meal Patterns

Cultural and group influences determine not only what foods are eaten, but they also determine the meal patterns, the number of meals in a day, and the methods of eating and utensils used. Travelers in Europe perhaps have watched an American order bacon and eggs and pay a price many times the cost of the European's continental breakfast of rolls and a hot beverage. The habit of having tea even at a business conference in Iran and in India surprises many Americans and sometimes is a bit trying to them when, in true American style of rushing about, a busy morning calls for several conferences. The meal hours for dinner at nine o'clock or later in some tropical countries often tries the patience of the American tourist, who may find himself the only diner if he eats earlier. The National Dairy Council once had a poster showing different kinds of breakfasts in a number of countries around the world and the time of eating in relation to Central Standard Time in the U.S. Miso soup may be a commonplace breakfast in Japan, but when a well-known U.S. soup company gave a "Soup Breakfast" at a national meeting, many people were surprised. Although some of us in the U.S. believe that the continental use of the knife and fork is perhaps more efficient and even more graceful, we stubbornly cling to what we learned as children.

The history of manners for eating and etiquette is an interesting study in itself. Sumner, in *Folkways*, said: "The conquest of the art of eating with propriety was accomplished by the introduction of forks. Before that, the bread was a tool with which to eat, and it required cultivated skill to handle it properly." The dainty use of fingers for eating in Moslem cultures is often amazing to Americans. Even differences in table service, such as the one dish that must last through a many-course Asian feast, sometimes cause Americans to raise their eyebrows.

There are also fashions in food and fashions in meal patterns. These may be based on the intellectual approach of the low-calorie breakfast or lunch. In the calorie-conscious food culture in the U.S., it is now fashionable to omit bread and desserts for dinner.

After the urbanization of many Americans made it impossible for the man of the house to eat at home at noon, the heavy meal of the day naturally came to be served at night. Although, quite logically, it could then be called dinner, many considered this an affectation; the name of this meal was often confused with that for light supper.

The usual seems natural to us, and the unusual seems unnatural or suspect. Yet habit rather than logic must be given credit for many of the group customs of foods eaten, manner of eating, or even times of eating. Ritchie Calder pointed out that abalone steak is an expensive item enjoyed by gourmets in California, but he doubted that they would enjoy the up to three-quarters of a pound of meat of the large African black snail, which has the texture and other qualities of abalone. In

Coastal West Africa, however, this snail is a festival food as is our Christmas turkey. In some areas no one can be found at home when weather conditions make a large harvest of these snails available.

The staple food of a country usually enjoys high prestige. This is true in Uganda, where steamed plantains, called *matoke,* are a staple food, as is cassava in Ghana and bread in Greece. Poi, made from taro, once was a staple food of Polynesian Hawaiians. Now that it has become expensive and scarce, it is not commonly eaten in Honolulu but is still highly prized and ascribed by some people to have a nutritive value beyond that warranted by its actual nutritive content. There has been discussion of trying to create a greater market for it by promoting its use as a food for allergic infants, who apparently tolerate it well.

In addition to cultural, ethnic, and family influences on food habits, individuals differ, as we all know, from the moment of birth. Good and poor digestion, food allergies and idiosyncracies, the rate of the body's use of food for energy, the ease of adjusting to the environment, the degree of intelligence, the difference in imagination, the effect of education in making the individual aware of the body's needs, and drives such as the desire to attain status all combine to give an individual his own peculiar eating pattern. Mothers who try to feed a family made up of strong-minded individuals are well aware of these differences, as are those whose business involves serving food to the public. Reactions to coffee, good or bad, served by different restaurants point to the fact that the descriptions are colored by more than the coffee brew itself. It has been found experimentally that some individuals rate the same brew of coffee as weaker when it is served in thin cups than when served in heavy pottery mugs.

Probably everyone has a unique pattern of food behavior which is shared with only a few others. Individual differences in some cases may obscure the common food habits and attitudes of a shared culture which are brought about in a group by similar physiological makeup and environment.

To summarize group and individual differences in food patterns, we quote from the FAO Bulletin Basic Study number six, "Education and Training in Nutrition":

> What people are willing to eat is determined by a complex system of attitudes, ideas, and assumptions that form the local cultural patterns. These include religious restrictions, taboos, ideas pertaining to the merits or demerits of a food, and other attitudes which are as yet little understood.

OTHER INFLUENCES

Geography

In addition to the other factors discussed, it is well known that geography exerts a fundamental influence on food habits. Although the inhabitants of Puerto Rico and Hawaii come from entirely different ethnic backgrounds, there is a great similarity in the tropical fruits used in each of these countries. In Southeast Asia, where rice and not wheat flourishes due to the water soaking of the lands by the monsoon rains and hot temperatures, the people are rice eaters. The introduction from the New World of maize into sections of Africa and of the potato into Europe where the climate favored their production brought about fundamental changes in the diets of the people. Sugar cane, now cultivated in many tropical countries, was said to have been brought by early travelers from India. The liberal use of pineapple, even in iced tea, and other tropical fruits in Hawaii at once suggests the influence of climate and geographic conditions on food habits. Where else will wild huckleberries be so commonly eaten as in the mountainous areas where they grow abundantly, or salmon be such a favorite food as in the water-surrounded Pacific Northwest and Alaskan coastal area?

Climate and seasonal production also affect food habits, especially when methods of preservation and storage are not highly developed. In many places, foods can be eaten only in season. In parts of the Near East, grapes and fresh figs, although abundant in season, can be eaten only during two months of the year.

Technological Development

Technological development exerts a pronounced influence on food habits and is one of the strongest forces causing change. The introduction of the freezing process for perishable foodstuffs profoundly affected our use of canned and fresh vegetables, fruits, and meats. The development of refrigerator cars also meant that fresh fruits and other foods from faraway places could be sold cheaper. The American housewife with a freezer ample for storage also can reduce the number of her shopping trips and her total time of the preparation of family meals when she prepares several meal-size portions of food at one time and freezes these for future use. When adequate refrigeration has come within the reach of a majority of families, frozen foods have become popular. This food preservation method makes it possible, as an example, for a well-known U.S. brand of frozen chicken to be served at a Sunday dinner in the hills of Accra, Ghana. Perhaps it should be pointed out that the introduction of these necessarily more expensive convenience foods into a developing country only widens the gap in foods used by high- and low-income families. Air transportation has also changed food patterns, as evidenced by the foods now available in Alaskan markets as well as by papayas from Hawaii and Granny Smith apples and kiwi fruits from New Zealand in mainland U.S. markets.

Technological developments are, of course, basic to the production of enough food for all the people in a country. The reclamation or better use of the arable land, the use of fertilizers and insecticides, the making available of needed water, the supplying of good seed, the improvement of the methods of sowing, the use of improved cultivating and harvesting equipment, the provision of adequate marketing facilities with money for seeds and machinery, and the development of facilities to distribute the food produced all profoundly influence the foods available to a people.

The kind of transportation also markedly affects food habits. The Egyptian who never travels may never taste citrus fruits even though he lives only a short distance from where they are grown. In India, the millet, wheat, and rice grown in different regions of the country are not available in other parts, even though the people from different sections might use the other grains and be better nourished by varying their diet.

For the fortunate people who live in technically developed countries, a worldwide diffusion of foods is taking place due to the increased ease of traveling and the possibilities of air transport of foods from one country to another, as well as purposeful transportation of seeds, plants, and food animals. The men of the armed forces who have known the foods of Korea, Vietnam, and other places in Europe and Asia often come to like them and want them when they come home, so restaurants serving widely varied cuisines have become popular. Food patterns are also affected when traditional methods of preservation are no longer used. The once familiar sun-dried corn of the farm belt in the U.S. is eagerly purchased when available by some people who remember it from their childhood.

Uses of Food

The primary use of food is always first to satisfy hunger and then to satisfy the needs of the body for growth, maintenance, and energy.

These we choose to call the nutritive uses of food because nutrition of the body is involved here. Dorothy Lee said:

> Culture may present food mainly as a means of the stilling of hunger, or of getting nutrition, or as a way to psychosomatic health; it may regard eating as a duty or a virtue, or as a gustatory pleasure, or as a social or a religious communion.

There are, however, many other uses of food; only a few of these are discussed here.

Food is used to promote friendliness and social warmth or, as it has been called, the ritual of hospitality. Or we may say that food is used in many ways to promote interpersonal acceptance. This becomes so strong a motive that most of us offer food or drink quickly when friends call. A relationship develops between the giver of the food and the recipient. In fact, we all accept food more readily from our friends than we do from strangers because it is easier to develop a relationship with friends.

The common use of food as a gift varies from a neighborly present of homemade bread to the elaborate and expensive packages, often of strange and unusual foods, given at Christmastime. These foods, the purpose of which is to signify friendliness, are usually choice or especially attractive or perhaps rare, exotic, or fraught with nostalgic memories. At Christmastime, the advertising pages of gourmet magazines are filled with pictures and descriptions of expensive macadamia nuts from Hawaii, of genuine aged Smithfield hams from Virginia, of live lobsters from Maine, or of Black Sea caviar. On the other hand, the home magazines display and explain in detail how the homemaker can make attractive gifts of inexpensive foods in her own kitchen. Whether the food gift is expensive or homemade depends on how and by whom it is used.

In some societies, homemade food products are considered inferior; to these people, processed and packaged foods are considered items worth giving. To others, homemade foods are considered especially desirable. Gifts of foods, however, are always considered delicacies by the giver and are not staple items of diet; the filling of a need even seems to negate the spirit of the gift. Christmas baskets for needy families are usually better received if some unusual foods for a treat are included.

The prominent part food plays at funerals and during the days preceding the funeral is well known. As a visible offering of sympathy, often our first thought is to give the grief-stricken family some food.

The importance of inviting newly made acquaintances to eat in our homes is recognized. It has been said that to eat with a person is to say, "I am your equal." The tension felt by many a young wife when she first invites her husband's boss and his wife to dinner and the extent of her efforts to provide the best meal she can are mute evidence of this. Will they accept? Will they like our kind of food? What shall I prepare? Am I equal to making a satisfactory menu? Will I be able to make the food good enough? What will he talk about? Will he be a friendly guest? I wonder what she's like?

All of the restrictions of the hierarchy of dining rooms in a business, government firm, or hospital have some of this philosophy of equals eating with equals behind it. Who can eat in the executive dining room? Perhaps guarded secrets are kept by this closed system, but it must be admitted that there is still the philosophy that only equals eat together.

It is well known that the barring of Negroes from some restaurants has caused some of the worst race riots. As Harry Golden said, it is only when people sit down together in a restaurant, at a family table, or in a schoolroom that they must do so as equals; standing together usually has not caused trouble. In some societies, social class is a greater barrier to eating together than is race.

Many people working in different aid programs, such as the Peace Corps, have found that the local people are especially sensitive to the behavior of the outsiders when they are invited to eat in local homes. It is said that the American refusing to eat the prized sheep's eye at a Near East meal can undo much former work to cement friendship.

Many hostesses enjoy giving outstanding dinner parties as a means of creative expression. On the other hand, some extremely wealthy people give great parties to keep their names in the public press. This is not new, for when the Roman Lucullus (for whom Lucullian feasts were named) realized that his wealth was nearly dissipated and that he could no longer continue to give his splendid parties, he splurged one last time and then committed suicide.

It is equally true that we accept foods from our friends most easily and suspect and reject food offered by enemies. The latter was especially true in early times when royalty, threatened by their enemies, had tasters whose job it was to test food for poison. The closing of many German restaurants during World War II was necessitated by these strong feelings.

In some U.S. groups today, foods are being used as a protest against

"The Establishment." The rise in popularity and the use of so-called *organic* or health foods can be seen as a protest against the use of chemical fertilizers and added preservatives. Another example of protest is the macrobiotic diet which some young people follow without understanding the deficiency of needed nutrients in it.

Attaining Status

One use made of food is to attain status. Food is often used to promote an individual's or group's welfare. It is said that in Ruanda the Urundi keep cattle not for meat or milk but as a bank account, a symbol of family wealth. The improvement of status rather than friendship may even be involved in gifts of food or invitations to meals. Those who strive to climb the social ladder, advancing also their economic status, shun the foods of the poor. Nothing less than the best steak is offered. Some people try to build a reputation as gourmets by serving exotic foods. These may be even infrequently liked, expensive, and difficult to prepare; excellence of flavor may be sacrificed for the visible signs of the unusual. In some groups, there is nothing to indicate that this is unacceptable social behavior.

Achieving Security

Closely associated with the uses of food to promote interpersonal relationships and to raise one's status is the use of food to promote security. The individual, as explained through the Maslow theory (see below), who knows where his next meals are coming from is on his way to acquiring security. A feeling of security is associated with orderliness or a lack of anxiety and tension over whether food will be forthcoming. Certain foods foster security more than others, even apart from their ability to satisfy hunger. For many people, milk is the primary security food. Many of us watched the Red Cross handing glasses of milk to soldiers returning from the Asian Theater of World War II almost before they had come off the gangplank. The eagerness with which these men— long deprived of family and familiar foods—took this milk gave ample proof of its meaning to them. Harriet Bruce Moore said: "The unhappy, suffering, far-from-home-and-loved-ones soldier looks back to *milk* as in many ways expressing the comfort, security, and contentedness of life as it was at home." Milk, because of its association in early life, may foster security for some; but other people, when questioned, name foods such as potatoes or meat. Sweets must have a rather deep meaning for many, as evidenced by the liberal use of them during times of tension.

In times of crises, familiar foods are even more highly valued. During World War II, the quartermaster's corps conducted extensive research to determine the meanings of specific foods to the men in the Armed Forces. The value of food in maintaining morale was well understood.

During the summer of 1966, the author asked a class at the University of Hawaii what food signified security. The immediate answer was "rice." As is well known, the Chinese and Japanese predominate ethnic groups in modern Hawaii. These students then told of the hoarding of rice when a shipping strike threatened to reduce its importation.

Relieving Tension

That food is often used to relieve tension is commonly known. Research has shown that as many as 75% of a group studied said that they ate more when under tension; the 25% who tended not to eat under tension admitted that they *sometimes* did use food to relieve boredom. Such use of sweets, even in young children, is well known. This dietary habit has been credited by some to be basic to the problem of obesity in the affluent countries. The fact that from one-fourth to one-third of many people's calories come daily from snacks may result not so much from hunger as from relieving boredom or tension. Increasing interpersonal sociability certainly plays a part in the heavy snacking pattern of Americans.

Influencing the Behavior of Others

Another use of food is to influence the behavior of others. Some mothers express their love of family through the preparation of food. It has been sarcastically said that the mother who is angry may serve liver, spinach, and bread pudding, but when she wants to please her husband or her family, she may serve steak, baked potatoes, and ice cream.

Sweet foods often are used as rewards, even as a personal reward, when a day has been especially hard. Generations of children have been admonished to eat their vegetables so they could have dessert. Some physicians give a child an all-day sucker for being good.

Young children learn very early that to eat or not eat their food is an easy way to elicit a reaction from anxious parents. In fact, many children are past masters at controlling adults through their eating. Food also can be a powerful weapon for punishment, either by the withholding of eagerly sought food or the forced eating of unwanted food.

Adolescents often find the use of food a good way to express rebellion. Many people who work with this age group believe that some over-eating, with the resulting obesity, is the result of such parental conflict and the child's rebellion.

In business, clients are sometimes entertained with expensive and luxurious meals. This makes it difficult for the client to refuse a request. Some commercial companies have made a rule that food and drink may not be accepted as gifts from customers or prospective customers. The reason for this is obvious.

The discussion of the Maslow theory of human needs can be helpful here. Abraham Maslow in *Motivation and Personality* (1970) discussed human needs. His classification is useful in considering why people eat as they do. He classified human needs into the (1) physiological needs, (2) safety needs, (3) belongingness and love needs, (4) esteem needs, (5) self-actualization needs.

Hunger here meaning an urgent need for food, is one of the most dominant of the physiological needs; it is a survival need. When a man is truly hungry, his need for food dominates his entire being. In the extremities of hunger, a man thinks only of himself, having forgotten even family and loved ones. It is useless to ask him to think of anything else until his hunger is satisfied at least to the extent that he is again physiologically comfortable.

As Maslow said: "For the man who is extremely and dangerously hungry, no other interests exist but food." Maslow also said, "He dreams food, he remembers food, he thinks about food, he emotes only about food, he perceives only food, and he wants only food." It is easy to understand why politics, community welfare, and even love of fellow men are of no immediate concern to the truly hungry man. Also see pages 281–283.

The next needs in this hierarchy, the safety needs, may be considered also as *security* needs. Once a man's hunger has been satisfied at least temporarily, he can become interested in attaining the security that he will have his next meal today and so on tomorrow and in the days ahead.

Maslow discussed the infant's need for undisrupted routine or rhythm as an illustration of the safety need. This is a basic reason why regular meals are necessary for a happy child. The anti-social behavior of hungry slum children is largely due to the lack of satisfaction of this basic need. The on-and-off programs for relief of hunger often are upsetting to a hungry group for the same reason. Security, as we have said before, can be obtained by the storing of food so that future meals are assured. As the economic situation of the individual improves, he may move upward in the satisfaction of his food needs. Yet in times of disaster, he becomes anxious over his future food supply. The hoarding of sugar during or just before food rationing went into effect during World War II is proof that people are soon brought back to fear for the security of their food supply. The overloading of American cupboards, pantries, and freezers perhaps may be traced to this motive and gives evidence that the need has not been fully satisfied. The fact that the insecure individual chooses a familiar over an unfamiliar food may well be explained by the need for a feeling of safety.

When the physiological and safety needs are fairly well satisfied, as Maslow said, the needs for belongingness, for love, and for affection appear. Food is used constantly to satisfy belongingness needs. Members of closed groups carefully guard their food habits to remain "in" or to "get in." All of us worry what to serve at a meal if we do not wish to deviate from a group's expectations, especially when we do not know what they expect. As an individual becomes more and more secure, she can dare to serve what she wants to; she can substitute lower-calorie fresh fruits for the rich, high-calorie desserts usually served.

The esteem needs next in the hierarchy are well illustrated by the "best cooks" contests. We have already discussed food to attain or maintain status; promoters of contests to see who is the best cake or cookie baker in the country must be well aware of the strength of this motivation. Perhaps the use and promotion of proficiencies in the preparation and presentation of food is a commendatory way to build a sagging ego in the adolescent.

The last need in this hierarchy of needs was called *self-actualization* by Maslow. Some students studying food and man have been found to understand the term *self-realization* better than the term used by Maslow. At this stage, the individual dares to make up his own recipe, to serve exotic foods, and to indulge in complicated procedures of food preparation. Townsend's 1928 statement expresses what we are trying to say: "The educated cosmopolite does not hesitate to try strange foods. Not so, the savage, the child, the ignorant. In these three classes, food prejudices often curious and irrational abound." Perhaps we should add that the savage, the child, and the uninformed are not secure in their sense of belonging, nor have they attained a fixed status among their often hostile associates. Therefore, they dare not be different in what they eat. Children who have unusual foods at home are the most venturesome in trying new foods at school. There probably is no age limit on being a gourmet if one dares to be one. Evidence of the increasing popularity of foods from other countries probably bespeaks the fact that increasing travel increases belongingness and raises self-esteem, perhaps even gives great satisfaction to the security need. For the further discussion of this classification of human needs and how Maslow interpreted the satisfaction of them, the student is referred to his *Motivation and Personality*, 1970 edition.

Some students have found the following terms and the diagram helpful:

	self-realization	—social need
	esteem or status	—social need
	belongingness	—social need
	security	—physiologic and social need
	survival	—physiologic need

The arrow pointing downward in the hierarchy of needs diagram was put there to remind us that our surplus food in an affluent society could be wiped out in a disaster such as a nuclear holocaust; we would then be brought down rapidly to the survival stage. One is reminded of the letters-to-the-editors and popular opinions expressed in the press several years ago when there was a campaign to stock bomb shelters with food. Some people said they would not assume responsibility for any except their own families.

Expressing Creativity

Although we have mentioned creativity several times in relation to food, it probably warrants more discussion. Whenever man's hunger and his need of food for security are both satisfied, he then dares to use his creative abilities in preparing food. He tries new foods and combinations of them.

The history of the Romans is replete with excessively extravagant feasts for the wealthy class. The development of complicated methods of preparing food in history and in modern times often puzzles the student. Perhaps the fact that everyone eats, except in fasting, and also that food is an intimate part of daily life leads some to degrade food preparation as a lowly task. Yet chefs of renown and those who can create beautiful and delicious foods are well rewarded in most modern societies. The ancient Romans and Greeks gave special recognition to good chefs. See page 43.

Cookery can be an art, else why were 206 new cookbooks published in 1965, and why did the cookbook that topped that list in sales sell nearly 12 million copies during the first year? In late 1966, *Time* (November 25) used a cover picture and story on Julia Child, whose TV cooking program had become a rage. Many of the newly published cookbooks are written to appeal to those who want to be creative in food preparation.

Mothers often show their impulse to create or to show love for their family through food preparation. They prepare an especially delicious dish, serve a meal of a meaningful pattern, or have an appropriate food for a special occasion. Families come to expect a particular food on special occasions, and deep meanings thereby come to be attached to it. Thus, the love of the mother is associated with certain foods, and these are often lifetime favorites in spite of the children's wandering far from the parental home.

SYMBOLISM AND PRESTIGE FOODS

A complete body of symbolism has surrounded foods both in historical and modern times. Bread, commonly called "the staff of life" in societies where it is a staple food and not just an accompaniment, assumes high prestige. In some of these cultures, bread is used in religious and social rites; it is placed as an exhibit or decoration at a banquet. In the Lord's Prayer, we say, "give us our daily bread," meaning all food. An old proverb says, "as good as bread." In groups where bread is highly regarded, even crumbs are precious and always are carefully gathered up when they fall on the floor. The story is told of a group of U.S. senators each being given a loaf of bread upon leaving a Greek island by boat and of the great insult inflicted when one threw his overboard because he felt he did not need it.

Nizzardini and Jaffee, writing in the mid-1940's on Italian food patterns for the Committee on Food Habits, said that in the group where Italian bread is eaten every day and every meal, an emotional tone surrounds it. These people consider it wrong to waste any food but sinful to waste bread; and the *thrifty* housewife gets this appellation because she uses much bread rather than other accompanying foods.

Bread, it is there agreed, is a prestige food for some people. In some cultures, it must be white to enjoy the highest prestige. White sugar also has enjoyed a long history of prestige. Meat is a prestige food with many people. Roast beef in England was long regarded as food for land owners and rich men, so it was small wonder that ration points were carefully hoarded in war time for the Englishman to buy his Sunday roast. Even now in the U.S., roast beef and steak dinners often command and get the highest prices at most restaurants. The finest of caviar has such prestige that in 1972, it was being sold for $75.00 per pound in Seattle, Washington.

The molded cooked peacocks with feathers replaced in elaborate pastries, as Cussler and DeGive reminded us, showed "how culinary artifice assumed prestige in sophisticated Roman society." They also said that "*changing the appearance of food* usually involves complex techniques proportionate to the degree of civilization, so that highly milled and refined foods hold an approved position." It must be pointed out that an adverse reaction to highly processed foods may later begin. Now in the U.S. whole-grain breads often command a higher price than white bread. Bennett said that foods of in groups acquire prestige and those of out groups affect the attitude toward them. Foods used at ceremonial functions—e.g. weddings, picnics, family gatherings, holidays—acquire high prestige. He believed that foods are more important as symbols than as carriers of nutrients. He said that symbolic interest in food operates largely as a way of relieving tension.

In some cultures, certain foods are supposed to have magical qualities and be influences either for good or evil. Not all of this association is from primitive cultures or from early times. Even recently, those who opposed pasteurization of milk were heard in public testimony to endow *raw* milk with the ability to turn gray hair back to black. Certain foods, like the fertilized duck egg which is regarded highly by some groups in the Philippines, are said to possess aphrodisiac qualities. It is a rather common belief, though untrue, that visceral meats are less "energy giving" than muscle meats. Many Americans have a revulsion concerning eating the brains of animals.

A discussion of the meaning of food cannot bypass the question of food taboos. These taboos usually surround animal foods such as meat, eggs, fish, and milk. Many of these culturally imposed dietary restrictions are connected with sex and reproductive function. Some foods are taboo for women, some for boys just entering adolescence, some for fathers or prospective fathers. There are numerous tribes who restrict menstruating women from even coming in contact with some foods. Many of these restrictions concern milk and cows, whose welfare is thought to be inimical to that of women. There are also restrictions concerning the foods pregnant or lactating women may or may not eat.

Some taboos may have been based on valuable experience, whereas others have arisen from superstitions, myths, and folk tales. In his *African Notebook*, Albert Schweitzer presented cases of individuals who unknowingly broke taboos and died within a short time.

Another aspect of foods is interesting to contemplate because it is related to the symbolism of food. Norman Cameron, in *The Psychology of Behavior Disorders*, said:

> Our language is full of ambiguous allusions to social acceptance and rejection, to verbal assaults, to gastric need for food, and to the spiritual need for sustenance. Thus we eat our words and swallow our wrath, the Lord spews us forth, we sink our teeth into a problem, drink in a message, find an explanation indigestible, and reject it with biting comments. When the human being, with all of his verbal ambiguities in his behavior, becomes confused, he often acts out as social operations what was intended to be only verbal metaphors.

In many ways, our English language would be weaker did we not use words basically concerned with food and eating where there is no connection with food. Harriet Bruce Moore said: "Every one has 'his taste' and from infancy until death he concerns himself with seeking and enjoying the kinds of food that are most pleasurable to him." She went on to explain this need by the frequency and naturalness "with which we use our eating sensations to categorize and describe other experiences." She summed this up thus:

> We speak of "taste" in many areas of flavors to describe people and situations —spicy, flat, sour, sweet, delectable, and so on. We speak of sensation associated with food—of coolness, bland, tart, smooth as cream, an oily personality, and so on.

We also tend to categorize our foods in ways only some of which have rational meaning. The meaning of the terms "hot" and "cold," when applied to foods of such people as those of India, are difficult for an American to fathom or connect with his use of the term hot meaning spicy or hot in degrees of temperature. Foods such as meat are said to be strength giving. Foods are luxury or essential, primary or secondary, farm or store foods. The latter terms were used more formerly than they are now. Some foods such as peanut butter, milk, and cooked cereals are children's foods, while steak, potatoes, and pie are men's food, and casserole dishes, salads, vegetables, and cakes are for women.

The meanings of food are usually consistent and stable within a group, and the individuals in the group understand these meanings and make the same interpretations.

The symbolism of salt is one of the fascinating stories in all lore concerning food. It has been said that since it is man's earliest condiment, the hunger for it is almost universal. It is well documented that human settlements were made close to the sources of salt. Some primitive people obtained a salt mixture from ashes when they could not get salt from mining it or evaporating sea water. Many North American Indians, who were unfamiliar with our salt, used alkaline potash instead. The word salt is derived from the Greek word for "sea." Homer referred to salt as "divine" and separated those nations which knew salt from those which did not.

Once salt was eagerly sought and even used as money. The Roman salt cellar was the symbol of hospitality and friendship. To be seated "above the salt," that is between the salt cellar and the host, was to be honored. In ancient days, salt was used as a form of purification, as a medicine, and in embalming after death. Wars have been fought for salt rights. Traeger said: "In some places salt is so scarce that it is considered as much a treat as children in our own culture regard sugar candy." He also says that "little cakes of salt, each stamped with the likeness of the emperor, were once used as money in China." Pepper also soared in ancient times to heights of fame, and reparations after wars often were made partially in payments of pepper.

Jean A. S. Ritchie, in 1950, in her classic presentation in the FAO Bulletin, *Teaching Better Nutrition*, has summed up the cultural significance of food. She says:

> Because of its fundamental role in the struggle for existence, food has acquired a significance in human society beyond that of providing nourishment for the body, which is reflected in many patterns of human behavior. Food may be closely associated with feelings of security and prestige. It has an important place in religious observations. It is linked with countless super-

stitions and prejudices. Thus, it can arouse many emotions—pleasure, envy, confidence, and even violent fanaticism. Their relationships must be taken into account in attempting to alter food consumption.

Jennie I. Rowntree said it just a little differently:

Food is eaten for enjoyment, for emotional release, for social prestige, and for attention, adverse or otherwise. Food is refused because of such unconscious emotions as the pleasure of paining others and showing self-assertion.

Poppy Cannon, in the article in *Saturday Review* entitled "Revolution in the Kitchen," said:

Never was a cliché more fatigued—or truer—than the one that bids: Tell me what you eat and I'll tell you what you are. Not only biography and genealogy but the whole field of anthropology could, if one knew the code, be deduced from food. Food is a mirror that reflects a thousand phases of personal, national, and international history. Geography is reflected in the food; so is climate, the local flora and fauna, religion, superstitions, and taboos; wars, victories, defeats, invasions. The food remembers where people traveled, who their grandmothers were, and from what part of the world their ancestors hailed.

FESTIVALS AND FEASTS

The story of a people could also be written in terms of their feasts and those who attended the celebrations. In general, feasts have been held from pagan times until now to:

1. Celebrate a particular religious event.
2. Celebrate a harvest in the fall of the year.
3. Offer appeasement and glory to a god at the winter solstice when in early times the people feared the sun would desert them.
4. Bless the sowing and celebrate the bursting of spring.
5. Honor the dead and pay homage to ancestors.

Other feasts, peculiar to one cultural group or nation, celebrate certain important national happenings such as the winning of independence. Certain foods come to be associated with each type of feast. Thus, at the time of harvest festivals, traditional and meaningful foods are used. Wild turkeys were used by the Pilgrims in Massachusetts as perhaps their best fall source of meat. This set a precedent for us in the U.S. in the use of turkey for our Thanksgiving dinner. Long before the Christian era, our present harvest festivals had their counterparts in pagan countries where the gods of the harvest were worshipped with curious and varied rites. Although residents of the U.S. may think of Thanksgiving as our special festival, practically all European countries have a similar one. These are celebrated there more frequently in the rural than in the urban areas. When the President of the U.S. proclaimed Thanksgiving as a national holiday, it became more of a national festival than it is in most other countries.

In the old calendar, the sign for the winter solstice was a circle with a dot in the center. This represented the sun. A symbolic cracker, called a bretzel or pretzel, was made at this season in the form of a circle with a cross in the center to represent the four seasons. The present pretzel is somewhat of a variation of this original form, but no longer is this food used so symbolically, at least in general.

Many winter holidays are gay with lights as well as foods, as is St. Lucia Day in Sweden, Divali in India, and the religious holiday at Christmas all over Christendom. Often a meat fairly heavy with fat, such as goose, forms the traditional food for Christmas. Foods which take long and loving preparation are used in many countries at Christmas and other winter festivals. In Virginia, which has been "Christmas making" for 350 years, the ways of celebrating are as steeped in custom as are the mince pies in spirits. Mince pie, a Christmas food in England since ancient times, is made from ingredients from the East which symbolize the gifts of the Wise Men to the Infant Jesus. The name, at first "shrid pye" or "shredded pie," later was changed to "minced or mince pie." At first, these were made in the form of the manger. It is said that when the upper part or upper crust was solid, it was called the coffin. But when it was cross latticed, it was supposed to represent the hayrack of the stable. Later, mince pies became known as "idolatry in crust" because of their association with the Church of Rome.

The Ukranian housewife sprinkles straw under her best embroidered tablecloth for the Christmas table. She also strews straw on the floor and places a sheaf of wheat in corners of the room. It is said that these rites are very old and may represent Christ's humble birth, but some of them may even date back to pagan harvest festivals.

The use of wine and Christmas turkey fat sprinkled on the Yule log is an old English custom. The Croats and Serbians are said to have sprinkled corn and wine on the Yule log while uttering wishes for an abundant harvest the next spring.

Marian Schibsby, writing for the American Council for Nationalities

Services on the old-world Christmas customs of many ethnic groups, told an interesting story of the Armenians. She said that after the Church service it is the custom to make visits; these are known as "hand-kissing visits" because the young folks are supposed to kiss the hands of their elders on whom they call. These visitors bring gifts of fruit: oranges for the women and lemons for the men. Also on that day, children bring gifts of poppyseed bread, pastry, and roast chicken, among other things, to their godparents, who reward them with gifts of money or handsome new clothes.

Schibsby mentioned a custom of the Czechs and Slovaks who, like many groups, use December 24 as a fast day. Some groups are admonished not to eat until they see the first star. The Czech and Slovakian children are urged to abstain from food until evening so that they may see the "golden pig," but Schibsby did not say what this is. Perhaps the highly prized baked carp is what they were to wait for. This meal, which takes weeks of preparation, is said to be well worth waiting for. The table decoration is made of dried fruit with loaves of special Christmas bread called *Vanocka* after the word for Christmas, *Vanoce*.

The traditions centering around Easter are similar to those which, in pagan times, honored the Goddess of Spring. The very word "Easter" is said to come from the name of this goddess, Eastre or Ostara. The spring holiday foods are often young lamb and fresh, newly grown vegetables if available. These are symbolic of youth, no doubt.

In many religions, feasts to honor the dead include the setting of foods which, after the supposed departure of the spirits, are eagerly consumed by the needy living.

Too many feasts may become a threat to good nutrition in several ways. One is, of course, overeating. In some cultures, so much food is saved for feasts that undernourishment in between is common. In general, foods which are used for feasts are:

1. Scarce—which puts a high priority on them.
2. High quality—the best jar of pickles saved for Christmas dinner.
3. Often expensive—which makes them desired.
4. Difficult and time consuming to prepare—where the love of the cook can be demonstrated.

Abstinence from some kinds of foods before a festival has been practiced throughout recorded history in many different settings. Many people abstain from certain foods, usually animal foods, until the first star is seen the evening before Christmas. Abstinence from animal foods before the spring festival is found in a number of cultures as it is in Lent before the Christian Easter. Denying oneself the favored animal food is considered good self-discipline and increases one's devotion to a belief. It has been said that authoritative religions all use the denial of the gratification of appetites in order that one may live above carnal desires and escape the fear of complying with instincts.

It has been said that among the most valued gifts the immigrant brought to the U.S. were their folkways and folklore. The best and finest of their customs and traditions associated with their festivals now have become woven into the culture of the U.S. Many people are now working to preserve these differences in ethnic foods and customs.

STUDY QUESTIONS

1. Explain how food patterns are culturally oriented.
2. What differences in your own food patterns have come from your own family background?
3. How can the Maslow hierarchy of needs be used to explain food practices?
4. Why is a study of festival foods important in understanding the culture of a group?
5. On page 156. Poppy Cannon is quoted. Can you justify her statement with illustrations from the literature?

TOPICS FOR INDIVIDUAL INVESTIGATION

1. Describe in detail the food habits of one ethnic group of people, pointing out similarities as well as differences from the food habits and foodways with which you are most familiar. Give the background or reasons for the difference wherever you can.
2. Plan in detail a program to improve the food habits of a particular group of people using the Willerman-Lewin method.
3. Describe a program where making a food or several foods available caused a real change in food habits.
4. Trace the changes in consumption of five foods in the U.S.

160   Food & Man

during the first six decades of the twentieth century. Give basic reasons for these changes.

5. Show how a group of people such as the Amish or those of the Amana Colony in Iowa influence the foods of their neighbors. Also show how these distinct patterns of ethnic groups settled in a defined area are influenced by their neighbors.

6. Use any popular American cookbook to try to discover foods introduced by some immigrants.

REFERENCES AND SUGGESTED READINGS

A.H.E.A. *Family Holidays Around the World.* Wash., D.C., 1964.

Babcock, C. G. Food and Its Emotional Significance. *J. Amer. Diet Assoc.,* 24: 390, 1948.

Bennett, John W. Food and Social Status in A Rural Society. *Am. Soc. Review,* 8: 561–69, 1943.

Bruch, H. Obesity in Childhood and Personality Development. *Amer. J. Orthopsychiatry,* 11: 467, 1941.

Burgess, A. and R. F. A. Dean, Eds. *Malnutrition and Food Habits.* Macmillan, New York, 1962.

Calder, R. *A Starving World.* Macmillan, New York, 1962.

Cameron, N. *Psychology of Behavior Disorders—A Biosocial Interpretation.* Houghton-Mifflin, Boston, 1947.

Cannon, P. Revolution in the Kitchen. *Saturday Rev.,* p. 54, Oct. 24, 1964.

Cassel, J. Social and Cultural Implications of Food and Food Habits. *Amer. J. Pub. Health,* 47: 732, 1957.

Committee on Food Habits. *Manual for the Study of Food Habits.* National Research Council Bull. 111, National Academy of Sciences, Wash., D.C., 1945.

Committee on Food Habits. *The Problem of Changing Food Habits.* National Research Council Bull. 108, National Academy of Sciences, Wash., D.C., 1943.

Cussler, M., and M. DeGive. *Twixt the Cup and the Lip.* Twane, New York, 1952.

Dupont, Jacqueline, Ed. Dimensions of Nutrition—Proceedings of the Colorado Diet. Assn. Conference, Fort Collins, Colorado, Associated University Press, 1969.

English, O. S. Psychosomatic Medicine and Dietetics. *J. Amer. Diet. Assoc.,* 27: 721, 1951.

Eppright, E. Factors Affecting Food Acceptance. *J. Amer. Diet. Assoc.,* 23: 579, 1947.

Fliegel, F. C. *Food Habits and National Background.* Pa. State Univ. Agr. Exp. Sta. Bull. 684, University Park, Pa., 1961.

Food for Peace, Annual Report on Public Law 480. U.S. Government Printing Office, Wash., D.C., 1965.

Galdston, I. Motivation in Health Education. *J. Amer. Diet. Assoc.,* 25: 747, 1949.

Galdston, I. Nutrition from the Psychiatric Point of View. *J. Amer. Diet. Assoc.,* 28: 405, 1952.

Golden, H. *Only in America.* World Publishing, New York, 1958.

Graubard, M. A. *Man's Food—Its Rhyme or Reasons*. Macmillan, New York, 1943.

Hollinger, M. and L. J. Roberts. Overcoming Food Dislikes: A Study with Evaporated Milk. *J. Home Econ.*, 21: 923, 1929.

Hottes, A. C. *Christmas Facts and Fancies*. A. T. DeLaMare, New York, 1954.

Jelliffe, D. B. Parallel Food Classification in Developing and Industrialized Countries. *Amer. J. Clin. Nutr.*, 20: 279, 1967.

Jelliffe, D. B., and F. J. Bennett. Cultural and Anthropological Factors in Infant and Maternal Nutrition. Proceedings of Fifth International Congress of Nutrition, Fed. Proc. 18: 185, 1961.

Jelliffe, E. E. *Patrice—Cajanus Newsletter of the Caribbean*. Food and Nutrition Institute, Mona, Kingston, Jamacia, Vol. 4, No. 3, 1971.

Jensen, Lloyd B. *Man's Food. Nutrition and Environments in Food Gathering Times and Food Producing Times*. Garrard Press, Champaign, Ill., 1953.

Kane, H. T. *The Southern Christmas Book*. David McKay, New York, 1958.

Khurody, D. N. *What's behind a Bottle of Milk*, 3rd Ed. Government Central Press, Bombay, India, 1958.

Khurody, D. N. *The Retrospect and Prospect of Bombay's Milk Supply*. Government Central Press, Bombay, India, 1958.

Kluckhohn, Clyde. *Mirror for Man*. Fawcett Publications, Inc., Greenwich, Conn., 1974.

Lee, D. Cultural Factors in Dietary Choice. *Amer. J. Clin. Nutr.*, 5: 166, 1957.

Lowenberg, M. F. Food Preferences of Young Children. *J. Am. Diet. Assoc.*, 24: 430–434, 1948.

Maslow, A. H. *Motivation and Personality*. Harper & Row, New York, 1970.

Masouka, Jitswichi. Changing Food Habits of the Japanese in Hawaii. *Am. Soc. Rev.*, 10: 759–765, 1945.

May, J. M. The Geography of Food and Cooking. *Int. Record Med.*, 170: 231, 1957.

Mead, M. Dietary Patterns and Food Habits. *J. Amer. Diet. Assoc.*, 19: 1, 1943.

Mead, M., Ed. *Cultural Patterns and Technical Change*. UNESCO, Paris, 1953.

Mead, M. Factors of Food Habits. *Ann. Amer. Acad. Pol. Sci. Soc.*, 225: 136, 1943.

Moore, H. B. Psychologic Facts and Dietary Fancies. *J. Amer. Diet. Assoc.*, 28: 789, 1952.

Nizzaridini, G. and N. F. Joffe. *Italian Food Patterns and Their Relationship to Wartime Problems of Food and Nutrition*. Committee on Food Habits, National Research Council, Wash., D.C., 1943.

Perl, Lila. *Rice, Spice and Bitter Oranges*. World Publishing Co., New York, 1967.

Pirie, N. W. *Food Resources Conventional and Novel*. Penguin Books, Baltimore, Md., 1969.

Radke, M. and E. K. Caso. Lecture and Discussion as Method of Influencing Food Habits. *J. Amer. Diet. Assoc.*, 24: 23, 1948.

Radke, M. and D. Klisurich. Experiments in Changing Food Habits. *Science Monthly*, 43: 193, 1936.

Renner, H. D. *The Origin of Food Habits*. Faber & Faber, London, 1944.

Ritchie, Jean A. S. *Learning Better Nutrition*. FAO Nutritional Studies No. 20, FAO, Rome, Italy, 1967.

Ritchie, Jean A. S. Teaching People Better Habits of Diet. *J. Amer. Diet. Assoc.*, 26: 94, 1950.

Roberts, Lydia J. *The Dona Elena Project*. Univ. of Puerto Rico, Rio Piedras, P.R., 1963.

Rowntree, Jennie I. The Human Factor in Nutrition Study. *J. Home Econ.*, 41: 433, 1949.

Schibsby, M. *Foreign Festival Customs*. American Council for Nationalities Service, New York, 1951.

Seifrit, E. Changes in Beliefs and Food Practices in Pregnancy. *J. Amer. Diet. Assoc.*, 39: 455, 1961.

Simoons, F. J. *Eat Not This Flesh*. Univ. of Wisconsin Press, Madison, Wis., 1961.

Spicer, D. G. *Feast Day Cakes From Many Lands*. Holt, Rinehart and Winston, New York, 1960.

Sumner, W. G. *Folkways*. Mentor Books, New York, 1960.

Sweeney, Mary. Changing Food Habits. *J. Home Econ.*, 34: 457, 1942.

Traeger, James. *Foodbook*. Grossman Publishers, New York, 1970.

Todhunter, E. N. *The History of Food Patterns in the U.S.A.* Proceedings of the Third International Congress of Dietetics, Newman Books, London, p. 13, 1961.

Townsend, C. W. Food Prejudices. *The Scientific Monthly*, 27: 65, 1928.

United Nations Education and Scientific and Cultural Organization. The Milk Conservation Program—An Appraisal of UNICEF/FAO Assisted Milk Conservation Programs. Private Communication, 1948–1960.

U.S. Office of Education. *A Study of Methods of Changing Food Habits of Rural Children in Dakota County Minnesota*. Nutrition Education Series Pamphlet No. 5, 1944.

Wellin, E. Cultural Factors in Nutrition. *Nutrition Reviews*, 12: 129, 1955.

Young, C. M., B. G. Waldner, and K. Berresford. What the Homemaker Knows About Nutrition. *J. Amer. Diet. Assoc.*, 32: 218, 1956.

4
Development of Man's Knowledge of Nutrition

Our concern is with man and his food. Let us first look at man himself. What is man? This question has been asked throughout the ages. Philosophers and theologians have argued about the question. Scientists in medicine, anatomy, and physiology have dissected man, experimented on him, and treated him to see how he is put together. Social scientists have analyzed him to see how and why he behaves as he does. Educators have worked with him to discover how he learns.

Man has been classified in many ways. One's view of man probably depends on one's background of education, training, and experience. Here is one viewpoint on man. He is:

Aggressive—his explorations, discoveries, and long history of wars speak for this characteristic.

163

Compassionate—the generous, sometimes self-sacrificing nature of what man will do for his fellowmen is attested to throughout history.

A reasoning, thinking being—the advances in science and our rich stores of knowledge are proof of this feature.

Creative—art, literature, music, architecture, and the inventions we are heirs to are results of this creativity.

Inquisitive—were it not for man's inquisitiveness, exploration of the earth and outer space and all the discoveries of science never could have been made.

A spiritual being—man's belief in some force, power, spirit, or God has placed him above all other creatures in the world.

Gregarious—family, home, community, and city life are evidence of this.

Communicative—powers of speech and written language, further developed into all the mass media of communications, are an essential part of man and his progress.

A physiological being—much of what man is and his actions depend on his physical structure and its physiological functioning.

At different periods in history, one or another of these characteristics of man has tended to be predominant. But always his physiological nature has expressed itself. Man's hunger drive is basic to his existence. Food determines his survival because food nourishes the body. There are many kinds of food, and they differ widely in their nutritive value. Knowledge of the nutritive value of food is a twentieth-century achievement. Throughout the ages man ate what he could get. Undoubtedly it was by trial and error that civilized man gained some understanding of how foods differed; he learned from experience that certain kinds of food were necessary for health. But not until this century did man identify the different nutrient constituents in foods and learn how they were used physiologically for the highly complex processes in the body.

Always man's inquiring mind has asked: "What is it?" "Why?" "How?" His search for the answers to these questions about food in relation to health is the story of the development of the modern science of nutrition. Today, the basic concepts* are summarized in the simplest terms as follows:

1. Nutrition is the way the body uses food. We eat to live, to grow,

*Statements made by the U.S. Interagency Committee on Nutrition Education, 1972.

to keep healthy and well, and to get energy for work and play.

2. Food is made up of different nutrients needed for growth and health. Nutrients include proteins, carbohydrates, fats, minerals, and vitamins. All nutrients needed by the body are available through food. Many kinds and combinations of food can lead to a well-balanced diet. No single food has all the nutrients needed for good growth and health. Each nutrient has specific uses in the body. Most nutrients do their best work in the body when teamed with other nutrients.

3. All persons, throughout life, have need for the same nutrients, but in varying amounts. The amounts of nutrients needed are influenced by age, sex, body size, activity, state of health, and heredity.

4. The way food is handled influences the amount of nutrients in food, its safety, quality, appearance, taste, acceptability, and cost. Handling means anything that happens to food while it is being grown, processed, stored, and prepared for eating.

WHY HISTORY?

History gives meaning to the present. Through knowledge of the past, we gain understanding of what is happening today. History has more than a utilitarian purpose; it is the record of the progress of man's endeavors and work, his ideas, visions, failures, and achievements. Athena sprang full armored from the head of Zeus, according to Greek mythology, but knowledge never has sprung full fledged from the brain of man. It has been acquired step by step.

The history of nutrition is the story of men with questioning minds at work on the problems that affect the lives and health of all people. This is an exciting story interwoven with medicine, anatomy, physiology, chemistry, bacteriology, and agriculture. Men of almost every nationality contributed to the story because, as Pasteur said, "science knows no national boundaries." They were men of different temperaments and personalities, some with little formal education and others of high specialization; they were physicians, chemists, sailors, explorers, tradesmen, rich aristocrats, teachers, pharmacists, and lawyers. But they were all men with curiosity and a will to find the answers to questions that arose in their minds.

This chapter will deal with some of the high points of discoveries that have brought us to our present state of knowledge. We are not quite sure when the story began, but reliable records date back to early Greek and Roman times. The story can be pieced together through study of Babylonian and Egyptian tablets, ancient scrolls and papyri, journals of explorers and early voyagers, records of wars and famines, diaries and letters of men in all walks of life, scientific papers, and medical records.

Nutrition is a twentieth-century science. Since nutrition is vital to man's life and well being, why should nutrition be so late in developing? The answers are several:

1. Nutrition is dependent on the isolation and measurement of nutrients, which could be achieved only after the development of modern chemistry and the invention of scientific instruments for the quantitative study of minute amounts of chemicals present in food and the human body.
2. Nutrition deals with the living organism and its physiologic functions. Therefore, progress was dependent on advances in the biological sciences.
3. Much that is known about nutrition and health was learned from the study of disease, so progress in clinical medicine had to come first.
4. Man's concern for his fellowmen, rather than concern for science and technology as such, is a development of the twentieth century.

History without dates is meaningless. Dates help to put events in a time sequence and to relate them to other events. Use them as a guide to increased understanding of man's progress in acquiring knowledge of food and its nutritional significance to his health and all his achievements.

THE BEGINNINGS OF MODERN SCIENCE

The story of the history of modern nutrition begins with the seventeenth century, often called the Golden Age of Science, when modern science began to develop because instruments were invented to make experimentation and measurement possible.

The Greeks and Romans believed in using diet in the treatment of disease, although they had no understanding of which foods were really helpful or why. An early Greek physician introduced the idea of four elements: fire, water, earth, and air. These four elements made up the four qualities: hot, dry, cold, and wet. But science could not progress far on such concepts as these. In the second century A.D., Galen, a physician from the Greek kingdom of Pergamos, dissected animals and wrote on the anatomy of man. He wrote many books on medical topics with so much authority that for the next 1200 years his teachings and writings were accepted as the final word on the subject.

From the time of the downfall of the Roman Empire (476 A.D.) through the Middle Ages was the period of the spread of Christianity, and there was little attention to medicine or science. Voyages of exploration, particularly the discovery of America by Columbus (1492), turned men's thoughts to broader horizons. The invention of movable type in the fifteenth century made the printed word available to more people and thus helped the wider spread of knowledge and ideas.

And now for the seventeenth century. Elizabeth I, or "good Queen Bess" as she was sometimes called, died in 1603, and the reign of the Stuarts began in England. The period of ocean voyages and land discovery was now to be joined by a new type of discovery—scientific discovery. No longer were men willing to accept what Galen said; the voice of authority gave way to the experimental approach. Galileo (1564–1642) in Italy made a telescope to study the stars. Anton Leeuwenhoek (1632–1723), the Dutch tradesman, spent his time grinding lenses and making a kind of microscope so that he was the first to see "little animals" in pond water. He studied all kinds of plant and animal tissue; he was a careful, patient observer who wrote simple, honest accounts of what he saw; and he was a man who described himself as having "a craving after knowledge which, I notice, resides in me more than in most men."

William Harvey (1578–1657) proved, by demonstration and carefully planned experiments, that the blood circulates through the body (1628), going from the heart by way of the arteries and returning by the veins. Harvey thus laid the foundation for later understanding of how food materials are transported to every cell in the body. Robert Boyle (1626–1691), the "father of chemistry," experimented for the joy of finding out things and invented an air pump. Sir Isaac Newton (1642–1727) gave us the theory of gravitation and wrote his great work on mathematics.

The experimental method, crude though it was at first, was now being used. Scientific societies were formed and had their scientific journals for reporting results of experiments. The *Mayflower* arrived in 1620 in what was to become the United States of America; Harvard College was founded in 1636. These are some of the high spots of the seventeenth century, the beginnings of science and freedom for men to use their inquiring minds and to test their ideas.

HOW FOOD IS CHANGED INTO MAN

Ham and eggs eaten by Susie Jones for breakfast are on their way to becoming Susie Jones. Magic? No—it is a process whereby the chemical constituents of food are rearranged within the body to form the chemical constituents that make up a human being. The complex and intricate processes are well understood today, but current knowledge has been achieved only by patient study through the centuries. Sanctorius (1561–1636), an Italian physician, probably was the first man to do nutrition studies on humans. For weeks he weighed himself, his food, and all body excretions. But neither the equipment nor the basic information in science was available to help him solve the problem of differences between his body weight and what he ate and excreted. One hundred years passed before the next steps were taken to discover how food is changed into man.

Digestion

How could solid food be changed in the stomach or some other part of the digestive tract and then get into the blood stream to be circulated in the body? Many wondered about this problem. But how little it was understood is illustrated by the following statement:

> Some physiologists will have it that the stomach is a Mill—others that it is a Fermenting Vat—others again that it is a Stew-pan—but in my view of the matter it is neither a Mill, a Fermenting Vat, nor a Stew-pan—but a stomach, Gentlemen, a Stomach.

This was the way John Hunter (1728–1793), English surgeon and lecturer, informed his students and colleagues that he did not know what the stomach did.

A few men found some ways to try to answer the question. One of these was René Réaumur (1683–1757) of France. He was educated in law but could afford to study what interested him most, and that was natural science. He had a pet bird, a kite, which could regurgitate food after swallowing it. Réaumur made some metal cylinders and placed food inside them. Then he put wire grating at each end so that the food could not fall out but would still be exposed to the action of digestion in the stomach when swallowed. Meat was put into the tubes; when regurgitated by the bird, it was found to be partially dissolved. There was no odor of putrefaction and the tubes showed no evidence of crushing or pressure, thus disproving the current theories that digestion was a grinding action and was putrefaction. Réaumur also put sponge in some of the tubes; in this way, he soaked up some of the gastric juices. He found that this juice was acid in nature and would partially dissolve meat in a test tube. New theories are slow to be accepted. Although Réaumur's evidence did not change current ideas, he had introduced a new method of investigation.

Twenty-five years later, Lazzaro Spallanzani (1729–1799) of Italy continued the work and methods begun by Réaumur, and he also experimented on himself; he swallowed small linen bags containing meat and bread. He confirmed Réaumur's findings and wrote a book that showed that digestion was a chemical process and not fermentation.

The next big step forward came in 1822. It was the result of an accident, but a man with vision, curiosity, and scientific interest was there to take advantage of the unusual occurrence. The accident happened to Alexis St. Martin, a French Canadian trapper who was shot in the chest and abdomen. The young Army surgeon who treated him was William Beaumont; the place was a frontier village in northern Michigan; the time was 1822. Although the injury was believed to be fatal, Beaumont's treatment and care of the patient brought about his recovery. However, a small hole in the abdominal wall and into the stomach remained open. Through this opening, Beaumont could insert a thermometer and measure the temperature; he could also see what foods and conditions stimulated the flow of gastric juice and the rate at which different foods were digested. He made 238 observations and experiments, and many of his inferences still are considered to be correct today. Undoubtedly Beaumont could have learned even more about the digestive process but, understandably perhaps, Alexis did not enjoy being studied in this way and went back to Canada.

Chemistry developed rapidly in the nineteenth century. Soon chemists were able to identify the acid in gastric juice as hydrochloric acid, but they also found that some other agent was responsible for the actual process of dissolving food. This agent was found to be an enzyme which was named pepsin (1835).

Advances from that time forward were comparatively rapid, and the chemistry and physiology of digestion are well understood today. Also, much has been learned of the psychological influences on the digestive processes.

Calorimetry

What happens to food once it is absorbed and circulating in the blood stream was even more puzzling than the question of digestion. At about the time Spallanzani was doing his experiments, this question was receiving the attention of Antoine Lavoisier (1743–1794) in Paris. Other scientists (Priestley and Scheele) had discovered oxygen but did not understand it nor correctly identify it. Lavoisier discovered the true nature of oxygen. Moreover, he had the vision to interpret and the ability to systematize the knowledge of his time so that modern chemistry could develop. At the height of his scientific career, Lavoisier was a victim of the French Revolution and was beheaded on the guillotine. The work he started was continued by others. Lavoisier showed that accuracy in weighing on analytical balances and exact measurements were essential in science. And above all, his experiments laid the foundation for understanding the processes going on inside the human body. For this he has been called the "father of nutrition."

Breathing is natural to everyone; without air, man dies. This was an ancient discovery. But what does air do and what is it? Men of the seventeenth century had studied the problem and found that a lighted candle enclosed in a vessel was soon extinguished. Others enclosed a mouse in a jar of air over water and found that when part of the air was used up the mouse died. Lavoisier's experiments and his keen mind for interpreting what he found showed that breathing or respiration is a chemical process that uses oxygen; the process is called oxidation. Oxygen is essential for the changing of food nutrients into the body structure of man. The sum of all these many chemical processes is metabolism; Lavoisier was the first to measure metabolism in man. He measured the amount of oxygen consumed by his laboratory assistant when sitting at rest and also the amount of carbon dioxide he breathed out at the same time. From these and other measurements on animals, Lavoisier was able to show that oxidation within the body is a source of heat and energy. Lavoisier's experiments also showed that more oxygen is used when one eats food and when one exercises or does work. This was the beginning of calorimetry or measurement of heat and work in the body, which eventually led to the measurement of calorie values of foods.

Other scientists soon added to the foundations of knowledge established by Lavoisier. The center of research passed for a time to a group of German scientists who first built a calorimeter large enough for a dog to be enclosed in and then one in which a man could be enclosed. The oxygen used and carbon dioxide exhaled could be measured precisely, as well as the body heat at all times and under differing conditions of diet and of work. Graham Lusk (1866–1932) of Connecticut studied calorimetry in Germany. When he returned to the U.S., he had a calorimeter built and then investigated the metabolism of healthy and diseased animals and children.

NUTRIENTS IN FOOD

The Search for Protein

Although a scientist discovered the gas called nitrogen in 1772, it was not known that this element had anything to do with nutrition until 1816. At that time, a French physician and teacher of physiology, Francois Magendie (1783–1855) published some of his research findings. When he fed dogs single foods such as sugar and water or olive oil and water, the animals died. Magendie concluded that animals needed nitrogen in the diet. He knew that both body tissues and many foods contained nitrogen, and he suggested that the nitrogen of the tissues probably came from food. The nitrogen-containing foods were called albuminous foods; just 22 years (1838) after Magendie's work, a Dutch chemist, Mulder, gave the name *protein* to the nitrogen-containing material in these albuminous foods.

The word protein comes from the Greek word meaning first. But protein does not take first place in nutrition. No nutrient is first because nutrition requires that there be adequate amounts of a number of nutrients. However, protein is essential, and children stop growing when it is not supplied in their diets. In many countries today, especially those dependent upon cereals and root crops, good quality protein is

Lazzaro Spallanzani (1729–1799)
of Italy; early investigator of
physiology of digestion.

Jean B. D. Boussingault (1802–
1887) of France; first to conduct
balance studies on animals.

Men of many nationalities and different fields of investigation laid the foundation for the science of nutrition.

Christian Eijkman (1858–1930) of Holland; Nobel prize winner for work leading to the discovery of vitamin B$_1$.

W. O. Atwater (1844–1907) of New York; earned the title "Father of American Nutrition."

lacking and the health and vigor of the people are impaired. Kwashiorkor (described in Chapter 8), a disease of children, is associated with lack of protein and calories in food.

A new pathway was opened by this work on nitrogen-containing foods. Chemists began to identify the various constituents or building blocks that make up different proteins; these blocks are called amino acids. Some 22 amino acids have been identified in food. Some of these amino acids can be synthesized in the body from nitrogenous material supplied in the diet. Others must be supplied preformed in food; these are called the essential amino acids.

Chemical analysis and animal feeding experiments have been the methods for learning about proteins. Albino rats have been used most frequently in the twentieth century because they are small, easily handled, grow rapidly and therefore show any deficiency quickly, and eat almost any kind of food mixture. Advances in chemistry make it possible to separate the pure constituents of food. By feeding these in varying combinations, the essential nutrients for an adequate diet were identified. The amount of protein needed by animals or man can be measured. The amount of nitrogen is determined in the food that is eaten, and similar analysis for nitrogen is made on excreta. If what is consumed equals what is excreted, then there is obviously a balance and the diet is adequate. If more is excreted than is being eaten in food, then the body is losing protein and more must be eaten to meet the body's needs. Using these basic methods, rapid advances in knowledge of proteins have been made in the last 50 years. But research is still continuing on the amino-acid makeup of foods, the amounts needed, and the various ways in which protein foods may be combined in the diet to provide all the amino acids. Although foods of animal origin are the best sources of the essential amino acids, recent studies have shown that a judicious mixture of different plant proteins can be made and that mixtures of cereals and other plant foods can be prepared that are nutritionally adequate (see Chapter 9).

Is Fat Necessary?

Carbohydrates—starches and sugars—form the basis of the diets of people the world over, except for the Eskimos in the Arctic regions where these foods will not grow. Cereals (wheat, rice, corn, oats, rye, and barley) and tropical root plants are the easiest and cheapest of all foods to grow. Their great value is that they are a cheap source of calories, and calories are necessary to satisfy hunger and provide energy for man.

Fat was one of the earliest food substances to be recognized because of its oily or greasy nature. The fat on meat is readily seen, as is the cream on milk. Oil, which is liquid fat, is found in nuts and the seeds of many plants such as cottonseed and soybean. These foods are usually more expensive to produce than are the cereals and root crops.

By the middle of the last century, scientists were beginning to look much more critically at proteins, fat, and carbohydrates and to question how they were formed in the body, where they came from, and whether they were necessary in food. At first it was thought that the fat of an animal's body was obtained from fat in food. But farm animals grew fat eating grass, and grass certainly had little fat in it. Using the method of feeding diets of known food composition, Boussingault, in France, fed diets that were free from fat to geese; the geese grew well and stored fat in their bodies. He obtained the same results with ducks. In other countries, similar experiments with fat-free diets for dogs and farm animals gave clear evidence that the animal body can synthesize fat from carbohydrate. The same is true for human beings. If the body is given more carbohydrates, that is, more calories, than are needed for work and body functions, the excess is changed chemically in the metabolic processes to fat and is stored in the body as fat.

This does not mean that fat itself is unnecessary in the diet; fats are high in energy value, providing two and one-fourth times as many calories per unit of weight as do carbohydrates or proteins. Fats are enjoyed because they give flavor and palatability to food. Some fats carry certain vitamins and also an essential unsaturated fatty acid. (Unsaturated fatty acids are ones in which two or more pairs of carbon atoms in the carbon chain of the molecule can add additional hydrogen atoms.)

Mineral Elements

In the early 1800's, three classes of foodstuffs were recognized and called saccharine, albuminous, and oleaginous substances; these are now known as carbohydrates, proteins, and fats. The nineteenth century was a period of rapid discovery of the chemical nature and properties of these substances and of other elements necessary for growth and health. Chemical analysis and feeding experiments with animals were the techniques used to discover a new group of substances, the ash constituents or mineral elements, essential for the nutrition of man.

When plant material was burned, it did not disappear entirely; some ash always remained. Chemists at this time (1800) began to look at this ash and try to find out what it was composed of. They were also curious about the chemical nature of bone, blood, and other body fluids. At the same time, other investigators were using the new technique of feeding experiments with farm animals. One of these investigators was Boussingault (1802–1887), the French chemist, physicist, and mining engineer, to whom reference has already been made. He is credited with being the first to apply knowledge of chemistry to the feeding of farm animals. In his experiments, he compared the growth and health of animals when one lot was fed a diet containing ordinary salt and another lot received no salt. Salt made an obvious difference in the appearance and well-being of the animals. In similar types of feeding experiments, he found that iron was essential in the diet.

Other investigators found that calcium and phosphorus were needed for skeletal growth. Iodine was discovered in the thyroid gland of man. Sheep died unless cobalt was present in the soil on which their food grew. Many men in many places identified new mineral elements necessary for life, and new discoveries still are being made. At least sixteen of these elements are now known to be part of the body structure or the body fluids, and they must be supplied in man's daily food. Some of these, such as copper, zinc, and manganese, are present in such small amounts that they have been called trace elements or microelements.

One more group of food nutrients had yet to be discovered—the vitamins. Although they were the last group of nutrients to be isolated and named, their story is perhaps the longest and started earlier in history than that of any other food constituent.

DEFICIENCY DISEASES AND DISCOVERY OF VITAMINS

Man's history has been marked by his struggle to obtain food and to ward off disease. Until this century, hunger, famine, and disease were major factors in keeping down the numbers of the population in many countries. Much disease has been eliminated or controlled since the discovery of the bacterial origin of disease and the development of sanitation, drugs, and antibiotics.

Another group of diseases is being eliminated through knowledge of nutrition; these diseases are called the dietary-deficiency diseases because they are caused by the lack of vitamins or other nutrients in the diet. Some of these diseases such as scurvy, pellagra, and rickets have been known for many years. Since 1912, the vitamin associated with each has been discovered; that is the story told here. Other dietary-deficiency diseases include beriberi, endemic goiter, and kwashiorkor. These are discussed in Chapter 8.

Scurvy

Scurvy has been known for centuries. Because it affected sailors on long voyages, it has been called the scourge of sailors. However, this disease has been just as much a calamity for soldiers, explorers, and civilian populations when they have been deprived of fresh foods, especially fruits and vegetables.

It is always easier to look back and see how and why problems existed than it is to understand them at the time. So it is natural to ask why there is no mention of scurvy in Columbus' voyage of discovery across the Atlantic in 1492. He had three ships with a complement of 88 men. They sailed on September 6 and reached the West Indies October 12—a voyage of little over one month. They also stopped at the Canary Islands for repairs, fresh water, and food. Healthy men on a voyage of that length did not succumb to scurvy. But on longer voyages scurvy took its toll.

Vasco da Gama, the great Portuguese navigator, sailed from Lisbon in 1497 to the East Indies. He lost 100 out of 160 men while on a voyage around the Cape of Good Hope because his men were continuously at sea for four months without fresh food of any kind.

Jacques Cartier, the French explorer, is well remembered in the history of scurvy because he learned from the Indians how to cure it in his crew on their voyage during 1535 and 1536 to Canada.

> During this period there died to the number of twenty-five of the best and most able seamen we had, who all succumbed to the aforesaid malady (scurvy). And at that time there was little hope of saving more than forty others, while the whole of the rest were ill, except three or four.

Cartier saw an Indian walking about in good health whom he had seen ten days earlier ill with the same disease his men suffered from. The Indian told him that he "had been healed by the juice of the leaves of a tree and the dregs of these, and that this was the only way to cure sickness." Cartier obtained some branches of the tree and prepared the drink from it for his men.

> As soon as they had drunk it, they felt better, which must clearly be ascribed to miraculous causes; for after drinking it two or three times, they recovered health and strength and were cured of all the diseases they had ever had . . . in less than eight days a whole tree as large and as tall as any I ever saw was used up, and produced such a result, that had all the doctors of Louvain, and Montpelier been there, with all the drugs of Alexandria, they could not have done so much in a year as did this tree in eight days; for it benefited us so much that all who were willing to use it, recovered health and strength, thanks be to God.

The particular tree used has not been identified with certainty. Some thought it to be the sassafras tree, others the hemlock. Leaves and twigs of pine, willow, and evergreens have been analyzed and shown to be good sources of vitamin C, the vitamin that cures scurvy.

Practical experience worked well for some voyagers. John Woodall, ship's surgeon, wrote a book in 1617 in which he gave advice for preventing scurvy: "The use of the juice of lemon is a precious medicine and well tried, being sound and good." But Lord Anson, who sailed in 1740 with three ships to explore the Pacific and also to raid and capture Spanish galleons, paid no attention to such suggestions. He had a force of 961 officers and men; within a year 626 were dead, most of them from scurvy.

No matter how exciting the stories, descriptions, or folklore about foods or treatment of disease, science rightly demands experimental evidence before accepting statements. In the case of scurvy, this evidence was provided by Captain James Lind in his book, *A Treatise of the Scurvy,* published in 1753. Lind was the son of a Scottish merchant. He studied medicine, entered the Royal Navy, and became a ship's surgeon and then physician in charge of a Royal Naval hospital. He was a man noted for his clear thinking, knowledge, and ability. In his book, we have the description of the first clinical experiment carried out under controlled conditions. It still stands today as a model of careful planning of a nutrition experiment with control of all conditions, completeness, and conciseness and accuracy of recording. It is worthy of study not only for its place in history and its information but also for its style. Lind wrote:

> On the 20th of May 1747, I took twelve patients in the scurvy, on board the *Salisbury* at sea. Their cases were similar as I could have them. They all in general had putrid gums, the spots and lassitude with weakness of their knees. They lay together in one place, being a proper apartment for the sick in the fore-hold; and had one diet common to all *viz.*, water-gruel sweetened with sugar in the morning; fresh mutton-broth often times for dinner; at other times puddings, boiled biscuit with sugar; and for supper, barley and raisins, rice and currants, sago and wine, or the like. Two of these were ordered each a quart of cyder a-day. Two others took twenty-five gutts of *elixir vitriol* three times a-day, upon an empty stomach; using a gargle strongly acidulated with it for their mouths. Two others took two spoonfuls of vinegar three times a-day, upon an empty stomach; having their gruels and their other food well acidulated with it, as also the gargle for their mouth. Two of the worst patients, with the tendons in ham rigid (a symptom none of the rest had), were put upon a course of sea-water. Of this they drank half a pint every day, and sometimes more or less, at it operated, by way of gentle physic. Two others had each two oranges and one lemon given them every day. These they ate with greediness, at different times, upon an empty stomach. They continued but six days under this course, having consumed the quantity that could be spared. The two remaining patients took the bigness of a nutmeg three times a-day, of an electuary recommended by an hospital surgeon, made of garlic, mustard seed, balsam of Peru, and gum myrrh.
>
> The consequence was, that the most sudden and visible good effects were perceived from the use of the oranges and lemons; one of those who had taken them, being at the end of six days fit for duty. . . . The other was the best recovered of any in his condition; and being now deemed pretty well, was appointed nurse to the rest of the sick. . . .
>
> As I shall have occasion elsewhere to take notice of the effects of other medicines in this disease, I shall here only observe, that the result of all my experiments was, that oranges and lemons were the most effectual remedies for this distemper at sea. I am apt to think oranges preferable to lemons, though perhaps both given together will be found serviceable.

Despite this clear-cut evidence of the value of citrus fruit for curing scurvy, it was not until 50 years later that the Royal Navy adopted the regular practice of daily provision of lemon or lime juice for all sailors. And this is the origin of the term "limey," so long applied to British sailors and sometimes even today to anyone from England.

The Gold Rush days of California, 1849–1850, brought a sudden increase of 100,000 persons to that part of the country. Food shortages, especially of fruit and vegetables, developed quickly; the deaths from scurvy in the mining camps have been estimated conservatively at 10,000 men. The last part of the overland trail to California was marked with the graves of those who died of scurvy. It is of interest that scurvy and the Gold Rush were factors in starting the citrus industry of Southern California; the demand for lemons led some pioneers in 1849 to plant large orchards of citrus fruit.

Acceptance of new knowledge is sometimes very slow. Military forces apparently thought of scurvy as a sea disease and did not provide protection against it. Consequently, throughout Europe and America, the story of wars is also a record of scurvy. In the American Civil War, 30,714 cases of scurvy were reported and 338 deaths were attributed to this disease. In the Franco-Prussian War of 1870–1871, the besieged city of Paris suffered severely from scurvy. In the Russo-Japanese War, half the garrison of 17,000 soldiers suffered from scurvy after the siege of Port Arthur. In World War I, 1914–1918, thousands of troops were incapacitated by scurvy; it affected the armies of Russia, Turkey, Romania, Germany, Austria, Italy, and France. The troops from India fighting in Mesopotamia with the British army had 7500 cases of scurvy in a 19-week period.

It has been said that "science knows no national boundaries." The same is true of scurvy and other dietary-deficiency diseases. Lack of an essential nutrient in the diet affects anyone no matter what his nationality, color, occupation, place of living, age, and sex. Scurvy often affected men more than women because the men were absent from home and regular meals, and their hard work produced the effects more quickly. Today scurvy is not unknown in infants whose mothers fail to give them orange or other fruit juice. It is also seen in men and women who fail to use fruits and vegetables in their diets because of poverty or because they live alone and do not take the trouble to obtain an adequate diet.

In 1907, two Norwegian investigators searching for the cause of beriberi found that guinea pigs fed a diet of only grain and water developed scurvy but that this could be cured by feeding them green-stuff. This was one of those "lucky chances" in research because guinea pigs, monkeys, and man are practically the only creatures that must have vitamin C-containing foods supplied in their diet. Almost all other animals can synthesize this vitamin in their bodies. This discovery with guinea pigs opened the way for a quick and easy means of studying foods as a source of vitamin C. Finally, in 1932, an American scientist, C. G. King at the University of Pittsburgh, crystallized pure vitamin C from lemon juice. And at the same time, Szent Gyorgy in Hungary was making the same discovery using sweet red peppers. This vitamin is now named ascorbic acid and can be synthesized in the laboratory.

Pellagra

Pellagra is a disease somewhat more recently recognized than scurvy because it occurs mainly where people use corn (maize) as a staple of the diet, and corn was introduced into Europe after the discovery of the Western Hemisphere. Pellagra was described first by Gaspar Casál of Spain in 1735; he attributed it to faulty diet after observing its occurrence among poor peasants who lived chiefly on maize. The disease was common in Italy in the eighteenth century and continued to occur in that country until wheat and other foods were introduced into the high-maize diet. The Italians named the disease pellagra, meaning "rough skin," because this is one of the characteristics of the disease. In the nineteenth century, pellagra was common in Romania, Hungary, Turkey, Greece, and Egypt; it still exists where large amounts of corn-meal are eaten.

In the U.S., pellagra was described first in 1907 by a physician at a mental institution in Alabama. It increased in the southern states among low-income families, both white and Negro, until in 1917 there were 170,000 cases recorded and many deaths. The U.S. Bureau of Public Health appointed Joseph Goldberger to investigate the cause of this malady. Many physicians thought it was an infectious disease, but Goldberger found that doctors and attendants in asylums where the disease frequently occurred were free from pellagra. Moreover, he was unable to transfer the disease from pellagrins to himself. He did not find pellagra wherever the diet included meat, milk, and eggs. All the evidence pointed to a poor diet, high in cornmeal, as the cause. By feeding experiments on animals and humans, Goldberger showed this to be true. It was first thought that something in good-quality protein foods such as meat, milk, and eggs prevented pellagra and that a pellagra-preventive vitamin would be found in these foods. Although this was not quite the answer, these proteins were found to contain an amino acid, tryptophan, which could be changed into the pellagra-preventive vitamin within the human body. The vitamin was discovered through studies with dogs which suffered from a disease called black tongue which is similar to pellagra in man. In 1937, Elvehjem of the University of Wisconsin found that nicotinic acid would cure black tongue in dogs. Clinicians then used this nicotinic acid on pellagra patients, and they were cured of the disease.

Rickets

Rickets is rarely seen today but was once a common disease of children in England and Europe. Bowed legs were the most visible signs of rickets, but many other parts of the bone structure also were affected. Rickets was most frequently observed during the middle of the eighteenth century when the industrial revolution began in England, and the rapidly increasing number of textile mills employed many women and children. Cities became crowded, slums developed, many families never saw sunlight, and rickets began to occur in children.

What was the cause of rickets? By some happy chance, cod liver oil was found to be beneficial. The Manchester Infirmary began using cod liver oil, 50 to 60 gallons annually, for treatment of rickets, joint diseases, and rheumatism. The oil took from four weeks to six months to have any effect. Many theories were given for the action of cod liver oil; some thought it was the iodine in the oil, others that it was the fatty acids. Not until 1922 was the answer found—a vitamin.

Where there is plenty of sunlight, there is no rickets. At the end of World War I, children in Vienna and Berlin were found to have severe rickets; they were treated by exposing them to lamps that produced ultraviolet rays, the same as those from sunlight. This process is called irradiation. Experiments with animals that were fed diets which produced rickets showed that it was just as effective to irradiate the food before giving it to the animals as to irradiate the animals. The puzzle was a complicated one. Rickets occurred where there was poor hygiene, crowded living conditions, and poor diet. Cod liver oil cured rickets and so did sunlight or the ultraviolet light from lamps.

In the 1920's, with knowledge of other vitamins as a guide, vitamin

D was found in cod liver oil. Certain foods, and also the human skin, contain substances called sterols. When these sterols are exposed to sunlight or ultraviolet rays, one of the sterols is changed to active vitamin D. Thus, two centuries of experience with the disease of rickets finally yielded the answer: vitamin D is necessary so that the body can use the minerals calcium and phosphorus to form normal bone. Today it is approved practice in the U.S. to give all infants some form of vitamin D such as irradiated sterol or the pure vitamin in solution. Infants and children are given milk to which vitamin D has been added. Thus, another of the dietary-deficiency diseases has been eliminated for all who use the knowledge of nutrition.

Discovery of Vitamins

It was in 1906 that Frederick Gowland Hopkins, biochemist of Cambridge University, England, and Nobel Prize winner, reported that there was an unknown something in food essential for life and health. By 1912, he was able to support this statement with experimental data. He fed milk to young albino rats and they grew well. But when he fed them the purified constituents from milk, the animals not only failed to grow but soon died.

Another investigator, Casimir Funk, a Polish chemist working at the Lister Institute in London in 1911, was trying to find the substance present in the outer coating of rice which was known to be a cure for beriberi. His reading, thinking, and experimenting led him to believe that beriberi, scurvy, and rickets were all caused by something that was lacking in certain diets. These substances, present in certain foods, he named *vitamines* in the 1912 publication; this name was later changed to *vitamins*. Funk was not the first to propose that there was something in food essential for health, but he was the first to express clearly this idea so that it received attention in the scientific world. The name and idea of vitamins soon captured public interest.

The time was ripe for such an idea. But why had there been such a long delay in acceptance of the possibility of dietary deficiencies such as vitamins? It is not easy to explain why an idea presented at one time gains immediate acceptance and at another time is rejected or unnoticed for years or even centuries. In the second half of the nineteenth century, Louis Pasteur, the great French scientist, clearly demonstrated to all the world that diseases were caused by microorganisms. At the same time, Robert Koch of Germany identified many bacteria and showed how to fix and stain them for study under the microscope. Pasteur and Koch founded the science of bacteriology. In a world that had just awakened to the concept of disease caused by invading organisms or bacteria, it was not easy to accept an idea which was the complete reversal of this, namely that disease could be caused because something was *not* present.

Acceptance of the vitamin theory could not be delayed very long after 1912. Since 1907, Dr. Elmer V. McCollum and co-workers at the University of Wisconsin (and later at Baltimore) had been trying to find exactly what were the constituents of an adequate diet for cattle. The first interest of these investigators was to help farmers; only when the first vitamins were discovered did McCollum realize their significance for human health and become one of the great leaders of the day in human nutrition. McCollum and Marguerite Davis used synthetic diets, ones made up of purified materials. When lard was used as the source of fat in the diet, the experimental animals ceased to grow. But if fat from butter or fat extracted from egg yolk was used, growth was normal. Many experiments of this type led to a scientific report in 1913 telling that a special factor was present in some types of fat and not in others. Two years later, continued research provided evidence that there were two different factors essential for normal growth, one associated with fat and the other with milk sugar. McCollum called these factors "fat-soluble A" and "water-soluble B." McCollum also introduced the term "protective foods." This term clearly expressed the newly developing ideas of nutrition that foods differed in their value in the diet. In 1918, he wrote: "Milk and the leaves of plants are to be regarded as protective foods and should never be omitted from the diet."

At the same time that McCollum and Davis were making their first vitamin studies, similar investigations were being carried on independently by Osborne and Mendel at New Haven, Connecticut, and were in agreement with McCollum's findings. Thus, the first two vitamins, A and B, were proven to exist. Then many investigators in various countries took up the search for further information about these vitamins and for other vitamins. Soon vitamin C, the cure for scurvy, and then vitamin D, associated with the prevention of rickets, were described. Vitamin E, necessary for reproduction in animals, was added to the list in 1922.

By 1926, what had been called vitamin B was shown to consist of at least two separate factors. Although investigators did not know the chemical identity of these vitamins, they knew that they existed because of the effect on animals when foodstuffs containing these vitamins were withheld from the diet. Experiments were conducted using rats, mice, guinea pigs, monkeys, hamsters, chickens, pigeons, and farm animals. Studies with dogs led to the discovery of the vitamin that prevents pellagra. The physiological effect of the different vitamins, the comparative vitamins in different foods, and the effect of heat, cooking, drying, and other treatments on the vitamin content of foods were measured by feeding experiments. Search for other vitamins also continued. Microorganisms such as yeasts, molds, and bacteria were used because they too needed vitamins for their growth. Because the microorganisms grew much more quickly than animals, results could be obtained in a few days or hours instead of the weeks for animal studies.

The most recent vitamin to be discovered was vitamin B_{12}, or cyanocobalamin, which was identified in 1948 and found to be essential in the prevention of pernicious anemia.

While biological assays were going on in the animal laboratories, chemists were at work seeking to extract the vitamins from food, purify them, obtain the pure crystalline material, and determine the chemical formula for each. In 1926, a Dutch worker obtained crystals of vitamin B_1, which prevents beriberi. But it was not until 1936 that Robert R. Williams, who had spent a lifetime in the search for this vitamin, was able to produce it in quantity and determine its formula. The chemical structures of all the known vitamins now have been determined; they can be manufactured in the laboratory for use in research and medical treatment. However, the best way for every individual to obtain vitamins is from food. Meals that include meats, milk, fruits, vegetables, cereals, and butter or margarine can supply all the needed vitamins for the normal individual. Foods wisely chosen have the advantage of supplying not only vitamins, but also the other essentials for health, namely energy or fuel value (measured in calories), protein, and minerals.

NUTRITION IN MAN

Chemical analysis and feeding experiments have shown what nutrients are needed and in what quantities. But how to find out what goes on inside the human body was for a long time a puzzling question. How could one see inside man? Then, in 1934, a new tool become available that made this possible, at least indirectly. Harold Urey, a chemist at Columbia University, discovered "heavy hydrogen," and for this he was awarded the Nobel Prize. Heavy hydrogen, now called deuterium, has all the properties and reactions of ordinary hydrogen except that it has a different weight or mass. This means that an atom of heavy hydrogen can always be identified wherever it is in food or the body tissues.

A young biochemist, Rudolph Schoenheimer, took some of the heavy hydrogen and placed it by chemical procedures in certain fatty acids and fed these to mice. After a period of this feeding, the animals were killed and analyzed, and the amount and location of the heavy hydrogen were determined. In this way, it was found that the heavy hydrogen had become part of the fat tissues of the body, even in those organs and areas that were believed to be fat-storage depots. This work introduced a new concept into nutrition—that there is a constant state of change within the cells of the body. There is a dynamic state in the body with constituents from food rapidly exchanging places with similar constituents already in the cells. This same type of experiment also was done with heavy nitrogen and the proteins. Many chemical changes were followed in the body by this method. It was as if a label were tied to nutrients in the food and they could be followed in their chemical processes throughout the body. Radioisotopes now serve the same purpose. These can be located in the body, its tissues, fluids, or bony structure because of their radioactivity. Thus, the biochemist has a new tool with which he can follow what is happening to food nutrients in the body; in other words, he can "see" inside man.

Learning from Man's Eating Experience—Dietary Studies

In the last decades of the nineteenth century, careful studies were made of what different people ate. The reasoning was this: People who were able to work hard and appeared to be in good health must be eating the kind of food they needed. Therefore, food of such people was weighed and measured; the calories, total protein, fat, starches, and sugars also were calculated. Nothing was known then about vitamins or differences in protein; the calories were thought to be the all-important item. It is of interest that the calorie intakes calculated in these diet studies were almost the same as the caloric needs determined in the calorimeter studies done in Germany. Dietary studies were made for many groups in this country around 1900 by W. O. Atwater, "father of nutrition," in the U.S. Atwater designed a bomb calorimeter, so called because of its shape. It was a tightly sealed container in which small weighed amounts of pure foodstuffs could be placed, ignited by an electric spark, and burned in oxygen. All the heat produced in this way by the oxidation of the food could be measured. Thus were obtained the familiar calorie values of food: four calories for each gram (about one-thirtieth of an ounce) of protein and of carbohydrate and nine calories per gram of fat. These calorie values of foods were used, and are still used today, to calculate the calorie value of a day's diet.

Dietary studies are currently used as a way of finding out if individuals are obtaining all the nutrients they need in desired amounts. The amounts of protein, fat, minerals, and each vitamin, as well as calories, are calculated. Dietary studies are a useful and practical tool in nutrition investigation.

Quantitative Requirements for Nutrients

What are the constituents of food that are essential in the diet? This was one of the first questions that challenged investigators, but science is quantitative. How much of each nutrient is needed was the next question. This is more difficult to answer, and research still is going on to determine amounts needed of some of the vitamins and mineral elements. The basic technique is the same as that already described for animal feeding. Purified diets are used, and for the nutrient studied, the amounts are varied to find how much is needed for growth and health of experimental animals. Then similar experiments are made on man. Here there are many difficulties encountered. Amounts of nutrients needed differ with age and rate of growth, with activity, body size, and a number of other influencing factors including biochemical individuality.

Summary of Achievements in Nutrition

Man has progressed from food for survival to knowledge of nutrition for health. The four nutrition concepts given at the beginning of this chapter summarize in elementary terms where we stand today with regard to what is known of the science of nutrition.

Man's knowledge of nutrition as a science was negligible until the nineteenth century and has developed fully only in this century. Its growth has been dependent largely on chemistry, physiology, and

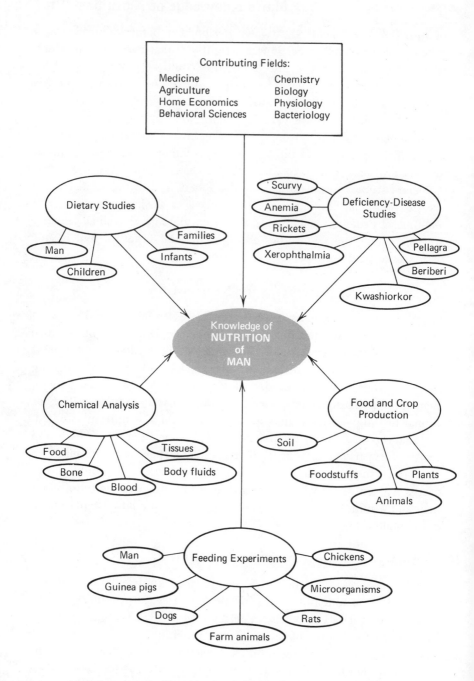

Methods and areas of investigation that led to the development of the science of nutrition.

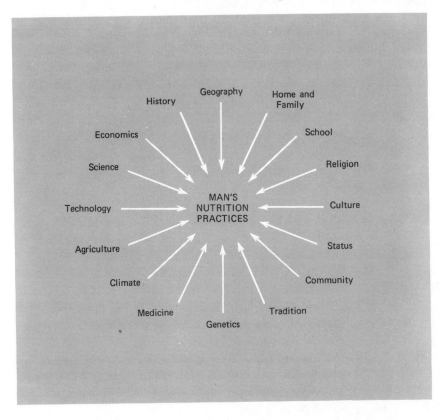

medicine; nutrition had to wait for these sciences and the concept of the experimental method to develop. Also there had to be available the kind of laboratory apparatus and equipment necessary for quantitative measurements. Men, ideas, and tools at the right time and place have been the essential ingredients for progress and scientific discoveries. The figure on the opposite page is a graphic summary of some of the many and varied studies that have led man to his present knowledge of the science of nutrition.

It is now known that nutrition is essential for growth, health, and well being of all people. However, it must be added that nutrition alone cannot guarantee good health because many other factors are involved (hygiene, freedom from infection, accident, and other health hazards).

Progress in nutrition science is a continuing process, but there is an immediate challenge now. This challenge is how to make available to all people everywhere enough food of the right kind, and how to educate all people to select and enjoy foods for nutritive value.

The story of the history of nutrition shows how we have acquired our present sum of knowledge. Nutrition affects man's health, ability to work, behavior, and learning ability. But knowledge is not enough; man's use of knowledge is not always guided by his reasoning ability. Many other factors influence how and to what extent man uses his nutrition knowledge and what he practices in food selection for himself and his family. Some of these influencing factors are shown in the preceding diagram and will be discussed in succeeding chapters.

STUDY QUESTIONS

1. In the nineteenth century, chemical analysis could not measure all the nutrients present in food. Why was this and how was the problem solved?

2. This chapter has stressed some problems encountered in the development of nutrition science. List these and others you find in your reading. Explain why these were major problems at that time.

3. Men of the past were seeking for the unknowns about food values and nutrients in relation to health. What can you envision as unknowns in this field that should be explored today?

4. Read the journals of some early explorer of land or sea or the diaries of early American colonists. How would you evaluate their food and its nutritional value?

5. What were the chief nutritional problems at different periods in American history such as the early colonial days, the overland trail period, the industrial expansion era, and the growth period of large cities?

6. Prepare a chronological chart showing major discoveries in nutrition and other events happening at that time. What are the relationships between nutrition progress and other historical events?

TOPICS FOR INDIVIDUAL INVESTIGATION

1. Describe your concept of man and how much he can or should be influenced by nutrition. Develop in depth your concept of a well-nourished individual.

2. In what ways does the history of nutrition help you understand other events in history? Choose one of these events and develop the relationship.

3. Choose one of the nutrients and critically trace its history of discovery; or choose one of the discoverers in nutrition science and describe and evaluate his work in relation to his life and personality.

4. Polar explorations have failed many times because of nutritional difficulties. Select a polar expedition, describe its preparations and route, and then evaluate the nutritional problems, why they occurred, and whether or not they were inevitable at that time.

5. In what ways has the stage of nutrition knowledge influenced the outcome of wars or exploration? Choose one of these events and trace the relationship between the event and nutrition.

REFERENCES AND SUGGESTED READINGS

General

Aykroyd, W. R. *Conquest of Deficiency Diseases.* F.F.H.C. Basic Study No. 24, WHO, Geneva, 1970.

Biggar, H. P. *The Voyages of Jacques Cartier.* Published from the original translations, notes, and appendices, by authority of the Sec. of State under the direction of the Archivist, Ottawa, Canada, 1924.

Drummond, J. C. and A. Wilbraham. *The Englishman's Food. A History of Five Centuries of English Diet.* Jonathan Cape, London, 1939.

Essays on the History of Nutrition and Dietetics. Amer. Dietet. Assoc. Chicago, 1967.

Galdston, I., Ed. *Human Nutrition Historic and Scientific.* N.Y. Academy of Medicine Monograph III. International Universities Press, New York, 1960.

Hill, Mary M. ICNE Formulates Some Basic Concepts in Nutrition. *Nutrition Program News.* U.S. Dept. of Agr. pp. 1–2, Sept.–Oct. 1964.

Lusk, G. *Nutrition.* Paul Hoeber, New York, 1933.

McCollum, E. V. *The Newer Knowledge of Nutrition.* Macmillan, New York, 1918.

McCollum, E. V. *A History of Nutrition.* Houghton-Mifflin, Boston, 1957.

McCollum, E. V. *From Kansas Farm Boy to Scientist, An Autobiography*. Univ. of Kansas Press, Lawrence, 1964.

Orr, J. B. *Feast and Famine, The Wonderful World of Food*. Rathbone Books, London, 1957.

Todhunter, E. N. The Story of Nutrition. *Yearbook of Agriculture*. U.S. Dept. of Agr., p. 7, 1959.

Todhunter, E. N. Some Aspects of the History of Dietetics. *World Review of Nutr. and Dietet*. 5: 32, 1965.

Scurvy

Hess, A. F. *Scurvy Past and Present*. J. B. Lippincott, Philadelphia, 1920.

Lind, J. *Treatise of the Scurvy*. Edinburgh Univ. Press, London, 1753. Reprinted as a Bicentennary Volume, C. P. Stewart and D. Guthrie, Eds. Edinburgh Univ. Press, 1953.

Beriberi

Harris, L. J. *Vitamins and Vitamin Deficiency, Beriberi*. P. Blakiston, Philadelphia, 1938.

Vedder, E. B. *Beriberi*. Wm. Wood, New York, 1913.

Williams, R. R. *Toward the Conquest of Beriberi*. Harvard Univ. Press, Mass., 1961.

Pellagra

Parsons, R. P. *Trail to Light—A Biography of Joseph Goldberger*. Bobbs-Merrill, New York, 1943.

Sebrell, W. H. Biography of Joseph Goldberger. *J. Nutr*. 55: 3, 1955.

5

Food, Man, and Religion

The various religions of the world have a profound influence on man's dietary practices and customs. Over the centuries of man's recorded and unrecorded history, many religions have decreed what foods man could or could not eat, what foods he could or could not eat on certain days of the year, and frequently how certain foods must be prepared for consumption. Many of these dietary habits have become symbolic of the religion itself.

What are some of these religious influences on diet? What are the religious bases for these dietary practices? How did they develop? What is the significance today of these influences? These are a few of the many questions that seem important to examine when developing a deeper understanding of the relationship between food and man.

It has been said that religious beliefs and practices are perhaps the least understood aspects of the cultures of other peoples. On casual examination, the various religions of the world appear widely different. Each has its own beliefs concerning the supernatural, its own sacred objects, its own symbolism, its own priests, ministers, or holy men, its own seemingly mystical rituals and prescribed activities, and its own moral values. However, if a more detailed study of the world's religions is undertaken, many of these apparent differences dissolve and a large number of similarities appear.

What is meant by the term religion? It undoubtedly has different meanings to many people. No attempt is made in this section to discuss all the intricacies of this subject. According to Webster's dictionary, religion is the service and adoration of a god through worship in obedience to divine commands found in the sacred writings and through the following of a way of life regarded as incumbent on true believers. It further states that religion is a conviction of the existence of a supreme being or some supernatural influence which controls the destiny of all.

Brown, in *Understanding Other Cultures,* states that every religion provides ways by which man can try to relate to a supreme being or some supernatural force. Many of the practices and beliefs of the various religions of man are attempts to explain those things which man himself cannot understand or control. Each religion has evolved certain rituals or customs which are important to the members of that religion. The observance of these rituals and customs is believed to be mandatory since they express and reaffirm the various beliefs of the religion.

Food, which was early man's most precious and often scarce possession, has become associated with many of these religious rituals or customs. The practice of giving food or abstaining from food has provided man in his everyday life with a symbolic way to indicate his devotion, respect, and love to his supreme being or supernatural power. Furthermore, the act of giving or abstaining from food has been used to insure the good will and protection of the all powerful on behalf of the individual. The religious practices of most religions are deeply imbued with many symbolic meanings; without an understanding of this symbolism, the practices of the religion by themselves may seem strange and peculiar. Brown gives an example of this. To a Christian, the symbolic meaning of the bread and wine in the Communion Service is clear. But to someone totally unfamiliar with this symbolism the words, "This is my body broken for you . . . This is my blood . . .," which are recited before the bread and wine are consumed, might indeed seem very peculiar.

FIVE MAJOR RELIGIONS

In this chapter, five major religions of the world and the relationship between these religions, food, and man will be discussed. These religions are Christianity, Judaism, Islam, Hinduism, and Buddhism. The areas of the world where these religions predominate are shown on the map. Relationships between food and other religions such as Shintoism, Confucianism, and various tribal religions undoubtedly exist and would be interesting topics to pursue. However, based on available figures (1969), these five major religions together were estimated to encompass about 60% of the world's population (see graph on page 197); and for this reason, they were selected as the basis for this discussion.

Christianity

Christianity is the most widely spread of all the major religions in the world today. Its adherents numbered in 1969 some 924 million— approximately one out of every four people in the world. Of these 924 million Christians, 63% were Roman Catholic, 23% were Protestant, and 14% were Eastern Orthodox.

It is not possible in this book to discuss in detail the influence of all the Christian religions on the food habits of their adherents. Almost everyone is familiar with the ruling of the Roman Catholic Church, which until recently required Catholics to observe certain fast days and to abstain from eating meat on Fridays in remembrance of the sacrificial death of Christ. However, in 1966, the U.S. Catholic Conference abolished this church law; now Catholics are required to abstain from eating meat only on the Fridays of Lent.

Among some Protestant denominations, such as the Seventh-day Adventists and the Church of Jesus Christ of the Latter-day Saints, certain dietary practices exist which are an integral part of their religious beliefs. The Seventh-day Adventists comprise the largest single body in the Adventist movement—that is, those who believe in the imminent second coming of Christ. The world membership in the late 1960s was approximately 1.6 million, with over 420,000 reported to be residing in the U.S. as of 1970. The church is active in world-wide evangelistic preaching, maintains 43 publishing houses, and conducts over 5000 schools ranging from elementary schools to colleges and universities. It has the third largest parochial school system in the U.S.

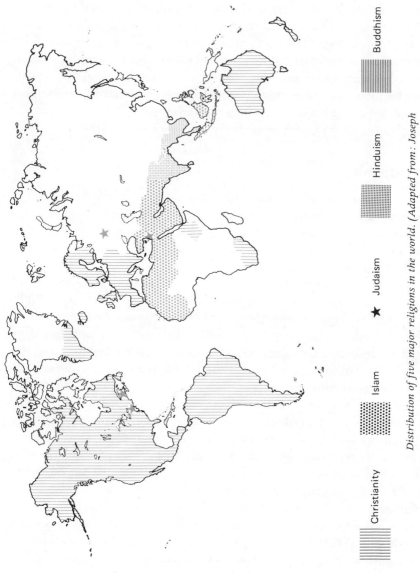

Distribution of five major religions in the world. (Adapted from: Joseph Gaer, How the Great Religions Began, Dodd-Mead, 1956.)

Christianity   Islam   ★ Judaism   Hinduism   Buddhism

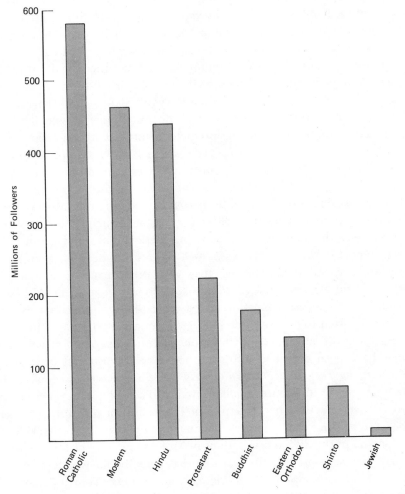

Number of followers of world religions, 1969.

In addition, the church operates 128 sanitariums and hospitals, a medical and dental school, and 34 nurses' training schools in many countries. It also sponsors a welfare organization actively involved in disaster relief thru the distribution of food and clothing. The funds needed for these extensive operations are obtain by a 10% tithe of the membership plus additional voluntary contributions. The institutions sponsored by this church are indeed numerous considering the total membership of the denomination.

Seventh-Day Adventists Church.   During the early part of the nineteenth century, a world-wide interdenominational resurgence occurred in the belief that the second coming of Christ as foretold in the Bible was near at hand. In the U.S., this movement was led by the Millerites, followers of William Miller, who predicted originally that Christ would return to earth on October 23, 1843. When Miller's prediction failed, many of his followers abandoned this belief; but others held fast to the idea. From one segment of these believers, the Seventh-day Adventists Church developed and was officially organized in 1863. The present Seventh-day Adventists believe that the exact time at which Christ will return to earth cannot be predicted, but that it is not far away.

One of Miller's converts to Adventism in 1840 was a young woman named Ellen G. Harmon. This woman, who was later to become the wife of James White, an Adventist preacher, was to have a profound and lasting influence on the Seventh-day Adventists Church. Mrs. White's eminent position in her church as one of the principal founders and guides was the result of over 2000 prophetic visions and dreams she was reported to have had over a 70-year span beginning in 1844. Seventh-day Adventists believe that Mrs. White had a prophetic gift and that through her God gave his inspired message to them. Although Mrs. White's formal education ended when she was only 9 years old, she is reported to have written over 100,000 manuscript pages by hand describing the substance of her visions and dreams. Many of her writings have been compiled into such books as *The Ministry of Healing, Counsels on Diet, and Foods, Counsels on Health.* Over 50 books containing her writings are available today. Basically, the Seventh-day Adventists practice the principles of Protestantism but differ in their belief regarding the imminent coming of Christ and his 10,000 year reign and in the divine inspirations of Mrs. White. One of Mrs. White's early visions contained the warning that man should worship God on the seventh day or Sabbath as originally stated in the Fourth Commandment and not on Sunday; so as their name implies, they observe Saturday, the seventh day of the week, as the Sabbath—a day of rest and prayer. Like many Orthodox Jews, they may prepare the Sabbath meal on Fridays and wash the Sabbath dishes on Sundays. The practice of footwashing is observed prior to the celebration of Holy Communion, which occurs four times a year. The Bible is the ultimate and absolute authority on matters of faith and practice and the true word of God. To the Seventh-day Adventists, the Ten Commandments are to be taken literally and provide the basis of man's duty on earth. Mrs. White's writings are considered to provide a clear explanation and commentary on God's word for modern man.

An all important concept of the Seventh-day Adventists' beliefs is that of healthful living. The biblical reference for this is taken from Corinthians 3:16–17:

> Know ye not that ye are the temple of God and that the Spirit of God dwelleth in you?
> If any man defile the temple of God, him shall God destroy; for the temple of God is holy, which temple ye are.

In 1863, Mrs. White wrote of a vision she was given:

> I saw that it was a sacred duty to attend to our health, and arouse others to their duty. . . . We have a duty to come out against intemperance of every kind—intemperance in working, in eating, in drinking, in drugging—and then point them to God's great medicine; water, pure soft water for diseases, for health, for cleanliness, for luxury. . . . I saw that we should not be silent upon the subject of health, but should wake up minds to the subject.

Shortly after this vision, the Western Health Reform Institute was established, the first of many such world-wide institutions sponsored by the church. This first institute was later to become the world famous Battle Creek Sanitarium in Battle Creek, Michigan.

To the Seventh-day Adventist, good health is a treasure, and violation of the laws of health surely leads to sickness. One's lifestyle should be directed toward maintaining and preserving health through eating the right kinds of foods in moderation and in getting a sufficient amount of exercise and rest. Accordingly, the Seventh-day Adventists believe that the original vegetarian diet prescribed by God is the best diet for health. They believe that the simpler one eats, the better his body will function and that, in the consumption of grains, fruits, vegetables, and nuts, one can find all the required food nutrients. With very careful planning of menus to include a variety of these foods, this belief is probably true, with the exception of vitamin B_{12}. Most Seventh-day Adventists are lacto-ovo-vegetarians, but some consume no milk or eggs; others, at the opposite end of the spectrum, consume meats. The book *Counsels on Diet and Foods,* published in 1938, contains a compilation of Mrs. White's writing about this subject. Seventh-day Adventists rely on legumes such as lentils, soybeans, garbanzos, and peas in addition to nuts, whole grain cereals, cottage cheese, eggs, and milk to provide enough good-quality protein in their diet. In the *Ministry of Health,* Mrs. White advocated the use of nuts in place of flesh foods, the substitution of olive oil for animal fats, and the consumption of bread made from whole-wheat flour and not refined flour.

The Seventh-day Adventists reject flesh foods for many reasons. The rejection is partly related to the statements in the Bible which forbid man to eat certain unclean foods such as the swine and also to the writings of Mrs. White, who pointed out that the consumption of meat could cause various diseases and could make man more animalistic and less sympathetic to the needs of others.

Tea, coffee, alcoholic beverages, and tobacco are all considered harmful to the health of the individual due to their stimulating action on the body. Water is considered the best liquid, especially if soft, and should be consumed at room temperature or slightly cooled either before or after a meal, but never with a meal.

The meals served in a Seventh-day Adventists' home are not highly spiced. Condiments such as mustard, pepper, and others which might be harmful to the stomach are avoided. Breakfast is usually a substantial meal, and the noon meal is the largest of the day. Supper is light in order to avoid overtaxing the digestive tract. A typical lacto-ovo-vegetarians' breakfast might consist of fruit juice, brown rice with honey and milk, stewed prunes, whole-wheat toast with margarine, and a cereal-base coffee substitute. The main meal at noon might contain Dinner Cuts, a baked potato, lentils, carrots, whole-wheat bread with margarine, milk, and a fruit such as watermelon. (Dinner Cuts are a commercially pre-pared vegetable protein product containing essentially wheat protein, produced by the Loma Linda Foods of Riverside, California. This Company, as well as the Worthington Foods of Worthington, Ohio, produces a wide variety of processed foods from wheat and soybeans which may serve as meat analogs in the diet.) Supper or the evening meal may consist of a soup and salad with cottage cheese or peanut butter on whole wheat crackers. Eating between meals is discouraged in order to allow the digestive tract proper time to digest and assimilate the food eaten at meal times. Mrs. White recommends that 5–6 hours should lapse between meals.

Eastern Orthodox Church.   To the average westerner, the Eastern Orthodox Church is probably the least familiar branch of Christianity and thus merits a closer look. Historically, Orthodox Christian Churches were established in the Holy Lands before Christianity spread to Rome.

But by 300 A.D., the two principal centers of Christianity were Rome and Constantinople, and they had already begun to compete with each other for absolute power and authority over all Christians. In 1054 A.D., this power struggle culminated in a division of the followers of Christianity into the Church of Rome and the Eastern Orthodox Church. Some main points of disagreement between the two groups were the origin of the Holy Spirit, the use of unleavened bread in the Communion Service, and clerical celibacy. The Eastern Orthodox Church believed that the Holy Spirit originated completely from God the father, that leavened bread should be used in the Communion Service, and that priests should be allowed to marry prior to ordination. The followers of the early Eastern Orthodox Church were the Christians of the Middle East, the Balkans, the northeastern Mediterranean area, and Russia. Eastern Orthodoxy is the state religion in many of these same countries today. All of the state churches are independent of each other and have their own separate patriarch or archbishop. But they acknowledge as their spiritual leader the Patriarch of Constantinople. The world membership in 1969 was 120 million; 3.6 million adherents resided in the U.S.

In the Greek Orthodox religion, numerous fast days provide ample opportunity for man to prove that he does not live by bread alone but that the soul can rule the body. With only two exceptions, every Wednesday and Friday of the year are considered fast days to commemorate the betrayal of Christ and His death upon the cross. In addition, there is a 40-day fast called the Great Lent which precedes Easter and there is another 40-day fast called Advent which begins on November 15. Two shorter fast periods in June and August also are observed.

On these fast days, no meat or animal products including milk, butter, and cheese can be eaten; fish, with the exception of shell fish such as clams, shrimp, and oysters, also cannot be eaten. Abstinence from olive oil although not olives, is observed by the more devout older Greeks. Because the olive and its oil are important staples in the diets of Greeks, the denial of olive oil represents a true sacrifice and an outward symbol of one's devotion to God. Another possible reason for abstinence from the oil is that many years ago olive oil commonly was stored in casks lined with the stomach of the calf; thus, the olive oil was contaminated in a religious sense by having been in contact with an animal product. Moreover, in earlier times olive oil was thought to increase sexual desire. Since every fast day is supposed to be a day of sexual abstinence, this may be another explanation of the avoidance of olive oil. A popular common meal in Greece on fast days is dried bean and lentil soup.

Easter, the most important event in the calendar of the Orthodox Church, occurs on the first Sunday after the full moon, which occurs on or immediately after March 21, but it may not precede the Jewish Passover. Thus, in some years Easter is postponed to the first Sunday after the Jewish Passover. The 40-day Great Lent period is preceded by a three week prelenten period of preparation and repentance. The third Sunday of this prelenten period is called Meat Fare Sunday (Apokreos). All meat in the house is consumed or disposed of on this Sunday and during the week following. On the following Sunday, Cheese Fare Sunday, all cheese, eggs, and butter in the house are consumed. On the next day, "Clean Monday," the family is ready to begin the true Great Lent and abstain from all animal foods until Easter Sunday. Fish is allowed on two days during this fast—on Palm Sunday and the Annunciation Day of the Virgin Mary. The Great Lent fast is in memory of the Lord's 40-day fast in the desert and of Holy Week. Lentil soup is always eaten on Good Friday to symbolize the tears of the Virgin Mary. The lentil soup often is served with vinegar to recall that Christ on the cross was given vinegar instead of the water He requested.

The Orthodox Easter fast traditionally is broken after the midnight Resurrection Service on Easter Sunday with mageritsa, a soup made with the internal organs of the lamb such as the tripe, liver, pancreas, lungs, and heart. Lamb is the traditional food on Easter. Another traditional Greek custom is the baking of thick, round, leavened loaves of Easter bread decorated with colored, hard-boiled eggs. The eggs are always dyed bright red, symbolic of the blood of Christ which redeemed the world. The eggs are dyed only on Holy Thursday and Saturday and are considered tokens of good luck in the home. The eggs are placed on the top of the bread dough, and then the bread is baked. The red color is used as a sign of mourning, and the egg symbolized the tomb of Christ. The breaking open of these eggs on Easter morning symbolizes the opening of the tomb of Christ and is an outward sign of belief in the resurrection of Christ. One person says, "Christos Anesti" (Christ is risen), the other person replies "Alithos Anesti" (Indeed, He is risen), and each cracks his egg against the other's egg.

All members of the Greek Orthodox Church are encouraged to receive Holy Communion every Sunday at the celebration of the Divine Liturgy. The altar bread used for this service is called Prosphoron, meaning the bread of offering. These round loaves of leavened bread are usually prepared by the women in their own homes from the purest ingredients. The bread must be free of all shortening, milk, sugar, and eggs. The preparation of Prosphoron serves to involve the laywoman of the church actively in an all-important religious rite because it is believed that the Holy Spirit descends during a particular prayer in the service and changes the bread into the body of Christ and the wine into His blood. As the dough of the Prosphoron rises for the second time, a Prosphoron seal is placed on top of the dough and left there until the bread is ready to bake. The Prosphoron seal marks the bread as indicated in the drawing. The center portion of the loaf represents a lamb and is the part of the loaf which becomes the body of Christ. The abbreviations IC and XC indicate Jesus Christ and the letters NIKA mean conquers. The priest at the Communion Service removes this section of the Prosphoron and places it on a paten along with the ten smaller triangular pieces. The larger triangular piece on the left of the center portion is in memory of the Virgin Mary; the nine pieces on the right are in commemoration of the Angelic Hosts and Saints of the Orthodox Church. The Prosphoron offering is brought to the altar before the service with two lists of names. One list is composed of the names of living friends or family members and the other list of dead ones. During the service, the people named in the lists are remembered; good health is wished for the living and pleasant repose for the dead.

Boiled whole grain wheat (Koliva) plays an important role in memorial services for the dead. It is customary in the Greek Orthodox Church to offer Koliva before the altar three, nine, and forty days, as well as six and twelve months, after the death of a family member. It also may be offered whenever desired thereafter. The Koliva symbolizes the resurrection of Christ. The offering of Koliva on the third, ninth, and fortieth day after death is related to the recorded appearances of Christ on earth after his crucifixion. The boiled wheat, symbolizing everlasting life, is mixed with parsley, chopped walnuts, zwieback biscuits, spices, sugar, raisins, blanched almonds, sesame seeds, and pomegranate seeds. The raisins and the pomegranate seeds are used as symbols of sweetness and plenty. A leveled mound of the mixture is placed on a silver tray and sprinkled heavily with powdered sugar. The sugar covering symbolizes the wish of the living that the departed will have a sweet and blissful life in heaven. In the center of the Koliva a cross is made with brown sugar or Jordan almonds. Beneath the cross, either the name or the initials

Children of Greek Orthodox Church with baskets of red eggs in preparation for Easter Sunday. (Courtesy Jack Kirland, Knoxville News-Sentinel, Knoxville, Tenn.)

The Prosphoron seal marks the altar bread.

Passover seder plate made in Vienna, Austria, in 1815. It has various containers for the traditional foods associated with Passover. (Courtesy Hebrew Union College Museum, Cincinnati, Ohio.)

A Jewish Passover seder meal when matzo instead of bread is eaten. (Courtesy the B. Manischewitz Co., Neward, N.J.)

of the deceased is placed by using either toasted almonds, brown sugar, or raisins. The Koliva is blessed by the priest at the morning service and is later distributed to friends of the deceased.

Judaism

The ancestors of the Hebrews, who can be traced back to about 2000 B.C., were seminomads roving the lands of Egypt, Syria, and Mesopotamia. The beginnings of Judaism, God's covenants with Abraham and later with Moses, are recorded in the first five books of the Old Testament. As God's chosen people, the Jews were commanded to denounce idolatry and polytheism, to worship only the one true God, and to ascertain and obey His will in all matters. The Torah, composed of the books of Genesis, Exodus, Leviticus, Numbers, and Deuteronomy, is the most sacred writing of Judaism and contains the basic laws which express the will of God to the Jew. The Torah, meaning guidance and direction, is considered by the Orthodox Jew to be the ultimate authority regarding all human conduct. This guiding principle of Judaism is read aloud at every Sabbath service in the synagogue; the entire five books are read in a year.

Other sacred books, such as the Talmud, were written at later times. Over the centuries, the early rabbis attempted to interpret, amplify, and adapt the teachings in the Torah to make them more meaningful to man in his daily life. These interpretations of the Torah became known as the body of oral law and were passed down from generation to generation by word of mouth. Sometimes in the latter part of the sixth century A.D., the body of oral law finally was committed to paper and became known as the Talmud. The teachings from the Torah and the Talmud range all the way from the Ten Commandments and the Golden Rule to detailed instruction regarding the proper attire to wear on the Sabbath.

Throughout most of their history, the Jewish people suffered persecution, isolation, enslavement, and, on several occasions, near extermination. Yet each time they survived and were delivered from their oppressors. To the Jew each of these experiences represent a reenactment of the deliverance of the Jewish people from bondage in Egypt centuries ago and serves to strengthen his belief that the Jewish people truly are the chosen people of God.

As the chosen people, the Jews have certain responsibilities to God. Judaism teaches that man is capable of perfection and that he alone is responsible for his actions. Man has a choice between what is right and wrong. Sin is attributed to man's innate weakness; no man can completely escape it. Although Judaism recognizes the existence of a hereafter, its main concerns are with man in his present life and the ways to guide him in fulfilling his moral responsibilities to God.

For the Jew, the Torah makes a distinction between those animals which are considered clean and are thus permitted to be eaten and those considered unclean and thus forbidden. Leviticus, Chapter II, and Deuteronomy, Chapter 14, give the Biblical basis for many Jewish dietary practices. Animals classified as clean are those that chew their cud and whose hooves are divided (cloven). If an animal satisfies only one of these criteria, he cannot be considered clean. Thus the cow, sheep, ox, and goat are clean but not the pig since he does not chew the cud. Although the camel chews his cud, he is unclean because he does not have cloven hooves. Also forbidden are most winged insects, reptiles, creeping animals such as the mouse, and birds of prey. Only fish with both fins and scales are permitted to be used for food. Thus all shellfish and eels are eliminated from the diet of an Orthodox Jew. Any meat from animals which have died either from natural causes or disease is considered unfit.

Blood is a sacred substance and is taboo for human consumption. Several references in Leviticus, Chapter 17, which give the basis for this dietary practice, are, "I will set My face against that soul that eateth blood" and "For the life of the flesh is in the blood." To the ancient Jews, killing was synonymous with the shedding of blood; the blood was thus considered the vital life of the animal. The internal fat of an animal is also taboo. Thus, only those soaps and scouring powders which do not contain animal fats may be used for washing dishes. Detergents are permitted.

Another Jewish dietary practice which can be related to Biblical teaching is that which prohibits eating meat and dairy foods together in the same meal. The exact reason for this practice is not clear, but it may be the result of the three statements in Exodus and Deuteronomy which warn not "to seethe a kid in its mother's milk." Not only can meat and milk not be eaten at the same meal, but meat cannot be prepared or served in the same dishes used for preparing and serving foods containing milk and other dairy products. Thus, in Orthodox Jewish homes, two sets of dishes, silverware, and cooking utensils are needed, one for use with meats and the other for use with foods containing milk and other dairy products. Each set of dishes and utensils must be washed separately and carefully handled so that one set does not become mixed with the other. An Orthodox Jew will wait six hours after eating meat before eating milk or any dairy food, but only a one-hour interval is necessary if milk is consumed prior to meat. This dietary regulation prevents anyone who has meat in a meal from having such things as cream in his coffee, dessert containing milk, or even butter on his vegetables.

The attempts of the early rabbis to interpret and expand the Torah in more specific terms, as mentioned earlier, resulted in the Laws of Kashrut as written down in the Talmud. The term *kosher* refers not only to those foods which are permitted by the Bible but also to foods which have been processed and prepared in the prescribed manner. Trayf is the term used to indicate either a food that is unclean according to the Bible or one which has not been prepared according to the ritually correct method.

A rabbi must supervise the slaughtering of all animals in order for them to be considered kosher. In fact, only one other ritual in the Jewish religion actually requires the participation of a rabbi, and that is divorce. The actual slaughter of the animal is done by a trained person called a shocket. One swift deep slash at the throat of the animal makes him unconcious immediately and allows the blood to drain from his body as completely as possible. The meat from animals so slaughtered is carefully inspected and then stamped with the seal of the shocket to indicate its ritual purity.

Meat to be truly kosher must also be treated further to ensure the complete removal of blood. Meat is soaked in cold water for thirty minutes and then allowed to drain on a slanting board. The meat is then generously sprinkled with salt. After one hour it is washed in cold water; then it is ready to be cooked. In the past, this task was usually performed in the home but it is now possible to purchase meat which has been treated in this fashion.

Although no Biblical reference can be found to justify the practice, the Jew is forbidden in the Talmud to eat the sciatic nerve of an animal. According to Epstein, kosher butcher stores in the United States sell only forequarters of meat; the ligaments and nerves of the hindquarters are very difficult to remove and must be removed if the meat is to be considered kosher.

From the earliest times, rabbis have devoted considerable time to determining what was acceptable as kashrut and what not. The increasing number of processed foods appearing on the market in recent years has made this problem perhaps even more difficult for the Jewish housewife. The problem has been alleviated somewhat by the use of certain symbols on the labels of processed foods. The commonly used symbols are U or K which refer to the Union of Orthodox Jewish Congregations and the O. K. Laboratories, respectively. The presence of these symbols on a label indicates that the food is kosher and that it has been processed following the Laws of Kashrut. The introduction of such products as margarine and nondairy cream substitutes has made it possible for the Jew to circumvent the dietary restriction regarding the use of meat and dairy products in the same meal. A nonanimal "gelatin" was put on the market which enables the Orthodix Jew to have congealed salads and desserts.

The Jewish holy days and festivals are rich in symbolical meanings, and food plays a major role in much of this symbolism. Every Sabbath is truly a day of rest and spiritual reunion in an Orthodox Jewish home. In most homes, Friday is spent preparing for the Sabbath, which begins at sundown and continues until sundown on Saturday. The Sabbath dinner on Friday evenings is prepared with great care. All food that will be eaten on the Sabbath is prepared and cooked ahead in accordance with the belief that the Sabbath should be a day of rest. The traditional items on every Sabbath table are two loaves of bread called challah. The custom of serving challah on the Sabbath goes back many centuries to the ancient practice of placing twelve challah loaves on the altar of the Temple in Jerusalem; each loaf represented one of the original tribes of Israel. The use of two challah loaves today is in remembrance of the double portion of manna which God provided the Israelites on Friday for the Sabbath during the 40 years they spent wandering in the wilderness.

The ten most solemn holy days of the Jewish year begin with Rosh Hashanah, the Day of Judgment, and end with Yom Kippur, the Day of Atonement. On Rosh Hashanah, the challah is also made but it is decorated with ladders or birds baked on the top to carry symbolically the prayers of the family to heaven. Bread and slices of apple are dipped in honey as a symbolic wish for sweetness in the new year. Yom Kippur is a day of complete fasting for all except children under thirteen years of age.

The symbolic role of food in the Jewish faith is perhaps most evident in the traditional practices observed during the eight-day Festival of Pesach (Passover) which commemorates the flight of the Israelites from Egypt as described in Exodus. The story of the liberation of the Jews is relived by all members of the family, especially at the seder meal, which is eaten on the first evening of this festival. The preparations in an Orthodox Jewish home for Passover are many. According to ritual laws, none of the foods used every day in the kitchen can be used during Passover. Especially prepared foods marked Kasher L'Pesach (Kosher for Passover) must be used.

No leavened bread can be eaten during this time in obedience to God's command to Moses. For centuries, the Jews have made an unleavened wheat bread called matzo. It was made especially for Pesach and prepared ahead of time in large enough amounts to last throughout the entire eight-day festival. This preparation was usually a project of the whole community; detailed instructions for its preparation are given in the Talmud. Today matzo is commonly prepared commercially under rabbinical supervision. It is possible even to obtain a special kind of matzo which has been prepared under the most exacting, ritually correct conditions, the wheat having been constantly washed during harvesting, milling, and baking. This latter type of matzo is used by some of the more pious, older Orthodox Jews.

Flour and other grains cannot be used in cooking during Passover. In place of flour, the Jewish housewife uses finely ground matzo called matza meal. No leavening agents nor malt liquors may be used during Passover. In fact, it is a custom for an Orthodox Jew prior to Passover to write out a bill of sale and sell all the leavened products he owns to a non-Jew for the duration of the Passover. The sale is proposed with the understanding that the goods will be returned to the original owner after the holiday. The rabbi handles the transaction for the members of his congregation at their request. All leavened products in the house are either eaten or discarded prior to the beginning of Passover.

Many Jewish homes have separate sets of dishes that are used only during the Passover. If everyday utensils have to be used during Passover, there is prescribed ritual for purifying them.

The seder plate is usually used twice a year, on the first and second nights of Passover. The beautiful, silver, Viennese seder plate shown in the picture dates back to 1815. It has various containers for the traditional foods that, over the centuries, have become symbolic of the Jewish exodus from slavery in Egypt. In the boatlike containers would be placed a roasted egg and a roasted lamb bone. The roasted egg is generally considered to be a symbol of the burnt offerings made in the Temple at Jerusalem; the lamb bone symbolizes the Paschal lamb which in ancient times was sacrificed at the Temple. The containers carried by the two women would be filled with maror and karpas, respectively. The maror (bitter herb such as horseradish) recalls the bitterness of slavery; the karpas (usually parsley or celery) represents the poor quality of diet the Israelites were fed during their years of slavery. During the seder meal, the karpas would be dipped into the container of salt water held by the hatted man and then eaten in remembrance of the tears shed by Jews while in bondage. The wheelbarrow pushed by the other hatted figure would contain charoset, which is a combination of finely chopped apple, nuts, cinnamon, and wine. The consistency of the charoset is likened to that of the mortar which the Israelites used in constructing buildings for the Egyptians. On top of the commanding figure of Moses in the center of the seder plate would be placed a wine cup called the cup of Elijah. According to tradition, the prophet Elijah would announce the coming of the Messiah on the seder night. Under the top of the seder plate are three shelves; on each shelf a piece of matzo, the bread of affliction, would be placed to represent the three divisions of Israel—priests, Levites, and laymen. The picture shows a father and his children celebrating Pesach and singing songs written in the Haggadah which contains the history and ritual of the Pesach festival. The seder plate is much simpler than the one from the last century, but all the symbolic foods are present.

The world Jewish population in 1969 numbered almost 14 million, making it the smallest of the major religions in terms of numbers. Within the last century, the Jews gradually emerged from the ghettos of Europe and emigrated to the U. S. in large numbers. Slightly over 5.7 million Jews now live within the boundaries of the U.S., mainly in the northeast.

As the Jew became more a part of the outside world, it became increasingly difficult for him to carry out many of the numerous ancient customs of his religion. The end result of this conflict between modern everyday life in Western Europe and U.S. and the necessity of following the rigid rules of Orthodox Judaism was the division of the Jews into three groups: Orthodox, Conservative, and Reform. All three groups are agreed on most matters of basic theology but differ in their interpretations of the ancient rituals and the value received from observing these rituals in today's world. The Reform Jew conforms least to the old customs and rituals such as those described. He does not practice the various dietary restrictions or obey the Laws of Kaskrut. In addition, various changes have occurred in the Reform Sabbath service. The Reform Jew rejects the use of prayer shawls and skull caps. The Torah is read in English as well as Hebrew. Organ and choir music are allowed, and men and women are allowed to sit together in the Reform Temple. The Conservative Jew is a blend of Orthodox and Reform Judaism. He still observes and practices some of the ancient rituals, including the eating of only kosher foods. But he has forsaken many of the other practices of the Orthodox Jew. Accurate figures on synagogue membership in the U.S. are difficult to obtain. It has been estimated that each of the three branches of Judaism has about 1 million members. However, many Orthodox congregations are not affiliated with any national organization; thus the number of Orthodox Jews may actually be higher than the number of Reform or Conservative Jews.

To the Orthodox Jew, the ancient practices and customs that regulate his diet are intended to test his piety and love of God. To him, they are part and parcel of the Jewish way of life and are some of many acts that God has directed his chosen people to perform. Until the last 100 years or so, these dietary practices unquestionably made it extremely difficult for the Orthodox Jew to have social and cultural relations with non-Jews. The Jews were prohibited in the Talmud from eating bread baked by a Gentile or even buying from him such items as milk and wine. The Laws of Kashrut, however, gave to the Jewish people a common bond which was visible to all and served to identify them as a particular group. This common bond no doubt has helped to unify and unite them in years past. To the Reform Jew, the Laws of Kashrut are outdated and archaic and a reflection of totemism. He believes that the customs which reflect the principles of the religion should change with the times. However, Reform Jews have not introduced any new customs to reflect these principles.

Islam

Islam, the youngest major religion in the world, is both a religion and a way of life for over 493 million people. It is the second largest religion in terms of numbers of adherents. Islam is perhaps almost as widely spread throughout the world as Christianity. It is the major religion of Saudi Arabia, its birthplace, and the surrounding Arab countries of Iraq, Jordan, Syria, Turkey, and Iran. In the course of some 1300 years since its founding, Islam has spread south to the African continent. Today it embraces the majority of the Egyptians, Algerians, Moroccans,

Libyans, and many other people south of the Sahara such as Nigerians and Ethiopians. The teachings of Islam moved eastward to Asia; today it is the major religion in Pakistan, Indonesia, and Malaya. The only European countries which today have a sizable number of Moslems are the Balkan States and Russia.

Mohammed, the founder of Islam, was born in Mecca, Saudi Arabia, in 751 A.D. During Mohammed's early years, he came in close contact with both Jews and Christians and was impressed with their belief in one god as contrasted with the many gods of the Arabs. Although a successful trader and merchant, Mohammed was prone to spend many days and weeks in solitude in the hills surrounding Mecca. One night while Mohammed was meditating on the nature of life and the destiny of man, God spoke to him through the Archangel Gabriel. Mohammed, convinced he was mad, attempted to kill himself but was stopped by a voice saying, "Thou art a prophet." The initial doubts of Mohammed were alleviated by later visitations of the Archangel; Mohammed became convinced that he was truly a prophet of Allah, the one true God.

At first, the teachings of Mohammed extended only to his family and friends, but gradually he began to voice his teachings in the marketplace of Mecca. At that time, Mecca was the crossroad of two great caravan routes, the spice route from Southern Arabia to Syria and the route from Persia to the Nile Valley. It was also to Mecca that many Arab pilgrims came to worship at the numerous shrines. These visiting pilgrims and the caravan traders helped in time to spread the teachings of Mohammed to the outlying areas. However, the merchants and wealthy men of Mecca, afraid that Mohammed's teachings of submission to one god would curtail the number of pilgrims who came to the city, ridiculed and ostracized him. In 622 A.D. Mohammed fled from Mecca to Medina with some of his loyal converts. It is from this date that the Islamic calendar begins. Mohammed united the tribes of Medina and became their spiritual as well as political leader. After a few military battles, he conquered Mecca. On his triumphant return, he destroyed all the idols and declared the shrine of Mecca to be a place holy to the one true God.

Mohammed taught that there was only one God, Allah, and that all men must submit completely to His will. The word Islam means submission, and the word Moslem refers to one who submits. The God of Judaism, of Christianity, and of Islam are all basically similar because the Arabs trace their origin back to the early Hebrews through Abraham's son Ishmael. Neither Christ nor Mohammed are considered divine by the Moslem—only spokesmen of God. Mohammed is, however, the greatest since he was the latest and the last of the great prophets of God.

The followers of Islam acknowledge the divinity of the Old and New Testaments but believe that the Bible is not the final expression of the will of God. The most sacred writing of Islam is the Koran. This sacred book, although probably not written during the lifetime of Mohammed, is believed to contain the words spoken to Mohammed by Allah. It is thereby the most authoritative and final expression of the will of God; it supersedes the earlier Biblical writings. The Koran consists of 114 suras or chapters which all (except one) begin with the sentence "In the name of Allah, the Beneficent, the Merciful." Parts of the Koran are read daily in all Moslem schools and mosques. One of the longest suras is the second one, entitled "The Cow" or the little Koran. It contains the main points of all the revelations made to Mohammed as well as instructions regarding the dietary regulations, the need for fasting, pilgrimages, and correct morals.

In the years following the writing of the Koran, scholars and other religious-minded men attempted to analyze and interpret the Koran and relate it in a more meaningful way to the daily life of the faithful followers. A growing list of traditions developed over the years based on what Mohammed either said or did or was reported to have done. These traditions became the patterns or guidelines for every Moslem to follow in almost every conceivable facet of life—a situation analogous to the Jewish Talmud.

The religious practices of those who profess to Islam are often referred to as the Five Pillars of Islam. The first of these is faith. All Moslems repeat once a day the creed "I bear witness that there is no God but Allah and that Mohammed is the Prophet of Allah." Allah is considered to be in complete control of everything. He has determined the fate of every man; whatever happens is the will of Allah. On the day of final resurrection, all men will be judged worthy of either heaven or hell.

Prayer is the second pillar. All Moslems are taught to pray five times a day; at dawn, noon, midafternoon, sunset, and nightfall. The call to prayer can be heard at these times in any Moslem city. A crier climbs to the balcony at the top of the minaret of the mosque and calls out the words by Mohammed, enjoining the faithful to prayer. Regardless of where a Moslem is, he is supposed to offer prayer. If he is not able to go to a mosque, he spreads down his prayer rug, thereby making that spot sacred, turns his face toward Mecca, and prays. Friday is the day of public prayer, and sermons are delivered in the mosque after the noon prayer.

Alms giving is the third pillar. Several passages in the Koran describe the benefits to be reaped by the giving of money to the poor, orphaned, and aged.

Fasting is the fourth pillar. The Koran promises rewards beyond bounds for fasting for God's sake. The Koran commands all faithful Moslems to observe the fast of Ramadan; Ramadan is the ninth month of the lunar Moslem year. Since Mohammed received his first revelation on the twenty-seventh day of this month, he declared in the Koran that the entire month should be one of complete fasting from sunrise to sunset. The fast includes abstinence from water and smoking as well as food. During Ramadan, it is believed that "the gates of Heaven are open, the gates of Hell closed, and the devil put in chains." The faithful observance of the Ramadan fast is believed to result in the remission of sin. In many of the larger cities in the Arab world, a cannon is fired several hours before sunrise to warn the people that the hour to begin fasting is approaching. The cannon is fired again at sunset to announce the end of the day's fast. The meals eaten after sunset are suppose to be light. A special type of leavened bread is eaten during this month. The observance of the Ramadan fast is perhaps the most strictly adhered to of all Islamic practices. This may in part be attributed to the numerous community activities involved in the observance of this fast, which place a strong pressure on all to conform. To fast during Ramadan is considered a yearly reaffirmation of one's allegiance to Islam; nonobservance of the fast could bring social disapproval or perhaps ostracism. Since the Moslems follow a lunar calendar, the month of Ramadan occurs at different times during the year. When Ramadan occurs during the summer and temperatures reach 100° or more, the self-discipline required to refrain from taking even a sip of water must be very great. Several other fast days exist for the Moslem, but none have as great a significance as that of Ramadan. The Koran exempts young children, the aged and sick, travelers, and nursing or pregnant women from the Ramadan fast; however, days missed because of travel, pregnancy, or lactation must be made up at a later time.

The last pillar of Islam is the pilgrimage or haji to Mecca. This trip is the height of religious exhilaration for the Moslem. Every year thousands come from all over the world to pay homage at the great shrine. In 1962, approximately 966,000 made this pilgrimage; the vast majority came from Saudi Arabia, but about 22% came from other countries. The area surrounding Mecca for 100 square miles is closed to all who are not Moslems. The Great Mosque of Mecca, which can hold over 35,000 people in its court, also contains the holiest shrine of Islam, the Kaaba. The southeast corner of the Kaaba contains the Black Stone, which is believed to have been given to Abraham and Ishmael by the Archangel Gabriel.

The Koran and the traditions, like the Jewish Torah and Talmud, contain statements which inform the Moslem of the clean and proper foods to eat and how they should be eaten. Animals that are forbidden are any that die of disease or strangulation or that are beaten to death. Blood is forbidden as well as swine. Islam like Judaism adopted the rejection of the pig; four passages in the Koran forbid the eating of pork. The pig is so abhorred that in some places even the word pig is avoided, and the animal is referred to as "the black one." Simoons, in his book *Eat Not This Flesh,* reports that a pious Moslem killed by a wild boar is said to remain in the fires of hell for 500 years to become purified. Moslems are also forbidden to partake of wine or other intoxicating beverages.

No animal food except fish and locusts is considered lawful unless it has been slaughtered according to the proper ritual, which is similar to that used by the Jewish shocket. The person killing the animal must repeat at the instant of slaughter, "In the name of God, God is great."

Among the Islamic traditions one finds statements regarding how one should eat. For example, the Moslem is commanded "to eat in God's name, to return thanks, to eat with the right hand and with shoes off, and to lick plate when meal is finished." Islam makes no distinction between men regardless of wealth, social position, race, or color and encourages the practice of all types of men eating together. All are brothers united in the worship of the one and only true God.

One cannot help but be struck by the similarity between some of the ritual practices of Islam and Judaism. This may be attributed to the fact that the two religions developed in the same part of the world and to the close contact of Islam with Judaism during the formative years of Islam.

Hinduism

Hinduism, considered by some the oldest living religion, originated in India approximately 4000 years ago. Its adherents in 1969 numbered some 437 million, with the vast majority of these people living in the

Indian subcontinent. Although to many of us it may appear that the Hindu worships several hundred deities, this is not strictly true. These numerous gods and goddesses are all manifestations of one supreme being which the Hindu calls Brahman—the Universal Spirit. According to ancient Hindu mythology, Brahman appeared in the form of the god Brahma and created the universe. Then in the form of the god Vishnu, Brahman sustained the universe for a period of 432 million human years; eventually, in the form of the god Shiva, Brahman destroyed the universe. The universe to a Hindu is cyclic. The present world was created by Brahma. It is now approximately 425,000 years from the time when Shiva will cause the destruction of the world, thus enabling another world to be reconstructed by Brahma. The Hindu believes that nothing which once existed is ever completely destroyed, it merely undergoes a change in its form.

Brahma, Vishnu, and Shiva have been referred to as the Hindu trinity. Of these three deities, only Vishnu and Shiva are worshipped today to any large extent. In addition to these two principal deities, there are reported to be some 300 other manifestations of deities which are worshipped in varying degrees. Orthodox Hinduism is subdivided into six different sects; for each sect, there is a particular set of deities that is considered most sacred. Most Hindus worship at least three deities: the god of his village or town, the god of his family, and a personal deity.

Intimately involved in the Hindu way of life and religion is the caste system. From ancient times, the caste system has provided a means of dividing society into unalterable levels of social status depending upon birth. An individual born into a caste was destined to remain a member of that caste throughout his life regardless of his efforts to advance to a higher caste. In all societies, birth undoubtedly influenced one's social status, but it was usually possible for an individual to improve his social position by one means or another. Not so with the Hindu. According to the early religious writings, four social orders or castes of Hindu society arose from the different parts of the body of Brahma. From his mouth were created the priests and teachers called Brahmins; from his arms sprang the warriors and rulers, the Ksatriyas; from his thighs came the farmers and traders or Vaisyas; and from his feet, the menial laborers, the Sudras, were born. All individuals born outside these four orders were considered to have been created from the darkness which Brahma discarded in the process of creation. These people were called outcasts or untouchables. Since 500 B.C., when the caste system was known to have been in effect, the four original castes have subdivided within themselves so that today nearly 3000 different castes are said to exist.

The word caste in Sanskrit means the equivalent of race, suggesting that the caste system may have originated from the racial pride and color prejudice of the Aryan conquerors of India thousands of years ago. Whatever its origin, the caste system became a basic institution sanctioned by the religion and woven into the Hindu way of life.

The members of each caste had a moral duty to perform which was unique for that caste. For each caste, definite rules and regulations existed, dictating to the member whom he could marry, what he could eat, and with whom he could eat and socialize. The Brahmins occupied a privileged position in the Hindu society and were considered the highest caste. Originally the Brahmins were not permitted to engage in any type of work other than study and religious teachings. People in the other castes were expected to support and sustain the Brahmins with gifts of food or money. The ancient laws and writings sacred to the Hindu encouraged the giving of these gifts to the Brahmins, promising great benefits or merit to the giver. For example, the gift of a cow or a piece of land to a Brahmin ensured that the giver would go to heaven. In more recent times, many Brahmins have abandoned the old idea of not working; today many Brahmins are engaged in the professions of law, medicine, and business. Many have positions in the government and in universities. However, they still retain their esteemed social position and rigidly follow many of the ancient practices regarding their social and home life.

The Ksatriyas, as the kings and soldiers, originally were obligated to protect the community and willingly give their lives to protect the Brahmins as well as the most sacred animal to the Hindu, the cow. The members of this caste were allowed to kill for food and were meat eaters. The duties of the Vaisyas were to make money and to improve the economic situation of the country. They were particularly encouraged to give gifts to the Brahmins and money for the building of temples. The moral duty of the Sudras was to serve the three higher classes with diligence and humbleness. This class in particular developed numerous subdivisions based mainly on various occupations such as carpenters and weavers; the profession of a Sudra had an important influence on his social status. In these early times, the outcasts or untouchables were considered so lowly that they were not even allowed in the villages and

towns except to do the most menial of labor. These people were not allowed to own land or to build houses and lived under wretched conditions.

The caste system of India has been likened in many ways to the social
structure of Medieval Europe; the princes, feudal lords, merchants, and
peasants of that period are comparable with the four main castes of India.
The Industrial Revolution contributed greatly to the dissolution of
Europe's caste system, but India's caste system has remained relatively
unchanged over the centuries. However, in 1949, as a result of the
vigorous efforts of Gandhi, the Indian government declared untouch-
ability illegal and expressed opposition to the social barriers of caste.
Social changes of this nature are accepted slowly; the caste system is still
a forceful factor, particularly in the villages, and affects the lives of
millions of Indians. Whether the caste system can survive the increasing
industrialization of India and the increasing mobility of Indians from
the villages to the cities is a question that cannot be answered at the
present time.

Fundamental to the Hindu religion are the ideas of reincarnation and
destiny. To a Hindu, his present existence is but one of many. After
death, his soul is liberated and eventually takes birth again in another
form. Thus, the Hindu goes through endless cycles of birth, death, and
rebirth. The ultimate goals of the Hindu are to attain liberation from this
cycle and to gain complete self-identification with the Universal Spirit,
Brahman. The form the soul takes at rebirth is the direct consequence
of a person's actions during his previous life. If a Hindu, whatever his
caste, performs his moral duty well and is pious during his present life,
he may be reborn in a higher caste. On the other hand, if he does not
behave according to his moral code, he may be reborn at a lower level
of existence, either human or animal. Thus, every thought and deed
committed by a Hindu are his own responsibility and he alone must reap
the consequences. This philosophy justifies to the Hindu all the in-
equalities of life, including the caste system. What a Hindu is in his
present life is the direct consequence of his actions in a previous existence, and his next life will be largely determined by his present actions.

To the orthodox Hindu, Brahman is all and everything. All living
things contain a part of this divine spirit. Thus, all life is sacred. To take
the life of even the smallest creature is tantamount to causing harm to a
part of Brahman. The belief in reincarnation also contributes to the

Hindu's abhorrence of the taking of life since he could never be sure that any animal he killed did not contain the soul of an ancestor reborn as that animal.

Of the numerous writings sacred to the Hindu, the Code of Manu contains many references which have an influence on the diet of the Hindu. A few examples follow:

> Wound not others, do not injury by thought or deed, utter no word to pain thy fellow creatures.
>
> One should cease from eating all flesh. There is no fault in eating flesh, nor in drinking intoxicating liquor, nor in copulation, for that is the occupations of beings, but cessation from them produces great fruit.
>
> Meat can never be obtained without injury to living creatures, and injury to sentient beings is detrimental to the attainment of heavenly bliss.
>
> There is no greater sinner than that man who, though not worshipping the gods or the manes, seeks to increase the bulk of his own flesh by the flesh of other beings.

Most pious Hindus, especially those of the Brahmin caste, are strict vegetarians who follow the nonviolence attitude and strict rules of the Code of Manu. The more devout Brahmins deny themselves eggs as well as all forms of meat since to eat an egg would be equivalent to taking a life. The members of the other castes may eat meat other than beef, but prejudice against this practice increases the higher the caste. The particular god which a family worships may influence whether they eat meat. Although the avoidance of pork and chicken in the diet is undoubtedly influenced by the religious attitude of the sanctity of life, it is also due in part to the idea that these animals are scavengers and thus unclean. Fish is consumed by some Hindus, particularly those in the area of Bengal.

Although all animals contain a part of Brahman and are sacred, the cow has been singled out as a particularly sacred animal. The exact reason for this is not clear. Records dating back hundreds of years before the birth of Christ indicate that cattle were slaughtered and eaten in India. However, the code of Manu, written sometime between 100–300 A.D., listed the slaying of cattle as an offense requiring penance. One can at best only speculate on the reasons for this change in attitude. It has been suggested that the cow took on a sacred aura because of his years of faithful service in helping man till the soil and providing him with food to feed his family as well as fuel, in the form of dried cow dung, to heat his home and cook his food. It also has been suggested that the

killing of cattle was prohibited to encourage the development of agriculture and the planting of crops for food.

According to Hindu mythology, the cow was created by Brahma on
the same day as the Brahmins and thus is an animal to be venerated above
all others. In fact, one of the several Hindu heavens is named after the
cow. The cow has become the symbol of motherhood in India. Mahatma
Gandhi referred to the cow as a poem of pity and the mother to millions
of Indian mankind. The early scriptures admonish "all that kill . . . cows
rot in hell for as many years as there are hairs on the body of the cow."
Thomas reports that no devout Hindu will pass a cow without touching
it and then touching his own head. The act of feeding a cow brings great
merit to a Hindu. The cow is sacred to all sects of Hinduism and to all
castes. Cows wander at will through most towns and cities of India,
often causing considerable damage to crops. In 1956, India had 159 million cattle, one-fifth of all the cattle in the world. Many of these cattle
were diseased and unproductive; perhaps of even more serious consequence, they were either consuming or destroying food needed by the
people. Every conceivable means is used in India to protect the cattle
from harm and slaughter. The Indian government in 1965 supported
sixty-two special farms for old, infirm, and unproductive cattle.

The kitchen in a devout Hindu Brahmin home is sacred. Since all food
contains a part of the Universal Spirit, Brahman, it must be prepared
and consumed with proper reverence. The women who prepare the
meal, as well as any who partake of it, must purify themselves by means
of ritual bathing of the entire body and often by putting on clean clothes.
A Brahmin usually does not accept cooked food from a member of any
lower caste but he will accept uncooked food. Even the shadow of a
lower caste person falling on the food of a Brahmin is said to render it
unfit for eating.

Ghee (clarified butter) and milk coming from the cow are sacred foods.
These ritually pure foods cannot be contaminated even by the touch of
someone from the lowest caste. Thus, a Brahmin may accept milk or any
food provided it is cooked with ghee from a Sudra. This sacredness of
milk is evidenced also by the fact that in some Indian villages milk is
sprinkled inside a house in which a child had died of smallpox. The
purifying effect of the milk is believed to make the house safe.

Ghee is preferred over all other animal fats. Although the Sepoy rebellion in 1857 was due to many factors, one cause was the aversion that
the soldiers had to other animal fats. A new rifle requiring greased bullets

had been introduced into the army. The tips of these bullets had to be bitten off before the gun was loaded, and the soldiers rebelled at the taste of the animal grease.

The coconut is another food considered sacred. It is used as a symbol of Shiva, the three eyes of the coconut being associated with the three eyes of Shiva. To be successful, all new enterprises should be started by breaking a coconut.

Meat, especially beef, is not the only food that is taboo to the orthodox Hindu. The code of Manu forbids to the higher castes the eating of domestic fowls, onions, garlic, turnips, mushrooms, and salted pork. The association of blood with the color of some lentils and tomatoes has made these vegetables unacceptable to some castes.

The Hindu has many days of fasting and prayer called Vratas. On these days, he is expected to observe either a complete fast or at least to abstain from eating cooked foods. The Hindu has no weekly day of rest comparable to Sunday in the Christian religions, but actually every day of the week is a holy day dedicated to one or another of the many gods. Brahmins and most women of the higher castes observe Vratas on certain prescribed days each month. To break the fast, a Brahmin has to be fed. Women of the lower castes can feed a Brahmin either ghee, coconuts, fruits, or some uncooked food.

Buddhism

Buddhism originated during the sixth century B.C. and in many ways was an outgrowth of Hinduism. Siddhartha Gautama, who was to become Buddha—The Enlightened One—was raised as a Hindu, the son of a wealthy Himalayan chieftain. At the age of 29, discontent with his luxurious life and deeply troubled with the misery and suffering of mankind, he renounced his worldly possessions and assumed the role of a beggar. He wandered throughout India seeking the advice and counsel of the wisest teachers and scholars as to the universal cause of misery and how it could be removed. For six years he denied himself friends and the comforts of adequate food, shelter, and clothing while he devoted his time to meditation on how misery and suffering could be abolished. On a night in May on which the moon was full, he seated himself under a bodhi tree and passed into deep meditation. Legend has it that he was overcome by a deep mystic rapture that lasted 49 days—enlightenment was captured and Gautama became Buddha. In the Deer Park of Sarnath near Benares, India, Buddha delivered his first sermon on "Setting in

Motion the Wheel of Righteousness." For the remainder of his life, he traveled throughout India teaching the Middle Way. In 250 B.C. Buddhism was made India's state religion. Although today less than 1% of India's population is Buddhist, Buddhism is the predominant religion in Ceylon, Burma, Thailand, Laos, Cambodia, and Japan. Its adherents numbered some 177 million in 1969.

Buddha taught that ignorance produces selfish desires which are the cause of rebirth, and it is this rebirth that causes sorrow and suffering. Man passes through many cycles of birth, growth, decay, and death. These teachings are embodied in the Four Noble Truths, which state that:

1. Existence is suffering.
2. This suffering is due to selfish desires.
3. The cure of suffering is to destroy these selfish desires.
4. This cure can be accomplished by practicing the Eight-Fold Path: right belief, right thought, right speech, right action, right means of livelihood, right exertion, right remembrance, and right meditation.

By following this Eight-Fold Path, man can gradually in his life after life on earth attain liberation from rebirth with its inevitable suffering and finally reach Enlightenment or Nirvana.

Basic to the understanding of Buddhism is the doctrine of Karma. Karma means literally "action or deed," but it implies both cause and effect. Briefly it means that what a person is today is the result of the sum total of his actions or deeds in a previous existence. This is the Buddhist's answer to the apparent injustices of his present life. If a man is born a cripple or poor or rich, he must simply suffer or enjoy the consequences because he alone is responsible. Every man is thus the master of his life to come. In order not to be reborn in a lower form or as a non-human but rather in a higher state moving slowly toward Nirvana, the Buddhist vows to follow the Eight-Fold Path including "right action." He vows to abstain from killing or doing injury to any living being, from stealing, from falsehood, from drinking intoxicating beverages, and from sexual misconduct. By the practice of "right action," the Buddhist gains and acquires the merit that will help him progress toward a higher existence in the next life. The accumulation of merit is paramount in the life of a devout Buddhist. Violation of these vows brings demerit. If demerit is accumulated in excess of merit, it may result in rebirth at a lower level.

The building of merit is accomplished through voluntary gifts with-

Buddhist monks are completely dependent upon voluntary contributions of food from the village people. (Collection of the author.)

out thought of immediate personal gain. By making a self-sacrificing gift to a beggar, the Buddhist shows that he is concentrating on someone other than himself and is not overly concerned with the accumulation of worldly goods.

Buddhist monks hold a very special role in the attainment of merit. The Burmese monk is considered by the villagers of Upper Burma to be the embodiment of all this is good and noble in man and one who is definitely on a higher level of existence. Thus, the custom of helping to feed and support a man of such exemplary conduct is considered natural and a high form of merit-making (Kutho). The Buddhist monk vows not to eat after midday although he is allowed to drink tea and coconut milk.

He pledges to remain aloof from all women. His worldly possessions are the three cloths that he wears, a begging bowl, a razor, a needlecase, a mat, and a small cloth used to filter his drinking water. Buddhist monks are completely dependent upon voluntary contributions of food and clothing from the people. Every morning the yellow-clad monks with their iron or brass beggar's bowls silently make the rounds of the houses in the villages. The monks are not allowed to announce their arrival in any way or give any thanks for food received. The woman of the house gives the very best of what rice, curry, or fruit she has available. (See the picture opposite.)

In the cities or larger towns in Thailand, the monks' meals may be prepared from food sent to the monastery by wealthy Buddhists. Some village households may send additional food to the monastery for the monks' midday meals. In fact, one hour before noon, a temple drum may be sounded to warn those who want to send food that the hour is approaching. Many families might not normally eat a meal at noon themselves but still would prepare food to be sent to the monks. In some northern Thailand villages, the monks no longer beg for their food each morning. Instead, a section of the village, consisting of 16 or so households, is assigned the responsibility of providing sufficient food for the monks on a particular day. The food is brought to the monastery early in the morning by the women and girls of the households. The monks are served by temple boys. Additional food also might be sent to the monastery on special holy days, and the monks might be invited to eat with a family on important family occasions.

The cost of maintaining the monks might represent an economic hardship in the eyes of a Westerner. DeYoung estimates that there were probably 400,000 Thai males in monasteries in 1955. Village boys in Thailand usually become temple boys at about the age of ten. In this capacity, they act as attendants to the monks and, in return, are taught to read and write and to learn some of the Buddhist scriptures. Many boys remain in the temple and qualify for novicehood. In Burma, parents are expected to sponsor their sons for novicehood. This is one of the highest forms of earning merit; the boys are encouraged to enter the monastery in order to provide their parents with the opportunity to obtain merit. The length of stay in the monastery may vary from only a few days to several months or a lifetime.

DeYoung estimates that the amount of food contributed to the monastery by each household in a Thai village in a year's time is probably equivalent to the cost of feeding one additional person for a year. Assuming that an adult male consumes approximately 1 pound of rice a a day, this amounts to at least 365 pound of rice a year or approximately $10.

Kutho, or merit, in lesser amounts can be obtained by giving food to nuns and beggars. Food is always offered immediately to a visitor in a Burmese home. Not to offer food is thought of as not the right action and is a source of Akutho or demerit.

The vow to abstain from taking life is reflected in countless ways in Buddhist countries. The growing of rice and other crops is regarded as the right livelihood because it does not directly involve the taking of life. Attempts to introduce the growing of ground nuts have been successful for this reason, whereas attempts to increase the production of livestock, such as pigs and chickens, have met with limited success. Pigs raised by villagers in Thailand usually are sold to a Chinese dealer for slaughter and marketing. In Thailand, a villager must buy a permit to slaughter a pig. Chickens are raised for sale by nearly every farm household in Thailand, but most farm families do not eat more than four or five chickens a year.

However, the vow to abstain from taking life is rigidly adhered to, as evidenced by the fact that fish is a common supplement to the Thai rice diet. According to Pfanner, Thai villagers reason that they do not kill the fish, they simply remove them from the water. In a Burmese village, a government program to control rodent destruction of ground nuts by use of rodent poison was accepted. In anticipation of resistance to the program, the government declared that any Akutho earned by killing the rats would come to the government and not the farmer. Most farmers, however, adopted the attitude that killing the rats was necessary; that by doing this, more money would be earned from the sale of ground nuts. The increased income could then be used to help acquire Kutho, thus balancing any Akutho gained by killing the rats.

POSSIBLE ORIGINS OF RELIGIOUS DIETARY PRACTICES

From the discussion of the five selected religions, it can be seen that they all prohibit some food either completely or on certain days. In every case, these foods are of animal origin. For certain groups in the

Hindu society and for Buddhists, no meat of any kind can be eaten; for all Hindu castes, beef is especially tabooed. The eating of pork or blood is considered despicable to the Orthodox Jew or Moslem. If the adherents of the Eastern Orthodox Church abstain from meat, fish, and dairy products on all the indicated days of fast, these foods cannot be eaten on about 136 days out of the year.

In almost every religion, statements of one type or another pertaining to man's diet can be found in the sacred books and writings. Because these dietary regulations were actually written down in these sacred books, which were often considered the word or will of the supreme being, the regulations have been preserved and perpetuated over the centuries. The religion itself has encouraged and contributed to the continuing observance of these dietary habits from the earliest times. However, this does not explain why the particular dietary practice came to be a part of the sacred writings of the religion. The real origins of these dietary practices are lost in antiquity; today one can only suggest possible reasons as to why these practices developed.

Man's environment prior to the development of each religion and the writings of the sacred books must surely have influenced his dietary habits. The founders of the various religions may have incorporated already existing dietary habits into the religion. Primitive man was oppressed by hunger and consumed almost any food that he could obtain. Usually no choice was involved. It was more a question of food for survival. Simoons suggests that the original prejudice against the pig developed among the pastoral peoples living in the arid regions of Asia. The pig was not a commonly eaten animal in their group but was in the diet of those who settled permanently in the area. Contempt for the food of the rival group may have made the pastoral people ridicule the eating of this animal; thus, the prejudice was established and may then have been incorporated into the sacred writings. The similarity between the dietary practices of Islam and Judaism suggests that Mohammed may have been influenced by the existing practices of the Jews.

An example of a religious festival which was practiced before the Old Testament was written and is still practiced today is the Jewish Pesach. The origin of the present-day Pesach festival, as related by Schauss, is really the combination of two festivals that were observed by nomadic Jews long before their deliverance from Egypt. The Festival of the Shepherds was one of these. It was observed in the spring when the kids and lambs were born. On the night of the full moon just before dusk, a sheep or goat was sacrificed and the animal roasted whole. All the family members had to consume the animal completely that night since it was forbidden to have any of the uneaten meat left by daybreak. One ritual associated with this festival was to mark the tent posts of all who partook of the feast with the blood of the slain animal. The other early festival was called the Festival of Matzos (unleavened bread). This festival also occurred in the spring at the time of the cutting of the barley and lasted about seven weeks, until the wheat was harvested. Prior to the harvest of the barley, the Jews removed from their homes any old bread or fermented dough. The first barley cut was given to the priest as a gift to God. This latter festival was a command festival conducted in a place of worship.

Schauss states that, over the centuries, as the Jewish people settled in towns and cities, the meanings and relevance of these early customs became obscure to the new generations. The Jews retained the old customs but reinterpreted them and gave them new meaning and emphasis Pesach thus became the festival which allowed each Jew to commemorate and relive the deliverance of the Jewish people from bondage in Egypt. Thus, the eating of the matzos during Pesach is retained, but not to assure a good harvest of wheat. Instead it is eaten to commemorate the fact that the Jews did not have time to allow bread dough to rise and so baked unleavened bread on the night they fled from Egypt. It seems inevitable that this sort of reinterpretation and reevaluation of the many customs and rituals in all religions must have occurred over the centuries since their founding. The recent decree which allows Roman Catholics to eat meat on Friday if they so choose is an example of this reevaluation process.

The fear of disease has been suggested as a possible reason why the early Jews, Moslems, and Hindus rejected the pig. This animal was a scavenger and may have been considered unfit as food since he ate all kinds of filth. The relationship between trichinosis and the eating of pork is well known to us today, but it is doubtful that early man knew of this relationship. It is possible that he did recognize a connection between the eating of pork and vomiting and diarrhea, which are early symptoms of trichinosis. But Simoons points out that these symptoms of trichinosis occur in only about 5% of the cases. Undoubtedly the problem of preserving meat and dairy products for the early Hebrews and Moslems was great, particularly with the climatic conditions of their environment. Spoiled meat was inevitable if it was not consumed rather quickly, but this would be true of all meats and not just pork.

Early man, as well as many groups of primitive people today, worshiped and regarded as sacred certain animals. This practice is referred to as totemism. Why a particular animal is singled out is unknown. It may be through fear or because of the pleasant association man has with a certain animal. The latter reason is the one most often suggested as to why the cow is a sacred animal to the Hindu. In many African tribes, cows usually are not killed and eaten but are kept as status symbols and an indication of wealth.

Certain dietary practices may have developed as a means of separating one religious group from another. Simoons suggests that the rejection of pork by the Moslems was adopted by Mohammed to distinguish Islam from Christianity. As pointed out earlier, various dietary practices may have originated to provide an effective way of holding the members of a religious group together. The observance of these practices in their everyday life gave a common bond to the group which, in turn, strengthened their religious beliefs.

THE FUTURE RELATIONSHIP

Since the early beginnings of each of the five religions discussed in this chapter, food has played an intimate role in the manner by which man has attempted to relate to his supreme being or supernatural power. For hundreds of years within each religion, the numerous symbolic ways of using food has had deep meaning to man. It is perhaps not surprising that food, so necessary for physical well being, should also have been used to attain spiritual well being.

Most of the discussion in this chapter has been concerned with the relationship of religion, food, and man as it has existed in these religions. But what of today and tomorrow? Are these religions having as great an impact on the dietary practices and habits of their adherents as they had in the past? The abolishment of the church law directing Roman Catholics to abstain from eating meat on Fridays and other fast days, the large number of Reform Jews in the U.S. who do not observe the Laws of Kashrut, and the custom of many Greek Americans to observe only a 7-day fast before Easter and Christmas instead of the 40-day fast suggests that, in the U.S. at least, the influence of certain religions on the dietary habits of their adherents is not as strong as it was. The situation in other countries is difficult to determine. If in the future the role of food in religion decreases, will man need to replace the spiritual values he once received from the observance of certain religious dietary practices with something else and, if so, with what?

STUDY QUESTIONS

1. What similarities and differences have the religions discussed made on the food practices and customs of their adherents?
2. What are the religious bases or reasonings for the various food practices and customs listed in Question 1?
3. What values have certain religious dietary practices had in the past to their adherents? Do you think that these values are important today? Why?
4. Roman Catholics have recently been given the opportunity to choose some other way of doing penance than abstaining from meat on Fridays. What are some of these choices? How widely have these other ways of doing penance been adopted by Catholics?
5. Why is the cow a sacred animal to the Hindu?

TOPICS FOR INDIVIDUAL INVESTIGATION

1. Examine in detail the religious influences of Shintoism and Confucianism on the dietary habits of their adherents.
2. Discuss how the tribal religions of various American Indian tribes influenced their dietary habits and agricultural practices.
3. Discuss the influences that some tribal religions of Africans have had on the production, distribution, and consumption of food.
4. Interview a Hindu, a Moslem, an Orthdox and a Reform Jew, a Seventh-day Adventist, a member of an Eastern Orthodox Church, and a member of the Church of Jesus Christ of the Latter-day Saints to determine what influence their religions have on their own dietary habits. Does the observance of these practices have certain values for them? If so, what? What are some difficulties they encounter in following these practices?

REFERENCES AND SUGGESTED READINGS

Ali, M. *The Religion of Islam*. Ripon Printing Press, Lahore, Pakistan, 1950.

Ansubel, N. *The Book of Jewish Knowledge*. Crown, New York, 1964.

Brown, J. C. *Understanding Other Cultures*. Prentice-Hall, Englewood Cliffs, N.J., 1963.

DeYoung, J. E. *Village Life in Modern Thailand*. Univ. of California Press, Berkeley, 1955.

Engle, F., and G. Blair. *The Jewish Festival Cookbook*. Paperback Library, New York, 1966.

Epstein, M. *All About Jewish Holidays and Customs*. KTAV Publishing House, New York, 1959.

Firth, R. Religion in Social Reality. *Reader in Comparative Religion* by W. Lessa and E. Z. Vogt. Row, Peterson, White Plains, N.Y., 1958.

Fitch, F. M. *Their Search for God—Ways of Worship in the Orient*. Lothrop, Lee and Shepard, New York, 1947.

Fitch, F. M. *Allah, The God of Islam*. Lothrop, Lee and Shepard, New York, 1950.

Gaster, T. H. *Customs and Folkways of Jewish Life*. William Sloane Associates, New York, 1955.

Gaster, T. H. *Festivals of the Jewish Year*. William Sloane Associates, New York, 1952.

Herndon, B. *The Seventh Day*. McGraw-Hill, New York, 1960.

Hughes, T. P. *A Dictionary of Islam*. W. H. Allen, London, 1935.

Karay, M. P., Ed. *Hellenic Cuisine*. Saint Helen's Philoptochas Society and Saints Constantine and Helen Parent-Teacher Association, Detroit, 1957.

Khaing, M. M. *Burmese Family*. Indiana Univ. Press, Bloomington, 1962.

Life. *The World's Great Religions*. Time, New York, 1957.

Nash, M. Burmese Buddhism in Everyday Life. *Amer. Anthropologist* 65: 285, 1963.

Nash, M. *The Golden Road to Modernity: Village Life in Contemporary Burma*. John Wiley, New York, 1965.

Pfanner, D. E., and J. Ingersoll. Theravada Buddhism and Village Economic Behavior. *J. Asian Studies* 21: 341, 1962.

Schauss, H. Pesach: Its Origins. Reprinted from *The Jewish Festivals*, Union of American Hebrew Congregations, Cincinnati, 1938. *Reader in Comparative Religion* by W. Lessa and E. Z. Vogt. Row, Peterson, White Plains, N.Y., 1958.

Simoons, F. J. *Eat Not This Flesh*, Univ. of Wisconsin Press, Madison, 1961.

Spence, N. *The Story of America's Religions*. Holt, Rinehart and Winston, New York, 1957.

Stephanou, E. *Belief and Practices in the Orthodox Church*. Minos Publishing, New York, 1965.

Thomas, P. *Hindu Religion: Custom and Manners*. D. B. Taraporevala Sons, Bombay, India, 1956.

Vanos, F., and L. Prichard. *Can The Greeks Cook*. Dietz Press, Richmond, Va., 1950.

Von Grunebaum, G. E. *Mohammedan Festivals*. Henry Schuman, New York, 1951.

White, E. G. *The Ministry of Healing*. Pacific Press Publishing Association, Mountain View, Cal., 1905.

White, E. G. *Counsels on Diet and Foods*. Review and Herald Publishing Association, Washington, D.C., 1938.

Women of St. Paul's Greek Orthodox Church. *The Art of Greek Cookery*. Doubleday, New York, 1963.

6

Food, Man, and the Influence of Business

Up to this point, man's physical need for food and some of the cultural, social, and individual reasons for his selection, preparation, and use of it have been considered. These factors alone do not totally explain modern man's relationship to food. What is it that causes us, as a nation, to consume millions of dollars worth of sugar-coated cereals or frozen pizzas each year? The answer is not clear, but the influence of business is clearly at work and has helped to make these products and thousands of others part of our everyday eating habits. How did business come into its position of importance? How does it influence the consumer in his food buying habits?

In order to answer these questions we must break down business influence into the discrete parts that make it up, and examine in detail.

233

These parts are:

- Business firm
- Product
- Promotion

The product can further be broken down into:

- The product itself
- Brand
- Package
- Price
- Retail outlet

THE BUSINESS FIRM

In order to understand why an individual behaves in a certain manner, it is necessary to understand his background. The same holds true for business.

The Function of Business

The function of any business is to produce goods or supply services. It does this in order to generate profits for its owners. Any business, large or small, engages in three activities in order to operate:

1. Financing itself
2. Production or supplying service
3. Marketing

The native in West Africa who decides to produce a cash crop must obtain capital to buy seed and other necessities. As M. P. Miracle pointed out, many times the money is borrowed from a cartel run by a powerful head—often a woman—which buys the crops once they are harvested. The business system in this situation is quite simple. Financing and marketing are taken care of by the cartel, and the native sees to it that his wives tend to the fields in order to produce the crops.

A U.S. corporation gets the capital it needs by issuing stocks or bonds or borrowing from financial institutions. This money is used to help build plants and buy machinery in order to produce its line of products.

The marketing strategy probably includes the use of both national advertising and salesmen placed in large cities around the country.

Note that both of these businesses have the three basic activities mentioned earlier in common. Corporations in the U.S.—especially the very large ones—have developed these activities to such a degree that their complexity and degree of sophistication are seldom equaled anywhere else in the world. The development and refinement of these activities can be traced through our economic history. Each has held the limelight at some point in our development.

Soon after our nation was founded, it faced a scarcity of goods and services. More people called for more and more products. In order to produce the needed goods, this period, which lasted until the end of the nineteenth century, was characterized by successful attempts to increase production efficiency.

Increased production efficiency was usually characterized by the introduction of machines to take the place of a number of men. Machines were expensive. Raw materials were expensive. Capital was needed to buy these things. The great financiers came on the scene. These men were experts in raising the capital that was needed to keep business producing, prospering, and growing.

The final activity left for refinement—marketing—came to a dominant position soon after World War II, and it has continued to hold its position of central importance. We have become a nation characterized by abundance. As Philip Kotler points out in his book *Marketing Management Analysis, Planning, and Control:*

> The economy is marked not by a scarcity of goods, but by a scarcity of markets. The major problem of most firms is to find sufficient customers for their output.

People in the U.S. and in other developed nations find themselves in a position vastly different from the situation that faces the people in less developed nations. The situation can be viewed in light of the *Hierarchy Of Needs* concept presented by Maslow. As was stated in a previous chapter, Maslow classified all human needs into physiological needs and social needs. The idea behind this theory of human motivation is that a minimum satisfaction of one need is necessary before the person can move up to seek satisfaction of the next need in the hierarchy. People in many countries of the world engage in the daily struggle to satisfy basic physiological needs or, perhaps, have "advanced" up to obtaining some level of security or safety in their lives. On the other hand, people in the U.S. and other developed countries, are sure that their physical needs will be satisfied and are attempting to be loved by their peers and, in many instances, have advanced to seeking esteem.

As Kassarjian and Robertson said in their book *Perspectives in Consumer Behavior:*

> In middle-class America, most individuals seem to be attempting to satisfy their love or esteem needs. If advertising at all reflects the American need structure, this becomes evident from a casual perusal of present-day ads. Seldom does one see an advertizing message like "Crispy crackers fill your stomach fuller than other products"; more typically one sees "Serve Crispy crackers with exotic cheese and impress your friends."

Comparison:
Less Developed Nations vs. Developed Nations
Their Relative Levels of Realized Needs

Maslow's hierarchy of needs	Less-developed nations	Developed nations
The Need for Self-Actualization Esteem Needs Belongingness-Love Needs Safety Needs Physiological Needs	⇧	⇧

In developed countries, marketing continues to overshadow the other two principal activities of business in terms of importance and will continue to do so. This point was brought out quite clearly in a National Association of Manufacturers Symposium when a participant said:

> In this exciting age of change, marketing is the beating heart of many operations. It must be considered a principal reason for corporate existence. . . .
>
> No longer can a company just figure out how many widgets it can produce and then go ahead and turn them out. To endure in this highly competitive change-infested market, a company must first determine what it can sell, how much it can sell, and what approaches must be used to entice the wary customer. . . .

Marketing Defined

Marketing, as defined in 1960 by the American Marketing Association, is the performance of business activities related to the flow of goods and service from producer to consumer in order to satisfy consumers and achieve the firm's objectives. Striving towards consumer satisfaction is the basic philosophy of modern marketing. If a company that is dependent upon the consumer to buy its product does not live by this philosophy, it will fail.

A bread manufacturer might feel quite smug. After all, people must have carbohydrates in their diet in order to survive. Yes, they need carbohydrates, but do they need bread? Bread is not the only source of carbohydrates. Even if it was, his bread is not the only one on the market. The customer in the typical supermarket can choose between a vast assortment of bread put out by a variety of manufacturers. Today's customer doesn't "need" his particular brand of bread. The lady wheeling her shopping cart down the aisle may not realize it, but when she picks up a loaf of bread she has said to one company "You have done well—I like your product" and has shown her indifference or displeasure to the other manufacturers by not choosing their products.

Steuart Henderson Britt in his book *The Spenders* summed up the philosophy that marketing men in our age of abundance must live by when he said: *the consumer is king.*

THE PRODUCT

The business firm in our society recognizes its dependence upon the consumer for its continued existence. It manifests this recognition through its marketing efforts. One of the primary tools available to the marketing man in his attempt to satisfy the consumer is the product his firm sells.

What Is a Product?

When a shopper goes to her local supermarket, she sees thousands of products on the shelves. Crackers are an example. What is a cracker? According to the list of ingredients on the side of the box, it is flour, shortening, salt, leavening, and perhaps various other things such as sesame seeds. It is also a particular brand of cracker with a distinctive name, packaged in a box or carton, and sold for a certain price in the store the shopper selected. A cracker is also intangible to the extent that the consumer not only buys the physical attributes contained in the product but also the psychological ones attached to it.

According to Ernest Dichter, President of the Institute for Motivational Research, in his *Handbook of Consumer Motivations:*

> Crackers are psychologically a sort of quick, lazy bread and are consumed as snacks or informally at social gatherings. A good part of their appeal comes from their tactile variety and taste. This implies the rhythmic sound and the sensation they have for the tongue and palate. Together with other products such as nuts or cereals, crackers signify the importance of emotional elements in the food field other than taste.

While thinking about crackers, we can turn our attention to a product that is often used to spread on them—peanut butter. This protein-rich food, which will probably continue to be popular and to serve as a basic part of youngster's diets, is at present made up of peanuts, dextrose, salt, and hydrogenated oil. Peanut butter is symbolic of youth. Kids usually love the stuff—or are made to believe that they love it. Sidney J. Levy told of one interesting incident in an article titled "Symbols by Which We Buy":

> One little 6-year-old boy protested in an interview how he had never liked peanut butter, but that his mother and sister had always insisted that he did, and now he loved it. Apparently a violent bias in favor of peanut butter is suitable to little boys, and may be taken as representing something of the rowdy boyishness of childhood, as against more restrained and orderly foods.

The little fellow's indoctrination probably included a psychological "push" toward chunky as opposed to smooth peanut butter because, as Dr. Levy also pointed out in his article, smoothness is generally understood to be more feminine so, as goods go, it seems fitting that girls should prefer the smooth peanut butter and boys the chunky.

The imagery and symbolism connected with crackers, peanut butter, and all the other foods we eat are just as much a part of them as are their physical ingredients. It is for this reason that a product should be defined much like William J. Stanton did in his book *Fundamentals of Marketing* when he wrote that a product is a complex of tangible and intangible attributes, including packaging, color, price, manufacturer's

The shopper makes her choice. (Courtesy Baking Industry.)

Crackers—just flour, shortening, etc., or more? (Courtesy Nabisco Inc.)

prestige, retailer's prestige, and manufacturer's and retailer's services, which the buyer may accept as offering satisfaction of wants or needs.

Brand

Students of the American West—via reading or devotion to television and motion picture westerns—are familiar with the concept of branding. Ranchers brand their cattle in order to prove ownership. Branding, however, began long before our nation was founded. The guild system, which flourished between 1200 and 1700, perfected its use. Each article produced by a guild member bore the guild mark or brand. Severe and often cruel penalties were enforced against "industrious" individuals who forged a guild's mark. This early form of branding achieved the same results as the modern version.

Definition.   According to the American Marketing Association, a brand is a name, term, symbol, or design or a combination of them which is intended to identify the goods or services of one seller or group of sellers and to differentiate them from those of competitors.

The term brand is comprehensive in that it actually represents a number of more specific terms. A brand name consists of words, letters, or numbers which can be vocalized. Jell-O, Campbell's, and Green Giant are examples of brand names. Brand marks appear as symbols, designs—things that can be recognized but not expressed when a person pronounces the brand. An example of a brand mark would be the friendly *Jolly Green Giant.*

The word trademark is often used synonymously with brand. This is technically incorrect because a trademark is actually a legal term which includes only those brands or brand marks which the law designates as trademarks.

Brand Images.   Brands, like products, produce images in the minds of consumers. Marketing men attempt to make these images "positive" so that their brand will be preferred over the others that are available.

Herta Herzog, when speaking to a group of marketing educators, said that a brand image

. . . is the sum total of impressions the consumer receives from many sources: from actual experience and hearsay about the brand itself as well as its packaging, its name, the company making it, the types of people the individual has seen using the brand, what was said in its advertising, as well as from the tone, format, type of advertising vehicle in which the product story was told.

All these impressions amount to a sort of brand personality which is similar for the consuming public at large although different consumer groups may have different attitudes toward it. . . .

The brand image contains objective product qualities. . . . These qualities themselves have rational as well as symbolic meanings which merge with the meanings created by all the other sources through which the public meets a brand.

What Do We Call It?   The problems a couple encounter in trying to determine the name for their forthcoming baby are similar to those experienced by the marketing man attempting to determine the "correct" name for his product. Some names just came into being by accident. Hannah Campbell, in her book *Why Did They Name It . . . ?* tells how the brand name Maxwell House came into being:

> In 1873 Joel Cheek was a traveling salesman with a wholesale grocery firm. Though he sold a variety of grocery products, coffee held a greater interest for him that any of the others from the very beginning. While on the road he often thought about trying his hand at developing his own blend of coffee. . . .
>
> Several years later he got his wish. . . . At first he limited his experiments to his spare time, but gradually they demanded more and more of his working day. . . . In 1882 he quit the partnership . . and after more years of experiments, found the blend of coffee that had fired his imagination.
>
> One of the South's finest hotels at this time was the Maxwell House in Nashville. . . . Joel Cheek went to this hotel one day and proudly offered them the new blend of coffee. The management decided to try it and within weeks the guests in the magnificent dining room were talking about the marvelous new coffee. "This Maxwell House coffee, sir," they said, "is superb!"

Although business has undergone a radical change since Mr. Cheek developed his blend of coffee, many companies still leave the choice of a brand name up to chance and hope for a flash of inspiration. Other more realistic firms do not leave names up to chance. They realize that a brand's name is extremely important to its performance in the marketplace. As was stated by Lippincott & Margulies, Inc. in their article "The Name's the Thing," which appeared in *Design Sense 24:*

> As products, services, even companies have become more alike in function, and appearance, the name has assumed new significance. Often it is the sole

The evolution of a brand mark—a trademark owned by the Green Giant Company (1926, 1960, 1970.)

*Different products,
different packages.*

*Products, brands—each
with their own identity.
(Courtesy Advertising Age.)*

tangible, differentiating element between one brand and another. In many cases, it is the only permanent tool which advertising, promotion, publicity and packaging can use to create the . . . brand identity . . . the product image.

There is a great degree of latitude available in terms of selecting a name, but as was stated in the Lippincott & Margulies article, it will not do its job unless it possesses three basic elements:

1. The appeal of both sight and sound.
2. The prospects of long-term consumer equity.
3. The expression of a specific unique image.

Sight appeal simply means that the name has to look good if it is to appear on packages, in ads, and on signs. Sound appeal, according to Lippincott & Margulies, is even more important than sight appeal; methods of word reproduction may change, but the sound of words does not. Marketing men may turn to the science of language—philology—for guidance. If a hard-selling message is desired, then hard, abrupt consonants such as *b*'s, *t*'s, and *k*'s should be used. To make a soft impression, sibilants such as *s*, *ch*, and *z* should be used. Long-term consumer equity simply means that the customer will never tire of the name. It will come about naturally if sight and sound appeal and a positive product image are attained.

One other element should be added to the list—protectability. In light of the tremendous amount of time and money invested in the development of a brand and its image, the manufacturer makes every effort to ensure that he has exclusive rights to it. The Lanham Act of 1947 aids the manufacturer in this regard. If his brand mark and/or name complies with a number of requirements, he will be allowed to register them in the U.S. They then become legal trademarks and are made the legal property of the manufacturer. The manufacturer, therefore, must come up with a name that meets the Lanham Act's requirements in order to protect his investment.

One of the great fears of any manufacturer is that his product's name will become generic—descriptive of a type of product—and he will lose legal rights to it. In cases such as this, the courts can rule that the name has lost its distinctiveness and become part of the public domain. Shredded wheat, for example, was once a name owned by the National Biscuit Company, but the courts ruled that it had become generic in nature and therefore no longer protectable under law.

Private Brands.   Private or store brands account for a very sizeable portion of food products sold. They are an especially important factor in canned goods. Most of the larger chain stores have had products produced under their own brand names for quite some time.

Several factors have accounted for the popularity of these brands. One is the fact that the stores can make a higher profit on the products carrying their own brand name than they can on manufacturer's brands and still sell them for less.

The consumer plays an important role here, also. Many shoppers are aware of the fact that the store's brand is usually produced by large, well-known manufacturers. The consumer has also become more sophisticated; she is beginning to depend on her ability to determine the quality of a product regardless of the brand name it carries. When asked "How would you compare brand name canned goods to private label canned goods?" in a survey done by the Chicago *Tribune,* one shopper answered:

> Pricewise a private label is cheaper, but the quality is the same or close to it. You actually pay for the advertising of the brand name, whereas for the private label you don't.

Nevertheless, manufacturer's brand names still account for the largest portion of total sales. People continue to prefer them. As one respondent to the *Tribune* stated when asked the same question:

> I think the name labels taste better. I am used to the brand name and when I change I don't like it as well. The brand name would be a higher price and has a better quality.

Packaging

The idea of placing products in containers to move them from one place to another has been with us since ancient times. Skins or leaves probably served as the first form of container. As civilization developed, so did man's development and use of materials for holding and transporting goods.

The beginning of modern packaging is generally attributed to a Parisian chef and confectioner, Nicholas Appert. In 1808, motivated by Napoleon's offer of 12,000 francs for a method of preserving food to feed his army, Appert developed a process that involved the use of a glass container.

The advent of mass production in centralized locations and the subsequent shipping of products to distant distributors heralded the need for new and better packaging. This need was not immediately met. Well into the twentieth century, most products were still packed in bulk containers.

We can all picture what it must have been like in the "good old days" around the general store. Everything had to be counted out or weighed. The cracker barrel, the flour sacks, the big old pickle barrel—a part of the past we are much better off without. The crackers in the barrel were often stale long before the consumer purchased them; the flour sacks attracted rodents; and who knows what dropped into the pickle barrel!

A New Area.   Although packaging has its roots deep in the past, the greatest growth in terms of innovation in the field has taken place in the last 25 years. The prime stimulus for this growth was the development of the supermarket. Inherent in the operation of the supermarket is the concept of self-service. The friendly grocery store clerk that gathered all the things the customer wanted while she waited for them is a thing of the past. The customer is now on her own. Businessmen realize that the package now is an important marketing tool, for it acts as an in-store salesman. The package must get the customer to stop and pick it off the shelf from among a number of competing products. The package does not work alone, for it is only part of the entire product, but it plays an extremely important role.

What the Consumer Wants.   The consumer has some very definite ideas about what she wants a package to do for her. According to Curt Kornblau in a paper delivered to the American Marketing Association:

. . . above all the consumer seems to want convenience and utility.

Consumers expect the package to protect the contents and keep them at their flavorful best. They want packages that are easy to open, easy to use and easy to close. They are less than happy with pry-off tops, set-in lids, cans that open with a key, packages that leak, . . . "Press here to open" directions which seem entirely unrelated to the facts.

Consumers want packages that will fit on the shelves of the average home and won't topple open because of poor design. They want information on the package that will help them decide whether to purchase the product and, having purchased it, how to use it.

Consumers want honest value. They are not favorably impressed, for example, with misleading information as to the number of servings in a package.

Business Answers.   Marketing men are well aware of what the consumer demands in the way of packaging, and they are making every effort to give it to them. New and better methods of packaging are constantly being developed. Before the end of World War II, meats and produce were seldom packaged for the consumer. Today, with the widespread use of plastics for bags and shrink-pack plastic films, the majority of meats and a large portion of the produce is sold in premeasured quantities, thereby making this part of the shopping trip much easier and more convenient.

Another new concept is the aerosol can. It was developed in 1942 by Lyle D. Goodhue in his attempts to develop a better method of controlling insects, which caused large numbers of our soldiers to contract tropical diseases during World War II. Today the aerosol can is used in a number of food product applications, such as cake frostings and cheese spreads.

Caution Needed.   Consumers do not necessarily accept all innovations as being good. This is especially true of packaging in the food area. People take eating very seriously. Consequently, they are often wary of changes. This caution is generated by the product, their feelings toward it, and the package.

While packaging of produce, for example, is being done in more and more stores, many customers are not too happy about it. Their discontent varies by product. The *Progressive Grocer* consumer dynamics study found that, while 78% of the shoppers interviewed preferred to have their carrots prepackaged, only 52% liked to buy lettuce that was already packaged and only 14% liked their peaches in some form of package. Walter P. Margulies discussed this factor in relation to ketchup bottles in his book *Packaging Power:*

> Look at ketchup bottles. Could a container be less utilitarian? However delicious, the contents are stubbornly molasseslike at cool temperatures. The amount of ketchup we might want is difficult, if not impossible to measure accurately in advance.
> Designers have naturally addressed themselves to the problem of the

ketchup bottle. The difficulties are obvious and many solutions are easy to reach. But in spite of higher utility, and economic and aesthetic superiority, new designs have been market failures. Ketchup that isn't in a ketchup bottle is viewed with suspicion by the public.

Beyond Convenience and Utility. Marketing men are concerned with giving the customer what he or she wants in the way of packaging. The wants and needs of the consumer, however, go beyond the physical aspects of the package and its features.

The package, like all the other elements of the product, plays an important role in shaping the image the consumer has of a particular brand. As was stated earlier, the package has been playing a much more important role in shaping the image of the brand in the consumer's mind due to the increase in self-service in supermarkets. In other words, the package must act as a communicator to the consumer. As Burleigh B. Gardner, President of Social Research, Inc., said in "The Package as a Communication":

> When we talk about a package as a communication, we are referring to a complex set of reactions in the mind of the beholder, all of which contribute to a feeling about the product inside. The nature of this feeling can contribute to the anticipation of what the product will be like and the satisfaction it will provide. In the case of many food and beverage products the package may actually affect the sensory response to the product. Thus the same soft drink in different bottles may taste different. With high volume consumer items, where there are many competing brands, even subtle differences in package communication can have an important impact on sales.

According to Gardner, there are four factors which affect a package's ability to communicate:

1. Material used
2. Form or shape
3. Colors used
4. Label

The Material. Mr. Gardner stated that

> . . . There are distinct differences in the meanings and imagery evoked by different materials. Thus, metal arouses feelings different than plastic, paperboard or glass. Each evokes a different set of associations ranging from

descriptive realism, i.e., hard, brittle, to the nonrational, emotion-laden ideas such as purity or warmth.

The Form. The consumer perceives and often accepts or rejects products on the basis of the physical shape of their package. Ernest Dichter in his book *Handbook of Consumer Motivations* tells about a test designed to determine the consumers' preference for various shapes of meat packages:

> Ground beef was put into three different types of packages. One was a well-structured rectangular package; the second was semistructured, flat, broken, and circular; and the third was completely unstructured, an amorphous-appearing mass. All three types were wrapped in the same material. The packages were arranged in random order and the housewives were asked to indicate their first and second choices. The overwhelming preference was for the structured package.

The Color. Color is an extremely important factor in communication to the consumer. As Walter Margulies states in his book *Packaging Power:*

> . . . Color is not only a visual perception, but a multisensory experience. People "feel" color as well as see it. Indeed, some people even hear color.
>
> Green is the symbol of abundance and health. . . . Green offers a perfect example of package color reflecting product in its almost universal application to green-vegetable containers.
>
> Orange is perhaps the most "edible" color, especially in its brown-tinged shades. It is evocative of autumn, pumpkins, and harvest; of things well cooked and good to eat.

The Label. The label is generally considered to be part of the package. Its primary function is to communicate to the consumer facts about the product inside the package; but as Gardner points out, the label also portrays a visual communication in two dimensions—form and color. The colors interact with the form in order to present a total configuration.

Packaging and the Public Good. It was stated earlier that consumers demand honest value. They are particularly unhappy with what they consider to be misleading information. The government has done a number of things to insure fair value for the consumer.

The Food and Drug Act of 1906 and its 1938 amendment, the Food, Drug, and Cosmetic Act, provided for regulations for labeling, but these were not totally satisfactory, so in 1966 Congress enacted the Fair Packaging and Labeling Act. This law provides for the Food and Drug Administration and Federal Trade Commission to set packaging regulations which they believe are necessary. It also makes labeling mandatory and allows industry voluntarily to adopt packaging standards which limit the multiple weights and measures that were being used.

There are many concerned citizens who believe that still more must be done in this area. Consumer protection groups throughout the country have brought to light many practices that they consider deceptive or fraudulent. Their protests have been instrumental in many changes that are now being instituted.

One of the changes is a move toward unit pricing. The average grocery shopper finds it next to impossible to compare prices between two brands of the same product if the packages contain different amounts of the product being evaluated. Unit pricing—showing the price per ounce, pound, quart, or other unit of measure—allows the shopper to determine which of the brands under consideration gives the best value for the money.

Another change that will have important consequences in the future is nutritional labeling. Under the Fair Packaging and Labeling Act, food made of two or more ingredients had to have those ingredients listed by their common or usual names in order of their predominance in the food. While this was a step in the right direction, many concerned individuals and groups pointed out that the consumer still did not have enough information to make a rational choice. Their efforts resulted in research and discussion and culminated in revised nutritional labeling regulations. Thus, all products which are fortified as well as those that make nutritional or dietary claims on their labels or in advertising must comply with the regulations. For all other food products, use of nutritional labeling is still voluntary. The following information must appear on the nutritional label:

- Servings in the container and the size of the servings.
- The amount of calories, protein, carbohydrates, and fat in each serving.
- The percentage of the U.S. Recommended Daily Allowances (U.S.

RDA) of protein, vitamins, and minerals in each serving. The vitamins and minerals that must be listed if the product contains more than 2% of the U.S. RDA are: vitamin A, vitamin C, thiamine, riboflavin, niacin, calcium, and iron. The list may also include: vitamin D, vitamin E, vitamin B_6, folic acid, vitamin B_{12}, phosphorus, and iodine.

These changes reflect needs in our society. Unfortunately, those most in need of this type of information are often the least able to use it because of lack of training. A tremendous amount of consumer education will be necessary. This process promises to take a long time because the "typical" consumer often does not take time to shop and compare prices and is very naive about the nutrients required by the human body.

Americans are also becoming quite conscious of the environment and the fact that it is in many ways being damaged. As Carol White in an *Advertising Age* article stated:

> . . . In the past few years, ecology has become a much more important consideration in making, marketing and disposing of packaging.
> The problem is double-edged: first, to make effective packaging without creating pollutants or raping our already depleted resources (this is where recycling comes in), and second, to dispose of what can't be reused in a way that doesn't disturb our delicately balanced environment.

Business is becoming aware of these problems and is beginning to face up to them. A great deal of research is being done on "ecologically sound" packaging materials, and companies are aiding local and national efforts to correct the damage that has already been done. Nevertheless, much more needs to be done and done in the very near future.

Price

The fourth factor that goes into making up the consumer's image of a product is the price he must pay to obtain it. Every consumer, to some extent, is concerned with the prices that he must pay for they act as limiting forces upon his unlimited wants. Alfred Oxenfeldt, et al. in *Insights into Pricing* reveal that attitudes about prices (actually the money that they represent) are formed in very early childhood long before the individual really understands their significance. These attitudes are very strong. Young children often look forward to a visit by an uncle or aunt who usually rewards them with a shiny dime or quarter.

Children can also sense the tension that may arise in a family because of a lack of money. The emotionalism of the situation is communicated to them.

The adult consumer's attitudes toward money and prices are based on the ones they formulated quite early in life. Some lead to miserliness, others to extravagance—but they are always strong. For this reason, some people place price at the forefront in their decisions concerning the purchase of a product, while others relegate it to a much lesser position.

The Economic Man.   When price is discussed, it is natural to think of turning to the economist, for this is his area of specialization. He should have the answers. He does—to a point. The economist generally considers the consumer to be an economic man—an individual who possesses all the information available in order to make a decision, which is based solely on rational motives devoid of any emotion. Unfortunately, the consumer rarely has all the information available on any given product and emotion often plays a very important part in the decision to buy a product.

Information.   Food as a general category is one area where the consumer usually has a great deal of information. She buys products each week so she has a chance to determine the quality of one brand over another to a certain degree. But even in areas of assumed expertise, the consumer is often lacking in information and therefore turns to some other measure of quality.

Numerous studies have shown that consumers consider the price of a product to be an indicator of quality. In a study conducted by J. D. McConnel, subjects were given numerous chances over an extended period to select among three brands of beer. The beers were identical except for prices and their hypothetical brand names. The majority of the people involved selected the higher priced beer over the other brands and gave it the most favorable ratings in terms of quality. Obviously, the saying "you only get what you pay for" is applied as a guideline by consumers in a great number of buying decisions.

Psychological Factors.   Why does this or that product cost 98c? Obviously, the price reflects the cost of producing, shipping, and marketing the product along with a profit margin for everyone involved in the process. But psychological factors are also taken into considera-

Don't be confused.
All cans are recyclable...

steel cans most of all.

Recycling is "old hat" to the steel industry. For the past 30 years, more than half the raw material used to make new steel has been old steel. Today's cans and cars and carpet tacks and thousands of other products are made from steel recycled from yesterday's cars and carpet tacks and thousands of other products—58 *billion* pounds' worth last year alone.

What's new is the steel industry's program to help collect used cans—all kinds of cans—and to recycle all the steel cans it can get.

Tinplate Producers
American Iron and Steel Institute

STEEL—<u>the</u> recycled material.

Business works with the ecology movement. (Courtesy the American Iron and Steel Institute.)

tion. In "The Psychological Aspects of Price," Chester R. Wasson discussed three psychological aspects of price that are of interest:

1. Quantum effects
2. Reverse direction perception
3. Fair price comparisons

Quantum Effects.   Wasson states that:

> This phenomenon takes its name from a principle long known in physics: under certain conditions, the effect of light energy is not continuous, but sometimes has to build up to a certain point to work, then causes a disproportionate end result. A parallel price effect phenomenon is familiar to every supermarket operator. A given product may not move at $1.05 but a package containing only four-fifths as much, clearly labeled as to quantity will readily sell at 98¢. One dollar is a quantum point as far as its customers are concerned.

Reverse Direction Perception.   Numbers often seem to possess magical qualities because of the manner in which people perceive them. As Wasson states, a $2.95 price may look cheaper to the buyers than a $2.45 price, a 29c price may look like less than 24c. A price that is actually higher on the numerical scale often proves to be lower on the consumer's psychological scale.

Fair Price Standards.   Consumers attempt to gain as much information about a product as possible. Often there is very little available. In order to come to a decision, consumers may determine psychologically what they believe a fair price to be and often will not pay more—or less— for it. Wasson gave an example of a product originally priced at $1.19. The manufacturers decided that sales were not high enough, so they tried an experiment with the price. They selected three groups of stores. In one group, the product was priced at $.89; in another, at $1.09; in the third, at $1.29. The stores selling the product for $1.09 sold far greater quantities than the stores with the lower and higher prices. Consumers felt that $1.09 was the "right" price. They probably considered the $.89 price too low to be a quality item and the $1.19 or higher too much money for that particular product.

The Retail Outlet

The words "retail outlet" in today's food industry are almost synonymous with the term supermarket. There is good cause for this equation. *Progressive Grocer's* 38th Annual Report of the Grocery Industry shows that 75.4% of all grocery sales in 1970 were made by supermarkets. The supermarket is actually a relatively new method of retailing food. According to Rom J. Markin in his book *The Supermarket: An Analysis of Growth, Development, and Change,* prior to the 1920's, the grocery business was the most backward form of retailing. Consumers had to go from one specialized shop to another for the products they desired. This meant trips to the butcher shop, the bakery, and the produce store. But things began to change in the 1920's because of changes in the environment.

The people of our nation were beginning to move from the farms to the cities in search of jobs. As a result, the market for products in geographically small areas was expanding, and the jobs in the cities generated higher incomes. As incomes rose, tastes for new and different foods came into evidence. Home refrigeration by electrical means did much to change the environment. The consumer no longer was forced to shop every day for perishable products. In addition, the automobile was to a large extent responsible for the development and rapid growth of the one-stop, complete food market. No longer were people confined to their immediate vicinity. The automobile allowed them to go to new shopping areas and make larger purchases.

As Markin points out, the supermarket evolved slowly through time. A number of distinct concepts helped to develop it into the institution we know today. One of these early concepts was cash and carry. This was an unusual departure from the accepted system. Normally customers ran weekly and monthly accounts, and even small orders were delivered. Another important innovation was self-service. Improved packaging methods and quality control made this method of shopping acceptable to the consumer.

As the supermarket became the accepted retail outlet for food, the small, independent grocery stores that at one time could be found in every neighborhood began to close their doors. They could not compete with the vast selections and low prices of the larger stores.

It is interesting to note that one of the strong points of the supermarket when it began—convenience—has caused a resurgence of the neighborhood store in a new form. The idea of going to a supermarket and standing in check-out lines for a loaf of bread or a carton of soft drinks is not very appealing to the consumer. Neighborhood stores— or more correctly convenience stores—which are often run by a husband and wife team have stepped in to fill this void. Located in high population areas, these stores stay open long hours—sometimes 24 hours 7

Retail outlets changed with the times, from 1899 to 1927 to 1970. (Courtesy the National Tea Company.)

In-store displays like this help increase sales. (Courtesy Procter and Gamble Co.)

days a week—in order to serve their customers. They have proven to be very acceptable to the consumer, as indicated by their growing numbers and increased sales. In 1957, according to *Progressive Grocer*, they accounted for .2% of total grocery sales, or $75 million. In 1970, they held 3.0% of the market—$2.6 billion in sales!

What the Shopper Looks for.   In all metropolitan areas of any size, the shopper is confronted with a large number of grocery stores. Yet invariably there is one store that she patronizes almost exclusively. The reasons for her selection of one store over another will vary based on age, income, and a host of other demographic and psychological factors, but certain generalizations can be drawn. The Chicago Tribune study of food shoppers in the Chicagoland area is most revealing. When consumers were asked why they shopped at a particular store more than any other, they gave the responses shown in the following table.

Reasons for Shopping at Primary Store*

	% of shoppers giving this reason
Closeness/Location	62
Selection	46
Value	37
Habit	35
Quality	35
Meat quality	30
Parking	29
Produce quality	20
Stamps	8

*Source: Chicago *Tribune* Study, *All About Food, The Chicago-land Woman and Her Grocery Store*, 1970, p. 21.

No one reason can be selected as *the* determinant in store selection. The following quote from the *Tribune* study shows how interrelated the factors are in the final choice.

I know where things are. It seems to carry all the brands that I like. It is closer to me. Because of the drugs and all their other little departments, like household things, I'd say they have a wide variety of things, of not only foods. It also has a mail box close to it and that's a dumb reason, but I always have something to mail; and because they cash checks there.

Store Image.   The factors given in the *Tribune* study are evaluative in their nature. They are used by the consumer for comparing one store with another. Theoretically, an objective study could compare stores based on these criteria, and one would emerge as the "best." This would ultimately result in the "best" store receiving all the customers while neighboring stores would be forced to close their doors. Yet in many areas, competing stores all manage to obtain a certain percentage of the available consumers and all survive. This occurs because the consumer's perception of a store—the image that it generates—may be quite different from its "score" if it were subjected to an objective evaluation.

In their book *Consumer Behavior*, Engel, Kollat, and Blackwell gave six factors that help to form a store's image in the mind of the consumer. They are:

1. Price
2. Advertising
3. Product and service mix
4. Store personnel
5. Physical attributes
6. Store clientele

Price.   The price level for a given store or chain is one of the determinants of the image it produces in the mind of the consumer. Price is an objective factor, yet the price level perceived by the customer and the objective or actual price may be quite different. As Engel, Kollat, and Blackwell state, consumers often form their image about a store's prices more on the basis of advertising, displays, advertising specials, and physical layout than from the actual level of the store.

Advertising.   The late Pierre Martineau pointed up the importance of advertising in image production in his book *Motivation In Advertising* when he stated:

> Whether he (the retailer) realizes it consciously or not, all of his advertising is creating an image of his store. One of the most important functions in the housewife's role is to know the stores. She learns to single out certain cues in the advertising which will tell her about the store's status . . . its general atmosphere, its customer body, even its physical qualities; and then she decides intuitively whether this is where she fits in.

Product and Service Mix. The products and services offered to the shopper help to determine the image that it generates in the mind of the consumer. In a recent interview, a shopper was asked why she picked one store over another that was closer to her home. She replied that the one closer to home carried a number of different brands "nice for people that feel that they must have this kind of canned corn or that kind of cake mix" but that their prices were higher and she refused to pay the difference because her family would "only eat the same old things week after week—no chance to get fancy."

Store Personnel. Engel, Kollat, and Blackwell state that:

> A store sometimes takes on the character of the clerks, stock boys, and those management personnel who are seen by customers. The way clerks react to customers sometimes characterizes a store as friendly, impersonal, helpful, up-to-date, or disinterested.

Physical Attributes. The physical attributes of the store tend to reinforce the consumer's perceptions of other image-producing factors or cause them to be questioned. When considering the exterior of the store, Walters and Paul in their book *Consumer Behavior An Integrated Framework* stated that:

> The architecture, signs, and windows and doors, as well as the general condition of the building, all speak to consumers. The architecture of the exterior sets the image theme. Materials such as steel and aluminum still tend to be viewed as modern but cold. Concrete and glass are seen as modern but warm building materials.

The interior of the store must be coordinated with the exterior in order to present one image to the consumer. The arrangement of shelves, islands, special displays, the color of the walls and floors, and the type and intensity of lighting all go into making up the store's image. Through these factors, a store can create the image of being bright, clean and modern or become classified as crowded, dingy, and dirty.

Store Clientele. Consumers are very much aware of their fellow shoppers. Since individuals tend to belong to distinct social groups, it is only natural for them to choose the grocery store they shop at in light of the influence exerted by the group members. These influences tend to help form the image of the store in the minds of the consumers and allow them to know in which store they do and do not "belong."

PROMOTION

Promotion is the last major factor that must be covered in order to complete our overview of the influence business has on man and the food he eats. Kernan, Dommermuth, and Sommers define promotion as any identifiable effort on the part of a seller to persuade buyers to accept the seller's information. They go on to state that:

> the central element in this definition is persuasion. Would-be buyers must be persuaded of both the meaning and the value of seller's products or services. This requires communication of information—either directly from the seller to the buyer or from the seller to some intermediary who can be expected to influence the buyer.

Promotion of food is undertaken by both the original seller of the products—manufacturers—and intermediaries—the grocery stores.

Types of Promotion

The word promotion is used to denote a number of different "tools" that are available. In the food industry, the two primary tools used by both manufacturers and retailers are advertising and sales promotion.

Advertising.   According to the American Marketing Association, advertising is

> ... any paid form of nonpersonal presentation and promotion of ideas, goods, or services by an identified sponsor. It involves the use of such media as the following:
>
> Magazine and newspaper space
> Outdoor (posters, signs, skywriting, etc.)
> Direct mail
> Radio and television
> Programs and menus
> Circulars
>
> This list is intended to be illustrative, not all inclusive.

Manufacturers of food products that are distributed nationally and have wide appeal to a multitude of consumers may use all or most of the media listed above in an attempt to persuade consumers to buy their products. The stores, however, limit the types of media they use because their market is local rather than national in scope.

The primary medium used by grocery stores is newspaper advertising. This medium evokes immediate response by the reader. Most advertising by grocery stores in newspapers plays upon this sense of immediacy. Each week, usually on Wednesday, a large number of retailers have their ads displayed. According to the Supermarket Institute, 63% of their total members' advertising is placed in Wednesday's paper. The ads are usually quite crowded and are price oriented. They are designed to shout "sale" to the consumer and allow for price comparisons.

Not everyone in the food industry is convinced that this creative strategy is the correct one to follow. In *Chain Store Age*, D. Parson's keynote address to a National American Wholesale Grocers Association meeting was quoted as follows:

> Supermarket ads are directed at the consumer audience of 35 years ago, and talk to the housewife as if she were on relief.
>
> But the days of dramatic price comparisons (with the corner grocery) are long since gone, now that supermarket is competing against supermarket.

Creative strategy is changing, but it is taking place very slowly. As Markin pointed out in his book:

> . . . Greater attention is being placed on the selection of the items, size of advertisements, art work, and other factors. Some operators, in a bid to gain increased customer acceptance and appeal in their food advertisements, are moving rapidly to the use of color in newspapers.
>
> Others in an effort to increase the effectiveness of their newspaper advertisements, are going to the dramatic use of illustration, increased white space, variety of type sizes, and humorous cartoons.

The second most important medium for local retailers is handbills and circulars. They can be tailored to the store's creative strategy and be distributed to people in the immediate vicinity of the store—the most likely customers.

Radio is also used as a medium, but it has some distinct drawbacks for the retailer. He can only advertise a limited number of products in a given commercial and must pay for "deaf ears" since many listeners are distant from his store and do not represent potential customers.

Television suffers from the same drawbacks that radio does in the eyes of the individual retailers. The problems are actually magnified in the case of television because the audience is usually larger and more geographically scattered. Nevertheless, television and radio are used and often quite effectively by chain stores that have a number of stores throughout a viewing or listening area.

Sales Promotion.   The American Marketing Association defines sales promotion as

> . . . those marketing activities other than personal selling, advertising, and publicity that stimulate consumer purchasing and dealer effectiveness, such as display . . . demonstrations, and various nonrecurrent selling efforts not in the ordinary routine.

According to Markin, the most often used forms of in-store supermarket promotion activities are: in-store displays; premiums; trading stamps; and contests.

In-Store Displays.   It is difficult to enter any grocery store without being visually bombarded by in-store displays. Special displays can usually be found in any area that might be left vacant—along windows, on the end of aisles, and often in the aisle itself—along with special displays in the regular display areas.

There is a reason for all of these displays. Most importantly, these displays catch the consumer's eye, and it has often been proven that they lead to a tremendous increase in the sale of the displayed product. As Markin points out, some of the other reasons for their increased use are:

- To increase sales of related product lines
- For decorative purposes; enhance the appearance of the store
- To create a buying psychology on the part of the customer through psychological techniques of mass, color, and arrangement
- To create a "price" atmosphere

The manufacturers, through their salesmen, help the retailer plan and set up store displays. They furnish posters, racks, etc., to aid the retailers and thereby aid their own cause.

Premiums.   Another form of sales promotion that is usually inspired by the manufacturers is the use of premiums. Open up any magazine and you will find a coupon allowing a bargain price on some product. Coupons are also given in newspapers or sent to the consumer's home. Retailers look upon this tool with mixed emotions. While premiums or coupons increase their sales, they have a great deal of paperwork associated with them—paperwork that takes up time.

Trading Stamps.   The concept of giving trading stamps was developed around the turn of the century, but it was not until the mid-1950's that they really came into their own. Retailers in search of an added incentive to give to customers saw the trading stamp as the answer. Store after store employed stamps because they did not want their competitors to lure customers away. The use of stamps, however, has been declining in recent years. According to *Progressive Grocer* in their 38th Annual Report of the Grocery Industry:

> When the majority of supermarkets offered stamps in the early 1960's, their ability to attract customers leveled off. As prices began to increase in 1966, retailers began to drop stamps in favor of low prices, a trend still in operation.

Contests.   Contests, like trading stamps, are attempts by the retailer to keep his present customers and to lure new ones into his store. Just as in the case of trading stamps, store after store tends to jump on the contest bandwagon when one store or chain introduces the concept into a particular area.

The consumers of today, however, look on contests with mixed emotions. They accept them, but in our cost-conscious world, most of them would rather have a decrease in the prices they pay than a miniscule chance of winning a trip to some far off place in the sun.

STUDY QUESTIONS

STUDY QUESTIONS

1. Why has the consumer become a king in the eyes of businessmen?

2. Differentiate between: a brand name, a brand mark, and a trademark.

3. What elements should be considered by businessmen when naming a product?

4. Do people always act rationally when evaluating the price of a product? Discuss.

5. The best supermarket is not always the best in the eyes of the consumer. Why?

TOPICS FOR INDIVIDUAL INVESTIGATION

1. Study the history of business in the U.S. in greater detail. Show how each phase helped to build the system to its present state.

2. Pretend that you are a particular product and point up the things that consumers look for—and avoid—when selecting "you."

3. Think up a name for a new snack food based on the guidelines given in the chapter.

4. Study the topic of packaging in detail. Take into account both the consumer's desire for convenience and her concern for the ecology of our country.

5. Go to a supermarket and interview a number of people. Determine why they are shopping at that particular store and then compare the answers you received with the reasons given for store selection in the chapter.

REFERENCES AND SUGGESTED READINGS

Alexander, R. S., Compiler. *Marketing Definitions. A Glossary of Marketing Terms.* American Marketing Association, Chicago, 1960.

All About Food—The Chicagoland Woman and Her Grocery Store, Chicago Tribune Company, 1970.

Britt, S. H. *The Spenders.* McGraw-Hill, New York, 1960.

Britt, S. H., Ed. *Consumer Behavior And The Behavioral Sciences Theories and Applications.* John Wiley, New York, 1967.

Britt, S. H., Ed. and J. L. Lubawski, Collaborating Ed. *Consumer Behavior in Theory and in Action.* John Wiley, New York, 1970.

Buell, V. P., Ed. and C. Heyel, Coordinating Ed. *Handbook of Modern Marketing.* McGraw-Hill, New York, 1970.

Buskirk, R. H. *Principles of Marketing, The Management View,* 3rd Ed. Holt, Rinehart & Winston, New York, 1970.

Campbell, M. *Why Did They Name It . . . ?* Fleet Press, New York, 1964.

Consumer Dynamics in the Super Market. Progressive Grocer in cooperation with the R. H. Donnelley Corp. and The Kroger Co., New York, 1966.

Cook, V. J. and T. F. Schutte. *Brand Policy Determination.* Allyn & Bacon, Boston, 1967.

Dichter, E. *Handbook of Consumer Motivations. The Psychology of the World of Objects.* Copyright © 1964 by E. Dichter. Used with permission of McGraw-Hill Book Company, New York.

Engel, J. F., D. T. Kollat, and R. D. Blackwell. *Consumer Behavior.* Holt, Rinehart and Winston, New York, 1968.

Fair Packaging and Labeling Act, Public Law 89–755, 89th Congress S. 985, Nov. 3, 1966.

Gardner, B. The Package as a Communication, in M. S. Moyer and R. F. Vosburgh, *Marketing For Tomorrow . . . Today. 1967 Conference Proceedings.* American Marketing Association, Chicago, 1967.

Gist, R. R. *Marketing and Society A Conceptual Framework.* Holt, Rinehart & Winston, New York, 1971.

Herzog, Herta. Behavioral Science Concepts for Analyzing the Consumer, in Duncan, D. J., Ed. *Proceedings—Conference for Marketing Teachers from Far Western States.* University of California, Berkeley, 1958.

Kassarijian, H. H. and T. S. Robertson. *Perspectives in Consumer Behavior.* Scott, Foresman, Glenview, Ill., 1968.

Kernan, J. B., W. P. Dommermuth, and M. S. Sommers. *Promotion An Introductory Analysis.* Copyright © by J. B. Kernan, W. P. Dommermuth, and M. S. Sommers 1970. Used with permission of McGraw-Hill Book Company, New York.

Kornblau, C. Packaging and Supermarkets: The Package in the Market Place, in G. L. Baker, Jr., Ed., *Effective Marketing Coordination. Proceedings of the 44th National Conference.* American Marketing Association, Chicago, 1961.

Kotler, P. *Marketing Management Analysis, Planning and Control.* Prentice-Hall, Englewood Cliffs, N.J., 1967.

Levy, S. J. *Promotional Behavior.* Scott, Foresman, Glenview, Ill., 1971.

Levy, S. J. Symbols by Which We Buy, in Stockman, L. H., Ed., *Advancing Marketing Efficiency. 41st National Conference.* American Marketing Association, Chicago, 1958.

Lubawski, J. L. The Consumer in the Marketplace, J. C. Penney's *Forum* Spring/Summer, pp. 18–19, 1971.

Mandell, M. I. *Advertising.* Prentice-Hall, Englewood Cliffs, N.J., 1968.

Margulies, W. P. *Packaging Power.* Copyright © 1970 by Walter P. Margulies. Reprinted by permission of The World Publishing Company.

Markin, R. J. *The Supermarket: An Analysis of Growth, Development, and Change,* Revised Ed. Washington State Univ. Press, Pullman, Washington, 1968.

Martineau, P. *Motivation In Advertising.* Copyright © 1957 by P. Martineau. Used with permission of McGraw-Hill Book Company, New York.

McConnel, J. D. The Price-Quality Relationship in an Experimental Setting. *Journal of Marketing Research* Vol. 5, pp. 300–303, 1968.

Miracle, M. P. Market Structure in Commodity Trade and Capital Accumulation in West Africa, in R. Moyer and S. C. Hollander, *Markets and Marketing in Developing Economies.* Richard D. Irwin, Homewood, Ill., 1968.

New Look for Chain Ads. *Chain Store Age* Vol. 45 pp. 66–67, April, 1969.

Oxenfeldt, A., D. Miller, A. Shuchman, and C. Winick. *Insights into Pricing from Operations Research and Behavioral Science.* Wadsworth, Belmont, Cal., 1965.

Preston, L. E. *Markets and Marketing An Orientation.* Scott, Foresman, Glenview, Ill., 1970.

Preston, L. E., Ed. *Social Issues in Marketing.* Scott, Foresman, Glenview Ill., 1968.

Robertson, T. S. *Consumer Behavior.* Scott, Foresman, Glenview, Ill., 1970.

Sandage, C. H. and V. Fryburger. *Advertising Theory and Practice,* 8th Edition. Richard D. Irwin, Homewood, Ill., 1971.

Stanton, W. J. *Fundamentals of Marketing,* 3rd Edition. McGraw-Hill, New York, 1971.

Super Market Institute, *The Super Market Industry Speaks. Eighteenth Annual Report.* Super Market Institute, Chicago, 1966.

The Name's The Thing. *Design Sense 24.* Lippincott & Margulies.

Thirty-Eighth Annual Report of the Grocery Industry. *Progressive Grocer* Vol. 50, pp. 59–106, April, 1971.

Tomorrow's Corporate Marketing Operations. A Symposium. Marketing Committee, National Association of Manufacturers, December 1968.

Wasson, C. R. *The Economics of Managerial Decision: Profit Opportunity Analysis.* Appleton-Century-Crofts, 1965.

Walters, C. G. and G. W. Paul. *Consumer Behavior an Integrated Framework.* Richard D. Irwin, Homewood, Ill., 1970.

White, C. Ecology Switches Signals for Food Package: "Self-destruct." Reprinted with with permission from the November 1, 1971 issue of *Advertising Age.* Vol. 42, No. 44, p. 54. Copyright 1971 by Crain Communications, Inc.

Wish, J. R. and S. H. Gamble, Eds. *Marketing and Social Issues: An Action Reader.* John Wiley, New York, 1971.

7

Chronic
Hunger

Hunger is a condition of misery and suffering, a condition of human degradation. The effects of it reach around the world—to those who suffer its wretchedness and also to those who escape it—for hunger is the concern of men of goodwill everywhere.

Hunger is not an uncommon condition. In 1966, Fischnich of the Food and Agriculture Organization reported that 20% of the people in the less-developed areas were hungry and that 50% manifested evidences of specific nutritional deficiencies. In 1971, the FAO, reporting on the state of food and agriculture, indicated that, since 1967 in all developing regions except the Far East, the trend in per caput food production has been stable or falling, giving reason for concern. The effects of hunger on the physical condition of individuals, the behavioral changes observed during experimental hunger, the possible influences of

269

hunger on mental development, the Biafra famine, and Hunger-U.S.A. are dealt with in this chapter. Causes for the existing prevalence of hunger will be discussed, as will some programs now in operation in various countries aimed at lessening the incidence of hunger.

THE TERMINOLOGY OF HUNGER

Thus far we have spoken only of hunger. A term sometimes used synonymously is undernutrition. Both are interpreted to signify the effect of the intake of an insufficient quantity of food. When there is hunger, there is undernutrition. However, undernutrition may be from causes other than insufficient food—for example, an infection of intestinal parasites which nourish themselves on the nutrients of the host can in some cases prevent normal intestinal absorption.

When there is an inadequacy in the nutritional quality of the diet, deficiency of certain nutrients such as protein, minerals, or vitamins, the term malnutrition is used. Undernutrition and malnutrition are not mutually exclusive; people who are undernourished also may be malnourished. Malnutrition is discussed in Chapter 8.

EFFECTS OF HUNGER ON PHYSICAL STATUS

The effect of hunger on individuals is variable. The response depends on the duration and severity of the lack on the one hand and on the capacity of an individual to adjust to the deprivation on the other.

Growth

Failure to thrive is a sensitive indicator of undernutrition in the young. Children who grow in spite of hunger grow less and so are smaller than well-nourished children of the same age. Economically disadvantaged children, children who live in parts of the world where there is a shortage of food, and children who suffer the results of war and disaster reflect the stunting effect of insufficient food. Meredith of the University of Iowa examined a dozen research studies dealing with growth and economic level. The pattern common to all was that the children of higher-income families were taller and heavier than their counterparts in the lower-income groups. Thus, the children whose parents were in professional and managerial positions were larger than the less economically well-off children of the unskilled and semiskilled workers. And the children who were in school in the better residential districts were larger than the children in schools in the poorer residential areas.

Infants and young children in developing countries present dramatic, even though at this moment rather indirect, evidence of the effect of nutrition on growth. Breast-fed infants in developing countries grow in the early months of life at a rate within the norms established in the U.S. However, a break in the growth rate occurs after six months of age, with the rate falling below the U.S. standards. The cause is believed to be lack of proper food. This pattern was observed in the children of Lebanon. A survey of child-feeding practices in all parts of Lebanon revealed that at six months of age 90% of all infants were at the breast. By one year of age many had begun to sample adult fare. These foods, however, were lower in nutritive value than breast milk and often were carriers of infectious microorganisms.

Experimental studies with animals extend our information on the physical effects of hunger. To be sure, it is always a question as to whether the findings apply to the human, but they at least can be considered indicative. When the diet of experimental animals is restricted so that the body weight is held constant, certain parts of the body are found to persist in growth. In studies using dogs as the experimental animals, the dogs were found to grow longer and taller and leaner. In recent studies with pigs and chicks McCance and his co-workers in England found the weight of the bones, the heart, and the brain to increase in spite of the stationary body weight.

There is the continuing question as to whether restriction of food intake in early life affects the ultimate size attained. The recovery growth of eight children of ages ten months to three years under treatment for marasmus and kwashiorkor was observed in Jamaica. During the recovery period, the children grew 15 times as fast as normal children of the same age and five times as fast as normal children of a similar height and weight. These children attained the expected weight for height; when they reached this size, their food intake fell abruptly and their growth rate dropped to a level comparable to that of normal children of that height and weight.

At the University of Cape Town, South Africa, the growth of 53 children who were admitted to the hospital with kwashiorkor and severe growth retardation at ages one to four years was followed over a period

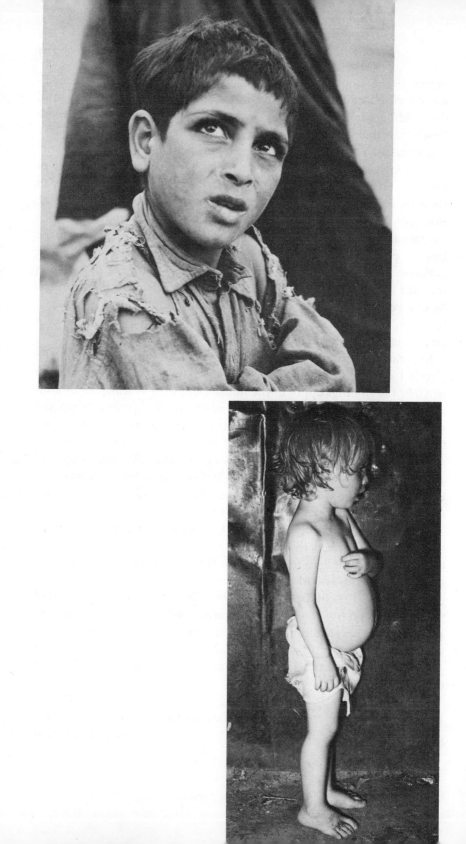

A worried mother brings her child to be treated for malnutrition.
Above. *(Courtesy AID.)*

Hunger—a condition of misery and suffering, of human
degradation. Top left. *(Courtesy Agency for*
International Development.)

Malnutrition in a child of a family of day laborers on
farms. Bottom left. *(Courtesy FSA-HEW.)*

of time. In ten years, approximately one-half of the children were within the normal range for height and weight for age. The reason for the growth failure of the remainder of the children is being investigated. "Long-term observation of malnourished infants suggests that severe caloric deprivation during most of the first year of life is likely to cause permanent stigmata in height and head size," Graham of Johns Hopkins University indicates. And adds that, "An episode of severe protein deficiency, unless accompanied by prolonged and severe caloric restriction, is much less likely to leave permanent defects."

Body Composition

During hunger, there is a loss of fat and protein from the body and an accumulation of water. In the classical Minnesota study of the effects of semistarvation, 32 young men consumed a diet of 1570 kcal over a period of 24 weeks; fat and protein were lost from their bodies. During the first few days of the restricted diet, there was considerable water loss. This loss decreased with the progress of the experiment, reaching a point where there was water retention (Table 1). It has been observed that in severely malnourished infants the water content is approximately 85% of the body weight, whereas the normal is around 65%.

Bones also change in composition with hunger, becoming more fragile. Radiographs of 95 infants and children hospitalized in Guatemala City with protein-calorie deficiency showed a picture of juvenile osteoporosis. It is the type of weakening observed in animals with experimentally produced protein-calorie deficiency.

Pregnancy

Fertility does not appear to be impaired by undernutrition. Casual observations indicate this situation, and demographic studies give circumstantial evidence of it. In the developing countries where hunger exists, the annual birth rate was estimated to be about 40 per 1000 population in 1963. In the other countries of the world, the annual birth rate was estimated to be about 17 per 1000 population.

During World War II, a careful study of the problems of fertility and and pregnancy in relation to nutrition in the Colony of Singapore was made. Food was scarce and expensive. There was no evidence that fertility was reduced. However, when the deprivation was near starvation level in Rotterdam and The Hague in the winter of 1944 and the spring

TABLE 1   Composition of Body Weight Loss at
Successive Periods of Undernutrition (Mean Values)

| Days | Percentage of total loss in | | |
	Fat	Protein	Water
Experiment—53 days			
1–3	27	9	64
4–6	40	10	50
7–12	53	13	34
Experiment—54 days			
1–3	25	5	70
11–12	69	12	19
22–24	85	15	0

From: A. Keys, "Undernutrition," in Duncan: *Diseases of Metabolism*,
5th Ed. W. B. Saunders, Philadelphia, p. 681, 1964.

of 1945, amenorrhea developed in about one-half of the women, with a consequent fall in the birth rate due to a lower rate of conception.

If fertility persists in spite of hunger, it is logical to question the effect on the infant born. The infants born to severely deprived mothers in Holland in 1944–1945 were small. In general, it seems that the baby of an undernourished mother is on the whole surprisingly normal but small. The socio-economic level is reflected in the birth weight within ethnic groups (Table 2). Although other factors are involved, it seems safe to conclude that the amount of food eaten by the mother is important in the difference between the birth weights of babies of the well-to-do and the poor.

It may well be asked if small birth weight has any significance for the later well-being of the child. A followup study was initiated in 1959 in Wake County, North Carolina, by Robinson and Robinson. The children studied were eight to ten years of age. By that age, 24% of those who had birth weights significantly less than normal suffered major physical defects; the incidence in other groups was only 2–3%.

Stillbirth and neonatal death rates also vary with socio-economic levels. Where the standard of living is high, the rates are low; where the standard of living is low, the rates are high. Poor nutrition is believed to be a responsible factor in the high incidence of stillbirths and neonatal deaths among those with low standards of living.

TABLE 2   Mean Birth Weights According to Socio-Economic Status

Place	Population	Subjects	Mean Birth Weights (grams)
Madras	Indian	Well-to-do	2985
		"Mostly poor"	2736
South India	Indian	Wealthy	3182
		Poor	2810
Bombay	Indian	Upper class	3247
		Upper-middle class	2945
		Lower-middle class	2796
		Lower class	2578
Calcutta	Indian	Paying patients	2851
		Poor class	2656
Congo	Bantu	"Very well nourished"	3026
		"Well nourished"	2965
		"Badly nourished"	2850
Ghana (Accra)	African	Prosperous	3188
		General population	2879
Indonesia	Javanese	Well-to-do	3022
		Poor	2816

From: World Health Organization. *Nutrition in Pregnancy and Lactation.* Tech. Rept. Series No. 302. Geneva, Switzerland, p. 14, 1965.

The British investigators Thomson and Hytten believe that nutrition in childhood influences the incidence of stillbirths among women. They use demographic data of Britain as their guidelines. They begin with the 1930's when there was a period of substantial unemployment; malnutrition was prevalent among the poor. During the subsequent war years, the rate of stillbirths fell from 38 per 1000 in 1940 to 28 per 1000 in 1945. During this period, there was food rationing, and pregnant and lactating women were given priority on supplies of protective foods, cheap or free milk, and vitamins. The authors believe that the good diet accounted for the fall in the rate of stillbirths. During the ten years following World War II, there was little change in the rate of stillbirths. There was economic austerity after the war, but the authors believe that the nutritional status of women during pregnancy and lactation did not suffer. In recent years, the stillbirth rate in Britain has been falling rapidly again.

Thomson and Hytten do not present an explanation for the current fall in the rate but do present an hypothesis. The basis for their proposal rests in part on the findings of an earlier work of Thomson in which he studied 489 women in Aberdeen, Scotland. He divided them into two groups, those with normal and those with abnormal clinical histories. Undernutrition was not found to be related to obstetrical performance; however, there were indications that stature of the mother did bear a relationship. The authors hypothesize that girls who are reared under favorable conditions and have a good diet "attain a high level of health and physiological efficiency" by the time they bear children; on the other hand, those who are stunted due to malnutrition fail to attain their full adult size. Thomson and Hytten point out that the mothers of the 1960's grew up after World War II. They are taller and heavier than those who grew up before that time. Other earlier studies have shown also that short women have higher rates of stillbirths than do tall women.

One last point about pregnancy which is of particular importance for undernourished women is the capacity of the body to use more efficiently the food nutrients provided to it during this period. As indicated from studies of the nutrients protein, calcium, and iron, a higher percent is absorbed from the gastrointestinal tract and more retained in the body by the pregnant woman than by the woman who is not pregnant. Such studies have not been done with the undernourished woman. However, it is safe to assume that there are minimal levels of need which, if not provided, would harm the mother or the unborn child.

Work Capacity

Significant anywhere, but particularly in developing countries, is the adverse effect of hunger on work capacity. The debilitation of undernutrition has been observed under naturally occurring conditions and has been explored under conditions imposed in the experimental laboratory. Hunger lessens the work capacity of man.

Keller and Kraut studied the coal miners of the Ruhr district of Germany during and immediately following World War II. In 1939, when the rations provided an average of 4500 kcal, approximately 2300 kcal of this amount remained for work after the requirements for basal metabolism and other activities were fulfilled. The daily amount of coal removed by each miner was 1.9 ton. In 1944, when only 1900 kcal were available for work, 1.65 ton of coal per man were mined. Workers in a steel plant were also studied. In 1939, when the worker's rations supplied 1900 work kcal daily, the steel production amounted to more than 120 tons per man per month. However, in 1944, when only 1150 kcal were available daily for work, production was less than 80 ton monthly per man.

The men in the experimental study of semistarvation carried out by Ancel Keys and his co-workers at the University of Minnesota suffered a marked loss of physical strength and endurance during the 24-week deprivation period. Voluntary exercise became less with the progress of the study. The men felt weak and tired. Although they moved cautiously, they bumped into objects and tripped over things.

The behavior of troops on short rations while in field operations reveals the incapacitating effect of too little food. Kark tells of the controlled study carried out in 1942 in the Canadian Arctic as follows:

> One company was given an excellent ration, the others lived on calorically deficient rations. By the end of the week it was obvious to us that those living on the poor rations were deteriorating, but all the measurements we made could not distinguish between the three companies. Then after a particularly grueling day they came into the bivouac area for the night, cut down spruce trees for their shelter, ate supper, and bedded down. The next morning, after they had left, we found that each platoon of the well-nourished troops had built proper shelters to protect them from the wind and the cold. The platoons of the next best nourished company started to build shelters, but halfway through they were so tired that they stopped. The most caloric deficient soldiers were so tired when they came into the bivouac area that they just took spruce branches, laid them on the ground, and slept unprotected.

Infection

A common affliction of the hungry is infection. In parts of the world where the incidence of hunger is high, the incidence of infections is also high and the outcome more grave than among the well nourished.

Infantile diarrhea is an example of the causal relationship of hunger to disease. The undernourished child is more susceptible to diarrhea than the well-fed child. The diarrheal condition then increases the severity of the undernutrition because the rapid passage of material through the intestine does not permit the absorption of nutrients to occur as under normal conditions.

Diarrhea, the primary cause of infant mortality in developing countries, increases in incidence markedly at the time of weaning. This almost universal association has led to the adoption of the term "weanling diarrhea." The replacement of mother's milk by food less nutritionally adequate and likely a carrier of infectious microorganisms is believed to be a causative factor. Further evidence of the role of nutrition was the decrease in the incidence of diarrhea among children under five years of age when supplementary food was given to them. In the Mayan Indian highland village of Santa Catarina Barabona, Guatemala, the children received four days each week a supplement of milk, a banana, and a special cereal mixture fortified with yeast, calcium, and vitamin A which supplied an additional fifteen grams of protein and 450 calories. The mortality rate of the children of this village was notably less than that for the children of Santa Cruz Balanya who received no supplements (Table 3).

TABLE 3   Mortality Rates per 1000: May 1959–April/May 1963

Village	Mortality rate	
	Age 6–18 months	Age 19–36 months
Santa Cruz Balanya (control)	96.6	25.2
Santa Catarina Barabona (feeding)	30.3	10.4

From N. S. Scrimshaw. Primary Deterrent to Human Progress. *Pre-School Child Malnutrition*. National Academy of Sciences, National Research Council, Washington, D.C., p. 70, 1966.

The incidence of diarrhea in undernourished children is not only higher than in normal children but fatalities from it are also higher. In 1956 in Mexico City, the fatality rate in children hospitalized with diarrhea was 14–15% in those without evidences of undernutrition and as high as 52% in those severely undernourished.

In seeking some solution for the tremendously high incidence of infant mortality from diarrhea in developing countries, Sabin looked back into the history of this malady in the U.S. As late as 1920, the death rates due to diarrhea in New York City were comparable to current rates in many Latin American countries. An extraordinarily low level of diarrheal death in infants, however, was achieved in the U.S. and Canada by 1955. This reduction was associated more with other improvements in the standard of living than with the mere provision of pure water and sanitary disposal of excreta in the homes because these sanitary installations were already in existence in New York City before 1920. Sabin, searching for an explanation, says:

. . . it is necessary to ask, therefore, what public activity is most likely to contribute to a significant reduction in infantile diarrheal mortality before the great improvements in the general standards of living are achieved in the parts of the world now plagued by poverty, hunger, ignorance, and disease.

He concludes that:

> . . . if malnutrition during the first two years of life could be largely eliminated, and breast-feeding could be supplemented and followed by feedings free from heavy bacterial growth, there is reason to expect a very significant reduction in the current, tragic infantile mortality, even though 'dirty hands' might continue to transmit infectious agents for a long time to come.

Organisms capable of causing diarrhea can be recovered from fecal samples in the early months of life without clinical diarrhea occurring; later diarrhea does occur. It is proposed that the status of nutrition worsens after weaning, causing greater susceptibility.

There is need for exerting efforts to maintain conditions as sanitary as possible. A rather unexpected observation is that, in the majority of the infantile diarrheas, no pathogenic organism can be identified. It is hypothesized that intestinal organisms normally present and normally nonpathogenic may become pathogenic and cause diarrhea when present in abundance, as is commonly the case when the sanitation of the environment is poor.

It is believed that undernutrition is a factor in the high death rates due to measles in certain Latin American countries. This mortality rate is 418 times higher in Ecuador, 189 times higher in Guatemala, and 180 times higher in Mexico than in the U.S.

On the other hand, with experimental animals under controlled laboratory conditions, a general statement that well-fed animals resist infection better than those poorly fed cannot be made. In fact, there are instances in which the undernourished animal resists the infection even better than the well-fed one. For example, riboflavin deficiency in chicks was found to increase resistance to the organism of avian malaria; folic acid deficiency in monkeys was found to increase resistance to the virus of poliomyelitis.

ADAPTATION

The discussion thus far, has examined some of the physical effects of hunger. Hunger causes stunting of growth and changes in body composition. It decreases the capacity to work and increases susceptibility to infection. But how is it that persons consuming diets grossly inadequate can live and work? Actually, the body makes adjustments to maintain normality in its composition and its functioning. Cannon, the physiologist, originated the word "homeostasis" to describe "the types of arrangements by which this stabilization is accomplished." Distinguished students of the subject, Mitchell and Keys, have written extensively about it. For example, when the energy intake is inadequate, body movements are diminished. The basal metabolism per square meter of body surface is reduced. And as a consequence, the total energy expenditure is lessened and the amount of energy needed is decreased. Keys indicates that, when the weight is reduced by around 20% from a previously normal weight, it is possible to maintain the body on a diet of approximately 50% of the energy value of the previously normal food intake. The mineral and vitamin intakes were in the general range of the National Research Council Recommended Daily Allowances, with the exception of the intakes of riboflavin and vitamin A, which were about one-half the recommendations (1948). This relationship between weight loss and energy reduction "explains why the rate of weight loss progressively decreases when a normal person chronically subsists on an inadequate diet and why life may be maintained for very long periods of time on a greatly reduced food intake." In the case of protein, minerals, and vitamins, when the intake is limited, the body eliminates less and retains within the body a higher percent of the amount provided in the diet.

HUNGER AND BEHAVIOR

Hunger causes changes in social behavior which are as well identified as are the physical changes. Experiments which produced hunger in man, such as the Minnesota experiment, gave researchers an opportunity to observe the deterioration in social relationships and personal adjustment with the progress of hunger. Actually, two criteria for the selection of the young men in Minnesota were good mental health and the ability to get along reasonably well with others.

Hunger changed the behavior of these young men. The clamor of it distracted them from their attempts to continue their cultural interests, normal activities, and studies. There was preoccupation with food. And when it did arrive at the two meals per day, they were torn between gulping it and consuming it slowly. There were changes in emotional reactions and attitudes. The stresses of this semistarvation regime caused instability. Periods of depression were common; gloominess permeated much of their lives; they seldom smiled. There was little humor, and the negative approach to things was the common attitude.

The discrepancy between what they had once been able to do physically, wanted to do now, and were unable to accomplish was a source of great frustration to them. It was necessary to rest when ascending stairs; it was even difficult to lift the feet high enough to avoid stumbling on uneven sidewalks.

An attempt was made to relate changes in social behavior with loss of body weight. With increasing loss of weight, the behavior changed from slight disorder and strife to very serious disorder, then receded to slight disorder and finally to none.

Percentage loss of body weight	Civil disorder and strife
5	Slight
10	Moderate
15	Serious
20	Very serious
30	Moderate
40	Slight
50	None

Although most of the time the men were silent and sad, as the deprivation progressed there were periods of a few hours or a few days when they felt elated. Some thought that they finally had adjusted to the ration and expected that the state of elation would continue. But it did not. The weather affected moods notably. Warm, sunny days brightened the spirits; cold, damp, cloudy days caused greater depression.

The sociability of the men changed greatly. In general there was a feeling of animosity toward strangers; there was a special dislike for those who had food. It became "too much trouble" or "too tiring" to contend with other people, so the men became more withdrawn and alone. Personal appearance and grooming deteriorated as stress progressed.

The pressure of hunger was more than some of the men could take, even though all were of the finest character. One person not only bought food but stole it as well; he was not able to continue the experiment.

The intellective capacity, as measured by psychological tests, did not change during the starvation period nor the subsequent period of rehabilitation. However, it was difficult for the men to concentrate on the intellective task at hand because of preoccupation with food. The men described themselves during the stress of hunger, in contrast to their previous well-fed condition, as lacking in self-discipline and self-control, indecisive, restless, sensitive to noise, unable to concentrate, and markedly nervous.

During the rehabilitation period, many of the behavior symptoms of the starvation period persisted for several weeks. Similarly, it is reported that after relief had come to the Belsen concentration camp in 1945 the inmates continued to steal, hide, and hoard food. At the beginning of the rehabilitation, the inmates in the Minnesota project complained "without spirit, hopelessly—but later as their condition improved, their complaints became fierce, bitter, and resentful." One man in the Minnesota experiment characterized the difference between starvation and rehabilitation as "the difference between old age and adolescence."

Hingson, who headed medical teams to Liberia, Honduras, and certain Asiatic nations, observed among those peoples

> the listlessness, the apathy, the suspicion of strangers, the lack of interest in self-improvement in adults whose life expectancy is thirty-five to forty years. I have seen little ones with the tell-tale sign of malnutrition, the distended stomach, sit for hours, as in a stupor, not romping or playing as normal youngsters. And they are marked for life by this lack if they survive disease to which they are prey. They will be as their elders, apathetic, dull and no desire or capacity to work together to improve their lot. Persistent undernutrition indeed leaves its ugly mark, not only on the body, but on the mind and the personality.

HUNGER AND MENTAL DEVELOPMENT

The question of the effect of hunger in early life on mental development has aroused great interest in recent years. With the estimate that 60% of the total preschool population of the world suffer with protein-calorie malnutrition in various degrees of severity, there is reason for concern.

Pertinent to the question of the ill effect of early malnutrition on the functioning of the brain is this organ's unique manner of growth. In his classic work *Measurement of Man,* Scammon expresses the growth of the body parts at different ages in per cent of the total increment at maturity; the brain and its parts achieve approximately 80% of the total growth by four years of age. Among the pioneers in the study of the effect of malnutrition on the mental development of children was Cravioto and his collaborators in Mexico. One of their observations was of children 15 to 42 months of age who were admitted to the hospital with protein-calorie malnutrition. With nutritional rehabilitation for six months, the response to tests administered indicated improvement in mental development. In another study, twenty children, infants and children of preschool age, were admitted to the hospital with severe pro-tein-calorie malnutrition. During recovery from the malnutrition, psychological tests were applied and performance on the tests used as a measure of developmental progress. Improvement·in developmental achievement accompanied rehabilitation from malnutrition except for the children who entered the hospital at less than six months of age.

The permanency of the mental retarding effect of severe malnutrition is yet to be explored conclusively. However, there are optimistic indications. A group of children in Cape Town, South Africa, who suffered an episode of kwashiorkor between ten months and four years of age were observed again nine or ten years later together with a sibling control group of similar age and sex. Intelligence tests were applied to both groups; the results were similar. Using test scores as a criteria for judgment, there seemed to be no residual retarding effect from the earlier occurrence of kwashiorkor.

Studies with animals have shown that malnutrition can limit both the number and size of cells in the young. In the newly born rat, under-nutrition diminishes the rate of cell division, resulting in a permanent deficit in the number of brain cells. In the young rat after weaning, undernutrition limits the size of the cell, but this adverse effect is reversible by later improved nutrition.

Maternal protein restriction in rats retards both placental and fetal growth. Animals born of mothers on protein-restricted diets but nursed by normal foster mothers manifested a deficit in total number of brain cells at the time of weaning. The adverse effect occurred during the prenatal period when the diet of the mother was low in protein. Prenatal influences are difficult to study in the human. However, certain observations have been made of the cell count of the placenta and size of the fetus as influenced by undernutrition. Placentas from infants of low birth weight due to "intrauterine growth failure" have fewer cells than the placentas of normal infants.

A postnatal influence in the human on cell number has also been observed. Infants who died from food deprivation during the first year of life had a 15–20% reduction in total number of brain cells. Infants whose weight was 2000g or less at birth and who suffered severe malnutrition during the first year of life showed a reduction of 60% in total number of brain cells. These infants suffered both pre- and postnatal deprivations and hence were "doubly deprived."

It is difficult to design a research project that can isolate and determine the contribution of inadequate nutrition to intellectual development. Efforts are being made to do so through longitudinal studies with normal siblings serving as controls for the malnourished. (Cooperative Study of the Columbia Institute of Family Welfare (Bogata); Department of Nutrition, Harvard University; and the Graduate School of Nutrition, Cornell University). Another is the research of the Institute of Nutrition of Central America and Panama in which small, isolated villages, as much alike as possible in socio-economic, public health, cultural, and other bases, are being studied in pairs. One village in each pair serves as a control.

THE BIAFRA FAMINE

Many details and a high incidence of calorie and protein malnutrition occurred in the nutritional disaster of Biafra. A report made by Aall in December 1969, two and one-half years after the initiation of the Nigerian-Biafran War, indicated that starvation was the chief cause of death and that the majority of deaths were among children.

Pre-war agricultural conditions in Biafra contributed to the vulnerability of the people. Many farmers raised cocoa as a cash crop. Food crops could not be grown under the cocoa trees, nor was additional land available. Hence, the families were dependent on the cash income for needed food, which in some cases was insufficient. Also in some cases, the available money was diverted to uses other than food. Up to 80% of the foods supplying protein were imported, including all of the milk, much of the meat, most of the fish, and also large amounts of beans and peanuts. It is not surprising in view of these facts that famine and calorie and protein malnutrition should occur in Biafra during time of war.

During the food emergency the extreme conservatism of man in food habits was demonstrated. Some of the foods sent in for relief were new to the people; they were reluctant to accept them.

CHRONIC HUNGER IN THE U.S.

In 1967 and 1968, attention was directed to the existence of malnutrition in the U.S. (especially among low income groups) by governmental and foundational units and by a citizens' group. There followed then the formation of the Select Committee on Nutrition and Human Needs of the United States Senate. Hearings of this Committee and the report of the White House Conference on Food, Nutrition, and Health focused attention on the occurrence of malnutrition in the U.S. To assess the nutritional levels of disadvantaged families, the National Nutrition Survey was authorized under the auspices of the U.S. Department of Health, Education, and Welfare. The indication of economic status used in the survey was the Poverty-Index Ratio, which is a composite index based on income, family size, farm or non-farm, and sex and age of the head of household. The sample was made up of persons below the poverty level and persons above it; the distribution varied among states with the least below the poverty level in New York State (18%) and the most in South Carolina (75.9%).

Between 1968 and 1970, data were collected in ten states (California, Kentucky, Louisiana, Massachusetts, Michigan, New York City and New York State, South Carolina, Texas, Washington, and West Virginia). Households interviewed numbered 23,192; within these households, there were 83,597 individuals. The nutritional status of about one-half of the persons (46%) was assessed. The preliminary report (1971) which presents some of the findings includes: four of the numerous biochemical measures used (hemoglobin, vitamin A, vitamin C in the blood, and urinary riboflavin); the height and weight data of pre-school children (numerous body dimensions were measured on all the persons selected for assessment of nutritional status); and dietary intake of selected nutrients (protein, iron, vitamin A, and vitamin C, and energy) for the individuals in the households interviewed in five states (Texas, Louisiana, New York, Kentucky, and Michigan).

The preliminary findings show the individuals in the below-poverty portion of the sample studied to have a higher incidence of biochemical values at deficient or low levels. and a greater percent of preschool children with low height-weight measurements (in comparison with the Iowa Growth Charts) than the respective portions of the above-poverty group. The adequacy of the diets in energy, protein, and vitamin A content were found to be little influenced by socio-economic status. The below-poverty group had a greater percentage of individuals not meeting the standard for adequacy of vitamin C intake than the above-poverty group. As for iron, there appears to be a consistent relationship between dietary iron intake and socio-economic status in all age groups and in all geographic areas. These data from the National Nutrition Survey are preliminary and incomplete; they can be considered indicative but not conclusive.

SOME CAUSES OF HUNGER

Hunger is a major cause of human suffering in the world. It degrades the human and all but precludes the achievements of excellence of which man is capable. The cause is simple—a lack of sufficient food; the solution—providing sufficient food—is difficult.

There are the problems of:

1. Increasing the production of food and controlling the rate of population increase to bring the two into balance.
2. Motivating the population to change beliefs and practices.
3. Providing enough money to buy food.

Food Production and Population

The world agricultural production was characterized in 1970 by continued increase in the developing countries as a whole and at a standstill in the developed countries—those with market economies. However, when agricultural production is considered in relation to population growth, there exists a marked disparity between the lesser and more developed regions in food supply per person. The rate of population growth at the turn of the century was less in the lesser developed regions, but the relative rates shifted in the 1930–1940 decade. Since that time, the rate of population increase of the lesser developed regions has exceeded that of the more developed, as shown in Table 4. A continuation of the same relationship in population growth is predicted for the present decade.

TABLE 4   Natural Increase in World Population

	Natural increase in percent	
	More developed regions	Less developed regions
1800–1850	0.7	0.5
1850–1900	1.0	0.4
1900–1910	1.3	0.7
1920–1930	1.2	1.0
1930–1940	0.8	1.2
1940–1950	0.5	1.2
1950–1960	1.3	2.0
1960–1970[1]	1.0	2.4
1970–1980	1.0	2.5

[1] According to recently revised population projections from a Concise Summary of the World Population Situation in 1970. Population Studies No. 48, United Nations, 1971, New York, p. 3.

The need for a better balance between agricultural production and increasing needs of the population is considered critical by students of the problem. Over the period from 1960 to 1970, the trend of per capita food production in the developing countries of both the Far East and Near East was static; in Latin America, there was a slight increase; in the African countries, production per capita fell slightly. Since population growth accelerated very little between 1960 and 1970 (it rose from 2.4% to 2.5% per year in Africa and the Far East; from 2.7–2.8% in the Near East; and remained unchanged at 2.9% in Latin America), the failure of per capita food supplies to increase reflects mainly the failure of food production to rise in these regions.

That agricultural production can be increased notably in production-deficit countries has been demonstrated. The program of the Rockefeller Foundation in Mexico presents a record of increasing production in the three basic food crops, corn, wheat, and beans, to the point of complete self-sufficiency; before the initiation of the program in 1943, it was necessary to import considerable quantities of each of these products.

One of the basic problems to increased agricultural production is education. The opportunities for the rural population to study even at the elementary level are limited in developing countries. The farmer, the agricultural extension worker, and the professor who teaches and does research in the universities are all in need of expanding opportunities for study. Mangelsdorf of the Harvard Botanical Museum, speaking on genetic potentials for increasing yields of food crops and animals, explains succinctly this urgent need. He indicates, according to the report of his presentation by Walsh in *Science,* that at present it is possible to breed superior plants but the rate at which agriculture can be improved "is dependent in no small part on the general level of literacy and education in the population and the willingness of governments to provide generous support for agricultural education and research. To change the ways of man is infinitely more difficult than to reshape our domestic animals and plants by genetic techniques."

Population, too, is an adjustable factor. In four of the most populous Asian countries—India, Pakistan, China (mainland), and Japan—the governments have sponsored various measures aimed at encouraging limitation of births. A lowered rate of population increase is expected to aid economic and social advancement. In Japan the birth rate dropped from 30.1 per thousand population in 1945–1949 to 17.2 per thousand in 1957. The high degree of industrialization and economic development and the high level of education of the people are cited as facilitating the movement in Japan. There is concern about Latin America. Population has been increasing there at an annual rate of 2.5%, while agricultural production has been rising at the rate of only 2.0%.

Education is the basic need for bringing into balance the supply of food and the demand for food. Education is a slow process, but it has lasting effects, as expressed by a Chinese proverb, "If you are planning for a year ahead, sow rice; for ten years, plant trees; for a hundred years, educate the people."

Motivation to Change

Change is necessary if the living conditions of the world's deprived millions are to improve. For those members of communities where poverty and hunger have long existed, they have become a way of life. People have developed attitudes, beliefs, and practices which yield to them a certain amount of security. To change these beliefs and practices poses a risk, and the person who lives in fear of starvation cannot afford "to risk new methods or new crops which some stranger tells him will give better results; he feels that he must stick to whatever he knows will feed him, however inadequately." He has learned by experience, by observing, and by doing things for himself. However, as reported in the 1963 FAO publication, *Malnutrition and Disease*, it has been shown that "once a start has been made, and the vicious cycle of poverty-malnutrition-more poverty is broken, confidence dispels apathy, activity replaces inertia and new expectations provide a continuing incentive to further experiment and achievement."

Economic gain may be an incentive for crop improvement. When a crop is grown for the market rather than for home consumption, the adoption of the new variety is usually extensive. In an Indian village studied by the anthropologist Duke, improved wheat for home consumption was not accepted happily because of the undesirable taste, whereas sugar cane, a cash crop, was quickly adopted by the people.

STUDY QUESTIONS

1. By definition, how do undernutrition and malnutrition differ?
2. Is there evidence that infection is associated with hunger?
3. What are some of the behavior changes observed in men during a semistarvation regime?
4. Is there evidence that hunger impairs fertility in the human?
5. What do research studies show as to the effect of hunger on the amount and quality of work that man is able to perform?

TOPICS FOR INDIVIDUAL INVESTIGATION

1. Prepare arguments supporting the necessity of working concertedly to free the world from hunger.
2. The body when subjected to the stress of hunger makes adjustments to preserve normality. Enumerate as many of these adjustments as possible.
3. Discuss the relationship of hunger and world peace.
4. Relate the problem of hunger and the progress toward self-sufficiency.
5. Discuss two great famines showing the social, economic, and political implications.

REFERENCES AND SUGGESTED READINGS

Aall, C. Relief, Nutrition and Health Problems in the Nigerian/Biafran War. *J. Trop. Pediatrics,* 16: 70, 1970.

Bhabha, H. Science and the Problem of Development. *Science,* 151: 541, 1966.

Birch, H. G. Field Measurement in Nutrition, Learning and Behavior. In N. S. Scrimshaw and J. E. Gordon, Eds., *Malnutrition, Learning and Behavior.* M.I.T. Press, Cambridge, Mass., 1968.

Brown, R. E. and J. Mayer. Famine and Disease in Biafra: An Assessment. *Trop. and Geogr. Med.,* 21: 348, 1969.

Burgess, A., and R. F. A. Dean, Eds. *Malnutrition and Food Habits.* Macmillan, New York, 1962.

Cravioto, J. and B. Robles. Evaluation of Adaptive and Motor Behavior During Rehabilitation and Kwashiorkor. *Amer. J. Orthopsychiat.,* 35: 449, 1965.

Dema, I. S. *Nutrition in Relation to Agriculture Production.* Food and Agriculture Organization, Rome, Italy, 1965.

Dube, S. C. Cultural Factors in Rural Community Development. *So. Asian Studies,* 16: 19, 1956.

Food and Agriculture Organization. *Malnutrition and Disease.* Freedom from Hunger Campaign, Basic Study No. 12, Rome, Italy, 1963.

Food and Agriculture Organization. *Nutrition and Working Efficiency.* Freedom from Hunger Campaign. Basic Study No. 5, Rome, Italy, 1962.

Food and Agriculture Organization. *Third World Food Survey.* Freedom from Hunger, Basic Study No. 11, Rome, Italy, 1968.

Food and Population. *Scientific American,* 226: 45, 1972.

Foster, G. M. *Traditional Cultures: and the Impact of Technological Change.* Harper and Row, New York, 1962.

Frisch, R. E. Present Status of the Supposition That Malnutrition Causes Permanent Mental Retardation. *Amer. J. Clin. Nutr.,* 23: 189, 1970.

Garn, S. M., M. Behar, F. Viteri, and M. A. Guzman. Compact Bone Deficiency in Protein-Calorie Malnutrition. *Science,* 145: 1444, 1964.

Geber, M. and R. F. A. Dean. The State of Development of Newborn African Children. *Lancet,* 1: 1216, 1957.

Goldsmith, G. Where Are We In the Race Against Starvation? *Amer. J. Pub. Health,* 61: 1478, 1971.

Graham, G. G. The Later Growth of Malnourished Infants; Effects of Age, Severity, and Subsequent Diet. In R. A. McCance and E. M. Widdowson, Eds., *Calorie Deficiencies and Protein Deficiencies.* Little, Brown, Boston, Mass., p. 314, 1968.

Hansen, J. D. L., C. Freesemann, A. D. Moodle, and D. E. Evans. Symposium On Growth and Development. What Does Nutritional Growth Retardation Imply? *Pediatrics,* 47: No. 1, Part II, 299, 1971.

Harrar, J. G. *Strategy for the Conquest of Hunger.* The Rockefeller Foundation, New York, N.Y., 1963.

Hingson, R. A. Unpublished statement. Quoted by H. A. Hunscher in Protein and Politics —a Theory. *Food and Nutr. News,* 38(2) 1, 1966.

Jackson, R. L. Effect of Malnutrition on Growth of the Pre-School Child. *Pre-School*

Child Malnutrition. National Academy of Sciences, National Research Council, Washington, D.C., p. 9, 1966.

Kark, R. M. *Food and Hunger in a World of Turmoil.* World Review of Nutrition and Dietetics by G. H. Bourne, Vol. 6, p. 1, Hafner Publishing, New York, N.Y., 1966.

Keys, A., et al. *The Biology of Human Starvation.* Univ. of Minnesota Press, Minneapolis, Minn., 1950.

Keller, W. D. and H. A. Kraut. *Work and Nutrition.* World Review of Nutrition and Dietetics by G. H. Bourne, Vol. 3, p. 69. Hafner Publishing, New York, N.Y., 1959.

Latham, M. C. and F. Cobos. The Effects of Malnutrition On Intellectual Development and Learning. *Amer. J. Pub. Health,* 61: 1307, 1971.

McCance, R. A. *The Bearing of Early Nutrition on Later Development.* Proceedings of the Sixth International Congress of Nutrition. Williams and Wilkins, Baltimore, Md., p. 74, 1964.

Meredith, H. V. Relation Between Socio-Economic Status and Body Size in Boys Seven to Ten Years of Age. *Amer. J. Diseases of Children,* 22: 702, 1951.

Mitchell, H. H. *Comparative Nutrition of Man and Domestic Animals.* Academic Press, New York, N.Y., 1962.

8

Malnutrition
and Disease

Malnutrition is found everywhere around the entire globe. In general, however, it is found to the greatest extent where poverty is the rule and not the exception and where ignorance and superstition are rampant. After the articles in the popular press within recent years, there can be few people who have no cause for concern for malnutrition in the U.S. Malnutrition is considered partly responsible for health hazards in the American Eskimo which resemble those seen in the rest of the U.S. 50 years ago. Malnutrition is also one cause for the heavy toll which diseases take in children of migrant workers, American Indians, and older citizens. For further discussion, see page 332.

Jan Myrdal, in an article in the August 13, 1966, *Saturday Review,* threw out a challenge:

293

In the concrete world in which we live we all know which is the main conflict. The few are rich, the many are poor. The few live long, the many die young. The majority of the population of our world is starving. The majority is downtrodden, trampled upon, exploited. And this majority is becoming conscious. It is questioning the whole structure of the world society.

It was said in 1962 at a meeting at Iowa State University, convened to discuss food as one tool in international economic development, that:

A substantial body of medical evidence and opinion exists showing that over large parts of the globe great numbers of people get inadequate diets, inadequate in terms of climatic environment and of the physical strains imposed upon them by social institutions and economic circumstances which are simultaneously the cause and the results of limited economic development.

Several terms should be understood before we discuss this problem further. People who are *undernourished* are simply getting too few calories to maintain normal body weight and normal activity. The *malnourished individual* may get enough calories but insufficient amounts of needed nutrients such as minerals, vitamins, and proteins or some of the critical amino acids in the proteins. This individual does not develop normally during the growth period and is unable at any time of life to maintain himself in good health and to resist disease.

Using any criteria which can be proposed to separate the poorly fed from the well fed of the world, it will be found that today millions of people are underfed. Malnutrition is an even more serious problem because ignorance and superstition add to the burden of not enough food.

A group of experts from the U.S. Department of Agriculture prepared a world food budget for 1962 and one for 1966. After analyzing food available and used, they stated that only 40 countries had adequate food supplies. These countries are largely in the temperate zones and include those in North America, the USSR, Oceania, the southern parts of South America, South Africa, and Japan, except that Japan has a low consumption of fat by choice. On the other hand, 70 countries, including countries in Latin America, Africa, West Asia, Communist Asia, and the Far East, were rated as food-deficit countries. It was estimated that 2 billion people, or two-thirds of the world's people, live in these food-deficit areas.

It is in this setting of not enough calories and not enough of the right kind of food eaten that we want to discuss undernutrition and malnutrition. As we do this, we pay tribute to a famous nutritionist of the past, Dr. Russell H. Chittenden, who in 1907 wrote in his book *The Nutrition of Man:* "These three main functions constitute the purpose of nutrition. . . . Development, growth, and vital activity all depend upon food in proper amounts and proper quality."

Malnutrition leads to disease, either acute or subacute, which can only be diagnosed by medical examination. In the subacute stages of malnourishment, individuals may only be approaching an illness. As is so often seen in the developing countries, an infectious disease such as measles or whooping cough in children or the condition caused by hookworm or other body-invading parasites precipitates the illness in the person who has been gradually weakened by malnutrition. At the same time, malnutrition may determine not only the incidence but also the progress and severity of the disease. It may favor the invasion of the agent of the disease and favor the development of secondary infections, thus delaying recovery from the disease.

According to James Hundley:

The true roots of malnutrition ramify very deeply into the social and economic fabric of society. In practice, all of the so-called causes are interrelated and interdependent: Agriculture, climate, economics, cultural and social patterns, transportation, communications, education and even religion exercise influences.

Fundamentally, however, the main root of malnutrition is probably in agriculture. It is usually considered that the permanent correction of malnutrition lies with those measures necessary to increase agricultural production. Recently it also has been said that the question is one of "matching food with the mouths."

In general, the kinds and amounts of food needed to nourish the human body, even under diverse conditions of climate and environment, are now known. The Food and Agriculture Organization (FAO) of the United Nations has published lists of recommended amounts of certain nutrients for various parts of the world. The problems now are to make food available where it is needed and to teach people to eat it. For instance, in parts of Africa, Central America, and Asia, the diets may be fairly adequate in calories but sadly lacking in such needed nutrients as protein.

NUTRITIONAL PROBLEMS

Berg (1970) said that the nutrition issue is becoming more relevant as the developing countries reduce their grain shortage. He says that large nutrition projects are now receiving attention that was not given to small projects proposed before. He offers hope that, with a massive attack such as was launched on smallpox and malaria, malnutrition can be wiped out. He also says that without a bold approach the benefits will be only of "fringe importance." The hope undoubtedly lies in having national planners understand how fundamental malnutrition is to economic development. Ghosh (1946) in India estimated that 22.5% of the national income was required to rear children who could not live long enough to be productive.

The social scientists and the nutrition scientists working together need to produce hard scientific data to support the idea that malnutrition is an obstacle to national development. Berg believed that the programs need to be permanent, like the Rockefeller seed-breeding program. Often those on the top levels of government who assist in planning nutrition programs for a country now have the opportunity to work with other specialists on plans for agriculture, income redistribution, or even transportation, all of which have great influence on the problems of adequate nutrition of people. A number of U.N. and U.S. agencies who are interested in nutrition problems have recently succeeded in becoming involved in national planning for all development plans.

Berg and Muscat (1971) outline the steps in planning for nutrition programs. They say that the following should be done:

1. The nature, scope, and trends of the nutrition problems should first be defined.
2. Broad objectives should be stated in a preliminary manner.
3. The system under which these nutritional conditions exist should be described.
4. A choice of programs and policies relevant to the objectives should be made.
5. Alternative plans or policies involving interrelations with other agencies should be considered.
6. The limitations of the budget and political implications should

be considered before final plans under redefined objectives are made.

7. Redesign of objectives and plans can now be delineated.
8. Evaluation of the actions taken and redesign of plans and objectives in light of results of this study.

Alan Berg and Robert Muscat said at a Massachusetts Institute of Technology meeting (1971), "development planners traditionally have directed little attention to the problem of malnutrition, largely because they view it as a welfare problem and have budgeted accordingly. Only recently have planners begun to recognize that malnutrition may have significant developmental implications—'that it may be a basic impediment to national growth.'" They continue to say that often planners have believed better nutrition would come as an outgrowth of economic development. These authors and others have pointed out reasons which make complete dependence on the general rise of incomes an incomplete answer to eliminating malnutrition:

1. Malnourished people cannot increase their income to have food to meet even the minimum nutritive requirements. Malnutrition is a contributing factor to underdevelopment and a deterrent to a rise in family income.
2. Increased family income does not assure better nutrition.

In addition, increased agricultural output does not assure the disappearance of malnutrition. Studies have shown that the greater nutritional problems in the world today are:

1. General undernutrition where people simply do not have enough to eat.
2. Protein-calorie malnutrition where both the quantity and quality are not adequate, especially during growth.
3. Anemia, which results from an inadequate intake of good protein, iron, or certain vitamins. Growth increases the need for these nutrients.
4. Blindness, and eye conditions leading to it, due to a lack of vitamin A.
5. Skin conditions due to a riboflavin deficiency.

Other conditions such as beriberi, pellagra, goiter, scurvy, and rickets

| | Pellagra | | Beriberi | | Scurvy | | Vitamin A Deficiency |

Diet-deficit subregions, 1970. **Right above.** *(Adapted from: Economic Research Service, U.S. Department of Agriculture.)*

Geographical distribution of vitamin deficiencies (general impression). Above. *(Adapted from: World Health Organization,* WHO Activities in Nutrition 1948–1964, p. 27, 1965.*)*

The vicious circle illustrates the close relationship between health, economics, and social progress—how poverty engenders disease which in turn engenders more poverty. (Adapted from: World Health, *p. 11, Sept.-Oct. 1961.)*

Diet-Deficit Subregion

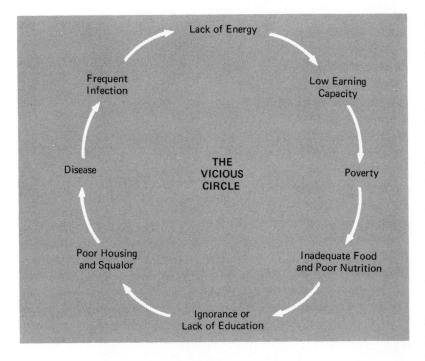

Lack of Energy

Low Earning
Capacity

Frequent
Infection

Poverty

Disease

THE
VICIOUS
CIRCLE

Inadequate Food
and Poor Nutrition

Poor Housing
and Squalor

Ignorance or
Lack of Education

TABLE 1   Intensity of Specific Nutritional Deficiencies in Selected Countries*

	Protein* malnutrition		Vitamin A		Goiter		Thiamine		Riboflavin		Niacin		Anemia (iron)		Vitamin C		Calcium	
	C†	A†	C	A	C	A	C	A	C	A	C	A	C	A	C	A	C	A
Brazil (N.E.)	I	III	I	II	IV	III	III	II	I	II	—	—	I	II	IV	IV	III	III
Bolivia	I	III	I	II	IV	III	—	—	I	II	—	—	I	II	—	—	III	III
Central America	I	II	I	V	I	II	—	—	I	II	—	—	I	II	—	—	III	III
Chile	I	II	I	II	IV	IV	—	—	I	III	III	III	I	II	I	—	V	V
Colombia	I	II	I	II	I	II‡	I	II	I	II	III	III	I	II	III	III	III	III
Ecuador	I	—	III	III	I	II	IV	IV	III	III	III	IV	I	—	—	—	I	II
Ethiopia	I	III	I	II	IV	III	—	—	—	—	—	—	—	III	I	I	IV	IV
India	I	II	I	II	III	III	IV	IV	V	V	IV	IV	I	II	V	V	III	III
Jordan	I	IV	I	II	IV	II	II	III	I	II	—	—	I	II	—	IV	III	III
Korea	I	III	I	II	—	—	III	III	I	I	—	—	I	—	—	—	—	—
Malaysia	III	IV	I	III	IV	IV	I	II	I	II	—	—	I	II	—	—	IV	IV
Mexico	I	II	—	—	—	V	—	—	I	—	—	—	—	—	—	—	V	V
Nigeria	I	II	I	II	I	V	—	—	—	—	—	—	I	II	—	—	V	V
Pakistan	I	II	I	II	III	III	IV	III	I	II	—	—	I	II	III	III	III	III
Peru	I	II	I	II	I	II	III	III	I	I	III	III	I	II	IV	IV	III	III
Poland	V	V	V	V	—	IV	—	—	—	—	—	—	—	—	—	—	—	—
UAR	V	V	V	V	IV	IV	—	—	—	—	—	—	—	—	—	—	—	—
Venezuela	III	—	III	II	I	II	I	II	I	I	—	—	III	II	—	—	—	—
Vietnam	I	—	I	II	IV	IV	I	II	I	I	—	—	I	II	—	III	—	—
Thailand	IV	—	I	III	I	I	I	II	I	II	—	—	—	—	III	—	—	—

From: A. Schaefer. Observations from Exploring Needs in National Nutrition Programs. Amer. J. Public Health 56: 1091, 1966. *Copyright 1966 by American Public Health Assoc., Inc.*

*These date are based on nutrition surveys.

†C = children; A = adults.

‡Now enriching salt with iodine.

I High priority—prevalence in children, 20 percent or more affected.
II High priority—prevalence in the entire population, 20 percent or more affected.
III Prevalence 10 percent.
IV Problem in isolated population groups.
V Deficiency known to exist—prevalence undetermined.

in a severe form are found in certain regions and are also damaging to the general health of the affected individuals.

Malnutrition is especially prevalent where the diet is largely composed of one of these five calorie-yielding staples of the world's food: rice, wheat, maize, cassava, or millet. It is now recognized that malnutrition in the preschool-age child is a serious deterrent to progress in developing countries; it impairs growth and the later capacity of adults to produce food and create a satisfactory *milieu* for good health. The maimed victims of malnutrition endured in early life lack the vigor and enterprise to raise themselves above the level of their parents.

It is obviously impossible to describe in detail all the diseases of malnutrition. We would like, however, to give a few facts about several of these conditions:

1. *Marasmus* is partial starvation or a gross, chronic calorie deficiency. This is seen especially in children where atrophy of muscles and a shriveled "old man" face are characteristic. In a 1963 report by UNICEF, it is said that physicians in the tropics and semitropics are "too familiar with the wasted limbs, emaciated body and features of the marasamic child."

2. *Protein-calorie malnutrition* is described and discussed in depth in the section on kwashiorkor later in this chapter.

3. *Beriberi* is also dealt with in detail in the latter part of this chapter.

4. *Endemic goiter* is discussed in detail later.

5. *Anemia* is currently a global problem among malnourished individuals, especially pregnant and lactating women and growing infants and children. In these individuals, the demands for the formation of hemoglobin, the iron-containing component of the blood, are greatest. The maintenance of an optimum blood supply depends on the capacity of the body to generate new cells with sufficient amounts of hemoglobin so that the blood can perform its oxygen-carrying function. Enough iron and high-grade proteins are often not found in poverty-restricted diets to satisfy the needs for this building of hemoglobin. In another type of anemia, vitamin C and one of the B vitamins (folacin) are the substances lacking in the diet.

6. *Xerophthalmia* is a deficiency disease which, in its most severe form, involves a drying of the membranes of the eye and other changes that cause destruction of the eye and ultimately blind-

ness. This disease is caused by a lack of vitamin A; young children are most frequently affected, although the disease may be seen in all ages. Some cases are found in Latin America and the Middle East, but by far the greatest incidence occurs in Ceylon, Burma, South India, Malaya, and above all Indonesia. Young children who have only occasional small pieces of fruit or green vegetable with a diet made up largely of a starchy food fall easy prey to xerophthalmia. In parts of the world where red palm oil, which is high in vitamin A, is produced and consumed, the condition is rarely seen. Night blindness and possibly decreased resistance to infection (though the latter is not well proven) are also results of a diet low in vitamin A.

Xerophthalmia is now considered one of the serious health problems of the world. All skim milk sent from the U.S. to countries where the need is great is now fortified with vitamin A as well as vitamin D. The mortality rate of malnourished children with this vitamin A deficiency is very high.

7. *Scurvy* is mostly seen in drought and famine areas of the arid countries of the Near East. However, some cases were reported in recent years in Canada and the U.S., mostly due here to ignorance and most frequently seen in the lonely old person who lives alone in the slums of industrial areas. Scurvy occurs when there is a low intake of vitamin C. This vitamin is known to be necessary for the formation of collagen, the cementing substance of the cell walls. Vitamin C is also needed for the maintenance of healthy gums and for the functioning of some glands. Growth causes greater need for vitamin C. Growing infants and children and pregnant and lactating mothers therefore show deficiencies most readily.

8. *Rickets,* seen in North America largely in the 1920's and 1930's, is a disease of infants and young children whose bones are growing rapidly. This disease is caused primarily by a lack of vitamin D, needed for the deposition of calcium in the bones. Vitamin D is found naturally in small amounts in only a few foods such as eggs, cream, and butter and in larger amounts in certain fish. Mostly, however, children do not receive enough vitamin D in foods unless they drink vitamin D-fortified milk as they now do in many parts of the U.S. The pro-vitamin of vitamin D occurs in or on the skin and is converted into active vitamin D by the

action of sunlight on the skin. Rickets is most severe in children whose diets contain little calcium. Except for the bones of fish and of poultry which are eaten in some parts of the world, milk is the chief food source of calcium. Rickets is found where there is little sunlight or where young infants and children are kept indoors as sometimes occurs even in sunny, tropical climates because of "purdah" or the social value of a pale skin. Rickets is said to occur in Ibadan, Nigeria, because mothers cover their children to shield them from the sun.

A survey in the U.S. done by the Academy of Pediatrics about 15 years ago, revealed a surprising number of cases of rickets. A 1965 survey in Seattle, Washington, on the seven-day intake of vitamin D of 150 children, ages birth through 17 years, showed a great variation in the amount of the vitamin ingested. In this city, almost all milk except some dry nonfat milk is enriched with this vitamin; some other foods are similarly enriched. A number of the children in this study, however, had several of these sources irregularly. Vigilance concerning the level of intake is evidently called for because it is possible for a child to consume too much as well as too little vitamin D.

9. *Pellagra* is essentially a disease of maize-eating people who are too poor to afford other foods such as meat, fish, or other whole-grain cereals which carry the needed vitamin, niacin, or supply sufficient amounts of the amino acid tryptophan which the body converts into niacin. Large numbers of cases of this disease occurred early in this century in the southern U.S.; it still is a problem in parts of Africa, India, Egypt, Portugal, Latin America, and Yugoslavia.

10. *Ariboflavinosis* is, as its name indicates, caused by the lack of riboflavin, one of the vitamins of the B complex. Tissue changes occur in the tongue, mucous membranes of the lips and mouth, and the skin around the base of the nose. Improvement in the diet causes a healing of these lesions. Although this disease is still referred to as a problem, there are fewer data available on its frequency and geography than for many other conditions. The association of this condition with a lack of vitamin A probably increases its importance.

11. *Obesity* in the affluent countries is currently one of the greatest problems in nutrition. It is said that 10–15% of the adolescent

population can be called obese, a higher incidence being found in girls. The relationship of this condition to heart disease and the degenerative diseases has directed much attention and research to it. Obesity is now known to arise from a complex interrelationship of psychological, physiological, environmental, and genetic factors as well as an excess of calories.

12. *Dental caries* is often listed as a disease of nutrition because its incidence can be reduced by 50% with adequate water fluoridation, limited use of sticky, highly sweet foods, and thorough cleaning of the teeth after the ingestion of food. Statistics on the incidence of this disease have caused it to be called the chief disease of nutrition in North America. Its incidence in other parts of the world is variable, being highest where the intake of refined carbohydrates is greatest. The fluorine content of the water supply is another factor in the incidence of dental caries.

Illness, with all of its attendant drains on the individual, the family, the community, and even the economy of a nation, would alone justify the world's attention to the problem of malnutrition. The high death rate in most developing countries, though decreasing, still is strikingly illustrated by the average length of life. It was said a few years ago that an infant in some Far Eastern countries had then as much chance to live to be 5 years of age as an infant born in the U.S. had to live to be 65 years of age. The exact ages in this comparison may vary as situations change, but the relative chances are still strikingly different.

As mentioned previously, inability to work and lack of energy are seen in malnourished people. Although these people often are called lazy, the wonder is not that they do not do more work on their low food intake but that they manage to do so much.

Without fail, growth is depressed when the young body is ill fed. Often this is the first sign of inadequate food. Formerly we paid little attention to slower physical growth and development in children in some countries; we even accepted, as if it were an innate genetic factor, that a man's wrist bones were the size of those of a ten-year-old boy in the U.S. Recent studies in post-war Japan and in many other parts of the world have shown that adequate food during growth can make a difference in the adult size of peoples formerly thought to be predestined to be small in stature.

Within the past several decades, severe loss of weight has been seen by most people, either firsthand or in newspaper pictures of prisoner-of-war camps. Almost no one presently can be unaware of it as a factor in nutrition. When horror pictures of this condition were shown in a class during the lecture on hunger, the college students were curious, interested, and not highly disturbed.

Within recent years, as discussed in the section on kwashiorkor, scientific evidence has increasingly shown that, in severe malnutrition, the potential for intellectual development can be permanently damaged in human beings. This, as has been shown conclusively in animals, is probably most severe when the malnutrition occurs in the very young infant under six months of age. The logic of impairment of growth of the brain when tissue in that organ is being formed at a rapid rate is certainly clear, and now scientific evidence is beginning to indicate that this hypothesis is probably true. It must be remembered that, by the end of the second year of life, the child's brain has attained 70–80% of its adult size and weight. A lessening of intellectual development potential, possibly causing in severe cases actual mental retardation, places an urgency on prevention of malnutrition.

Social behavior also has been observed to be changed in some diseases of malnutrition; this is almost universally seen with kwashiorkor, as discussed on pages 328–329. In milder forms of undernutrition, it is thought that low morale among the group may be one result. This leads to the vicious cycle so well illustrated on page 332.

It is difficult to describe the needs for a solution of the problem of malnutrition more succinctly and adequately than is done in "Malnutrition and Disease," which was published by WHO in 1963. It states:

> The solution of the problem of the hungry must take into account complex factors affecting almost every aspect of the life of man—climatic, economic, social and educational, religious and cultural. The solution will depend upon achieving cooperation between governments, national and international agencies, and workers in many scientific fields with the active participation not only of people in the developed countries but also the sufferers from malnutrition themselves.

BERIBERI

Beriberi today is only a name to many Americans; but to those who live in the rice-eating countries of the world, it can be a major cause of death and disability. This disease is discussed here because it is still a serious problem, as it has been through the centuries, in many countries of the Orient. Also, it is a good example of a disease of malnutrition. Beriberi is caused by a deficiency of one of the vitamins, thiamin, but is also complicated by lack of other nutrients when white rice is practically the only food.

In Chinese writings of the third, seventh, and eighth centuries, there are references to this disease, which was called *kak-ke*. The first European description of the disease was in a book written by a Dutch physician, Jacobus Bontius (1592–1631), and published in 1642. Bontius was physician with the East India Company and was sent to Batavia in 1627. He must have been a conscientious doctor because, when he realized how little he knew about tropical disease, he started to make a careful record of all he saw. An English translation of this book appeared in 1769. Bontius wrote: "The inhabitants of the East Indies are much afflicted with a troublesome disorder which they call the Beriberii." He described the disease as producing a loss of sensation in the feet and hands, a peculiar way of walking, and the whole body sometimes trembled. Beriberi, although well understood now, still occurs in many parts of the world. The cause is known; the cure and the way to prevent it also are known. But this disease is an interesting example of how food habits and customs have a stonger influence in the lives of people than scientific knowledge.

What Beriberi Is

Beriberi is a disease which affects the nervous tissues of the body. Four main types of the disease have been described. They are:

1. Wet beriberi, in which there is edema or swelling of the legs, hands, and abdomen due to accumulation of fluid in the tissues.
2. Dry beriberi, with neuritis, wasting and atrophy of the muscles, especially of the legs, and difficulty in walking.
3. Acute cardiac beriberi, with sudden onset of nausea and vomiting, enlargement of the heart, and increased heart rate.
4. Rudimentary beriberi, with mild symptoms of weakness in the legs, some swelling, abdominal pain, and heart palpitation. This form may exist for years or may suddenly develop into one of the other types and quickly become fatal.

The characteristic symptoms of beriberi are a tendency to edema, pain and loss of use of the limbs, and heart failure. Every combination of these symptoms may be found when examining a large number of cases of beriberi. We are not concerned here with clinical or technical details, but rather with the evidence that beriberi is a dietary disease, how this was discovered, and what the problems are today.

How Beriberi Was Identified as a Dietary Disease

From 1859, reports about the occurrence of beriberi in the Dutch navy appeared in Dutch medical journals. The suggestion was made that it was in some way caused by poor food, but nothing was done about this.

In Japan, beriberi or kak-ké was a serious problem, especially in the navy where there were several hundred cases per year and an average of 8.39 deaths per 1000 men. Kanehiro Takaki (1849–1920), a Japanese medical officer, entered the navy in 1872; during three years of service, he saw hundreds of cases of beriberi and so determined to learn everything that he could about the disease. Takaki went to England for medical study; when he returned to Japan, he was appointed director of the Tokyo Naval Hospital and later became director of the Naval Medical Bureau. Takaki carefully and systematically studied the disease of beriberi, its occurrence, and its location. He found that it was most frequent at the end of spring and summer, though some cases occurred in winter. He observed that soldiers, sailors, policemen, students, and shop boys suffered most. It was more common in large towns but was also present in small ones. And it occurred without any relation to the kind of living quarters or clothing. Takaki then turned his attention to the food of these people, especially the food of those in the navy. From calculations of the fat, carbohydrate, and protein in the rations, he saw that the carbohydrate food, rice, in the ration was very high and that there were not enough protein foods to make up for the body loss of nitrogen. He also saw that, the higher the ratio of carbohydrate to protein in the diet, the higher the incidence of beriberi.

Takaki proposed some dietary changes to the navy, but his ideas were not accepted; he therefore planned an experiment which would demonstrate whether his diet theory was right. The ability and clear thinking of Takaki are beautifully illustrated in the story of his carefully planned and controlled experiment. Two naval training ships were sent on the same long voyage across the equator and into the South Pacific so that any effect of different climate would be observed. The one difference was in the ration used on the ships. The training ship *Riujo* had 276 men and officers and sailed from Shinagawa, Japan, to Wellington, New Zealand, then to ports in Chile and Peru, and then to Honolulu. It returned to Japan after a voyage of 272 days. The customary naval ration was used on the *Riujo*, and there were 160 cases of beriberi and 25 deaths during the voyage.

The second ship, *Tsukuba*, followed the same course; all conditions were as nearly similar as possible except the ration was improved by increasing the amounts of meat, fish, and vegetables, adding some condensed milk, and decreasing the amount of rice. The voyage lasted 287 days and there were no deaths. But there were 10 cases of beriberi in men who had not eaten all parts of the new ration, particularly the milk and meat.

This clear demonstration of the value of improved diet in eliminating beriberi in the Japanese navy did not have much influence at the time it was published (1885–1888) because it was in Japanese journals and so not available to European workers. Also, this was the period of preoccupation with the bacterial origin of disease. Beriberi was believed to be due to an infection; then, when attention focused on food and especially rice in the diet, it was thought that some toxin in rice was the cause. With difficulty the final solution to the problem was obtained chiefly through investigators in three different geographical areas—the Dutch East Indies, Malaya, and the Philippines.

Rice is the cereal grain which is the main food for more than half the world's population; varieties of rice are numerous; terms to describe different forms of rice are sometimes confusing. The following descriptions give a general idea of terms and provide understanding of the relation of rice to the story of beriberi.

1. Paddy or rough rice—this is rice as it comes from the fields which are also called paddies; it is rice in the hulls.
2. Brown rice—the hulls have been removed but the outer coats of the grain and the germ are left. This form is very susceptible to attack by weevils and becomes rancid.
3. Polished or white rice—the germ and outer coats have been removed and the white starchy grain remains.
4. Parboiled or cured rice—this form is used mainly in India or in countries where there are large colonies of Indians. Rice in the hull is soaked, then steamed, and then dried in the sun; in this

process the vitamins are drawn into the center of the grain and are not lost in milling.

5. Converted rice—this is rice commercially processed in the U.S. using the same principle as in parboiling.
6. Enriched rice—in enriched rice, a premix is added to ordinary polished rice in definite proportions. The premix consists of specially treated rice grains that are impregnated with thiamin and other nutrients.

And now back to the main story and the work in the Dutch East Indies.

Dutch East Indies.   A key figure in the story of beriberi is Christian Eijkman (1858–1930), who, upon completing his medical training at the University of Amsterdam, was sent to the Dutch East Indies as an army surgeon. After two years, he returned to Holland to recover from malaria and became interested in the new science of bacteriology; he then studied under Robert Koch in Berlin. In 1886, Eijkman was appointed by the Dutch government as member of a commission to go to the East Indies and find the cause of beriberi which was responsible for so many deaths there. The commission thought beriberi was an infection; Eijkman remained in Batavia as director of the new research laboratory of bacteriology and pathology. For some reason not known now, domestic fowls were kept in the laboratory and were fed the waste food, mainly white rice, from the military hospital wards. The birds quickly developed polyneuritis gallarium, a disease similar to beriberi in man. This was reported in Dutch medical journals (1890) but apparently was not read by other investigators.

One story tells that an economy-minded administrator cut off Eijkman's supply of cooked white rice for his birds, so he had to buy cheap brown rice for them. To his surprise, the polyneuritis was cured. Eijkman was a bacteriologist and thought that there was a poison in the white rice and that the outer coatings of rice were an antidote. However, to Eijkman must go the credit for the experimental approach to study of dietary diseases by his being able to produce and cure polyneuritis in fowls and show that this was the same disease as human beriberi. Ill health caused Eijkman to return home, but his work was carried on by Gerrit Grijns (1865–1944), who continued the experiments with fowls. When Grijns fed the birds various native beans or brown rice, they maintained health; if polished rice from various countries was used, the birds died; addition of olive oil or mineral elements and salt mixtures to their diet did not help. Meat that was extracted with water and then dried gave no protection, nor did potato starch and milk sugar. Thus, it was shown that no dietary factor then known could prevent polyneuritis, and Grijns concluded that some unknown dietary substance was necessary. This study was published in 1901, but few were ready to accept or apply these findings. And being written in Dutch, as was Eijkman's work, the report could be read by few.

Malaya. W. L. Braddon, a British physician who had worked for many years in Malaya, observed differences in occurrence of beriberi among the racial groups living in Malaysia. The Malays used home-pounded (unpolished) rice and rarely had beriberi. The Tamils, who came from southeastern India, used parboiled rice and did not have beriberi. The Chinese used imported white rice and had a high incidence of beriberi. Europeans used little rice of any kind and did not have beriberi. The focus was on rice. but Braddon believed it was a poison associated with white rice that caused the disease.

W. Fletcher followed with studies on rice (1906–1907). Patients in an asylum were divided into two groups; one group ate polished white rice and the other group parboiled rice; the rest of the ration was the same for each. Over a period of six months, there were 53 cases of beriberi with white rice and none with parboiled rice. Fletcher theorized that there were three possible explanations: (1) there was a poison in white rice, (2) the ration was deficient in protein, and (3) white rice was so low in nutritive value that the patients were susceptible to attack by some organism. This was an excellent and convincing experiment.

Two other British physicians working near Singapore went a step further. H. Fraser and A. T. Stanton had the opportunity to study 300 laborers on road construction in two different camps in virgin jungle. The men were in new living quarters with good drainage and, on examination, all were in good health. They all were given a diet of rice, dried salt fish, onions, potatoes, coconut and oil, tea, and salt. The kind of rice, however, was different in the two camps. One camp had white rice, the other parboiled rice; those men receiving white rice developed beriberi, but those on parboiled rice did not.

Fraser and Stanton made extracts of rice and could find no traces of any toxic substance. They treated the parboiled rice to long extraction with hot alcohol; after this treatment the parboiled rice no longer protected fowls from beriberi. But if they added the alcohol extract itself to white rice, the birds did not get beriberi. In 1910, they reported that "our researches have conclusively shown that beriberi can be prevented by the use of unpolished rice and as surely produced by the use of highly polished rice." Here was the answer at last, or at least the first part of it. A little over a year later, Casimir Funk introduced the term *vitamine*, and many workers became active in this new field of investigation (see Chapter 4).

Philippines.   In the same period, beriberi was being studied in the Philippines. The Philippine Scouts (Filipino soldiers with American officers) had many hospital cases and a high death rate from beriberi (1902); when eventually (1910) their diet was changed to less rice and the rice was the under-milled form, beriberi rapidly disappeared. Infantile beriberi was also a serious problem. Feeding experiments in prisons, carried on quite independently but in similar fashion to those in Malaya, added further evidence to the dietary origin of the disease. But the work was to be carried much further in Manila.

Edward B. Vedder of the U.S. Army Medical Corps served in various capacities in the Philippines from 1904 to 1913 and was concerned with the beriberi problem. He studied everything written on the subject and found it so confusing that he said it was difficult "to sift the wheat from the chaff, or the rice from the rice polishings!" His book *Beriberi* (1913), is a classic on the subject. When R. R. Williams (1885–1965), a young chemist, received his master's degree from the University of Chicago, his first professional appointment (1908) was in the Philippines. There he soon became associated with Vedder who started him on the search for an isolation of the antiberiberi vitamin. This search lasted 26 years, until Williams found a way to prepare thiamin and determined its chemical structure and then its synthesis. His whole life was devoted to efforts to eliminate beriberi throughout the world. The discovery of the specific beriberi factor, first called vitamin B_1, then named thiamin is a story which belongs to chemistry. Vedder, Jansen of Holland, and Williams were outstanding figures in this story.

Because of Williams' success in synthesizing thiamin it can now be prepared cheaply. This led in 1941 to what has been called the enrichment program. During the years of World War II, the millers and bakers in America worked together with nutrition scientists on a plan whereby thiamin, iron, and niacin (and later riboflavin) could be added to flour, bread, and baked goods; the U.S. government made it mandatory during wartime that these products should be enriched. This was a measure to protect the health of all people against deficiencies in the diet because of wartime food shortages. Enrichment proved so beneficial that a number of states passed their own enrichment laws and continue to require enrichment of bread, flour, and cornmeal. And in a few states rice is enriched with thiamin because a practical way was found for adding thiamin to white rice.

If enrichment was beneficial to the population in the U.S., how much more beneficial it would be in those countries where beriberi was endemic. Williams believed in this solution and worked hard for it. One of the more exciting stories of a human nutrition experiment is one that Williams helped to plan and initiate in the Philippines. It began in 1947; the Bataan peninsula was chosen because it is somewhat isolated, with only one good road running the length of the peninsula so distribution of rice could be controlled. A survey was made of the incidence of beriberi, and cases equivalent to 12.7% of the population were clearly identified. Analyses of Bataan foods were made to determine their thiamin content, and clinical and biochemical measurements were made on a selected group of the people. The peninsula was divided into two areas. Beginning in 1948, the people in area A on the east coast were supplied with enriched rice, while those in the rest of the province, area B, received only white rice. When the groups were surveyed again a year later, there had been a marked drop in incidence of beriberi in the area which received the enriched rice and a slight increase in beriberi in the white rice area. For such large-scale experiments on people, it is difficult to control all factors; nevertheless, this experiment did show that it is practical and effective to increase the thamin intake by use of enriched rice.

Beriberi has not been confined to the peoples of the world who eat rice. It has occurred in Labrador and Newfoundland and, in isolated cases, in institutions in the U.S. when white bread and white flour have been used as the staples of the diet.

The current world situation regarding beriberi is best described by quoting from a report of the World Health Organization (1958):

. . . beriberi remains a serious public health problem in a number of rice-eating countries in South and East Asia, particularly in Burma, Thailand, and Viet Nam; and the disease is causing a large number of deaths in breast-fed infants between the first and sixth months of life. Surveys in Burma and Thailand by WHO officers support these conclusions. There are indications that the prevalence of beriberi is increasing, in association with the spread of small rice mills, in a number of rural rice-producing areas in East Asia. . . .

The causes of beriberi are fully established and methods of preventing it have been known for more than forty years. . . . There is ample evidence that beriberi can be eradicated. For example, while it was common in Japan in the early decades of the century, it is now a rare disease there as a result of changes in the national diet and preventive measures taken by the authorities.

Thiamin and Food

Thiamin functions in the body as part of certain enzyme systems, particularly in those which have to do with the utilization of carbohydrates. Therefore, the higher the intake of foods that are high in starch, as polished rice or unenriched white flour, the greater is the need for thiamin; and the higher the calorie intake, the larger is the amount of thiamin that must be supplied in the diet. This is why men or any one who is active or doing physical work need more thiamin or get beriberi if there is a dietary deficiency. Also, women under stress of pregnancy and lactation have increased need for thiamin. The nursing mother who lives on white rice produces milk which is almost devoid of thiamin, so her infant gets infantile beriberi; this is a high cause of infant mortality in some Asian countries.

Thiamin is present in many foods but usually in small amounts, and a few foods such as the fats and oils and refined sugars are devoid of thiamin. The cereal grains are good sources, but the thiamin is in the germ and outer coatings so that refined cereals such as white rice and white flour have lost their thiamin. Legumes such as various kinds of peas and beans, fresh or dried, and soybeans, lentils, and peanuts are significant sources. The animal foods, meat, fish, milk, and eggs, contain some thiamin; liver is higher in thiamin than muscle meat. And for some unknown reason, pork is a rich source; a liberal serving of pork supplies a day's requirement of thiamin. A variety of foods in the day's meals has many nutritional advantages, not the least of which is protection against a deficiency of thiamin. Enrichment of bread and cereals in the U.S. is one of the added protections provided in this country.

Thiamin has the chemical qualities of being soluble in water and destroyed by high temperatures and by some chemicals including soda used in the treatment of foods. Since it is water soluble, thiamin may be lost when large amounts of water are used in cooking vegetables or rice and the cooking water is thrown away. This water solubility of thiamin explains why thiamin containing foods should be eaten daily; this vitamin is not stored in the body—excess amounts are excreted.

Subclinical Thiamin Deficiencies

While beriberi is seen only in certain countries today, we must not lose sight of the fact that beriberi occurs when the diet is grossly lacking in thiamin. What about the people who get some thiamin but not enough? This can occur here or in any country; this condition is referred to as subclinical deficiency, meaning that the dietary lack is not so great as to cause definite illness, but the intake is not enough for good health. The effects of insufficient thiamin are hard to define, but clinical experiments show that low thiamin intakes may lead to loss of appetite, fatigue, irritability, and digestive disturbances (all of which may be caused by others factors, also). How much of this type of subclinical deficiency exists with regard to thiamin (or for that matter for the other vitamins and other nutrients) in many countries of the world is difficult to estimate; it is part of the problem of widespread malnutrition.

Dietary studies, where records are made of the kinds and amounts of food eaten by individuals or families and then the nutrient content of the diets calculated, indicate that many groups do not receive adequate amounts of thiamin (or of other nutrients) even though there are no obvious symptoms of disease. Such dietary studies are expensive, time consuming, require trained personnel, and, therefore, have not been made for populations in many areas. Biochemical measurements of the blood also provide information on adequacy of thiamin intake, but these are more expensive in equipment and personnel and so have been even more limited than dietary studies.

ENDEMIC GOITER

There are estimated to be 200 million cases of endemic goiter in the world today, according to a World Health Organization (WHO) report in 1960. This disease has been known for hundreds of years, but only in this century has the science of nutrition provided the evidence as to how this disease may be prevented. A century ago a French scientist provided the correct theory about the cause and prevention of endemic goiter, but his contemporaries simply did not believe him. This has recurred throughout science and man's history—discoveries have been

Goiter areas of the world. (Adapted from: World Health Organization, WHO Activities in Nutrition 1948–1964, p. 25, 1965.)

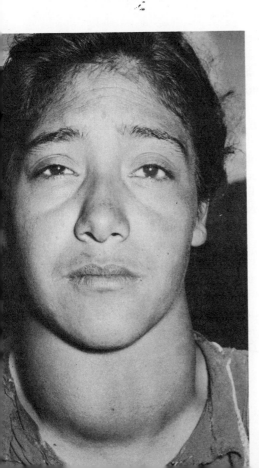

Several million cases of endemic goiter exist in the world today. (Courtesy World Health Organization.)

made but not accepted because the ideas have been ahead of their time.

The major cause of endemic goiter is a deficiency of iodine in the diet. This is a simple statement and one well verified by extensive experiments; by analyses of drinking water, soil, and food; and by clinical data. Study of this disease illustrates how much easier it is to understand discoveries when they fit in with the background of science and what we already know, and how difficult it is to accept that which is new when it is different from current beliefs.

Goiter is no respecter of persons or places (see map). It occurs in some part of almost every region and country of the world, so it obvious that climate or weather or temperature is not the causative factor. All people, whatever their race, color, creed, or socio-economic group, are susceptible to this disease. The high incidence of endemic goiter in the U.S. only 50 years ago led to the experimental studies in the Great Lakes region which demonstrated how this disease could be prevented.

The story of this disease and how to prevent it involves chemical elements and compounds, some physiological terms, and a gland of the body. Definitions and explanations of these terms will lead to fuller understanding of this deficiency disease.

1. *Iodine* is a chemical element first discovered in 1811 by a French chemist, Bernard Courtois, when he was preparing saltpeter for gunpowder for Napoleon's army.

2. *The thyroid,* a ductless gland at the base of the neck, uses iodine to make a hormone needed by the body for its normal processes. The name thyroid was given to this gland by an English physician, Thomas Wharton, in 1646; he was the first to determine the site, size, and weight of the gland.

3. *Thyroxine* is a hormone secreted by the thyroid gland, which must be supplied with iodine in order to make this hormone; Thyroxine was first prepared by Edward C. Kendall of the Mayo Clinic in 1914.

4. *Endemic goiter,* sometimes called simple goiter, is a condition of enlargement of the thyroid. Endemic means that it occurs in a large number of the people in a particular community or location. There are many other types of goiter and thyroid gland disorders which are different from endemic goiter in their effects and causes.

5. *Goitrogenic factors* are ones which produce goiter; the word goitrogenic comes from the Greek root *genic,* which means "giving rise to."

The Discovery of Iodine and the Cause of Goiter

Goiter is believed to have occurred for thousands of years and to have been described by the ancient Chinese, early Hindus, and the Egyptians. Difficulties in language, different meanings of words, and lack of knowledge in early times about the organs of the body leave us uncertain as to exactly how long this disease has been known.

At the beginning of the nineteenth century, biological and medical research had progressed to a stage where more exact and careful studies could be made on goiter. After Courtois discovered iodine (1811), a Swiss physician, Jean Francois Coindet (1820), recommended its use for treatment of goiter. However, the doses used were too large and there were harmful effects, so the use of iodine fell into disrepute. Some 30 years later, a French chemist, Gaspard Adolph Chatin, published results of research where he determined the iodine content of air, water, soil, and plants in many parts of Europe. He found that in Paris, where goiter did not occur, the people had a daily intake of iodine five times as high as the people of Lyons and Turin, where there was moderate goiter. In the alpine villages where there was much goiter, the people obtained only one-tenth as much iodine a day as the Parisians had. Chatin concluded that iodine deficiency was the cause of goiter, but his contemporaries rejected this idea.

Little progress was made in understanding the cause of goiter until 1895, when Eugen Baumann, a German chemist, analyzed the thyroid gland and showed that it contained iodine in small amounts. At last scientists had a connection between iodine and goiter. However, since goiter was not a fatal disease, it did not attract as much attention or study as did some of the more serious diseases.

In the U.S. there were serious problems in the cattle industry in various areas of the country, especially in Michigan and in parts of the West. There were heavy losses of young lambs, calves, and colts; piglets were born hairless and were stillborn or died within a few days. At this time (1907), a young medical research scientist, David Marine, in Cleveland, Ohio, began studies on the thyroid that were to lead to worldwide recognition that deficiency of iodine caused goiter. He first analyzed the thyroids of sheep, cattle, and hogs and found a relationship between iodine and the scructure of the gland. Then he spent several years, at the request of the Pennsylvania State Fish Commission, investigating the cause of thyroid disease in fish; this disease interfered with the raising of brook trout in the fish hatcheries. He eventually showed that the problem could be prevented by inclusion of iodine in the food of fish.

If iodine prevented goiter in farm animals and in fish, then surely the same must be true for man; but experimental evidence was essential. Dr. Marine began work in 1916 with school girls in Akron, Ohio. He surveyed all the girls from the fifth to the twelfth grades to find the incidence of goiter. There were 4,466 girls examined, and 56% had enlarged thyroids. With the approval of the local medical society, the school board, and the school superintendent, treatment by iodine (sodium iodide) was begun in 1917 for all girls who elected to have it. Examinations of the thyroid were made twice yearly. At the end of thirty months, Dr. Marine reported:

> . . . of 2,190 pupils taking 2 gm. sodium iodide twice yearly (given in 0.2 gm. doses daily, for ten consecutive school days each spring and autumn), five have shown enlargement of the thyroid, while of 2,305 pupils not taking the prophylactic 495 have shown enlargement of the thyroid. Of 1,182 pupils with thyroid enlargement at the first examination and who took prophylactic, 773 thyroids have decreased in size, while of 1,084 pupils with thyroid enlargement at the first examination and who did not take the prophylactic, 145 thyroids have decreased in size. These figures demonstrate in a striking manner both the preventive and therapeutic effects.

This was one of the first large-scale controlled studies on man of a dietary-deficiency disease.

D. Marine shared his results with R. Klinger in Zurich, Switzerland, where goiter was very severe in some areas. Klinger undertook similar treatments of school children and obtained even more striking results in prevention and improvement of goitrous conditions.

Some investigators believe that there is a relationship between goiter and cretinism and the accompanying feeble mindedness and deaf mutism. However, this has not been clearly defined, and more research is needed to clarify this question.

India is one of several countries which have attacked the problem of goiter. A pilot study was made between 1956 and 1962 to see whether iodized salt would be effective in preventing goiter. Two zones were chosen, and about 5000 people in each were examined for incidence of goiter. One zone received iodized salt and the other received ordinary salt for a five-year period. The people were then reexamined. In the zone where iodized salt was used, the number of goiter cases was reduced from 40% to about 17% of the population. In the zone receiving ordinary salt, the number of goiter cases remained at the same level it had been. The Indian government followed up this study by arranging to produce iodized salt for the people in several states of India.

Age and Sex Incidence

In areas where goiter is endemic, it may occur in individuals at any age; in highly goitrous areas, babies may be born with goiter. The highest incidence is in girls twelve to eighteen years of age and boys nine to thirteen years old. Pubertal changes appear to increase the need by the thyroid gland for iodine. Females are more susceptible to goiter than males.

Goitrogenic and Other Factors

Iodine deficiency results in goiter, but there may be other factors involved. There are naturally occurring substances in some foods, especially cabbage, rape, rutabaga, turnips, and related plants, which block the utilization of iodine by the thyroid. Certain sulphur-containing drugs act as antithyroid agents, apparently by interfering with the production of thyroxine.

There are genetic differences in susceptibility to goiter. Some research studies also show that infection and contamination of drinking water may be factors in causing goiter.

Food Sources of Iodine

The iodine content of foods depends on the soil in which they are grown; some plants, such as spinach, take more from the soil than others. Seaweeds are rich in iodine because they collect and concentrate iodine from seawater. All seafoods are good sources of iodine.

In general, the vegetables, especially green leafy ones and legumes, contain more iodine than cereals and fruits; meat and milk are between these groups. All foods are highly variable, and foods in the markets were grown in various areas. For this reason, a practical, economical way to make iodine available to everyone is to add it to salt. Iodine, in the form of potassium iodide, is added to table salt in the U.S. as a public health measure. No one is compelled to use iodized salt; plain salt is also available in the markets. But iodized salt is a wise choice; it is a means of restoring to salt what was present in the original crude substance before it was purified. Continuous educational programs are

Geographical distribution of kwashiorkor. (Adapted from: Food and Agriculture Organization.)

Child with kwashiorkor upon admission to the doctor's care.

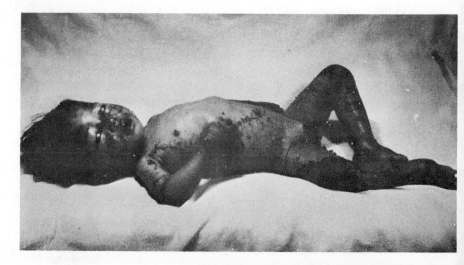

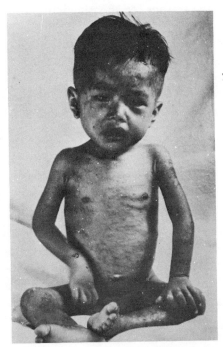

The same child four days later.

The same child after one month of care. (All photos courtesy World Health Organization.)

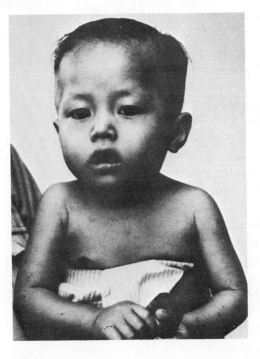

necessary to remind consumers of the reasons for choosing iodized salt for cooking and for table use.

Many other countries also use some form of iodized salt; a study group of WHO in 1952 recommended that "all food salts should be iodized compulsorily in any country or area in which goiter is endemic." However, many problems are encountered because in tropical countries the crude, moist salt used renders the iodine compound unstable.

KWASHIORKOR

One of the greatest enemies of good health in the world's children, protein-calorie malnutrition, came into the spotlight during the 1950's and especially during the 1960's. Kwashiorkor is a severe form of protein-calorie malnutrition. D. B. Jelliffe (1966) said that by "unofficial international agreement the term kwashiorkor is currently used almost universally for this particular extreme form of protein-calorie malnutrition of early childhood even though there is disagreement about minimum diagnostic criteria." Kwashiorkor is discussed in detail because such a discussion will show the complexity of such a disease and how the effects of it reach into all segments of a society. Students may wish to follow the methods used here to investigate other problems of vital concern in world health.

Presently in the U.S. the word kwashiorkor is being encountered in daily newspapers and in widely read magazines. In 1957, major attention was given to it in a full four-page article in the *Saturday Evening Post*.

In 1935 Dr. Cicely Williams used the word kwashiorkor for a disease for which, in a 1933 article, she had described the symptoms seen in twenty cases in Ghana (then called the Gold Coast). She said in 1935 that she used the word merely as a confession of ignorance.

It is known that this disease had at times some 50 different names all around the world. It had been called "fatty liver disease" or "sugar baby," "m'buoki" in the Congo, "dystrophie des farineux" in French, "mehlnahrschaden" in German, "nutritional distrophy" in India, and "distrofia pluricarencial infantil" in Latin America. The recognition that it was the same in Guatemala, India, or the Congo represented progress in clinical diagnosis of it.

The word kwashiorkor comes from the language of the Ga tribe, one of the principal tribes in Ghana. Different meanings have been ascribed to this word. One of them, "red boy," probably originates either from the red patches or the bleeding lesions on the legs or other parts of the body. In some children, the hair also may show either bands or tips of a reddish hue. Preference seems to be given by authorities to the red skin meaning. Many clinicians, including Williams, believe, however, that kwashiorkor really means the disease of the "deposed child" or the sickness of "the older child when a new baby is born." Some of the Ga people also say that the word really means "first-second." When Charity Dagadu, a Ga from Accra, Ghana, was a student in the author's class, she said that the Ga mother uses the word kwashiorkor to refer to the jealousy which the first child has for the new baby. According to her, many of these mothers think the disease is caused by this jealousy. In areas of the world where the disease is common, one may find it referred to as "that disease."

Regardless of the original tribal meaning of the word, it is now well described in medical literature, and the need to direct attention to its prevention is well recognized. It had been described as early as 1906 and thought it was caused by a high starch diet. Authorities now recognize that it is the imbalance of protein and carbohydrate in such a diet which causes the condition and not just the extra starch. An early article from Mexico described a disease with a "snakelike" skin which Williams had characterized as a "crazy pavement" skin. In 1918, reports of a similar condition came from Africa; a similar condition was described in Japan in 1923, in France in 1927, and in 1929 in Cuba. During the next two decades, reports came from Central and South America, from parts of the Caribbean such as Jamaica, from Hungary, from Greece, from India, from the Philippines, from Fiji, and from Spain.

In 1949, a commission of FAO, the "Expert Committee on Nutrition," met to discuss the reports of this disease which was evidently occurring in widely scattered parts of the world and which was found to respond promptly and completely when milk was given. This milk was usually provided as skim milk powder. Those on this committee must have remembered the 1933 article which Dr. Williams had written sixteen years before. As a result of the recommendations by the committee for further study of this disease, J. F. Brock and M. Autret made a survey in ten countries in Africa south of the Sahara. They then wrote "Kwashiorkor in Africa," which was issued jointly by FAO and WHO in 1952.

Shortly after this, similar surveys were done in Central America and Brazil.

Twenty-six people from twelve countries met in 1953 under the sponsorship of the Josiah Macy Foundation to discuss the prevalence, causes, and possible prevention of kwashiorkor. In 1955 at another meeting in Princeton, New Jersey, sponsored by the same foundation, the disease was recognized as a major problem in the world; the participants discussed methods of prevention. In 1956, a Committee on Protein Malnutrition of the NAS–NRC was created. Its assignment was "to organize and supervise a world-wide research program on high protein foods for the improvement of the nutrition of populations, particularly of growing children in food deficient countries." This work was supported by grants from the Rockefeller Foundation and UNICEF. More recently the same board appointed a Committee on International Nutrition Problems. An International Conference on "Meeting the Protein Needs of Infants and Preschool Children" was held in Washington, D.C., in 1960. After each of these conferences, the availability of their proceedings made the findings useful to the scientific community and to the science editors of the popular press. Protein-calorie malnutrition in one of its severe forms is now firmly labeled as kwashiorkor. Investigators have begun to probe the depths of its characteristics in its mild and severe forms, noting its consequences and its causes, both immediate and long-term. Kwashiorkor occupied a prominent place at the 1965 Western Hemisphere Nutrition Congress held in Chicago and at the 1965 and 1966 annual meetings of the American Public Health Association.

In 1963, another important step in the long history of kwashiorkor was taken at the Villa Servelloni in Bellagio on Lake Como in Italy. The group meeting there considered how to reach the preschool child because this postweaning disease was known to affect children from one to four years of age most seriously. Following the Lake Como Conference, at the Sixth International Congress in Nutrition meeting in Edinburgh, Scotland, plans were made for a 1964 International Conference on the Prevention of Malnutrition in the Preschool Child. This was held in Washington, D. C., in early December 1964.

The 1963 Lake Como and the 1964 Washington conferences, by focusing on the preschool-age child, gave prominence not only to kwashiorkor but also to other conditions of malnutrition in this age group, such as marasmus, xeropthalmia, anemia, and goiter. The lead sentence of the general summary of the report of this 1964 conference gave evidence of this:

> Malnutrition in the preschool child is one of the world's most serious health problems in developing areas. Not only is it killing and maiming the children today, but also, through physical, mental, and emotional damage, it will handicap the society of 1984 and the next generation.

This idea will be explained later in the chapter.

A conference at Schloss Tremsbüttel in Hamburg, Germany, in 1966 considered the administrative aspects of programs to protect the preschool child. After 1963, special programs to reach the younger children had been initiated in a number of countries. Now it was necessary to agree on practical procedures to carry on these programs so that they would be effective at once.

D. B. Jelliffe, who has spent years working with kwashiorkor, stated that "protein-calorie malnutrition in early childhood occurs most commonly in most tropical countries and in some it may be the primary public health problem although not recognized as such."

Because kwashiorkor, along with marasmus, is considered the most serious of the diseases afflicting preschool children in the world today, it will be discussed in detail. Everyone should be concerned about "that disease" "due to jealousy" "of a red boy" in Africa. It does affect all of us because anything which may handicap the society of 1984 on several continents also surely will handicap every citizen on earth.

The Prevalence of Kwashiorkor

Marcel Autret, Director of the Nutrition Division of FAO and one of the authors of the 1952 FAO/WHO report on "Kwashiorkor in Africa," in a paper prepared in 1964 for the personnel of the Nutrition Division of FAO, said:

> It has been admitted for ten years that malnutrition among preschool children —whether it is called kwashiorkor, protein malnutrition or calorie and protein malnutrition—constitutes the number one nutritional problem of our day. Now in these ten years has all been done that could be done to combat it? Certainly not. One had learned to identify the disease and to treat it correctly in a hospital; but one does not know what its incidence is in most parts of the world.

He also pointed out that one does not know what its incidence and therefore its relative importance are in a given country such as are known for malaria, tuberculosis, or for yaws. There is concern in 1973 because the new food products, rich in protein and made especially for children, really reach only a few of those who need them. Many others engaged in international health programs have made statements concerning the gravity of the problem and the lack of concentrated attention and effort to do something until recently. Paul Gyorgy stated that "70% of the preschool children in the developing countries suffer from various degrees of malnutrition." McLaren, studying a total of 146 Arab children suffering from protein-calorie malnutrition, found that 28.1% of the cases ended in death; and mortality was higher in boys than girls. During the 12-month period of study, 1,082 children under four years of age were admitted to the Luzmila Hospital in Amman, Jordan; 43% of them had one form or another of protein-calorie malnutrition according to his *Simple Scoring System* described on page 331. For all of these reasons it is difficult to determine the exact incidence of the disease. There is now, however, extensive literature on kwashiorkor.

We do know that it occurs most frequently in tropical and semi-tropical countries. Some cases of kwashiorkor were reported in the U.S. in the past decade, one in Kentucky in 1960 and one in the Bronx in 1966; in 1961, three cases were diagnosed in children from the Navajo Reservation. In 1969, Van Duzen and his coworkers made a systematic review of all cases admitted to the Public Health Service Indian Hospital in Tuba City, Arizona over the period of 1963–1967. This hospital was then one of six government hospitals providing health service to the Navajo Indians; the Tuba City hospital provided service to approximately 13% of all Navajos. Of 616 children with a diagnosis of malnutrition, 15 had kwashiorkor and 29 had marasmus. These authors believed that these cases were the end result of calorie and protein malnutrition associated with bacterial and viral infections. The author was told in 1972 by a prominent pediatrician in Ghana that depressed economic conditions were basic causes of many cases of kwashiorkor there.

As McLaren, from his work overseas, warned in 1966, the incidence of marasmus has been rising; he says the incidence of this disease has increased because of early weaning, a rapid succession of pregnancies, the return of the mother to work in industry, and her susceptibility to propaganda for artificial feeding. Because of the cost of the latter kind of infant foods, she often over-dilutes the food, which reduces the calories as well as the protein and also introduces a source of bacterial infections with impure water. McLaren and other medical people working in areas where malnutrition is prevalent have pointed to the following as causes of this increase of marasmus:

1. Rapid urbanization and the forsaking of old cultural practices.
2. Mothers now having more frequent pregnancies as polygamy is abandoned and monogamy taken up. This saps the mother's strength and affects her ability to breast feed her infant.
3. As a result, there is a reduced incidence of breast feeding even before the infant is one year old. The fact of the mother returning early to her work in industry is often the cause for this.
4. Feeding infants too dilute formula because of cost when infant is fed an expensive proprietary formula.
5. Formula infected with impure water which is added by the mother.
6. Often "starvation therapy" is used when the malnourished infant has diarrhea and other infections.

Clinical Features of the Disease

Certain characteristics of kwashiorkor have been observed by those who work with these children. In 1966, D. B. Jelliffe classified the clinical features of kwashiorkor into: (1) the constant signs, (2) the usual signs, and (3) the occasional signs. He said that the following signs may be regarded as diagnostic if found in early childhood in areas where the diet in infancy is mainly carbohydrate. They are:

1. Edema.
2. Growth retardation.
3. Muscle wasting with retention of some subcutaneous fat.
4. Psychomotor change.

The usual signs, though not necessary for diagnosis, are usually present singly or in any combination. They are:

1. Hair changes.
2. Diffuse pigmentation of the skin.
3. Moon face.
4. Anemia.

The occasional signs are present in some cases and not in others. They are:

1. Flaky-paint rash.
2. Enlarged liver with fatty infiltration.
3. Skin lesions such as fissures behind the ears and a "moist groin rash."
4. Associated vitamin deficiency.
5. Associated conditioning infections.

There is good agreement among those who work with kwashiorkor that retarded growth, showing first in a failure to gain weight before lack of increase in length is evident, is one of the first signs of the disease. This slow rate of growth is now believed to be caused by inadequate food and not a deficiency of a growth hormone.

Some studies have recently shown, as did Ashworth, et al, that children with kwashiorkor can, with adequate feeding, rapidly make up for the defects of body weight in relation to length. When the children they studied reached this stage of recovery there was some mechanism to reduce their appetites. They believe that "following malnutrition there is a stimulus to grow rapidly, but that this stimulus is reduced or removed when expected weight for height is reached." Workers in Africa have reported that children brought to the hospital at the age of eighteen months often show the weight of a normal five- to six-month-old infant. It has been pointed out that if the mothers and all who care for children in these vulnerable countries could be alerted to the seriousness of failure to grow and gain, much real kwashiorkor could probably be prevented. Additional work especially by such agencies as AID is being done now on educating mothers to the need for watching the preschool child's gain in weight. Clinics are concentrating on using new charts such as that devised by Morley, see page 391–394, and on mothers' education in their use.

Evidence is increasing every day which leads to the belief that, under optimum conditions, growth characteristics are the same in nearly all areas of the world. It is now thought rather generally that racial and genetic factors play only a small part in growth failure.

Another clinical symptom of the disease which is seen in practically 100% of the victims of kwashiorkor is *changed behavior*. The child becomes irritable, as Williams pointed out as early as 1933. In extremely severe cases, apathy develops and the child pays little attention to his surroundings. This condition was brought home to the author in a children's ward of the city hospital in Lagos, Nigeria. She saw a change in three days' time in a child with diagnosed kwashiorkor, from total apathy to emitting a whimpering cry. The cry is usually described as one which denotes a thoroughly wretched child, often said to exhibit peevish mental apathy. Brock and Autret, in their 1952 report, commented that this clinical aspect has often been neglected. More recently, most authors writing on the subject have mentioned this as one of the prominent features.

Edema, or retention of water in the tissues, is also frequently described as present. In fact, the child with kwashiorkor looks very different from the victim of marasmus, where wastage of subcutaneous and muscular tissue gives an appearance of extreme gauntness. In kwashiorkor, edema gives puffy legs and distended abdomen as well as the so-called "moon face" appearance.

Anemia is often associated with kwashiorkor. Adams, studying 148 African and Indian children with kwashiorkor, reported that the anemia found was mainly due to protein deficiency, with deficiencies of iron and folic acid playing a part in the condition.

Skin changes were described by the early writers as "crazy pavement" and "snake-like skin." These changes involve a coarsening of the skin in spots, with dark or heavily pigmented areas in some cases and light or dyspigmented spots in others. A change in appearance of the skin, which is more noticeable in Negro children than those of other races, has been called a "flaky-paint" skin. Spots, jet black in color, with sharply defined edges, appear on parts of the body. Erosion of the skin and later ulceration, forming open lesions or sores, may also appear on the affected areas. These secondary infections develop where the skin is broken, especially on those parts of the body which are exposed to the sunlight.

One of the other clinical features of the disease is the change in the color of the hair, as was discussed under the meaning of the name. The hair may be dyspigmented and become grayish white in color or it may take on a coppery reddish hue, either of which is strange looking in the black hair of a Negro child. The reddish tinge, which denotes a lowered amount of pigment available for the growing hair, is accounted for as one accounts for the red and yellow color in the leaves of trees which, in the fall of the year, lose their green color when the chlorophyll dies. The hair color may range from brownish black to brown to pale grayish brown or even to a straw color.

Two types of hair changes may be seen. One shows up in bands of different colors, aptly referred to as "banding" or the "flag sign." This results when the child receives inadequate protein and gives a striking record of the periods of hunger. Brock and Autret told in their 1952 report that, when ignorant and uneducated parents in Africa were asked whether the reddish hair was its natural color, they unhesitatingly replied that it was the result of the recent famine. The other type of change of color shows up in tipping of the hair.

Texture changes in hair also occur. The kinky, wiry hair of the African child becomes straight, soft, or even brittle; thin and sparse, it can be pulled out very easily.

Studies focused on the changes in the hair of kwashiorkor victims have shown statistically significant changes in tensile strength and significant differences in the diameter of anterior hair compared with the posterior hair, although the latter differences were not found in normal or even in marasmic children. Other workers have shown severe atrophy of the hair bulb with accompanying constriction along the shaft during the very short period of a 15-day experimental period of protein deprivation.

All of these hair changes have been observed less frequently in Latin America and India than they have in Africa.

Nowhere in the literature has the author found any statement concerning the shame which the African mother shows for the reddish tinge so that she dyes the hair black. In 1959 this was shown to her by the prominent pediatrician, Susan Ofori Atta, in a children's hospital in Accra, Ghana. She felt that this manifested shame gave her a good opening for teaching the mother how to prevent the reoccurrence of the reddish tinge.

Another clinical feature which is often found to be present is the enlargement and fatty changes of the liver. Trowell, et al, reported that, in the children they examined who had recovered from kwashiorkor, the liver tissue had returned to normal. Abnormality in other internal organs has also been noted.

There is an apparent association of avitaminosis A and kwashiorkor. According to Mahladevan and Ganguly: "The most common and almost inevitable nutritional disorder accompanying kwashiorkor is avitaminosis A." They also say that how kwashiorkor precipitates the vitamin A deficiency is not yet known. It appears that vitamin A is not well carried in the blood plasma of a kwashiorkor victim.

Probably the most alarming change which kwashiorkor may cause in the young child has only recently been recognized. There is an ever-increasing body of experimental evidence showing that severe malnutrition such as kwashiorkor, especially in the young infant, may cause irreparable brain damage and therefore a lessening of the potential for intellectual growth. This damage has been shown in animals to be most serious during what would correspond to an age under six months in the human infant. There is now reason to believe that this same kind of damage from inadequate food may occur in the human infant. Although much work remains to be done to show a direct relationship between protein-calorie malnutrition and permanent damage to the intellectual development potential, many authorities now believe that there is a real possibility that current research is proving such a relationship. Perhaps this is what Ritchie Calder meant in his 1964 statement: "By present neglect, we are exaggerating the problems of the future. We are caricaturing now the world society of 1984."

The Nutrition Review of February, 1969, in evaluating studies of mental development following kwashiorkor, urged caution and suggested that high priority should be given to research in which the nutritional variable is separated from genetic and many environmental variables. Such studies are now under way, as is discussed on page 196.

In 1968, McLaren raised the question of how to classify the large group of cases of protein-calorie malnutrition which could not be labeled, according to him, as either marasmus or kwashiorkor but were known to be "severe primary malnutrion." He and his coworkers have suggested a *Simple Scoring System* which includes three severe forms of protein-calorie malnutrition: *marasmus, marasmic-kwashiorkor,* and *kwashiorkor.*

In summary, then, prominent clinical features of kwashiorkor are:

1. Retarded growth and development which may include intellectual and hence social development.
2. Changed behavior, with peevishness and indifference to surroundings being most prominent.

3. Edema, especially in the extremities.
4. Skin changes, dyspigmentation, blotching, and lesions which permit secondary infections.
5. Changes in the hair color and texture.
6. Changes in the liver and other internal organs.

The Role of Infectious Diseases

An examination into the causes of death in children in countries where kwashiorkor is prevalent connects it with infectious diseases. In a study of 286 undernourished and malnourished children admitted to a hospital in India in 1957–1960, 123 were diagnosed as kwashiorkor (edematous and fatty type) and 163 as marasmus (wasted type); the mortality was high—23%. Within 48 hours after admission, 14% died, and 5% died suddenly in the hospital. The immediate causes of death were given as diarrhea, dehydration, and respiratory infections. It is well known that infection causes a decrease in appetite and water and mineral losses from the body or malabsorption of necessary nutrients from the intestinal tract. Arnold Schaefer observed that 40% of the children of Vietnam die from a combination of malnutrition and infectious diseases and that the death rate from measles in Guatemala was 325 times what it is in the U.S. and in most of Europe.

In south India, the maximum incidence of hospital admissions for kwashiorkor was noted to occur during the summer months when there were maximum breeding of the common housefly and maximum incidence of diarrhea. In Central America during a measles epidemic, no children in one village who were receiving supplementary feedings died, but there was a high fatality rate in a neighboring village where no extra food was being given to the children.

It has often been pointed out that the child whose body is weakened by malnutrition cannot withstand a bout of a serious infectious disease. Some have observed that even a vaccination during a period of grossly inadequate protein intake may cause a serious condition. It therefore has been proposed that, in countries where kwashiorkor is prevalent, vaccinations be done before very young children leave the mother's breast.

Causes of Kwashiorkor

The greater prevalence of this disease in children from one to four years of age points to the really basic cause. A study in Java (1963) gives a striking illustration of the ages of childhood when most deaths occur. In this study, 9% were infants; 36% were in their second year of life; 40% were in their third year; and 19% died during the sixth to seventh year.

In many developing countries in the tropics, it is the custom to nurse an infant at breast well up to two years or even more, usually until a new baby arrives. Because of this weaning at the arrival of the new baby, the child loses his chief source of protein. It may also be true that he has been gradually weakened since the age of six months because his mother's diet has been poor and the level of nutrients in her milk has decreased. But now, when he is suddenly removed from the breast, he suffers even more from a lack of needed nutrients and from the loss of his mother's love and attention. This sudden loss of close contact with his mother may be stark because she must, in her harried existence in a poverty-stricken environment, spend most of her time with the new baby and other household duties. The weanling child thus becomes suddenly neglected in several ways. He may be even taken out of the home to live with a grandmother or an aunt, which involves a real physical separation. Loss of appetite may also follow. Other changes in modes of living may affect this entire picture. It was reported in the WHO *Chronicle* of March 1966 that failure in lactation in communities in Africa was occurring with the increasing urbanization and the "erosion of traditional patterns of behavior." Improperly prepared artificial foods are being more and more used." In Kampala, the incidence of bottle feeding increased from 14% in 1950 to 42% in 1959. The shift was from kwashiorkor to marasmus often complicated by gastroenteritis.

As a substitute for the former breast milk, the newly weaned child is usually offered some kind of a starchy food. In many cultures, this kind of food is considered most desirable for a child of this age. Often this food, called "pap," is mixed with water, making a thin gruel. In the starchy-root-eating regions of Africa, this watery food may be made from cassava or manioc (tapioca is made from this) or from a large, white-fleshed root, called a yam, which also is low in protein. In Buganda, steamed plantains (a fruit similar to banana which must be cooked to be edible) called *matoke* are fed to the postweaned child. In South Asian countries, sweet potatoes are used, and in Latin America, Egypt, and parts of Africa, children receive corn or maize. Thin rice gruels may be fed in India. It must be said, however, that kwashiorkor is seen less among rice- and wheat-eating peoples than among the maize- and starchy-root-eating groups due to the difference in the quality of the protein of these foods. The rice gruel fed to children in India or other countries may be an inadequate food because the mother, in her ignorance, thinking that it will be more digestible, makes it into a thin food using much water.

All of these foods of the postweaned child have two things in common. They are:

1. High in starch and low in needed protein, these characteristics varying with the different foods.
2. Highly diluted with water.

Why is the weanling not given animal protein foods? In many areas, his family cannot afford meat, milk, eggs, or perhaps even fish; or these foods may actually not be available. In Africa, the tsetse fly, until international organizations such as FAO discovered and used methods for its control, made the raising of cattle practically impossible. In some places, although such foods as milk and eggs are available, the child does not get them because of the ignorance and superstition of his parents. In one tribe, eating eggs is considered a sign of greed because these people think it uneconomical not to let the greater food-producing chicken develop from the egg. In other groups, eggs are said to make girls licentious; as the author observed in a Zulu community during a 1972 food demonstration by a public health nutritionist, the older women shook their heads and looked disturbed when young mothers were encouraged to eat eggs. In Sierra Leone, eggs are not given to children below the age of five years because they are thought to cause them to steal. In Southern Rhodesia, it is believed that they cause baldness and sterility. When a local African in one area sees a person suffering from what a western observer conceptualizes as inadequate nutrition, the African may believe instead that the disease came about because the child's parents broke sexual taboos. There are kwashiorkor victims in cultures where milk is considered a disgusting food because it is a body secretion. In one tribe, only milk from cows of the mother's family's herd is considered fit food for her and her child. It is said that milk is so little valued by certain pastoral tribes in the north of Uganda that the people live on millet and give their milk to their herdsmen. Tribes such as the Masai, who use milk and blood and meat as a food, have no kwashiorkor, whereas their non-meat-eating and non-milk-drinking neighbors, the Kikuyu, have a high incidence. This was evident to the author in 1972 when she observed many Masai and their neighbors the Kikuyu and Mbutu; she saw the large-bellied children along the roadside. Differences in food habits of people living in areas next to each other make the contrast even more noticeable.

Another cultural factor which operates to promote undernourishment for the preschool child is that his order of demand on the scarce food of the family is low. The father, or the breadwinner, has first call, and all other adults get their share before the small child. For example, these people do not know that the growing body demands more good food relative to size than does the adult body. Stories are told that Masai men and warriors eat their fill of the cow they have killed before taking home any for the women and children.

It has been observed in some places that there is more kwashiorkor among boys than girls, probably meaning that the girl child, as she follows her mother around during the preparation of the family meal, gets handouts.

There is no doubt that the picture, as Gerlach has said, is one of "an intertwining web of social, economic, political, and magico-religious, technological, attitudinal, and environmental factors." We cannot, however, discuss here all of the factors which make the desirable protein-rich animal foods scarce.

As was said before, the poorest protein diet is furnished by the starchy roots of the cassava and the yam. One can only conjecture why peoples in parts of coastal West Africa came to depend on these starchy roots for their calories. In former days, did the well-buried roots represent a sure supply of calories when a plague of insects ate all parts of the plant which were above ground?

Prevention of Kwashiorkor

Solving the Problem. As can be readily understood, backgrounds of food habits are extremely complicated; yet they must be understood and the extent of the depth of their roots must be probed before any desired changes can be made. There is, therefore, no easy solution for the problem of protein-calorie malnutrition. It has often been pointed out that two types of goals must be set. There must be immediate relief, and there must be the long-term goal which looks to prevention in the future. Prevention involves a change in the fundamental structure of the society. The accomplishment of the short-term goal, however, may prepare the people to attack the larger problem and work toward its ultimate solution. The efforts to have the child weighed frequently during growth to determine his progress have been thought to show great promise.

Some people feel that the majority of preschool children in the developing countries pass through episodes of malnutrition of some degree of severity. How many of these suffer from real kwashiorkor is not known, as will be explained later. For protein-calorie malnutrition, one can find so-called modest estimates of 100 million and possibly a more realistic figure of 170 million. According to Arnold Schaefer, who has supervised many dietary surveys around the world, the overall figure of seriously malnourished children in countries outside the Communistic sphere currently is 269 million and will be 330 million in 1975. Cases of frank kwashiorkor are, of course, hidden in these figures, but malnutrition in general is, after all, the total problem.

The Fifth Session of the Joint Committee of the FAO/WHO Expert Committee of 1957 suggested in its report that "there is a need for simple, objective 'Nutritional Indicators' which can be used by general public health workers with a limited knowledge of nutrition." J. M. Bengoa, D. B. Jelliffe, and C. Perez suggested in 1959 the use of:

> five possible simple potentially useful indicators derived from the following sources: (1) vital statistics, (2) anthroprometric measurements, (3) clinical signs, (4) food composition, and (5) laboratory tests.

They stressed the need for further investigation and stated that "probably a combination based on data from all these sources would be most valuable."

It is easy to understand why data as to the number of cases of kwashiorkor in individual countries are even now not available. Uniformity and precision would depend upon the adoption and use of predetermined, simple, objective, numerically measurable, specific indicators.

As has been often pointed out by such recognized authorities as Nevin Scrimshaw and Arnold Schaefer, the exact number of diagnosed cases of kwashiorkor in relation to the child population of many developing countries is extremely difficult to determine. Many of these children may also have what is now designated as pre-kwashiorkor.

There are many obstacles to knowing how many actual cases of kwashiorkor exist in any one locality at any one time. Counts are usually taken on those children who come into the hospital. The number of cases admitted to the hospital varies with such factors as hospital beds available and whether the therapy of this hospital is understood and valued by the villagers. It is said that certain tribes in Africa are convinced that kwashiorkor is as inevitable as measles. The relation of kwashiorkor and infections is discussed further on page 332.

In most places, especially where medical personnel is extremely scarce, no one knows how many sick children in the community do not come to the attention of a physician for diagnosis. It has often been said that the analogy to an iceberg is pertinent here and that, for every diagnosed case, possibly 100 more are undiagnosed and therefore untreated.

Not much help in finding the incidence of the disease comes from the examination of records, of death. Often the cause of death is listed as measles or some other infectious disease. These diseases undoubtedly cause death because the child's body, so weakened with malnutrition, can not combat the infection.

For both kinds of programs, the cultural backgrounds of food habits and foodways must be understood. Also, parents who control the destiny of the preschool child in the family must be led, through education, to understand the food needs for growth and the causes of protein-calorie malnutrition. The demonstration of what dry milk and other protein-high foods can do for a kwashiorkor-ill child has to be used to persuade the father, most of all, that food does make the difference. The problem of reaching the father may be greater than that of reeducating the mother. Often, in the developing countries, the mother accompanies the child to the hospital and stays with him while he is being treated. It is quite fortunate, perhaps, that in many cultures the mother cannot think of abandoning her child to a spotless white hospital with strange people in forbidding-looking uniforms. Most public health workers feel that it is an absolute necessity for the mother to stay with the child so that she may be reeducated while the child is being cured. These mothers may feel insecure in leaving their children, as did the mother of a Negro child who was loath to leave her child in a modern, well-run, shipyard nursery school during World War II because "the teachers will not know how to comb the child's hair." This reason, though undoubtedly true, probably was only symbolic of a deep distrust.

It should be pointed out that the poor food the weanling receives probably does, in many cases, also reflect the poor diet of the entire family. Often simple procedures for storing or preserving food from times of plenty for use in the hungry months need to be taught.

Williams believed that the recent increase in malnutrition was the result of neglecting to provide maternal and child health services and due to the practical nonexistence of pediatricians in some areas. She also blamed fragmentation of services due to the modern tendency toward specialization. These, in relation to growth in the population and rapid urbanization, have made the problem greater. She urged more use of the nurse and also the spread of family-planning knowledge, which she delineates as helping families to have no more children than the parents want. She, as have others, cautioned that all problems of malnutrition cannot be cured, however, by even widespread use of family planning.

Many people have pointed out that attempts to relieve the problem of malnutrition should be started on many fronts at the same time. It has been said that, to combat malnutrition, it would take an army of extension workers in addition to medical and other health personnel for the needed teaching.

The Food for Peace program of the U.S. government, as Schaefer pointed out, may be no more than a temporary relief measure unless the requirements for a long-lasting program can be built in so that local governments are helped to assume increasing responsibilities. President Lyndon Johnson's February 1966 message to Congress also stressed this approach.

There are in operation now a number of general programs which are designed to increase the availability of the supply of local animal protein food. In this connection, mention should be made of all the dairy projects such as the one in Bombay, India, and those which were patterned after that one. This improvement of milk-producing animals and their care has been a great step forward. The efforts to increase the catch and production of fish both in the sea and in fish ponds is another notable effort. As recently as 1965, it was said in a medical journal from India that, although 1.5 million tons of fish are caught in the coastal waters off India, a large part of the catch is unavailable for human consumption because it is so perishable and because of the high cost of transportation. Another extensive effort is the preparation of fish-protein concentrate, which uses fish that might not otherwise be used for human food. The improvement and the production of meat, as well as the fostering of the raising of poultry and rabbits, can further increase the supply of animal food. Yet it is known that all these efforts are mere beginnings. We are told that the gap between the increase in population and the increase of available foods is widening each year.

All of this has a direct bearing on the prevention of kwashiorkor.

Indigenous Protein-Rich Foods.   For immediate relief of the problem of protein-calorie malnutrition, several kinds of protein-rich foods have been devised and tested. In these mixtures, the deficiency of amino acids in a vegetable protein needed for growth is made up by another one of the vegetable proteins used. Thus, the mixtures furnish all of the amino acids necessary for growth.

Centers for the production and testing of these mixtures have been set up with the assistance of the Rockefeller Foundation, WHO, FAO, and UNICEF. Some notable ones are in Guatemala City (Institute of Central American and Panama, INCAP); in Capetown, South Africa; in Dakar, Senegal; in Nigeria, West Africa; in Uganda, Central Eastern Africa; in Mysore and Coonor, India; in Mexico; and in Indonesia.

Because these offer perhaps the most specific solution to the problem, we will discuss them in detail. In no way, however, is it implied that the total problem be solved by this production of indigenous and acceptable protein-rich foods in every country where kwashiorkor or even mild protein-calorie malnutrition is found. Scrimshaw, however, believed that this is an encouraging development. The movement to find mixtures of foods grown locally which could be used to supplement the local low-protein originated at INCAP when he was its director.

The mixture *Incaparina* is currently being made of ground maize, ground sorghum, cottonseed flour, and yeast with calcium carbonate, lysine, and vitamin A added. It is recommended that three glasses of the prepared mixture, given to the child daily, would furnish a protein content comparable to that of three glasses of milk at a cost of approximately one and one-third cents per glass; in 1964, it was reported that milk, if available, would have cost three to four times as much. The Incaparina drink, made by adding one glass of water to twenty-five grams of the mixture and cooking it for fifteen minutes, is flavored to taste with sugar, cinnamon, vanilla, anise, or chocolate. In addition to the use as a drink, the dry mixture may be substituted (except in bread) for two-thirds of the flour in most recipes calling for wheat flour. Incaparina can also be made into puddings or added to soups. Incaparina has been used successfully to prevent malnutrition, and it has been

Proper child care can prevent malnutrition. (Courtesy World Health Organization.)

Molab, an Iranian girl at four months of age. Left. Molab, now at ten months of age. Food and careful nursing made the difference. Right. (Courtesy Food and Agriculture Organization.)

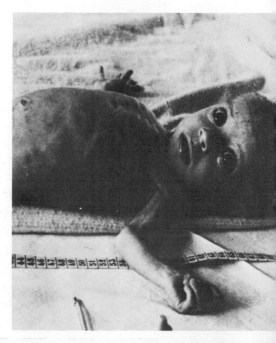

*Child enjoying Incaparina.
(Courtesy United Nations.)*

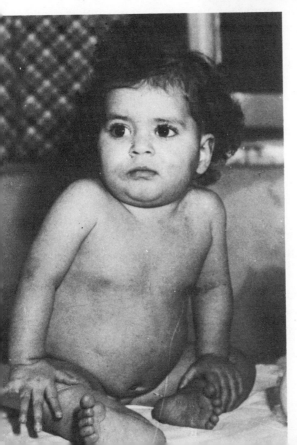

found to be highly acceptable to the populations where tests have been conducted. It is now on sale commercially in Guatemala and in several other Central American countries, and a group in the southern U.S. have produced and marketed it. However, Incaparina is not the entire answer to the problem. According to one statement, when 100,000 pounds a month were being distributed, only 2.5% of the children who needed it were getting it.

Within recent years, many other vegetable protein-rich mixtures have been developed and tried in various parts of the world. Some of the early products developed were Pro Nutro, used in South Africa; Temph, in Indonesia; Fortifex, in Brazil; Multi-Purpose Food, in India; Saradella, in Indonesia; and Laubina, in Lebanon. For the major source of protein, Pro Nutro uses soybeans, maize, groundnut, and powdered skim milk; Fortifex uses maize and soya flour; Laubina uses wheat, chick peas, and powdered skim milk; Incaparina, as was said, uses maize and cottonseed meal. Because of the wide variety and number of products presently manufactured, it is impossible to list all of them. See pages 339 and 414 under Programs for further discussion.

At the present time, trials using the press cakes after oils have been extracted from soya beans, cottonseed, peanuts, sesame, sunflower, and other seeds are proving encouraging. This press cake material furnishes a cheap source of valuable protein.

In 1966, attention was drawn to preliminary tests made in a number of countries on new high-protein blended foods. One, called CSM-Mix, made of gelatinized cornmeal, soy flour, nonfat dry milk, vitamins, and minerals, comes in powdered form and can be made into a drink by boiling it with water for one minute. The early good rate of acceptability of these foods has been encouraging and has caused the U.S. government and voluntary agencies to step up distribution. Such food was supplied to maternal and child welfare and school-feeding programs beginning in 1966.

To summarize and point to the requirements for these protein-rich foods, we quote from an article by the late R. F. A. Dean. He lists the following qualities as required:
The food should:

1. Be acceptable to children and to their parents.
2. Be cheap and processed from local ingredients.
3. Keep well even under poor conditions of storage.

TABLE 2   Examples of Protein Food Mixtures

Product	Country	Composition	Protein content (percentage)
Incaparina	Guatemala	Maize, cottonseed flour, vitamin A, lysine, calcium carbonate	27.5
	Colombia	Same, plus defatted soybean flour	27.5
	Mexico	Same, plus defatted soybean flour but without cottonseed flour	27.5
Fortiflex	Brazil	Maize, defatted soybean flour, vitamins, DL-methionine, calcium carbonate	30.0
Pro Nutro	South Africa	Maize, skim milk powder, groundnut, soybean, fish protein concentrate, yeast, wheat germ, vitamins, niacin, sugar, iodized salt	22.0
Protone	United Kingdom Congo	Maize, skim milk powder, yeast, vitamins, minerals	22.4
Arlac	Nigeria	Groundnut flour, skim milk powder, wheat and barley flour, vitamins, calcium	42.0
Lac-Tone	India	Groundnut flour, skim milk powder, wheat and barley flour, vitamins, calcium	26.0
Aliment de sevrage	Senegal	Millet flour, groundnut flour, skim milk powder, sugar, vitamins, calcium	20.0
CSM	United States	Maize (precooked), defatted soybean flour, skim milk powder, sugar, vitamins, calcium	20.0
Supro	East Africa	Maize or barley flour, torula yeast, skim milk powder, salt, condiments	24.0

From *Lives in Peril*, FAO/WHO/UNICEF—PAG—UNIPUB., New York, 1971.

4. Mix easily with staple foods.
5. Be bland.
6. Be capable of being used as a drink.
7. Be rich in proteins, minerals, and calories.
8. Contain protein of high quality.

It has also been pointed out by numerous workers in the field that the child with kwashiorkor usually also needs extra calories added to his present diet. Often the bulk of the food used to increase the calories and protein becomes too great for him to consume unless fat is used for the extra calories. Trials in India proved that the children observed could tolerate butter added to the diet. Some workers caution that with kwashiorkor the production of digestive enzymes that split fats is decreased; therefore, fats should not be fed for the first two to three weeks of treatment.

Recommendations.   In summary, a few of the many recommendations for the prevention of kwashiorkor will be given. No attempt is made, however, to give an inclusive list.

1. The national governments where the problems exist must be informed; most programs succeed better if they emanate from those national governments which build programs into national planning for improving nutrition.
2. Infectious diseases must be controlled.
3. The breeding and introduction of improved varieties of corn, wheat, and rice and the cultivation of soya beans and other legumes to improve the quality and quantity of protein-high foods available for children vulnerable to malnutrition should be encouraged. Efforts to produce varieties of corn higher in the amino acid, lysine, than we now have are important.
4. The introduction of better types of poultry, cattle, and swine and the development of a modern dairy industry including milk plants to produce skim and whole milk can help.
5. Above all, continuing mass education is needed. These programs must reach individual fathers and mothers to help them understand that protein-high foods are essential for the growth of children. It means reaching mothers to get them to wean their infants gradually on a diet rich in high-quality protein foods which are digestible and palatable to the infant.

6. Evaluation of existing programs has been called for by such authorities as Autret. Now there are plans for thorough investigation of programs with careful evaluations to find out specifically which programs have succeeded and why.

STUDY QUESTIONS

1. What are the basic causes for some of the problems in malnutrition in:
   a. The American Eskimo?
   b. The American Indian? (Choose a particular tribe.)
   c. The children of migrant workers?
   d. People over 65 in the lower socio-economic classes?

2. How do climate, economics, cultural and social patterns, transportation, communications, education, and religion affect the incidence and severity of malnutrition?

3. Why is xerophthalmia found in greater numbers of children in arid countries? How is goiter related to geography? Why has rickets followed initial industrial development? Why is obesity increasing rapidly during the decade of the 1960's in Europe?

4. Can you choose a country and describe the steps and procedures you would use to introduce iodized salt and get it used by the village homemakers?

5. Not all states in the U.S. have enrichment laws. Can you discuss the pros and cons for enrichment? Why is enrichment successful in this country but might not be in some other countries?

6. Why does protein-calorie malnutrition occur most frequently in tropical countries?

TOPICS FOR INDIVIDUAL INVESTIGATION

1. Write an article for laymen who have a nonscientific college education telling the story of pellagra so that they understand the importance of diet in this disease.

2. On a world map, show where each of the six principal sources of calories is consumed in greatest amounts. Indicate the flow of some of these foods from where they are raised to where they are consumed.

3. Discuss the chief causes of the five most frequent problems in malnutrition in the world today.

4. From reports from UNICEF, FAO, and WHO, list four or five ways in which programs in two countries are planned to prevent kwashiorkor.

5. Imagine that you are a nutritionist in some African country. Describe what you would need to know before you began a nutrition education program.

REFERENCES AND SUGGESTED READINGS

Malnutrition

Birch, H. G. and J. D. Gussow. Disadvantaged Children. *Health, Nutrition, and School Failure.* Harcourt, Brace and World, New York and Gurne & Stratton, Inc., New York, 1970.

Burgess A. and R. F. A. Dean., Eds. *Malnutrition and Food Habits.* Macmillan, New York, 1962.

Chittenden, R. H. *The Nutrition of Man.* Fredrick A. Stokes, New York, 1907.

Cravioto, J. Malnutrition and Behavioral Development in the Pre-school Child. *Pre-school Child Malnutrition,* National Academy of Sciences, National Research Council, Washington, D.C., 1966.

Dale, A. N. *Consumption of Vitamin D in Fortified and Natural Foods and Vitamin Preparations by Growing Children.* Thesis for Master of Science in Home Economics, Univ. of Washington, Seattle, 1966.

Food and Nutrition Board. Recommendations on Administrative Policies for International Food and Nutrition Programs. National Academy of Sciences, National Research Council, Washington, D.C., April, 1965.

Gyorgy, P. *The Problems. Pre-school Child Malnutrition.* National Academy of Sciences, National Research Council, Washington, D.C., 1966.

Gyorgy, P. and A. Burgess, Eds. *Protecting the Pre-School Child Programmes in Practice.* J. B. Lippincott, Philadelphia, Pa., 1954.

Hundley, J. M. Malnutrition—A Global Problem. *Fed. Proc.,* 18: 76, 1959.

Iowa State Univ. Center for Agr. and Econ. Adjustment. *Food, One Tool in International Economic Development.* Iowa State Univ. Press, Ames, Iowa, 1962.

Jelliffe, D. B. *The Assessment of the Nutritional Status of the Community.* WHO, Geneva, Switzerland, 1966.

Jelliffe, D. B. *Child Nutrition in Developing Countries.* U.S. Dept. of Health, Education, and Welfare, Washington, D.C., 1968.

Jelliffe, D. B. The Incidence of Protein-Calorie Malnutrition in Early Childhood. *Amer. J. Pub. Health,* 53: 905, 1963.

Jelliffe, D. B. *Infant Nutrition in the Tropics and Subtropics.* WHO, Geneva, Switzerland, 1955.

King, C. G. Future Programs. *Pre-School Child Malnutrition*. National Academy of Sciences, National Research Council, Washington, D.C., 1966, pp. 341.

Mann, C. V. The Health and Nutritional Status of Alaskan Eskimos, *Amer. J. Clin. Nutr.*, 11: 31, 1962.

Manneheimer, E. Programs for Combatting Malnutrition in the Pre-School Child in Ethiopia. *Pre-School Child Malnutrition*. National Academy of Sciences, National Research Council, Washington, D.C., 1966, pp. 137.

Milner, M. Food Technology and World Food Needs. *Food Tech.*, 17: 846, 1963.

Myrdal, J. Mood of the Writer. *Saturday Rev.*, Aug. 13, 1966.

Pre-School Child Malnutrition. Primary Deterrent to Human Progress. National Academy of Sciences, National Research Council, Washington, D.C., 1966, pp. 355.

Schaefer, A. Observations from Exploring Needs in National Nutrition Programs. *Amer. J. Pub. Health*, 56: 1089, 1966.

Scrimshaw, N. S. The Effect of the Interaction of Nutrition and Infection on the Pre-School Child. *Pre-School Child Malnutrition*. National Academy of Sciences, National Research Council, Washington, D.C., 1966, p. 63.

Scrimshaw, N. S. Present Programs. *Pre-School Child Malnutrition*. National Academy of Sciences, National Research Council, Washington, D.C., 1966, pp. 334.

Scrimshaw, N. S. World-Wide Opportunities for Food Scientists and Technologists. *Food Tech.*, 17: 850, 1963.

Scrimshaw, N. S. and J. E. Gordon, Eds. *Malnutrition, Learning and Behavior*. The M.I.T. Press, Cambridge, Mass., 1968.

Spencer, S. M. The Secret Killer of Children. *Saturday Evening Post*, Aug. 17, 1957.

United Nations International Children's Fund. *The Administrative Aspects of Programmes to Protect the Pre-School Child*. Report of a conference held at Schloss Tremsbuttel, Hamburg, Germany, 1966.

U.S. Dept. of Agr. *The World Food Budget 1962 and 1966*. Foreign Agr. Econ. Rept. No. 4, 1961, rev. 1962.

Williams, R. R. *Williams-Waterman Fund for the Combat of Dietary Diseases. A History of the Period 1935 through 1955*. Research Corporation, 405 Lexington Ave., New York, 1956.

Beriberi

Kinney, T. D., and R. H. Follis, Jr., Eds. Nutritional Diseases, Proceedings of a Conference on Beriberi, Endemic Goiter, and Hypovitaminosis A. Princeton, N.J. *Fed. Proc.* 17 (Part II): 3, 1958.

Oliveros, S. R., et al. *Beriberi*. Fifth Report of the Joint FAO/WHO Expert Committee on Nutrition. WHO Tech. Rept. Series 149, 1958.

Salcedo, J., et. al. Artificial Enrichment of White Rice as a Solution to Endemic Beriberi. Report of Field Trials in Bataan, Philippines. *J. Nutr.*, 42: 501, 1950.

Vedder, E. G. *Beriberi*. Wood, New York, 1913.

Williams, R. R. *Conquest of Beriberi*. Harvard Univ. Press, Cambridge, Mass., 1961.

Williams, R. R. Recollections of the Beriberi-Preventing Substance. *Nutr. Rev.* 11: 257, 1953.

Endemic Goiter

Endemic Goiter, *Fed. Proc.,* 17 (Part II, Supplement No. 2): 57, Sept. 1958.

McCollum, E. V. *A History of Nutrition.* Houghton-Mifflin, Boston, Mass., 1957.

Pitt-Rivers, R. and W. R. Trotter. *The Thyroid Gland,* Vols. 1 and 2. Butterworths, Washington, D.C., 1964.

Stanbury, J. B., et. al. *Endemic Goiter. The Adaptation of Man to Iodine Deficiency.* Harvard Univ. Press, Cambridge, Mass., 1954.

Stanbury, J. B. and V. Ramalingaswami. Iodine, in G. H. Beaton & E. W. McHenry, *Nutrition, A Comprehensive Treatise,* Vol. 1, p. 373, 1964.

Studies on the Prevention of Simple Goiter. Western Reserve University, Bull. No. 7, 1923.

WHO. *Endemic Goiter.* Mono. Series No. 44, 1960. WHO, Geneva, Switzerland.

Kwashiorkor

Adams, E. B. Anemia Associated with Kwashiorkor. *Amer. Jour. Clin. Nutr.,* 22: 1634–1638, 1969.

The Anemia of Kwashiorkor. *Nutr. Rev.,* 26: 273–275, 1968.

Autret, M. *Nutrition of the Preschool Child. A Consideration of New Approaches.* FAO, Rome, Italy, 1964.

Autret, M. and E. F. Horine, Jr. Some Observations on Problems of Planning and Evaluation in Programs for the Control of Malnutrition in the Pre-School Child. *Pre-School Child Malnutrition.* National Academy of Sciences, National Research Council, Washington, D.C., p. 288, 1966.

Behar, M. and R. Bressani. Experience in Development of Incaparina for the Pre-School Child. *Pre-School Child Malnutrition.* National Academy of Sciences, National Research Council, Washington, D.C., p. 213, 1966.

Benoga, J. M., D. B. Jelliffe, and C. Perez. Some Indicators for a Broad Assessment of the Magnitude of Protein-Calorie Malnutrition in Young Children in Population Groups. *Amer. J. Clin. Nutr.,* 7: 714, 1959.

Broch, J., and M. Autret. *Kwashiorkor in Africa.* WHO and FAO Rome, Italy, 1952.

Calder, R. Food Supplementation for Prevention of Malnutrition in the Pre-School Child. *Pre-School Child Malnutrition.* National Academy of Sciences, National Research Council, Washington, D.C., p. 251, 1966.

Dean, R. F. A. *Treatment and Prevention of Kwashiorkor.* WHO Bulletin 9: 767, 1953.

Dean, R. F. A. East Africa. *Med. J.,* 37: 378, 1960.

Diamond, I. and C. Vallbona. Kwashiorkor in a North American White Male. *Pediatrics,* 25: 248, 1960.

Diet in the Treatment of Disease-Part III. Kwashiorkor. *Quarterly Med. Rev.,* Bombay, India, 15: 1, 1964.

FAO. *Protein: At the Heart of the World Food Problem.* World Food Problems, No. 5, FAO, Rome, Italy, 1964.

FAO. *Lives in Peril.* FAO, Rome, Italy, 1970.

Jelliffe, D. B. The Incidence of Protein-Calorie Malnutrition in Early Childhood. *Amer. J. Pub. Health,* 53: 905, 1963.

Jelliffe, E. F. Patrice. Nutrition Education in the Hospital. *Cajanus—News Letter of Caribbean Food and Nutr. Inst.,* Vol. 4, No. 4, pp. 292–301, 1971.

Letter to the editor by D. S. McLaren. *Nutr. Rev.,* 26: 256, 1968.

The Liver in Protein-Calorie Malnutrition. *Nutr. Rev.,* 27: 223–225, 1969.

Mahadevans, P. M. and J. Ganguly. The Influence of Proteins on the Absorption and Metabolism of Vitamin A. *World Rev. Nutr. Diet.,* 5: 209, 1965.

Malnutrition and Disease, Freedom From Hunger Campaign Basic Study #12, Part III, Deficiency Disease, Protein-Calorie Malnutrition, 1963.

McLaren, D. S. Trends in Tropical Child Health (The Rise of Marasmus). *Jour. Trop. Ped.,* 12: 84–85, 1966.

McLaren, D. S., et. al. Short-Term Prognosis in Protein-Calorie Malnutrition. *Amer. J. Clin. Nutr.,* 22: 863–870, 1969.

Mental Development Following Kwashiorkor. *Nutr. Rev.,* 27: 46–49, 1969.

Morley, David. Comprehensive Care Through the Under-Five Clinics. Assignment Children. UNICEF, Jan/March, pp. 75–89, 1972.

Nutr. Rev. The Liver in Protein-Calorie Malnutrition, 27: 223–225, 1969.

Objective Measurement of Hair Changes in Kwashiorkor. *Nutr. Rev.,* 26: 330–332, 1968.

Recovery Rates of Children Following Protein-Calorie Malnutrition. *Nutr. Rev.,* 28: 118–122, 1970.

Scrimshaw, N. S. and M. Behar. Protein Malnutrition in Young Children. *Science,* 133: 2039, 1961.

Scrimshaw, N. S. and M. Behar. Worldwide Occurrence of Protein Malnutrition. *Fed. Proc.,* 18: 82, 1959.

Taitz, L. S. and L. Fineberg. Kwashiorkor in the Bronx. *Am. J. Dis. of Child.,* 112: 76, 1966.

Trowell, H. D., J. N. Davies, and R. F. A. Dean. *Kwashiorkor.* Edward Arnold, London, England, 1954.

Van Duzen, Jean, et. al. Protein and Calorie Malnutrition Among Pre-school Navajo Indian Children. *Amer. J. of Clin. Nutr.,* 22: 1362–1370, 1969.

Waterlow, J. C., J. Cravioto, and S. Frank. *Protein Malnutrition in Man.* Academic Press, New York, 1960.

Watts, E. Ronald. Education for Better Nutrition of Children in Tropical Africa. Assignment Children, UNICEF, Jan./March, 1972, pp. 93–103.

Williams, C. D. Kwashiorkor: Nutritional Diseases of Children Associated with Maize Diet. *Lancet,* 2: 1151, 1935.

Williams, C. D. Malnutrition and Mortality in the Pre-School Child. *Pre-School Child Malnutrition.* National Academy of Science. National Research Council, Washington, D.C., p. 3, 1966.

Williams, C. D. Nutritional Diseases of Children Associated with a Maize Diet. *Arch. Dis. Child.,* 8: 423, 1933.

Williams, C. D. The Story of Kwashiorkor-Courier-Central International De L'France. *Paris Courier,* p. 361, June 1963.

Wolfe, C. B. Kwashiorkor in a North American White Male. *Pediatrics,* 25: 248, 1960.

9

Programs to
Improve Nutrition*

When historian Arthur Toynbee said that the twentieth
century will probably be remembered most because it was
the first time in recorded history when man dared to use
his knowledge to benefit all mankind, he could have been
talking about the international as well as national programs to relieve hunger and malnutrition. Although many
of these programs have their roots in ideas and proposals
from previous centuries, the united efforts of the people
working in the twentieth century have brought more immediate and more far-reaching results.

---

*In this chapter, the style of writing is necessarily not uniform because sections have been written
by different authors. In the interest of accuracy in describing policies and programs, the senior
author in some cases sought assistance and approval of the editorial person of the agency. In some
cases, this person even secured the approval of his entire staff.

351

PROGRAMS OF INTERNATIONAL ORGANIZATIONS

FAO: Food and Agriculture Organization

Future historians looking back on this century will have to record the tremendous scientific advances and ventures into outer space as outstanding events. They will also have to give credit to this century as the one when man first achieved a worldwide program of international cooperative effort for the improvement of the nutrition of all people everywhere. FAO, with its dramatic design and Latin motto "let there be bread," is the Food and Agriculture Organization of the United Nations. This is the first agency of the United Nations that was established; it has the major responsibility for helping mankind the world over to get more and better food. FAO was established in 1945, but it did not just happen on that date. Its purpose and achievements are significant, but an understanding of events leading up to the establishment of FAO are essential if we are to understand man's progress toward developing a genuine concern for his fellowman's well being. The story that is the background for FAO had its beginnings some 50 years ago.

For many years, some professional organizations have held international meetings and have demonstrated that people of different nationalities could talk together on professional subjects of common interest. An International Institute of Agriculture (IIA) was organized in 1905 mainly through the efforts of David Lubin, a California businessman and farmer. He believed that, by collection and dissemination of international statistics about agricultural products, the farmers and food producers in various countries could be helped to obtain the best markets for their products. He gained the interest of the King of Italy, who provided housing for the Institute in Rome. However, IIA was concerned with food as a trade commodity rather than in relation to the health and welfare of people.

Wars have brought hunger, famine, death, and destruction to peoples and nations from earliest times, but in this century war has brought forth in many nations the genuine desire to work together for the common good. As a result of World War I (1914–1918), two international organizations were formed: the International Labor Organization (ILO) and the League of Nations, both with headquarters at Geneva, Switzerland. ILO was organized to deal with problems related to labor such as hours, wages, unemployment, child labor, old age pensions, and sickness benefits. However, in 1935, ILO did concern itself with the nutrition of workers and in 1936 published the report of a study, "Workers Nutrition and Social Policy."

With the establishment of the League of Nations, there was hope that at last a new world order would begin. But political problems eventually became insurmountable for the League; it was handicapped because the U.S. was not a member. Though the League failed, it did have many successes in the area of social and economic problems, particularly in health and nutrition.

In the Covenant of the League of Nations, it was stated that the League was "To endeavor to take steps in matters of international concern for the prevention and control of disease." A health organization was formed within the League for this purpose, and it was in this health section that the first international programs of food and nutrition had their beginning. In 1925, the Yugoslav delegation to the League requested a study of methods to be recommended in the interests of public health for the regulation of the manufacture and of the sale of food products. But it was not until ten years later that there was any widespread recognition of the need for nutrition studies. In 1935, a report, "Nutrition and Public Health," was published by Etienne Burnet and Wallace Aykroyd in the *Quarterly Bulletin* of the Health Organization. When the Assembly of the League met in September of that year, this report was the basis of discussion. Stanley Bruce of Australia delivered a speech in which he used the phrase "to marry health and agriculture" and went on to say, "by so doing, make a great step in the improvement of national health and, at the same time, an appreciable contribution to the solution of the agricultural problem." Bruce captured the interest and imagination of those assembled, and a resolution was passed to continue the nutrition work of the health committee and to bring a general report to the next meeting of the assembly.

In 1937, the League published a report, "The Relation of Nutrition to Health, Agriculture and Economic Policy," which became a best seller and inspired many governments to take practical steps to improve the diets of their people. Then World War II came, and the League of Nations was lost; but though it failed in its major goal, there were many solid achievements. And its international work in health and nutrition survived but in a new and different organization.

Preliminary Meeting

While World War II was still in progress, an event of profound significance in the history of mankind took place. This was a conference called by President Franklin D. Roosevelt and attended by representatives of 44 nations. The place of meeting was Hot Springs, Virginia, and the dates were May 18 to June 3, 1943. It was a meeting solely for the purpose of working together to secure lasting peace when the war was ended. Those attending the conference believed this could be achieved by raising the standards of living of the two-thirds of the world's population that was malnourished and in want.

Historic events of this kind come into being from a background of work of individuals—in this case, Frank McDougall. He was in Washington, D.C. in 1942 for discussions on an international wheat agreement; while there, he drafted a memorandum on a United Nation Program for Freedom from Want of Food. This plan was based on a lifetime of experience and on knowledge gained as the Australian delegate to the League of Nations (1929–1939) and as a member of the nutrition committee of the League. In his memorandum, McDougall outlined proposals which would make Stanley Bruce's marriage of health and agriculture a reality.

> Freedom from want of food must be given high priority in the actions taken to fulfill the pledges of the United Nations. For not only is food the most essential of human needs but the production of food is the principal economic activity of man . . . one of our most urgent immediate problems is the inability of the lower-income groups to buy sufficient food to maintain good health. Its solution will depend upon economic and social policies designed to increase purchasing power and to reduce the costs of production and distribution. . . . The need is to establish at once a United Nations Organization. . . . A Technical Commission on Food and Agriculture should formulate action programs designed to assist the nations to achieve freedom from want of food. . . . The necessity for immediate action cannot be over-emphasized. We must act now if we are to avoid the risk of losing the peace.

Eleanor Roosevelt saw this memorandum and realized that it incorporated some of the same ideas as given by President Roosevelt in his statement a year earlier on the Four Freedoms. She arranged for McDougall to meet President Roosevelt; the outcome was that the President of the United States convened the Hot Springs Conference in May 1943.

The conference recommended that the nations represented establish a permanent organization in the field of food and agriculture and that an Interim Commission be appointed to work out plans for such an organization. Frank McDougall was a member of the Interim Commission and helped to draw up the Constitution of FAO. (He continued to work with FAO in advisory capacities almost to the day of his death in 1958; the McDougall Memorial Lecture was instituted by the Council of FAO, Rome, 1958, to commemorate his work.)

FAO Established

The next step, following the work of the Interim Commission after the Hot Springs Conference, was taken in October 1945 when delegates from 42 countries met in Quebec, Canada. They ratified the constitution, which formally established the Food and Agriculture Organization of the United Nations. The preamble to the Constitution of FAO states:

> The nations accepting this Constitution, being determined to promote the common welfare by furthering separate and collective action on their part for the purposes of:
> Raising levels of nutrition and standards of living of the people under their respective jurisdictions,
> Securing improvements in the efficiency of the production and distribution of all food and agricultural products,
> Bettering the conditions of rural populations,
> And thus contributing toward an expanding world economy,
> Hereby established the Food and Agriculture Organization of the United Nations.

FAO is an autonomous independent organization which is a member of the family of specialized agencies of the United Nations. It has close ties with other specialized agencies, especially with WHO with which it has a joint committee on nutrition, with UNICEF, and with UNESCO. The member countries of FAO have pledged themselves to improve world agriculture, forestry, and fisheries through the pooling of their knowledge, efforts, and resources. Thus, they are making a basic attack on the problem of improving health through increased food production and improved quality and nutritive value of food.

Each member government supports the regular activities of FAO by paying into the budget a contribution proportionate to its national income. All members of FAO meet in conference every other year; the world food and agricultural situation is reviewed, and policies and activities are reexamined and changed as necessary. Each member country has one vote to elect the Director-General; a Council of 27 members meets one to three times a year. The present Director-General, the fifth in the history of FAO, is Addeke H. Boerma of the Netherlands.

It takes more than the stroke of pen and signatures on a document to make words become reality. Especially is this true when the desired reality is action and change in the lives of people. It takes time, patience, hard work, flexibility, willingness to adjust to the point of view of others, and a determination to overcome obstacles. Of these ingredients, FAO needed a liberal supply. There were barriers, disappointments, frustrations, and conflicting ideas, but the purpose and goal were always kept in sight. There have been some remarkable achievements. At the end of the first ten years of its work, FAO again met in Quebec to celebrate its historic founding and review accomplishments. That year, 1955, two books were published giving authoritative and exciting accounts of the work of FAO: *So Bold an Aim* by P. L. Yates for FAO, and *The Story of FAO* by Gove Hambidge. Those who read these books will find them extremely worthwhile; here we can give only a few examples of what has been done by FAO up to this time.

With a budget that was at first very limited, FAO carried on two main lines of work:

1. Gathering technical and economic information on food and making it available to all countries.
2. Advising and helping governments requesting action programs for food and agricultural development.

Each decade brings new problems in a changing world, and FAO is continuously seeking new approaches to solving the food needs of people. The World Food Program was set up jointly by FAO and the United Nations in 1963 as a way for many countries to share in bringing food to people in more than 70 developing countries. The stimulus came from the early efforts of the U.S. to aid starving countries. In 1954, the U.S. Congress passed Public Law 480, which decreed that surplus foods could be shipped to other countries as aid. The World Food Program meant that more countries could help and a greater variety of foodstuffs would be available. Today there are more than 90 countries providing aid, though the greater part of the resources come from 10 countries, with Canada and the U.S. contributing the largest amount. Thus, food is being used as an investment in development and is managed on a multilateral scale.

Food Aid is sent to developing countries to help them move ahead with their social and economic development. It works in a variety of ways. An example is seen in Peru, where the government has been carrying on a program of community development called *Cooperación Popular*. The villagers do the work of road building, and the World Food Program assists the project by providing food as partial compensation for their work. Each worker gets a daily ration for himself and for each of his dependents for every day of work on the project. The food consists of wheat, wheat flour, dried skim milk, dried eggs, dried fish, canned meat, and vegetable oil. The new roads link people in poor, remote villages to markets, schools, and health centers. The high-quality foods give extra energy to the manual workers and also improve the nutrition standards of young children and their mothers. Also, it is the peoples' own project. Each piece of work as it is completed receives a red and white sign with the words *"el pueblo lo hizo,"* meaning "the people built it." So far, some 2000 of these signs have been placed on roads, schools, medical centers, bridges, and drainage canals throughout Peru.

In other countries, land has been reclaimed from swamps and deserts, dykes have been built against floods and to provide water for parched fields, railways have been repaired, irrigation canals have been built, forests have been conserved and forest nurseries have been planted—in fact, wherever people are working to help themselves, food aid is also made available to help them. Food works to improve health and is a power in the social and economic development of the country. The World Food Program was started as a three-year program and then was extended "for as long as multilateral food aid is found feasible and desirable."

For this new decade of the 1970's, FAO is initiating what is called the Indicative World Plan for Agricultural Development. It has been learned that technology alone is not enough. Farmers must be given supplies, credit with which to operate, and there must be extension workers to give them the new knowledge on how to do it. They also need incentives to use the new methods; and in some countries, land reforms will be necessary. Also required is long-range planning at the international level. FAO has spent five years analyzing trends in agricultural production, consumption, and trade up to 1985 and has prepared the Indicative World Plan, which calls for increased production of high-yielding varieties of cereals and other crops, management of tropical forests, land reforms, and increased education and training in agriculture and food production.

FAO is a cooperative of 125 governments (as of 1972) which pool their efforts to meet the need of all people everywhere. The FAO catalog of publications lists many items including world food surveys, statistical bulletins and yearbooks, and reports of conferences and expert committees on nutritional requirements and nutrition education.

Freedom from Hunger Campaign (FFHC)

FAO works with governments and sends aid and technical help to a country only on request of the government of that country. However, FAO soon recognized the need to work directly with the people of all countries to help them realize the problems of world hunger and how hunger may be overcome by united effort. The affluent nations are unable to feed all the hungry millions in the world. Starvation and hunger can be prevented only by increased production in the developing countries. This was the way FAO saw it, and so they developed a plan which would help to mobilize people for their own development. The beginning was in 1960, when B. R. Sen, at that time Director-General of FAO, launched the Freedom from Hunger Campaign (FFHC) with support from the United Nations and its specialized agencies. Governments, voluntary organizations, industry, schools and universities, youth groups—in fact all sectors of the community in all countries of the world—were invited to participate in a joint effort of war on hunger and poverty.

Each country was invited to establish its own FFHC Committee. In a short time, these committees were set up in 80 countries, each country doing its own organizing and making its own plans for action. These plans were in general directed toward the following:

1. Teaching farmers new skills and teaching mothers better ways of feeding their families and meeting their nutritional needs.
2. Demonstrating results that can be obtained through use of fertilizers, better seeds, crop protection, irrigation, soil conservation, improved breeds and care of animals, improved methods of fishing and use of fish ponds, protective storage of foods, and international cooperation.
3. Helping to provide teachers and field workers, training programs, fellowships for study, and funds for seeds, tools, and equipment.
4. Persuading people individually or as groups, communities, organizations, and governments to cooperate and to act in the ways just described.

In 1963, FAO invited all governments to help in making FFHC known all over the world by issuing postage stamps that would in some way call attention to the campaign. This author has a collection of these stamps from 137 countries and islands; many are beautiful in color and design and almost all of them include in the design the heads of wheat which are the main feature of the FFHC emblem. These stamps have gone with letters from country to country, everywhere carrying the message of the world's food needs; they also are collector's items.

FFHC at the international level published a series of 23 Basic Study Booklets covering such subjects as hunger and social policy, malnutrition and disease nutrition and working efficiency, education and training in nutrition, and population and food supplies. These booklets provide factual data and information for discussion and action.

Action followed quickly. One story from the November-December 1966 *Freedom from Hunger* magazine illustrates the hundreds of ways that people in more fortunate circumstances are helping those in need. Casper Baldwin lives in Tanzania on the farm of a few acres belonging to his parents. His father never earned more than $2 a month in his life. Casper spent nine years in a leprosarium but is now completely cured. He did some farming while at the leprosarium and decided he wanted to be a farmer. Some cured patients were to be sent to farm-training centers. Casper heard about it, applied for training, and was accepted. He went with 23 ex-patients to Urambo, a big flat farm on cleared bushland, where a center had been built with some $225,000 from the people of Devon, England, donated under FFHC. Here Casper began a two-week course in gardening, poultry keeping, animal husbandry, and rabbit and pigeon raising. Everything he learned was feasible for the poverty stricken Tanzanian farmer; at Urambo he saw poultry houses made of saplings plastered with mud for walls; he saw vegetable gardens struggling in the heat and drought the same as his own garden. He also saw what was a real possibility for him. And so he made plans for his future; this is almost unheard of in a land where farmers consider planning ahead even for one year to be a blatant tempting of fate.

Casper Baldwin planned for three stages of development on his farm. Stage one would be to sell a few of his father's 80 goats to buy a cow as the start of a small herd. He and his wife would plant a vegetable garden, half an acre at first. He learned at Urambo that with proper care he could get three garden crops a year. He would also start some poultry and hoped in the first year to earn $6 a month. Stage two would also last a year, and he planned to expand his garden and raise his own poultry feed, plant fruit trees around his house as a windbreak, and raise a few pigeons for meat. His income should then reach $12 a month from sale of garden produce, eggs, poultry, and milk. (The principal of Urambo Center believes he can do this.) Stage three would be an expansion of all the activities of the first two stages, bringing an income of $20 a month. (The average farmer in his country earns only $5 a month.) Then, Casper Baldwin said, if he was successful that far, he would borrow money and go into bigger scale farming.

Urambo Center gave Casper Baldwin his training, and the Devon, England, FFHC committee that started the center continues to collect money for running expenses and supplies for the center.

FFHC has met a need, but much yet remains to be done. The FAO Council meeting in 1969 authorized the extension of the Freedom from Hunger Campaign for another ten years through the period of the Second United Nations Development Decade (1971–1980). The Campaign's motto as it enters this decade is 'Action for Development,' and there are now over 95 of these national FFHC committees, each organized in its own way but all coordinated internationally by FAO. These committees are now officially called Freedom From Hunger/Action for Development (FFH/AD). The FFH/AD committee in a developing country receives requests from some village, community, or organization for help on some project they want to do for themselves, such as better methods of fishing, or of storing crops and preserving food so as to prevent loss from rodents and insects or a child feeding program. The project request is forwarded to FAO, which then tries to find a sponsor in some other country which will provide the needed assistance.

In the U.S., a Freedom from Hunger Foundation was established with former President Harry S. Truman as honorary chairman. The first cash donation to this Foundation came from the people of the Virgin Islands. The committee is now officially known as the American Freedom from Hunger Foundation. It supports a wide variety of projects to alleviate the causes of hunger and malnutrition both at home and abroad, with emphasis on self-help projects of long-term value. Some of the projects in the U.S. are: an Indian nutrition research and education in North Dakota; an inner-city nutrition training center in San Diego; food co-operatives in Chicago and Buffalo; and high-protein food supplement in Texas. Among the foreign projects are: community canneries in Turkey; nutrition and health centers in Peru; demonstration home gardens in Malagasy; and school construction in Brazil, Ghana, and Peru.

Young World Appeal

The average age of the world population is under 30 years, and about 55% of the population of the developing countries are under 20 years of age, according to FAO. It is logical, therefore, and in fact it is essential to seek the cooperation of youth in the struggle to increase food production and improve living conditions. This is what Sen did when he was Director-General of FAO. Within FFHC committees, he proposed the formation of Young World Appeal Groups. At a meeting in Geneva in 1965, this plan was enthusiastically accepted by the representatives of religious groups, trade unions, youth and student organizations, education groups, and businessmen and businesswomen associations. Young people did not wait; immediately in many countries they began to inform themselves and their communities of world food needs. They worked to raise funds to aid projects in various countries.

Young World Development (YWD)

Development is a key word in international programs for the 1970's. The United Nations has its Second Development Decade, FAO has its World Plan for Agricultural Development, and Young World Development (YWD) is the name of the youth organization of the American Freedom from Hunger Foundation. In the words of YWD, "Development is not so much a word seeking definition, as it is a process whose results determine the shape of the future, and a challenge to be fulfilled by action and commitment. Development is a change for the benefit of human life and society. It is a revolution of hope, in the spirit of possibility." They say "Development is the new word for peace."

Beginning in 1968, YWD sponsored the now familiar Walks for Development. This is their way of involving the public and making known to other young people and adults what the world problems are and how to do something about them. Each participant in a Walk obtains a sponsor who agrees to contribute anywhere from a nickel to a dollar or more for each mile walked and certified by the Walk Committee. Some have walked 30 miles. Several million dollars have been raised in this way in the last three years. YWD distributes this money through the American Freedom from Hunger Foundation, and it is divided as follows: 42.5% goes to overseas projects, 42.5% is used for projects in the U.S., and the remaining 15% is used by AFFHF for administrative costs and for support of YWD's own program of action and continuing education:

YWD groups work at the community level with the goal of educating themselves and their community about human development. They believe this is the way to achieve change at the national and international level. There are eight regional offices of YWD in the U.S., and new groups are continuously being formed in each region. Groups choose their own projects to sponsor, following guidelines provided by AFFHF and their own YWD Advisory Board.

To the imaginative reader, this listing of the programs and some achievements of FAO, FFHC, AFFHF, and YWD must bring endless mental pictures of what is happening in homes, on farms, and in communities, cities, and regions of the world. Even the most hard-headed realist cannot fail to see that things are happening and that today there is hope where yesterday there was despair for scores of thousands of people in less developed countries of the world. Such a statement as this does not mean that we are blind to the failures, the difficulties, and the barriers to success (and one of the greatest handicaps is the shortage of trained workers and technicians). Nor does it mean that there is any possibility of a worldwide change tomorrow. To provide enough food for the world's people is a long, slow process which may take generations and decades of continued effort of FAO and other specialized agencies of the United Nations, as well as the fullest cooperation of all people everywhere. But in a world where man can walk in space, surely earth problems can be solved.

United Nations International Children's Fund (UNICEF)

It is estimated that, in 1970, of the 1420 million children (0–15 years) in the world, 1,108 million were born into countries still struggling with overpowering problems of sickness, illiteracy, and poverty. These countries include East Asia (excluding Japan), South Asia, Africa (excluding temperate South Africa), and Oceania (excluding Australia and New Zealand). This is not a new situation, but the giving way of the old fatalistic attitudes toward poverty and ignorance to new hopes and efforts is new. Now parents in Asia, Africa, and Central America dare hope for the advantages for their children which those in the more privileged countries have. These stirrings of hope have been aided by a new international consciousness and awareness of these needs. UNICEF, the only international agency whose sole purpose is to be concerned with the needs of children, has accomplished much in its 26 years of existence to promote this new hope in families all over the world.

In February 1946, President Truman appointed former President Herbert Hoover to head a survey mission to study the needs of children in war-torn European countries. Following the completion of this survey, Mr. Hoover, supported by other respected public officials, recommended that a special body be created within the United Nations to meet the emergency needs of these European children suffering from the ravages of the recent war. In mid-December of the same year, the United Nations International Children's Emergency Fund (UNICEF) was established by the United Nations General Assembly.

Although UNICEF is a part of the United Nations, it has had a semi-autonomous status. An Executive Board was appointed by the United Nations, Secretary General Trygve Lie, in consultation with this Executive Board, appointed as the first Executive-Director of UNICEF Maurice Pate, an American and an associate in the previous humanitarian activities of Mr. Hoover. Walter Judd, a well-known congressman from Minnesota, proposed that an initial $15 million dollars be contributed by the U.S. to get this work started. At the outset, the American contributions were more than 70% of the total.

In the first three years of existence, the resources of the Fund were devoted largely to bringing food, medical supplies, and clothing, on an emergency basis, to the children of fourteen war-ravaged countries of Europe and China. During the years from 1948 to 1952, some emergency relief was also furnished to refugee mothers and children of Palestine.

When it was evident that Europe was recovering, the needs of children in the economically underdeveloped countries created a new demand on the Fund. It has been pointed out that these so-called developing countries are and were simply developing much less rapidly than the economically advanced countries. In 1963, the combined income of the approximately 120 developing countries was in the area of one-fifth that of the more advantaged countries. Many families had less than $100 total yearly cash income. It is well known that where the minimum measure of "freedom from want" is not satisfied, children suffer most.

In 1950, therefore, the General Assembly extended the life of the Fund by three years and directed a shift in emphasis from emergency measures to long-term programs in the developing countries. At the end of these three years, UNICEF established its worth and the General Assembly voted to continue the agency indefinitely. At this time, the name was shortened to the United Nations International Children's Fund, but the well-known initials of UNICEF were retained.

UNICEF is governed by an Executive Board which meets regularly

once a year to set policy, consider requests, allocate funds, evaluate results, and establish the annual administrative budget of the Fund. The
actual day-to-day operation is the responsibility of the Executive-
Director. Maurice Pate, the first Executive-Director, continued to give
outstanding service until his death in 1965. At that time another American, Henry Richardson Labouisse, was appointed. During 1971, the
Executive Board approved program assistance totalling $66.8 million
to cover program aid for 95 projects in 62 countries. With previously
committed projects, UNICEF now provides assistance in 112 countries.

UNICEF is supported entirely by voluntary contributions from governments, organizations, and individuals. The "call-forwards" for program assistance for the calendar year of 1972 was estimated at $47
million; a further $9 million was allocated for program support services
and $5 million for administrative services. In 1971, 42.8% of the funds
available to UNICEF came from regular and special contributions of
governments.

In recent years, over 4 million American and Canadian children in
many thousands of communities, through locally sponsored Halloween
collection programs, have brought in over $3 million a year. In 1971,
3,600,000 children in every state in the U.S. were involved in these
programs, and $3,425,000 was collected. This popular program allows
children to have their own fun while contributing to the world's
needy children.

The story of UNICEF Christmas cards is also a heartwarming one.
In 1949, Jitka Samkova, a seven-year-old girl living in a village in
Bohemia, sent her own painting to UNICEF as a "thank you" for the
post-war help given to the children of her village. Many will remember
her joyful picture with the wreath at the top of a Maypole, which she
said was to show that the line of children being helped was endless.
UNICEF used her drawing, and in 1950 sold 130,000 Christmas cards
with that drawing on them. This project has shown remarkable growth;
the number of countries participating increased from 11 in 1950 to over
110 in 1966. The net income rose from $4,200 for the first year of the
campaign to $6 million in the 1971 campaign when 82 million UNICEF
cards were sold.

Social Welfare Programs.   Those who work in programs to improve
the nutrition of a group find that what people eat or do not eat cannot
be separated from the total environment of the group. The development
of social welfare programs has thus become a necessity in the total

UNICEF effort, and UNICEF now supports welfare programs in 50 countries. By 1971, 470 training institutions for welfare workers had been helped. The primary objective of this social welfare program is the keeping of families together to promote the good care (including, of course, feeding) of children.

UNICEF recognizes that a program can only be self-sustaining if the rising generation is given the needed skills and attitudes. Therefore, UNICEF has, in partnership with UNESCO (the United Nations agency primarily responsible for education), worked on a program to promote education. In 1971, UNICEF helped equip over 1080 teacher-training schools and about 37,900 associated primary schools, 24,700 of them for the first time. Over 670 prevocational training schools for young people have been equipped. Thus, children will be helped to prepare for useful lives once they have been saved from malnutrition and childhood diseases.

UNICEF has always, in addition to giving general help to countries in planning projects, furnished equipment and supplies needed to make a project viable. It also has provided stipends for the training of and, in some cases for an initial period, the salaries of key persons in training schemes. More than 430,000 national personnel have been trained with UNICEF stipends, with somewhat more than 100,000 completing this training by 1968. Nearly 1500 institutions training for various categories of health personnel have been equipped.

Other international agencies provide technical advice. In all of these programs, UNICEF has worked cooperatively with WHO, FAO, UNESCO, ILO, and the United Nations Bureau of Social Affairs both on specific projects and general policies for giving aid. Close cooperation among these organizations is thus achieved.

Policies.   UNICEF has certain basic policies. First of all, the countries receiving UNICEF aid must agree to use this aid equitably and efficiently on the basis of need without discrimination because of color, creed, nationality, or political belief. Once UNICEF's aid is discontinued for a particular project, each government continues it on a permanent basis. In fact, as is illustrated later in this chapter, one of the primary considerations before the UNICEF Executive Board approves a project is that it can and will become a permanent program under the government requesting the aid. So, as is said in the 1963 UNICEF report, the Fund "uses its resources to prepare the way for larger programs under national or international auspices." To encourage government interest

Hong Kong children choose their favorite books from a circulating library on wheels. (Courtesy social services department of UNICEF. Photo by Dorothy Lee.)

Treat for a good cause. (Courtesy UNICEF.)

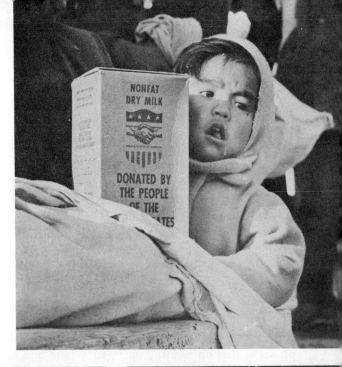

Milk from the Food for Peace Program for a Chilean youngster. (Courtesy Agency for International Development.)

UNICEF helps promote the teaching of nutrition and eating habits as in this project in Ghana. (Courtesy Food and Agriculture Organization.)

and commitments from the very outset, UNICEF requires that matching funds be contributed by the benefiting country. At the present time, these matching funds are two and one-half times the UNICEF contribution.

UNICEF operates no projects of its own within countries; its goals are to encourage and stimulate a local effort by giving the country international help which can be used as a lever to mobilize local resources on behalf of children.

UNICEF aid to benefit children so far has been given in the fields of health, nutrition, and social welfare. Although, in its early years of existence, most of the aid was given to projects in health and nutrition, today the base of operation is broader; attempts are made to assist governments to meet any of the needs of children which the particular country considers to be of high priority and for which practical, effective action is possible. The original purposes of UNICEF were concerned with the right of the child for survival, and this led to the emphasis at first on meeting emergency food and health needs. Maternal and child health services, as will be explained later, received major attention. The eradication of disease played a major role in the effort, with special attention being given to such diseases as malaria, tuberculosis, yaws, leprosy, and trachoma, all of which take a high toll among children.

Nutrition Programs.   Around 1955, UNICEF, in partnership with FAO, and WHO, along with various regional, governmental, and private organizations, undertook a united and expanded effort to combat protein-malnutrition in children in areas where milk was not sufficiently available. Later, in 1957, UNICEF, in cooperation with FAO and other technical United Nations agencies, set up what was called the "Expanded Nutrition Program."

A 1971 report, "UNICEF Work in Nutrition," said that the basic elements of this program are:

1. "food and nutrition education through primary schools, health clinics, voluntary clubs and groups."
2. "demonstration educational activities, often including school gardens, home and community gardens, orchards and small animal production (chickens, eggs, rabbits, fish ponds)."
3. "demonstration feeding programs for school children, preschool children and mothers, also serving to show how locally produced foods can be prepared to supplement inadequate diets."

4. "training at all levels from trained experts to the farmers and mothers."
5. "self-help and voluntary efforts stressed particularly at the village level."

They also say:

> In the actual implementation, FAO and WHO provide the technical advice and experts to assist in designing and conducting these projects. The role of UNICEF is in part to supply material assistance ranging from incubators for poultry and egg production to play equipment for day care centers, and aid for the training of personnel. This last is being recognized more and more as the most important facet of the program in terms of lasting impact.

Long term programs to combat malnutrition, first explored in 1957, now reach 61 countries in which 63 individual projects have been given assistance. In 1959, this Expanded Nutrition program approved projects concerned with the improvement of the teaching of health, nutrition, home economics, and school feeding in the schools and with the improvement of schools for training teachers for primary level.

Special Programs.   An Italian child once explained the word UNICEF as the American word for cow. Undoubtedly, to many mothers and children all over the world, the donations of dry skim milk made by UNICEF have spelled at least some relief from hunger and malnutrition. Dry skim milk was given to the children of Europe in the early post-war relief program. School feeding in Europe was one of the first ways of reaching children. It was early decided, however, that UNICEF should expand its operation to include the world. For this, large scale complete feeding programs were an impossibility. The use of dry skim milk as a supplement was even then recognized as one way of improving children's diets because it is an excellent source of both protein and calcium.

In 1953, because the U.S. had a surplus of skim milk powder, UNICEF was able to buy it at a nominal price. Later, in 1958 and in 1959, the Canadian government also made some dry milk powder available. Beginning in 1954, dry milk powder was available free at American ports for the UNICEF overseas child-feeding programs. The shipping charges averaged from two to two and a half cents per pound. In three years, beginning in 1957, UNICEF shipped 100 million pounds of this milk annually; it is said that, in 1959, 5 million children in 62 countries were receiving daily rations of it.

Because various factors reduced the production of milk in the U.S.

and in Canada in the last few months of 1959, there developed uncertainty about the quantity of dry milk powder which would be available. At this time, it was necessary for the UNICEF Board to agree to furnish the milk only to vulnerable groups. It became even more clear that efforts had to be expended toward helping countries solve their own milk problems. Thus, aid was given to numerous government-subsidized projects such as Anand Project in India, described on pages 131–134, as well as to projects promoting the use of fat-reduced milk or "toned" milk. The whole problem was even more clearly seen at this time as beyond the range of the assistance which UNICEF could give; the major problems would have to be solved by the countries themselves with technical assistance from FAO and with help in milk hygiene from WHO. By the end of 1965, UNICEF had aided milk-conservation programs in 38 countries giving major equipment for 34 milk-drying plants and 64 fluid dairies and auxiliary equipment to another 92 dairies. Also included was training in dairying methods and in quality milk control.

In spite of all of these efforts, however, it was evident that neither donations of dry skim milk nor the promotion of milk schemes in many countries could solve the problem of making available sufficient protein-rich foods, especially foods needed by pregnant and lactating women and growing infants and children. As a result, the joint effort of UNICEF, FAO, WHO, and the Rockefeller Foundation to produce and distribute new protein-rich food supplements (described on pages 413–424) came into being.

The 1965 Nobel Peace Prize was awarded to the United Nations Children's Fund. Maurice Pate, who had by then become known as Mr. UNICEF because of his great vision, unfaltering dedication, and astute business management of the Fund, had just died. The $54,500 of the prize was used as the basis for establishing a living memorial to him; the money was used to train people in the developing countries in fields of service to children.

The Scope of UNICEF. In summary, the following should be pointed out:

1. UNICEF is the only international agency devoted exclusively to helping children.
2. UNICEF assistance is given only on a government's request after a detailed plan has been submitted setting forth exactly how the

aid is to be used and with the assurances of the commitments and responsibilities of the government.

3. Full responsibility for running the health, nutrition, welfare, or education projects rests on the individual government.

4. Every country receiving aid must match UNICEF's contributions. Many do contribute up to two, three, or four times that of UNICEF.

5. UNICEF's aid is given without regard to political belief, race, creed, or nationality.

6. UNICEF is supported entirely by voluntary contributions, approximately 60% of which come from governments and the balance from organizations and individuals.

7. Each project is planned eventually to become an integral part of the country's health, nutrition, or welfare and education services. The projects should be so planned that when UNICEF aid stops the individual country can and will continue and expand the program.

In 1961, it was said by UNICEF that:

In order to obtain long-term benefits, UNICEF favors aid for projects which:

(a) are strategic in dealing with basic child care needs and have prevention as a principal objective.

(b) train personnel in order to supervise the quality and scope as well as the quantity of service.

(c) have an educational effect on the population and encourage its active participation.

(d) are adapted to the financial, technical and administrative capabilities of the country.

(e) set organizational patterns capable of being duplicated and extended elsewhere in the country.

The kinds of aid UNICEF is now giving are listed below.

1. *Health Services.* UNICEF supports a network of health services where expert advice and help are given to mothers and children. Technical equipment, supplies, and vehicles are provided for these services throughout the world.

2. *Disease Control.* UNICEF aids mass campaigns to control and prevent yaws, leprosy, trachoma, tuberculosis, malaria, and like diseases which take a particularly large toll among children.

3. *Nutrition.* UNICEF assists projects in the development and dis-

tribution of new foods needed for adequate nutrition through school and community gardens, fish culture, and poultry raising. It also distributes dry skim milk, promotes local milk production and processing, and aids the development and distribution of new protein-rich foods. Practical nutrition education is also promoted.

4. *Family and Child Welfare Services.* These are set up to help improve family life. For families needing such help, provision of day care or care for children outside the home is promoted. Assistance is also given to projects in community development, to mothers' clubs, and to residential children's institutions.

5. *Education and Vocational Training.* Projects for training teachers, doctors, nurses, midwives, and social workers are assisted. Vocational guidance and training for young people, both in school and for school dropouts, are provided.

6. *Emergency Aid.* When other aid is inadequate or not available, UNICEF may provide aid for children who are victims of earthquakes, floods, or other natural disasters. UNICEF, however, prefers to assist in the rehabilitation phases, leaving the immediate emergency aid to other organizations.

Those who have worked in UNICEF in the last 26 years begin to feel that a real beginning has been made, but that the developing countries still need help to establish many services for children on a permanent basis so that these services can be adapted to meet changing needs. They believe that many countries need permanent health organizations which, reaching out into rural areas, would deal with all aspects of child health. These countries are thought also to need a food and nutrition policy, functioning through all departmental services and effecting the improvement of food habits and the production of food so that both rural and urban children are benefited.

Sir Herbert Broadley, in a speech to nongovernmental agencies on UNICEF's role in the United Nations, said after discussing the projections of population in the world by the year 2000, that:

Thus, members of the United Nations family are faced with immense responsibilities. And of all international organizations, UNICEF perhaps carries the greatest burden, in that to some degree the future of civilization lies in its hands. This does not imply anything derogatory to the great work being undertaken by FAO in increasing the world's food supply, by WHO in banishing diseases and improving health throughout the world, or by UNESCO in spreading the benefits of education to the less developed countries. Whatever benefits may occur to the adult population as the result of all these activities, it is the children of today who are the most important in that the future of the world will be in their hands.

During recent years, UNICEF has evolved a new approach and a broadening of its policy based on the idea that child welfare projects would be more effective if the needs of the child were considered as a part of the overall development plans of a country. This has become known as the "Country Approach." This approach considers the vulnerability of the child and his potential as an agent for economic change.

The World Health Organization (WHO)

In 1971, the World Health Organization Assembly was composed of 131 member states and one associate member. The annual Assembly meeting, usually held in Geneva, Switzerland, establishes policy and decides on the program and budget for the following year. The WHO Board, comprised of people who are all qualified in health matters, meets twice annually to advise and act for the Assembly.

On May 7, 1966, WHO dedicated a beautiful modern headquarters building on the grounds of the Palace of the Nations in Geneva. This move from one of the original buildings occupied by the post-World War I League of Nations was symbolic of the long history of the international movement to improve and protect world health.

In 1972, more than a century after the first organized efforts to promote international health, there were 2832 professional posts budgeted for people carrying out programs at the WHO Headquarters and in 140 countries of the world. The 44 WHO expert panels, whose advice guides the worldwide work of WHO, are comprised of 2606 scientists, health administrators, and educators of many nations.

For WHO purposes, the world is divided into six regions. The regional office for Europe, including the USSR, is in Copenhagen, Denmark; for Africa, in Brazzaville, Republic of the Congo; for the Americas, in Washington, D.C.; for Southeast Asia, in New Delhi, India; for the Eastern Mediterranean, in Alexandria, United Arab Republic; and for the Western Pacific Region, in Manila, Philippines. These regional offices are responsible for planning and operating country projects; the Headquarters' technical staff stand ready to advise and help.

History of the International Health Movement.   The international health movement had its inception when Europeans realized that cholera was spreading from country to country. They also began to

What does the future hold for these children in nutrition and health?
Above and above right. *The proper food can help give this child a happy future.* Right. *(Photos courtesy Food and Agriculture Organization.)*

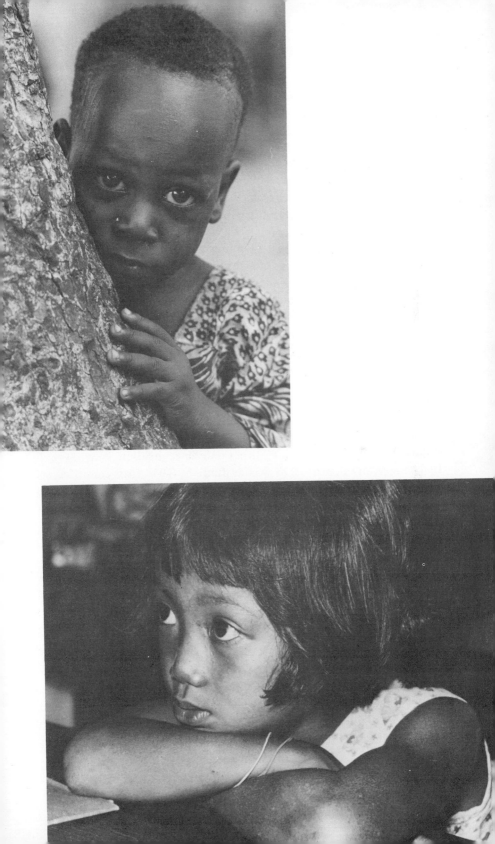

wonder how disease was related to sanitation, to climate, and to the physical environment in general.

Programs in social welfare arose in Europe when rapid industrialization brought overcrowding, poverty, suffering, and riots to the rapidly expanding urban areas. At this time, privately supported medical missions under newly organized private philanthropic groups began to expand their spheres of action beyond national boundaries. Even in this era of strong nationalism, it became increasingly evident that national governments could not solve their own problems. Because of this, the first International Sanitary Congress was called in Paris in 1851. The progress toward international planning and cooperation in matters of health was not continuous, but the general interest in international health spread and the present humanitarian objectives were coming to the fore. In 1919, at an intergovernmental health meeting, the idea that the masses must accept the need for the proposed health measures and even understand them was brought forth. Following World War I, the newly formed League of Nations included in its covenant a statement calling for international concern for the prevention and control of disease. In 1945, following World War II, when the delegates met in San Francisco to form the United Nations, the will to build the peace on firm foundations and a confidence that the use of existing scientific knowledge in health matters was held to be of paramount importance. Following an International Health Conference held in New York in 1946, the WHO Constitution was drafted; by 1948 fifty countries had ratified it. So on April 7, 1948, henceforth known as World Health Day, WHO was officially launched as an integral part of the United Nations with Dr. Broch Chisholm as its first Director-General.

The opening paragraph of the WHO Constitution says: "Health is a state of complete physical, mental and social well-being and not merely the absence of disease or infirmity." Upon retiring in 1953, in his last address, Dr. Chisholm said that all the principles included in the WHO Constitution "are based on this simple truth: in our shrunken world, health, like peace and security, is indivisible and mankind's fight against illness, its major enemy, can be won only through the concerted efforts of us all."

Nutrition in WHO.   From the first, nutrition has been recognized as important in the promotion of good health. In the proposals made for the 1950 program, the Director-General and the executive board of WHO, at the Second World Assembly in 1949, said: "Nutrition is perhaps the most important single environmental factor influencing health." To support this it was stated that discoveries of recent decades show the importance of nutrition in the reduction of the infant death rate and in the incidence of infectious diseases as well as in the productivity of adults.

Because of the gravity of the problems of food production, FAO was started in 1945 three years before WHO. Even before the latter was formed in 1948, observers from the WHO Interim Commission who attended the second annual conference of FAO proposed that a joint committee on nutrition be formed. Thus began the close cooperation between WHO and FAO which has been carried out by the Joint Expert Committee ever since.

In 1925, the Health Organization of the League of Nations began a study of nutrition, but active international interest really only began in 1935, with the circulation to governments and scientific bodies of a report of the Technical Commission. Sounding like modern concerns, in 1936 there was proposed study of the nutritional status of children, of nutritive requirements especially for young children, and of factors influencing nutritive requirements. Because the needs for nutrition emphasis in public health were already understood, at the World Health Assembly in 1948 nutrition was granted the same high priority as malaria, maternal and child health, tuberculosis, and venereal diseases. A nutrition section was immediately established within the Secretariat of WHO. At the first meeting of the Joint Expert Committee of FAO and WHO in October 1949 and at subsequent meetings, this committee made vital contributions, including:

1. Discussing individual and joint programs of the two organizations.
2. Giving expert advice on problems referred to them.
3. Examining problems of malnutrition of international concern and making recommendations for action to FAO and WHO.
4. Making suggestions for assistance to establish national food and nutrition organization in member countries.
5. Directing attention to training and education of personnel needed in national nutrition activities.

In 1959, some of the practical aspects of cooperation of the two agencies were critically evaluated and an agreement was drawn up, as stated in the book *The First Ten Years of WHO*. WHO agreed to concern itself with "nutrition as it affects health; the objective of FAO is to raise the levels of nutrition and standards of living, and to improve the efficiency of all food and agricultural products."

A specific example of the cooperation of WHO and FAO was shown when, in 1962, FAO and the United Nations launched the World Food Program. This was aimed at making plans for social and economic progress in developing countries and at relieving malnutrition by the organized use of surplus foods. WHO actively cooperated by : (1) examining the health implications as well as those concerning nutrition of the projects proposed, (2) following the progress of these projects, and (3) evaluating later the effects of these programs on the health of the populations involved.

For almost two decades now the Joint Expert Committee has been concerned with the extent of malnutrition and the indices for determining this. Its efforts have pointed to the urgent need for comparability on an international scale of methods of collecting data. Study continues on problems such as assessment of nutritional status and nutritional requirements and assessment of such diseases as goiter, xerophthalmia, nutritional anemia, protein-calorie malnutrition, and certain degenerative diseases. The increasing use of food additives led to the appointment, in 1956, of a joint committee to discuss the general principles which should govern their use. By 1964, recommendations for a number of food additives were drawn up. The use of pesticides also was studied by another committee, and principles governing consumer safety were established.

WHO also has cooperated with UNICEF, ILO, and UNESCO. The record of field projects conducted from 1948 to 1964 in member states by the Nutrition Section of WHO is impressive. Twenty-three short surveys (some with advice to the government) have been conducted; five comprehensive nutrition surveys and recommendations to governments have been made as well as an equal number of such surveys with aid in developing programs. Specific diseases have been studied in 14 countries; seven programs including *Nutrition and Parasitology, Dietetics, Social Anthropology, School Feeding,* and *Milk Conservation* have been completed. Aid has been given to 11 nutrition departments, nutrition institutes, or university units. The promotion of the training of health personnel in nutrition has a top priority rating now with WHO. Between 1947 and 1963, WHO provided 544 fellowships in nutrition, approximately two-thirds of which were held by people from the Americas, Africa, and Europe.

WHO emphasizes nutrition as an inseparable component of health which needs to be integrated by governments into their health plans; this is particularly stressed in the developing countries. During the past 15 years, WHO has employed approximately 150 nutrition experts as consultants to study malnutrition and to advise on its control and prevention.

As the result of all of these efforts, more attention is being paid in the developing countries to the teaching of nutrition in the medical schools and to building up contacts between medical schools in the developed and developing countries. Particular emphasis has been given to the need for pediatricians, maternal and child health specialists, and public health physicians to receive specific training in nutrition to enable them to handle the problems of malnutrition in mothers and young children.

For some years now, WHO has also recognized the need for training at various levels; with FAO, it has organized ad hoc training courses and seminars. From 1948 to 1964, seven training courses were held in Europe, Asia, and Africa. Eleven symposia and seminars were held in these regions in addition to Central and South America. Six training centers were established in the same regions; two surveys of training going on were conducted, one for India, the Americas, and Africa and the other for Europe.

A five-year program in nutrition for WHO was projected in 1965. It included proposals to:

1. Advise and assist member states to continue to define their problems in nutrition and to initiate action for the control and prevention of malnutrition.
2. Intensify efforts toward making prevention of malnutrition an integral part of national health planning as it relates to provision of basic health services, especially for mothers and children.
3. Increase efforts to provide adequate facilities to train medical and paramedical personnel in nutrition.
4. Continue research into the etiology of nutritional disorders and disease.
5. Promote knowledge of epidemiology of nutritional disease so preventive measures can be instituted.
6. Periodically assess the nutritional status of a population to determine the effect of changing conditions. In doing this, it is proposed to collect information on heights and weights of children in developing countries under differing socio-economic conditions. Norms for well-nourished children in these countries could

thus be established. Then longitudinal and cross-sectional studies could assess the value of specific programs.

7. Continue to study the interrelationship of nutrition and infection.
8. Study desirable weight gain in pregnancy, the effect of nutrition on fetal growth and birth weight, and the physiological cost of pregnancy and lactation in terms of increased need for nutrients.
9. Study energy requirements and essential nutrients for industrial workers in the interest of maximum efficiency. In consequence, it is hoped that it will be possible to recommend group feeding procedures to meet these needs.
10. Study effect of nutrition on degenerative diseases.
11. Continue to study acceptable levels of the major known essential nutrients with the hope that these can be established by 1970.
12. Draw up specifications for the toxicological evaluation of the antimicrobials, antioxidants, emulsifiers and related substances, bleaching agents, and food colors, as well as miscellaneous additives. Also continue work on the toxicity of pesticides.

Thus, the vital character of nutrition work in WHO continues into the future. In the December 1971 Program Review of the Nutrition Unit of WHO, the following were listed as of the highest priority:

1. protein-calorie malnutrition, because of its high mortality rate, its wide prevalence and the irreversible physical and (sometimes) mental damage it may cause;
2. xerophthalmia, because of its contribution to the mortality of malnourished children, its relatively wide prevalence and the dramatic irreversible damage (blindness) it causes;
3. nutritional anaemias, because of their wide distribution, their contribution to mortality from many other conditions and their effects on working capacity;
4. endemic goiter, because of its wide distribution.

Cooperative Relations of United Nations Agencies

Very soon after the creation of FAO, WHO, and UNICEF, it became apparent that committees to handle problems common to all of these organizations would be necessary. In 1960, Maurice Pate, then Executive-Director of UNICEF, said:

Over the course of the years a network of cooperative relationships has developed between UNICEF and the World Health Organization and also the Food and Agriculture Organization—relationships both of a formal and intimate character—to assure that the available international resources are aligned in the most effective ways possible in helping government projects.

Much of this cooperation has been accomplished through joint action programs in the developing countries. These commenced in the 1950's as "Expanded Nutrition Programs," and at first they were mainly concerned with school feeding activities. Realizing the potential that practical activities had in nutrition education, the International Agencies concerned decided to pay more attention to the food production components of such programs and in 1961 they were renamed "Applied Nutrition Programs." These may be defined as:

> Coordinated educational activities between agriculture, health and education authorities and other interested agencies with the aim of raising the levels of nutrition of local populations, particularly mothers and children in rural areas.

FAO/WHO/UNICEF Applied Nutrition Programs have been initiated in more than 70 countries, and consideration is presently being given to enlarge their scope through giving more attention to their introduction in urban areas.

These three agencies have also collaborated in assisting in training personnel from developing countries in food and nutrition. Apart from helping in the establishment of permanent training courses, these agencies have, when the need arose, helped to organize ad hoc training courses, seminars, fellowship programs, the development of teaching materials, and other means of assisting in providing trained personnel and creating facilities for teaching food and nutrition in developing countries.

The same Agencies collaborate in the Protein Advisory Group of the United Nations system. This Committee was originally set up by WHO to advise on the safety and nutritional usefulness for infants and young children of various protein foods and supplements. The Committee was enlarged in 1960 to include FAO and UNICEF. The Committee meets once or twice a year and has given and will continue to give the United Nations family advice and directives for developing programs in regard to protein-rich foods.

The responsibilities of the two agencies may be summarized thus: in FAO, the emphasis is on nutrition in relation to the production, distribution, and consumption of foods; in WHO, it is on nutrition in relation to the maintenance of health and the prevention of disease. In

Teaching schoolchildren to
raise gardens in Paraguay.
Above. *(Courtesy
UNICEF. Photos by Ling.)*

Seven agencies of the
United Nations cooperate
to teach Bolivians to raise
better potatoes. Left.
(Courtesy United Nations.)

appraising the problem FAO and WHO agreed to be jointly responsible for cultural and social aspects and for undertaking joint field studies pertaining to a particular nutrition deficiency, (e.g., kwashiorkor). They also undertook to join in program planning surveys in relation to UNICEF-assisted projects and in the determination of nutrient requirements.*

Nevin Schrimshaw said:

The most extraordinary and hopeful development in international nutrition has been the way in which, in the last decade, WHO, in cooperation with FAO and UNICEF, has led a vigorous and effective assault on the widespread problem of protein malnutrition and on the accompanying high prevalence of kwashiorkor and marasmus in young children in technically underdeveloped areas.

He also says that: "It is an inspiring record of accomplishment with the full effects only beginning to be felt."

Thus, on the practical level and to the benefit of all concerned, efforts towards cooperation in the field of nutrition have been attempted. As the ever-expanding population presents what seems to be almost insoluble nutrition problems, such cooperation is becoming even more imperative.

The story of cooperation within recent years is well illustrated by the Protein Advisory Group (PAG), whose story is worthy of detailing. The awareness of the world's protein problems, discussed on page 413–414, began in the 1950's when studies of kwashiorkor in Africa, Central America, and Brazil were first conducted and published jointly by FAO and WHO. The solution to this problem of weanlings called for the production of cheap, protein-rich foods. In 1955, the Protein Advisory Group, a joint commission of experts from all over the world, was created. Its original role was conceived as that of collecting information on raw materials to provide protein foods of high nutritive quality and to develop safe, protein-rich foods which were acceptable to the infants. Later it became apparent that the role of PAG must also involve the commercial areas of production of these products, and in 1967 and 1968, expansion of the scope of PAG was undertaken to include this broader role. The administration of PAG was then transferred to the Nutrition Division of FAO. At a 1970 meeting of PAG, the areas covered

*Report of an FAO/WHO Inter-Secretariant Meeting to discuss interagency cooperation in the field of food and nutrition, Rome 1966.

included human nutrition and child health; public health and food hygiene; management science, marketing, advertising, distribution, and consumer studies; and government food policies.

During the 18th meeting of PAG in 1971, the following statement was adopted:

> Large segments of the population in developing countries suffer from the effects of protein deficiency for want of adequate quality and quantity of protein in their diets. Projections based on current trends in demand and supply indicate that unless these trends are changed, the protein gap will become increasingly serious in the years to come.
>
> The nature and magnitude of the protein problem poses the greatest threat to vulnerable groups, particularly preschool children and expectant and nursing mothers, even when food balance sheets and family dietary surveys fail to show a deficiency. Moreover, agriculturally and economically, adequate protein of good quality will be more difficult to provide for a rapidly growing world population than the needed calories. The reasons for the existence of a protein problem must be understood clearly if serious errors in formulating national agricultural and food policies are to be avoided and grave consequences to the health and future of the under-privileged of all countries averted.

PAG has had marked success in achieving cooperation among international agencies as well as success in obtaining the services of experts outside these agencies. Because it is a small group, it has been able to call upon experts for advice and to respond rapidly to technical and scientific innovations relevant to the world protein problem. It can then inform the agencies best able to use this advice. It is now said in this sense to represent a world council on protein matters. For other activities of PAG, see pages 413–414.

Western Hemisphere Health Programs

All nations now share in the work of the United Nations and specialized agencies, but in the Western Hemisphere, health programs are developing which are directed toward meeting the particular needs of the millions of people in Latin America and the Caribbean.

The problems of Latin America are numerous, varied, and in many areas severe; there is a high incidence of infectious diseases, malnutrition and hunger, poor sanitation, poor housing and working conditions, illiteracy, and poverty. No one country has sufficient resources, facilities, and trained personnel to solve its problems immediately.

The Pan American Health Organization (PAHO). In March 1972, Bertlyn Bosley, Nutrition Advisor of the Regional Office of PAHO, kindly prepared the following statement of major nutrition activities of PAHO for 1967–1972. She said: "PAHO has greatly expanded its emphasis on the development of human resources in nutrition needed to implement services in all of the countries." Some of the activities which Dr. Bosley listed are:

1. In 1966, a conference in Caracas was held on the training of nutritionists and dietitians. Attending were directors of the then 22 schools of dietetics in Latin America. The purpose of this conference was to determine what type of education was needed for the training of nutrition personnel, both for work as dietitians in hospitals and as nutritionists in public health. This conference succeeded in the following:

   a. Developing a plan for the education through a four-year university program of nutritionists/dietitians.

   b. Twenty-three schools have now established a four-year university program in this area of study. These schools are located in eight Latin American countries.

   c. All the schools have graduated at least one class and some two to three. These graduates are now working in the integrated health services combining both preventive and curative programs which have been developed. They provide consultive service to local community program staffs from their regional or district offices.

2. The 1967, PAHO with FAO, the Williams-Waterman Fund, and the University of the West Indies of Jamaica and Trinidad established a Caribbean Foods and Nutrition Institute on the two campuses on which this university is located.

   The primary function of this Institute is:

   a. to train for the area middle-level people, not nutrition specialists. These include nurses, sanitarians, agriculture extension personnel, home economics teachers, and welfare workers.

   b. to coordinate food production and availability with the improvement of nutritional status of the people in the English-speaking area in the Caribbean.

   c. to make, as time permits, surveys of food availability and nutritional status.

Research is also now being carried on in the use of intramuscular injections of iodized oil for persons living in areas where goiter is endemic and it is not feasible to iodize the salt. Studies are also being conducted on nutritional anemia, food fortification, and anthropometric measurements in reference to growth and development of Latin American children.

The nutrition section, which now includes five people at the regional office of PAHO, also has held a number of technical conferences and published guidelines for the conduct of nutrition services at the local level as these have become needed.

The nutrition section of the quadrennial report to the director (1966–1969) says that during those years the areas of special interest have been protein-calorie malnutrition, nutritional anemias, endemic goiter, hypovitaminosis A, ariboflavinosis, and dental caries.

The Institute of Central America and Panama (INCAP).   In April 1972, the following material was furnished by INCAP:

> The six countries of the Central American Isthmus created in September, 1949, a unique scientific organization for the purpose of studying the nutrition problems of the area, finding ways of solving them, and assisting the member governments in applying the measures recommended for this purpose. This is called the Institute of Nutrition of Central America and Panama (INCAP). The government of the Republic of Guatemala offered to provide the necessary buildings to house the Institute. The offer was accepted and, by common agreement, Guatemala became the seat of INCAP. The W. K. Kellogg Foundation provided fellowships for the training of the basic scientific staff and for laboratory and library equipment. Dr. Nevin S. Scrimshaw was appointed as its first director, in which post he remained until 1961, when Dr. Moisés Béhar, Director in 1972, was selected to follow him. INCAP is administered by the Pan American Sanitary Bureau (PASB), Regional Office for the Americas of the World Health Organization. Its research, educational, and applied programs are guided by a Technical Advisory Committee of experts in nutrition and allied fields, and a Council, composed by representatives of the member countries and a representative from the PASB, meets annually to discuss all aspects of the programs under way.
>
> INCAP's specific aims are to promote and encourage the development of nutritional science and its application in member countries by means of scientific research on foodstuffs, nutrition, clinical and biochemical studies, and by training technical personnel, in collaboration with universities, agricultural institutions, and other scientific groups concerned. In fact, it

has become a training center in nutrition and allied fields for the Central American area.

Some of INCAP's achievements, which have provided a stimulus and a pattern for many other countries and regions of the world, have been: the production of a protein-rich vegetable mixture called Incaparina (a detailed description of which is given on page 414); the iodization of salt for the prevention and control of endemic goiter; the production of a milk substitute called Tenerina (for the feeding of young calves); the nutritional improvement of corn and bean varieties—the basic staples in the habitual diets of the Central American populations—and, as its most recent development, the fortification of sugar with vitamin A.

Agency for International Development (AID).   AID is an agency of the U.S. Department of State. The general purpose of AID is "to help developing countries achieve economic strength and momentum so they can provide for a better life for their own people, using their own knowledge and their own resources." This statement was made by David E. Bell, then the AID administrator, on February 21, 1966, in Memphis, Tennessee. He added, ". . . and at that point, we want to end our aid." It has been possible in the history of AID and its predecessor agencies to terminate assistance and for nations to proceed independently. Spain, Greece, Taiwan, Iran, Israel, Mexico, and Venezuela no longer require economic assistance. Turkey and Korea are approaching self-sustaining economies. Some of the former recipient countries are now helping other nations who are in the developing stages.

Program emphases in AID are in the general areas of agriculture, food production, health, and education. Food production is the aspect of the nutrition program directly related to agriculture and the record has been a successful one in increasing production. Improved seed is used, regular spraying is practiced, fertilizer is applied, the land is irrigated, roads from farm to market are built, and an agricultural extension education program is conducted. The experiences of AID have demonstrated the kinds of assistance, the kinds of national investments, and the kinds of national policies that can produce a rapid growth in food production.

In 1970, in AID's publication *The Protein Gap,* it was said that 20% of the population in the developing countries was undernourished and that 60% was malnourished. The authors of this publication again emphasized that "the prospects for economic and social development are bleak if the needs of preschool children and of nursing and pregnant women for balanced nutrition, above all for protein, cannot be met."

They also pointed out that, although there is promise of increased agricultural yields and of more effective family planning, the challenge is still staggering, although the solutions seem attainable. The protein gap, they say, is still the great problem, especially when the population of the underdeveloped nations is increasing at more than 1 million people per week. FAO has a target of a total of 112 million tons of protein as the world requirement by 1975, which is an increase of 27 million tons over the level of 1970. Most of this will have to come from conventional agriculture, animal husbandry, and fisheries, but especially from the production of cereals and the improvement of the quality of protein in them. Charts I and II from this publication show better than words just what this means.

CHART I*   The Gap

	Developed Countries	Developing Countries
Calories	2941	2033
Total protein per person, daily grams	84.1	52.4
Animal protein only, per person, daily grams	38.8	7.2
Population in millions	1089	1923

*Taken from *The Protein Gap*, p. 5, 1970. Agency for International Development, Bureau of Technical Assistance.

CHART II*   Number of Malnourished Children in Developing Countries 1966–1975 (Rough Estimate in Millions)

Number of children by age group	1966	1968	1975
0–6	342	350	425
7–14	325	338	390
Total: 0–14	667	688	815

*Taken from *The Protein Gap*, p. 5, 1970. Agency for International Development, Bureau of Technical Assistance.

The experiences of AID have demonstrated the kinds of assistance, the kinds of national investments, and the kinds of national policies that can produce a rapid growth in food production. To explore the feasibility of developing and marketing new high-protein foods, from 1966–1971 an AID program made 14 grants of $60,000 each to U.S. food companies. At present, AID reports that four or five of these will apparently result in viable enterprises. In a personal communication to the author, it was said that, although

this may appear to be a modest achievement, with benefits initially available only in urban areas to people with some purchasing power, significant progress has been made in:

1. Advancing the concept,
2. Identifying obstacles to developing new technologies,
3. Practical application of some of the concepts that have been developed in the Research and Development programs of the food industries.

The AID Office of Nutrition has also launched a program to provide grants to food industries in developing countries to stimulate new protein-food enterprises there. These projects will include feasibility studies as well as provide funds to purchase technical assistance. It is hoped that this three-year program, planned to provide 30 to 40 such grants, will result in bringing approximately a dozen new foods into production.

AID has also taken the lead in a program to demonstrate the feasibility of fortification of staples such as wheat-fortification in Tunisia, corn-fortification in Guatemala, and cassava-fortification in Brazil.

Not only does AID's research program provide "a means for developing acceptable protein concentrates and for determining optimum levels of fortification," but in addition, evaluation of the nutritional impact of these products is being conducted. These data are made available through international workshops and by the encouragement of visits of representatives of countries contemplating fortification as well as visits by teams of experts of countries engaged in such projects.

The major portion of the fortification program will be completed by mid-1975.

Health and Education Projects.   Another effort of the Office of Nutrition of AID 1972 is in the broad area of nutrition education. Before methodology can be developed for testing nutrition education in the improvement of food habits, an in-depth evaluation of the research in this area must be done. This entire project will culminate in field testing in those countries where the nutrition education methods will be used.

An important cooperative program with this office in AID and the Maternal and Child Health Services of the Department of Health, Education, and Welfare is the use of growth charts to assess the physical well-being of the children. A major conference on this subject was held in 1971. The use of the ILESHA growth chart (see illustration on following pages), developed by Dr. David Morley for use in Nigeria, is now promoted by AID. Two million copies (in English and French) have been printed and distributed. These charts, now requested from all parts of the world, have been used in Nigeria in the Under-Fives Clinics and are kept as a record by the mother. The monitoring of weight gain is said by D. B. Jelliffe to be extremely important in early detection and therefore prevention as well as recovery from such severe forms of protein-calorie malnutrition as kwashiorkor and another major pediatric problem, nutritional marasmus. Experience with these two clinical syndromes has shown that months and sometimes years of failure to gain weight normally precede their onset. The use of such growth charts can also help to educate and convince policy-makers in a country, all levels of health workers, and parents as well as supporting agencies of the importance of the prevention of malnutrition.

American Land Grant Universities, under contract with AID, are helping in the creation of agricultural training institutions, centers for practical research, and agricultural extension services to help the farmer translate research findings into action on the farm. It was found in Bangladesh that demonstrations of improved methods were accepted best when farmers themselves conducted them rather than when some model plot was used at the research institute. It is reported that "to the farmers of Mymensingh (Bangladesh) line-sowing, the use of fertilizer, small pump irrigation, and other innovations were worth copying only if they worked for a neighbor whose farm and whose means were on the same small scale as their own." Agricultural credit is of fundamental importance. If the farmer wishes to use better seed and to apply fertilizer but has not the money to buy them, his efforts are paralyzed. In the Philippines, the agricultural credit program was instrumental in the acceptance of the high-yield rice, resulting in a marked increase in agricultural production. It is jointly supported by AID and the private banks.

MAJOR ILLNESSES TO BE
ENTERED ON CHART

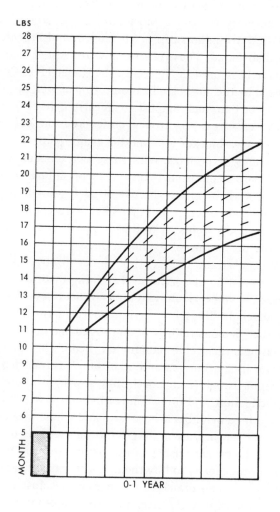

Child health and weight record the first five years—Ilesha chart. (Courtesy AID.)

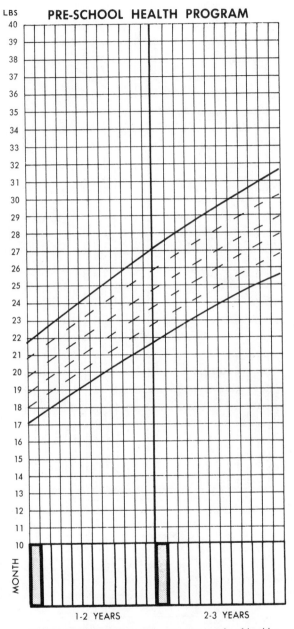

PRE-SCHOOL HEALTH PROGRAM

LBS

1-2 YEARS   2-3 YEARS

UPPER LINE—This represents the average weight of healthy and well-fed children.

LOWER LINE—The weight of children should be above this line. A steady upward progress of the weight record is more important than its position.

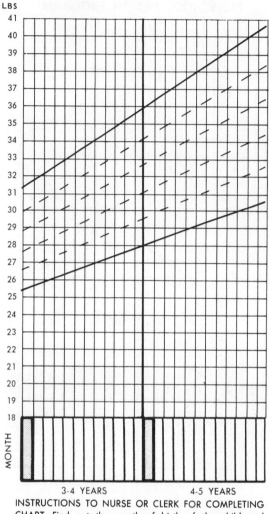

INSTRUCTIONS TO NURSE OR CLERK FOR COMPLETING
CHART—Find out the month of birth of the child and
fill this into all the black-edged spaces, then fill in the
other months. Also mark off the years as shown.

When the child comes for weighing make a large dot in
that month's column against the weight. Connect this with
the last dot.

A number of American food processors are experimenting with inexpensive protein-rich cereal products that could be popularized in the less-developed countries. For these industries, AID gives priority consideration by guaranteeing coverage for private American investments in food-processing improvements in other countries.

SOME INTERNATIONAL PROGRAMS
OF FEDERAL AGENCIES

A few of the international programs are reviewed here to indicate another type of assistance. The 1954 Agricultural Trade Development and Assistance Act, usually known as Public Law 480, was passed by the 83rd Congress. Under this law, foreign currency was to be accepted in payment for surplus American food sold to countries friendly to the U.S. and needing the food. This currency was to be deposited in the country of origin. It could be used for projects to benefit the people of that country. Several departments of the U.S. government have carried on programs in a number of countries. Some of these programs use P. L. 480 funds and others do not.

In 1966, 16.5% of the U.S. commodities were paid for in dollars and the remainder in the currency of the country receiving the commodity. In 1971, 70% was paid for in dollars. Wheat comprised 40% of the commodities sold in 1971.

The National Institutes of Health (NIH)

The National Institutes of Health are currently sponsoring studies on anemia in relation to parasitic infections and malnutrition in Egypt. The development of protein-rich foods in India is also being investigated along with metabolic studies on vitamin A and nutritional deficiencies in general. Other research projects currently being pursued include a study of calcium metabolism in periodontal disease and in osteoporosis in Israel, the effect of indigenous fats and oils in nutritional problems in Pakistan, and the pediatric approach to health problems in Pakistan.

The National Institute of Child Health and Human Development, in their own international program, not under P. L. 480, has a large grant at INCAP. This significant study, after a thorough investigation of methods, now concerns itself with the possible relationships between malnutrition, social variables, and intellectual development in a rural village population. The study, planned to extend over a seven to ten-year period, is comparing children, all under six years of age, in which one group is nutritionally supplemented and the other is not. Social stimulation is also a part of this project.

The latter Institute has and is now stimulating and supporting research projects concerning the relationship of malnutrition and mental retardation in the U.S. as well as in Mexico, Jamaica, Guatemala, Colombia, and Lebanon. The problems of infant malnutrition in Chile and nutrition and child growth and development are now under investigation.

The experience gained in the Guatemala and the Colombia projects has led to a similar project currently in operation in Harlem, New York.

Another important development in the nutrition activities of the National Institutes of Health concerns a cooperative effort between the U.S. and Japan. "The United States and Japanese governments have appointed biomedical scientists to constitute a U.S.-Japan Cooperative Medical Science Committee," according to a May, 1971, report on the first five years of the U.S.-Japan Cooperative Medical Science Program, 1965–1970. This cooperative project has been conducted under the Geographic Medicine Branch of the National Institute of Allergy and Infectious Diseases, National Institutes of Health. Under the U.S.-Japanese agreement, scientific projects will be supported, meetings held, and consultant and panel members supported to attend these joint meetings.

The joint Malnutrition Panel of this U.S.-Japan Cooperative Medical Science Program is one of six panels. Their high priority areas for research in developing countries of Asia are related to the:

1. Determination of the effects of malnutrition in children on mental development, learning, behavior, physical capability, and performance.
2. Determination of the effects of malnutrition on resistance to infection and the mechanisms responsible.
3. Investigations of prevalence, etiology, and methods for effective prevention of nutritional anemias.
4. Requirements for essential nutrients under prevailing conditions and improvement of methods for evaluation of conditions and improvement of methods for evaluation of nutritional status.

5. Development and evaluation of protein sources and new protein foods including amino acid fortification.
6. Mechanisms and limits of biochemical adaptation to malnutrition.
7. Studies of the distribution, importance, and methods of control or elimination of naturally occurring toxic substances in legumes and other plant foods with special emphasis on mycotoxins (toxic substances from molds).
8. The genetic improvement of the nutritive value of cereal grain.

The Maternal and Child Health Service of the Department of Health, Education, and Welfare

In October 1969, the health programs of the Children's Bureau were transferred to the Health Services and Mental Health Administration in the Department of Health, Education, and Welfare, and with this transfer went the international activities in maternal and child health. The Maternal and Child Health Service, like its predecessor the Children's Bureau, has no operating program in nutrition services overseas but carries on in the international field many activities of a consultative advisory nature and also has a research program which corresponds to its domestic responsibilities. In the foreign research program, which uses U.S.-owned foreign currencies generated by the sale of U.S. surplus agricultural products (P. L. 480), the grants made are designed to give practical answers for improving maternal and child health services useful both to the foreign country and to the U.S. Among these are some dealing with nutrition, such as anemia in pregnancy, the relationship between nutrition and resistance to infection, and the nutritional requirements of "small-for-date" infants.

Through an arrangement with AID, the Maternal and Child Health Service has on its staff a nutritionist with competence and experience in maternal and child health and experience in working overseas.

The Maternal and Child Health Service cooperates with such U.S. registered voluntary agencies as CARE, Catholic Relief Services, Church World Service, and their local counterparts. The Maternal and Child Health Service also serves as a focal point in the U.S. government for cooperation with UNICEF. Similarly, proposals dealing with child nutrition which are considered by WHO and FAO are also reviewed by the Maternal and Child Health Service.

U.S. Department of Agriculture Economic Research Service (ERS)

The following statement came from the secretariat of the Interagency Committee on Nutrition Education, U.S.D.A. Agriculture Research Service.

The involvement of ERS in dealing with nutrition problems occurs mainly through its Nutrition and Agribusiness Group. This group provides technical services to the Agency for International Development, both in Washington and in its missions abroad, in planning, executing, and evaluating projects aimed at improving nutritional status in developing countries. Through its activities, the Nutrition and Agribusiness Group encourages the application of modern developments in food science and technology to innovative programs of nutrition improvement. It has assisted in planning field trials of amino acid fortification of wheat in Tunisia, rice in Thailand, and corn in Guatemala, and of protein supplementation of cassava in Brazil. It encourages and assists the efforts of United States and foreign private industry aimed at developing low-cost protein foods such as soft drinks, infant weaning foods, textured protein products, and fortified pastas. Major ongoing projects include:

1. evaluation of consumer acceptability of the blended cereal food CSM (corn-soy-milk) distributed under the Food for Peace Program;
2. study of overall rural development approaches which include nutrition improvement as an indispensable component;
3. evaluation of the nutritional impact of the Green Revolution; and
4. assisting initiatives to further nutrition improvement through cereal breeding and/or fortification.

Food and Nutrition Board

The Food and Nutrition Board of the National Academy of Sciences, National Research Council, had its origin in 1940 when this country was on the brink of war. At that time, a Committee on Food and Nutrition was appointed to have as its major concern the national situation with regard to the extent and causes of malnutrition and how to improve the nutrition of all our people. A study was made of the research that had been published on the quantitative needs for nutrients for all age groups, in order to maintain our population in vigorous health and also to estimate the quantities of various foods that would be required to supply the necessary nutrients. From this study came the Recommended Dietary Allowances approved in 1941 and first published in 1943. These Recommended Dietary Allowances have been revised periodically ever since in order to take advantage of new research and new interpretations of nutritional research. The seventh revised edition was published in 1968, and a new revision came out in late 1973.

The Food and Nutrition Board has been concerned primarily with the application of nutritional science in the U.S., but international cooperation on problems of food and nutrition also has been a strong feature of the Board's continuing program. A committee on protein malnutrition has administered grants from the Rockefeller Foundation to assist nutrition scientists in some 20 countries in combating protein malnutrition, particularly in mothers and preschool children. This has been done in cooperation with FAO, WHO, and UNICEF. The Board's committee on international nutrition programs serves in an advisory capacity to the AID Office of Nutrition providing nutrition information and position papers or documented reports. This committee is also working on international dietary standards. Another committee on food protection has for more than 20 years actively worked on the many problems associated with maintaining the safety of the nation's food supply. Other activities of the Food and Nutrition Board are illustrated by the title of some of its current publications: "Maternal Nutrition and the Course of Pregnancy," "Dietary Fat and Human Health," "Toxicants Occurring Naturally in Foods," "Food Chemicals Codex," "Use of Human Subjects in Safety Evaluation of Food Chemicals."

Members of the Food and Nutrition Board are appointed from among leaders in the fields of food and nutrition, and they serve without compensation beyond their actual expenses. The Board is an advisory body which promotes research in food and nutrition and interprets nutritional science in the interest of the public welfare. It may act on its own initiative or at the request of public and private agencies. Financial support for publications and for meetings comes from agencies such as the Nutrition Foundation, the Milbank Memorial Fund, and the Research Corporation. Support for special projects and purposes may come from private agencies and government contracts and grants.

PRIVATE FOUNDATIONS

Two independent foundations that are contributing materially to programs for increasing the quantity and quality of food produced in the developing countries of the world are the Ford Foundation and the Rockefeller Foundation. They both are, and have been for several years,

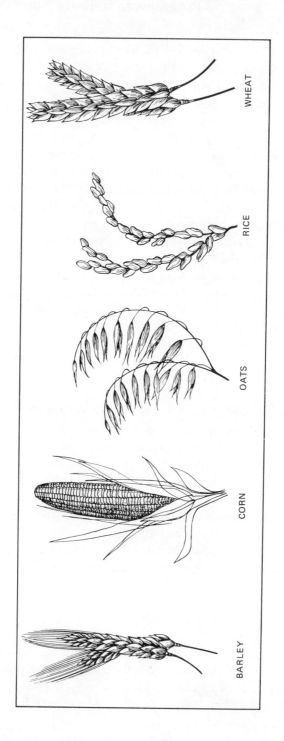

WHEAT

RICE

OATS

CORN

BARLEY

working at the invitation of governments to support needed research, give technical expert assistance, and provide training for local scientists and technicians. Each foundation has a number of separate projects to which it gives support, but in many cases they give joint support.

Ford Foundation

The Ford Foundation is a private nonprofit institution dedicated to public well-being; it seeks to identify and contribute to the solution of certain problems of national or international importance. The Foundation works principally by granting funds to institutions and organizations for experimental, demonstration, and developmental efforts that give promise of producing significant advances in various fields. One of a number of areas in which the Ford Foundation gives support is agricultural production of food in developing countries.

In 1951, the Foundation began its work in helping agriculture. One of the first grants was to India, at the request of then Prime Minister Nehru, to aid in the development of human resources. Emphasis has been on education, rural development, public health, small industries, and urban problems, all of which, indirectly at least, help to improve the food supply and nutritional well-being of the people through improved production, purchasing power, and knowledge. The government of India initiated an Intensive Agriculture District Program, and the Ford Foundation provided the financial support. Earlier efforts to help farmers had concentrated on trying to change only one agricultural method at a time. The new program used latest methods based on research and adapted to the conditions in each different district. The new practices were all taught at the same time by the demonstration plot method, where the farmers could see and follow what was happening. They saw the importance of using better seeds, cleaning and treating seeds for protection against diseases, using improved implements, using fertilizers at the right time and in the right quantities, using water more effectively, and taking suitable plant protection measures. The program succeeded because the farmers learned how to do it, and they got results in higher crop yields and thus increased income. The publication *Roots of Change* by the Ford Foundation will enable the reader to catch a glimpse of what can be achieved by men of vision and knowledge when they help their fellowman to help himself.

Currently the Foundation is shifting from activities in individual countries to those that have a regional or worldwide impact. Also, some nutritional programs are being initiated. Research is being sponsored on the social and economic aspects of malnutrition in Latin America. In Brazil, grants are given for cooperative research with other nutrition centers and groups specializing in food production and marketing. At the University of Chile, the Pediatric Research Center has received a grant to develop and test new protein sources from local fish and from crops that can be incorporated in milk and bread products. Nutrition will also be studied in relation to other factors such as family, income, education, and housing.

Rockefeller Foundation

For more than 50 years, the Rockefeller Foundation has administered its funds to support national and international programs that will benefit mankind. Through the years, the emphasis has shifted to meet the needs and problems that arise with changing times. Only the food production and nutritional aspects of the Foundation's programs will be discussed here. In 1963, the Trustees of the Foundation described their plans for the future and said

> We propose during the years ahead to strengthen that part of the Foundation's program which is directed to human nutrition. This will mean increasing the quality and quantity of those foods which feed the world and improving human health and vigor through application of the physical, biological, and social sciences basic to nutrition. It will involve the search for new knowledge leading to better use of land and water resources, development of non-conventional agricultural techniques, and investigation of the changing environment in which we live.

Read any *Annual Report of the Rockefeller Foundation* to see what is being done to help solve the world's hunger problem, or read *A Partnership to Improve Food Production in India* to understand the comprehensive programs in one country.

Fish is an important source of protein. Fresh water and brackish water ponds in Southeast Asia and Pacific countries can be a means of providing an inexpensive fish supply. The Foundation has funded research in experimental pond fisheries in Taiwan and the Philippines, with the focus on ways to increase the yield from these ponds through more efficient management techniques and through biological research on the breeding and growth of fish.

Sorghum grain is a basic food of man in Africa and India because it can be grown in areas where maize (corn) fails because of drought and very poor soil conditions. The Rockefeller Foundation has supported intensive research to develop new, hardier, and higher yielding breeds of sorghum, which can be grown under varying climatic and soil conditions. Thus, land now unable to produce food may be brought into profitable production.

The Foundation not only sends leading scientists to various countries to work on research projects designed to improve and increase food production but it also helps to train local scientists on the spot and provides scholarships and fellowships for study elsewhere.

For the 1970's, the Rockefeller Foundation has set as its priorities the following: (1) solve major technological problems that block progress; (2) extend benefits of modern farming to small landholders; (3) improve the protein quality of the available food supplies; and (4) enlarge the training opportunities in agricultural and nutritional sciences in developing areas, particularly at the graduate level. These goals will be implemented by proven methods and will include: (a) establishment of a network of international institutes; (b) cooperation in regional research, training, and food production; (c) support of agricultural educational institutions; and (d) funding of selected research projects in universities in USA.

Coordinated Programs of the Ford Foundation and the Rockefeller Foundation

The keynote for success in helping increase the world's food production in the 70's is cooperation and coordination of efforts. The problem is too big for any one group or country to do it alone. In the last few years, the Ford Foundation and the Rockefeller Foundation have shared the responsibility for a number of programs. They have pioneered in establishing autonomous international research institutes in cooperation with local governments in four regions of the world. The local governments provided the land and the two foundations provided the financial support for the buildings, equipment, and operation.

These four International Research Institutes are:

1. The International Rice Research Institute in the Philippines (IRRI). This Institute is described in more detail below.
2. The International Maize and Wheat Improvement Center (CIM-MYT), established in Mexico in 1966. This work was started some

25 years ago by the Rockefeller Foundation and now has Ford Foundation support also. They have developed "triple dwarf" wheats with very short stem and high yield. These wheats have helped increase food production in Asia, North Africa, and Latin America. A new cereal grain, which is a cross between wheat and rye and is called tricale, has been developed.

3. The International Center of Tropical Agriculture (CIAT) in Colombia, South America was established in 1968 to improve crop and livestock production in tropical Latin America. They also are trying to improve the protein content of corn, cassava, and beans.

4. The International Institute of Tropical Agriculture (IITA), established in Nigeria in 1968, is conducting research aimed at increasing the output and quality of tropical food crops, particularly rice, food legumes, maize, yams, and cassava. They also are studying soil management systems for tropical conditions to prevent erosion, increase fertility, and conserve water.

Each of these Institutes is independent, but all work together and exchange information and seeds. The innovations that stand out so clearly from these programs is the cooperation of the two Foundations and of national governments and the understanding that research is basic to all progress; programs must be established where the need is, and one must work with what people have and adjust to their habits and traditional familiar foods.

International Rice Research Institute (IRRI).   One of the projects jointly supported by the Ford Foundation and the Rockefeller Foundation is the International Rice Research Institute. This Institute was incorporated in 1960 and dedicated in 1962 as a world center for the study and improvement of rice by the government of the Philippines with the cooperation of the Ford Foundation and the Rockefeller Foundation. It is located at Los Baños, 40 miles southeast of Manila.

A visit to IRRI is an exciting event. One looks out over close to 200 acres (80 hectares) of experimental farm and sees endless experimental plots with rice in every stage of growth and maturity and every type of treatment of the soil, seeds, and plants. Here 10,000 varieties are being studied, using varying types of cultural practices and water and soil management. On some plots, one sees carabao pulling plows through the heavy wet soil.

IRRI is primarily a research center seeking to obtain more abundant rice yields through improved cultural practices and by development of new and improved varieties. The search is for a variety that: (1) has stiff straw so that it will not lodge or fall over, (2) is early maturing to allow more than one crop a year, (3) has maximum resistance to disease, and (4) has optional response to fertilizer. A very promising variety has already been developed called IR8; it resists lodging, matures in 120 days, flowers without regard to seasonal changes in light, and has a high yield experimentally of nine to ten metric tons per hectare and, with proper management, five to seven metric tons on farms in Southeast Asian countries. From viewing the rice plots, one enters the cool white buildings containing laboratories where chemists, geneticists, microbiologists, soil scientists, and the many other research scientists of seven nationalities conduct intensive investigations. The Institute offers resident training in rice research methods and techniques and provides symposia and international conferences.

In the library, one finds practically everything that has been written, in 23 major languages, in the technical literature on rice. The reading room is filled with students of many countries; here is the center for information on rice.

From the complexities of science and research, one enters another building where the agricultural engineers work on every type of equipment and machinery for tilling, cultivating, harvesting, and threshing rice.

At IRRI, everything centers on rice, and one catches a glimpse of what the future holds for the 60% of humanity for whom rice is life. This cooperative research endeavor is supplying the information which can be applied to produce more and better food to feed the people of the world's rice bowl.

The Ford Foundation contributed funds for the land, buildings, and initial equipment and, with the Rockefeller Foundation, now shares equally in the operational and maintenance costs.

VOLUNTARY AGENCY PROGRAMS

Cooperative for American Relief Everywhere (CARE)

In early 1972, the headquarters office reported that CARE helped feed 28 million people in 36 countries, of which 24,395,000 were children. A major aspect of CARE's work today lies in its shared-cost programs—programs made possible from joint contributions by CARE and the governments and communities in aided countries. It is estimated that $2.96

CARE furnishes milk for all ages in Colombia. (Courtesy CARE.)

Happy faces of children receiving CARE packages in Korea. (Courtesy CARE.)

has been contributed by those aided for every $1.00 CARE has invested from its donor funds.

CARE does not believe in aiding impoverished people without any contribution from them. The agency will feed them when they have little or nothing, but always its goal is to aid them so that they maintain their self-respect and are not reduced to the status of accepting sheer charity. If, for example, a village asks CARE to build a school, the national government of that country must contribute some of the cost, and the villagers must donate the land and the labor required for construction. Then and only then will CARE provide its expertise and construction materials. Village people have enormous pride in such a school— it becomes "*our* school" built by "our" hands. They acquire developing capacity to plan and do for themselves. Needy people around the world are willing to work and sweat in doing the job of securing the facilities they need to stand on their own feet. All they ask from CARE are tools, materials, and the expert guidance for which the agency is well known.

The year 1971 marked a milestone in CARE service: 25 years ago, the first CARE food packages were delivered in Europe to help save millions from starvation after World War II. Since 1946, CARE aid has reached into Asia, Latin America, the Middle East, and Africa. The experience gained each year has guided the growth of the CARE packages into programs that span the range of human needs— not only food but health, skills, and knowledge to help the hungry feed and support themselves.

To make CARE possible, 41,250,000 Americans and Canadians have contributed a cumulative total of approximately $282 million. Their concern has enabled CARE to enlist host government contributions and U.S. donations of produce from farm abundance for an overall total of more than $1.25 billion worth of assistance to the needy in 73 countries.

Table 1 shows the relative amounts of money spent for different forms of help by voluntary agencies.

Church Service Organizations

For the past several centuries, both Protestant and Catholic missionaries have had a record, apart from their religious efforts, of providing medical and educational aid in many countries and also of vigorous and successful help in agriculture in countries such as China, Japan, India, and Africa.

TABLE 1* Title II, Public Law 480—Number of recipients in fiscal year 1969, voluntary agency foreign donation programs approved as of Dec. 31, 1969

	Total	CARE	Catholic relief service	Church world service	UNICEF	Lutheran world relief	All other agencies
Maternal/child care	6,470,684	4,027,712	1,846,868	122,636	417,751	38,965	16,752
Schools	25,893,395	21,044,965	3,780,114	398,579	300,287	201,700	167,750
Other child feeding	1,798,760	756,965	720,556	219,987	13,844	61,173	26,235
Economic/community development	4,798,717	93,755	3,775,412	618,600		238,750	72,200
Educational development	37,500		30,500	5,000		2,000	
Health development	46,700	6,500	28,800	8,400		3,000	
Refugees	519,900	250	33,550	5,000		5,500	475,600
Disaster[1]	3,226,000	222,680	1,003,320	1,000,000	1,000,000		
Institutions	474,420	134,254	227,103	43,633		45,372	24,058
Health cases	373,600	29,599	267,814	41,375		30,537	4,275
Other[2]	1,093,365	548,100	469,086	29,159		40,250	6,770
Total recipients	44,733,041	26,864,780	12,183,123	2,492,369	1,731,882	667,247	793,640

[1]Includes approximately 3,000,000 Nigerian recipients benefiting under all Public Law 480 title II programs (Government to government, World Food Program and voluntary agency).

[2]Family individuals and feeding centers.

*From Food for Peace, the 1969 Annual Report on Public Law 480.

By 1907, a number of U.S. mission boards had initiated agricultural programs and centers for agricultural training. Space does not permit discussion of these programs nor of the continuing efforts of church groups today, working independently and also in cooperation with national and international agencies in disaster and famine relief, in training programs, and in the establishment of educational institutions where agriculture and home economics are taught. These are but a few of the ways in which the religious bodies of the world are striving, along with many other agencies and organizations, to free the people of the world from hunger and malnutrition. The following are some of the groups with active programs now:

Jewish—American Jewish Joint Distribution Committee
Catholic—Catholic Relief Services
Lutheran—Lutheran World Relief
Seventh Day Adventist—Seventh Day Adventist Welfare Service
Church World Service
Friends—Friend Service Committee

It was said in 1963 that the work of the Church World Service was reaching nearly every needy country and that it was moving from giving direct relief to helping the people help themselves. This is being done through loans, vocational training, medical and dental clinics, and agricultural projects intended to increase food production. Many American religious denominations help in the distribution of surplus foods to needy people.

Church World Service and Catholic Relief Service have also worked with UNICEF and other voluntary organizations which in turn enlist the aid of the food industry. All of these groups working together are making great contributions to the Food for Peace program.

The Salvation Army

The Salvation Army, a religious organization with a vast good-will and social service program, began its work in 1874 in Wales. Today the services of the Salvation Army extend to all continents of the world. Feeding people in need—the victims of disaster, the poor, the young who are without care, and the old—is one general service of the Salvation Army. Early in 1972, the National Office of the American Salvation

Army reported that they were maintaining over 500 food distribution centers and feeding about 15 million people.

The American National Red Cross

The American National Red Cross entered the field of nutrition education in 1908 when it authorized instruction in dietetics as a part of the Home Nursing Service. During the war period, 1917–1918, the Red Cross helped in the recruitment of hospital dietitians and nutrition instructors. At that time, some local chapters furnished free milk and hot lunches to school children as an emergency measure. In 1920, the American Red Cross Nutrition Service was set up as a separate service with a national director. The program expanded in personnel and services with some local chapters maintaining a full-time nutritionist. Classes in nutrition were taught for both children and adults. In 1932, because of lack of funds, the National Nutrition Service was discontinued except for the retention of a consultant at the national headquarters. In 1941, it was reinstituted and community nutrition programs were initiated. During the war period, the American Red Cross carried on an active community nutrition program. Since 1950, a consultant in nutrition has been maintained at the national headquarters. Local chapters recruit and register nutritionists and dietitians as instructors of canteen courses.

In addition, the American Red Cross has special programs for migrants, service to military families, meals-on-wheels, and for youth. For the latter, they publish two magazines which carry articles promoting good food habits.

The International Red Cross is active in 112 nations to relieve human suffering which includes among other provisions furnishing food where needed.

GENERAL PROGRAMS IN INDIVIDUAL COUNTRIES

As the need for an adequate diet for all peoples has become known and as surveys done in many countries have pointed out dietary inadequacies, new programs for prevention as well as cure of the problems of malnutrition have been devised. Practically every country now has a group working on these problems from several angles. There may be efforts to:

1. Improve the quantity and quality of food at its source.
2. Prepare mixtures of high nutritive value and test them for acceptability.
3. Produce a highly nutritious food new to a region.
4. Make nutritious foods available where needed.

For all of these efforts, needs must first be investigated through dietary surveys. Then efforts in coordinating services of raising food, marketing, and distribution, as well as educating the public to use the food, are vital. As has been so often said, those programs which originate at high government level but which consider at every step the people who are to eat the food are the only ones that succeed.

FOOD AND POPULATION

Enough food for all continues to be a major world problem. It is not possible in this short section to discuss population control or even the entire problem of producing enough food to feed all the world's people. This discussion will be limited to a few of the efforts to produce more food of higher nutritive value.

The warning often has been given that unless a greater and more concentrated effort is made on the international basis, food shortages and actual famine can occur. This will occur when the developed countries, after they feed their own people, can no longer buffer the food shortages in the developing countries. It is generally recognized that the increased food must come from farming, but there is hope to avert the disasters of food shortages and famine if agricultural technology can be improved fast enough in the hungry nations.

Those who are in a position to understand the situation, as Bennett, 1969, and Althschul, 1969, point out that population control alone is not the solution. The need for food is an immediate and increasing need, whereas the effects of population control can be realized only some years hence. It is understandable that we really do not know the extent of the problem because statistics on population and especially of crop yields are crude and probably inaccurate from some of the developing nations in Asia, Africa, and Latin America. When a group is faced with survival, they do not quickly reveal the extent of their food reserves.

Bennett, as president of the World Food Panel, which began its work in 1968, said that "Perhaps the single most fundamental conclusion that emerged from the study of the World Food Panel is the realization that hunger and malnutrition and the so-called population explosion are not *primary diseases* of the developing countries, rather they are symptoms of an underlying malady, *lagging economic development.*" In order to solve the latter problem, an entire new structure must be built, and this is infinitely more complicated and difficult than anyone at the beginning imagined. Bennett has pointed out, and others have agreed, that food shortages and rapid population growth are separate but interrelated problems and must be solved by individual action in each country.

Increasing Protein Food

In September 1970, the Protein Advisory Group of FAO/WHO/UNICEF said in their Statement No. 8 that "In developing countries cereals are the staple foods of 95% of the population; they contribute about 75% of the calories in the diet and from 40–70% of the proteins. Increased production of cereals is the principal solution to world hunger, and at the same time will make an important contribution to filling the protein gap. In coming years the annual increase must be much higher than the 30% rate observed during the last decade, if the world cereal needs are to be fully covered by 1985. Since suitable agricultural land is limited in the regions of greatest shortage of foods, any increase in production must rely heavily upon the introduction of varieties with higher yield potential."

Altschul, 1969, said that "an increase in animal protein can only take place where there is an excess of grain over and above the needs for human food or when conditions are favorable for grazing animals."

Some of the other sources for protein are called "unconventional protein sources" in the 1968 Report to the Economics and Social Council of the Advisory Committee on the Application of Science and Technology to Development in the bulletin called "International Action to Avert the Impending Protein Crisis."

PAG Statement 13a, April 1972, comments, "Presently, the world protein resources used for human consumption are estimated as follows:

Vegetable Sources	68%
Cereals	45%
Oil seeds	13%
Legumes	5%
Other	5%
Milk	15%
Meat	11%
Eggs	2%
Fish	4%

Thus, approximately 96% of all protein supplies for man are derived from conventional plant and livestock sources, and 4% are derived from fish. It is clear that in the foreseeable future the major contribution to protein nutrition must come from these sources and that efforts to improve conventional protein supplies are of greatest importance."

Different Protein Foods

Incaparina.   Protein malnutrition, especially among young children, is a major problem in Central America, where protein foods of animal origin are scarce and expensive. In its earliest studies, the Institute for Nutrition in Central America and Panama (INCAP) found a high incidence of protein malnutrition in the countries it surveyed. How to prevent this disease was the challenge. At the National Institute of Agriculture in Guatemala, work was done in 1950 to find sources of protein for animal feeding. It was realized that a similar approach might be used to meet human needs, so this Institute of Agriculture and INCAP cooperated in their search for indigenous products high in protein but low in cost. Many combinations of foodstuffs were tested biochemically and clinically until a mixture of ground dried corn (maize), ground sorghum, cottonseed flour, torula yeast, calcium salts, and vitamin A was found satisfactory.

The product itself resembles a food which is a customary part of the diet in Central America, an "atole" or beverage made of cornmeal and water. The new vegetable-protein mixture was given the name Incaparina. Its nutritive value is similar to milk both in amount and quality of protein; one pound of Incaparina as protein of biological value equivalent to that of 18 glasses of milk. The crucial test was whether the product would be accepted by children and adults. Acceptability trials were made in several communities in cooperation with the Ministry of Health in Guatemala. Children drank Incaparina willingly.

Incaparina is low in cost; it is manufactured commercially and sold in packages containing enough mixture for three glasses at a cost of a little over one cent per glass. Increased production and extended consumption can probably lower the price. INCAP receives no profit from the sale of Incaparina. Although commercial firms are authorized to produce and distribute Incaparina, they must submit their product for periodic analysis by INCAP so that standards of quality are maintained. The product is manufactured commercially in Guatemala and Colombia; and other countries are now conducting marketing trials.

Multi-Purpose Food. During World War II, Clifford Clinton, President of Clinton Cafeterias, gave Henry Borsook, the eminent biochemist at the California Institute of Technology, a $5000 special grant to develop a nutritious food. This food was to be made from nonrationed ingredients and have a cost low enough to be practical. Clinton, the son of missionary parents in the Orient, had made free meals in his cafeterias available to the needy. After the war broke out, when food rationing went into effect, he realized that he could not continue his previous charity.

Borsook compounded what was named Multi-Purpose Food (MPF) from toasted soy grits, calcium carbonate, vitamin C, niacin, vitamin A, riboflavin, vitamin B_6, thiamine, vitamin D, potassium iodide, and vitamin B_{12}. This mixture is 50% protein. It was made to have low-moisture content so that it would store well and need little storage space. Multi-Purpose Food can be used as a gruel, sprinkled over ready-to-eat cereal, or used in milk for a cereal topping. It can also be stirred into milk, tomato juice, or fruit juice to be used as a drink. It is, of course, precooked and ready to eat, and it has been found in tests to be acceptable to many people. It is also cheap.

Clinton organized Meals for Millions, a nonprofit organization, whose mission was to distribute Multi-Purpose Food in areas where malnutrition was present. Now after 20 years, Multi-Purpose Food has been distributed in over 130 countries, according to a December 1966 statement made by the General Mills Company. During 1946–1959, it was made by a well-known spice manufacturer in California. In 1959, the

General Mills Company took over its production when they agreed to produce it more cheaply and to pay the Meals for Millions a royalty on the commercial sales of this product. It is now also produced in India, Japan, Mexico, and Brazil.

Multi-Purpose Food is now sold to independent relief organizations, such as Church World Service, to be donated to local missions for relief feeding. Tom Dooley and Albert Schweitzer used it in feeding their patients. It has been used as a means of combating kwashiorkor.

The Freedom Meal.   In his message to Congress on February 10, 1966, President Johnson said: "We will continue to encourage private industry, in cooperation with government, to produce and distribute foods to combat malnutrition." This message called for the expansion of shipment of foods to countries needing them where there were efforts in self-help. It also proposed the elimination of the surplus concept of food and a continued expansion of markets for American agricultural products.

Shortly after this, the research program of the State Department of Agriculture and Economic Development of Nebraska contracted with the Midwest Research Institute of Kansas City, Missouri, to develop a food to be called a Freedom Meal. By mid-June, the product had been compounded according to specifications.

This meal, a cereal product with 20% protein content, contains 25% milo (sorghum), 25% corn, 25% wheat, 15% soy meal, and 10% nonfat dry milk. Vitamins and minerals are also added. All of these foods are produced in Nebraska; therefore, the production of this product benefits Nebraska's farmers as well as furnishing food to be used by the world's needy.

This blended cereal can be eaten after cooking for one or two minutes. The shelf life is the same as for any dry cereal. It meets the requirements set up by the U.S. Department of Agriculture for a foodstuff in the Food for Peace program. These are:

1. Wheat or corn should be the basic component.
2. It should contain 20% protein.
3. The protein supplementation should be provided by a combination of soy and nonfat dry milk.
4. Vitamins and mineral supplements should be included.
5. It should have a bland flavor and a low bran content.

6. It should be partially cooked and ready for serving after one or two minutes of boiling.

Later, the millers and grain processors in Nebraska and the government officials were called to a meeting by the Governor of Nebraska to work out details of the contracts. This group in Nebraska was the first group to work on this problem. They also developed a survival cracker called Nebraskit, which they say will keep for five years. This cracker contains wheat flour, corn flour, corn sugar, hydrogenated fat, salt, nonfat dry milk, and dried whey. Following the introduction of the Nebraskit, a milk bar was developed from corn sugar, fat, powdered malt, nonfat dry milk, and dried whey, which was reported to have a shelf life of six months.

Increasing and Improving Cereal Grains

Borlaug in his 1970 Nobel Peace Prize acceptance speech observed that, despite the fact that civilization as we know it could not have come into being or survived "without an adequate food supply, man until rather recently did relatively little to control biological and physical catastrophies connected with food production." He cited especially the recent spectacular progress made in increasing wheat, rice, and maize production in several of the most populous Southeast Asian countries. He credits the popular press with describing this as the Green Revolution, a term he and others have thought possibly "premature, too optimistic, and too broad in scope." Yet it must be pointed out that the increased crop production of wheat and rice alone in India, Pakistan, and the Philippines and later in Afghanistan, Ceylon, Indonesia, Iran, Kenya, Malaya, Morocco, Thailand, Tunisia, and Turkey is reason for some optimism.

There are several difficulties to considering this as the great solution to the world food problem. Even though the larger yield of grain and the genetic improvement which increases nutritive value are a great step forward, there are certain problems which must be overcome. The use of more fertilizer in many of the tropical-subtropical countries where these new seeds are being used and irrigation in dry countries are too expensive for the use of the small farmer who is the one in most need of help.

One difficulty is the need for greater capital resources to grow the new varieties of wheat, rice, and maize. This capital is needed for fertilizer, pesticides, and water for which new wells must be drilled and irrigation systems installed. Modern farm equipment is also needed. It has been also pointed out by Borlaug and other experts that in countries such as India, the cereal grains regrettably are replacing some of the important protein-high legume crops as chick beans, pigeon peas, beans, and lentils which have in the past made a real contribution to the adequacy of the diet of these people. The Green Revolution will be carefully scrutinized by sociologists, economists, and agricultural experts in a new worldwide United Nations project to be concluded in mid-1973.

Many have pointed out that man cannot afford to become over-emotional regarding the use of insecticides to control the insects which threaten his food supply because the food supply may thus be reduced to a dangerous level.

In summary, Brown (1970) said "Thus the new seeds promise to improve the well-being of more people in a shorter time than any other single technological advance in history." He stated that these seeds can replace despair and hope, but that this will happen only "if a sustained effort is mounted by the rich and the poor countries together."

Foods from the Sea

In 1968, about 64 million metric tons of fish, one of the oldest and most plentiful sources of food, was harvested from the sea; of this, 40 million metric tons were used for direct human consumption and 24 million metric tons were used largely as processed fish meal for animal feeds. FAO experts estimated that, in 1971, only one-half as much fish was taken as could be. The chief problems are that fish is a highly perishable food and therefore requires great care in harvesting and transportation, and some of the fish is not palatable to human beings. Because the proteins of fish are of high nutritive value, efforts have been made to make this protein available where it is needed.

Fish Flour and Fish Protein Concentrate.   Holden (1971) says that "fish flour and fish protein concentrate (FPC) was hailed during the days of the New Frontier as the possible miracle solution to the world's nutrition problems." She continues with a story many have read in the daily newspapers: "Since then, its development has bogged down in a morass of economic and technical realities, and interest in the product has been kept alive in the United States almost solely by continuing research efforts on the part of the government." A study of the present day literature corroborates these statements. Sidwell, et al. (1970) reported a nutritive value nearly or wholly equal to that of casein, and they seemed to think that the flavor and texture was acceptable with the addition of 5–10% FPC in bread, pasta, crackers, cookies, soups, tortillas, and beverages. With chocolate flavor, the latter was very acceptable. The color of some products, however, was adversely affected.

The lack of success of FPC is usually credited to the fact that commercial production has not proved profitable.

In the U.S., many regulations, some imposed by the Federal Food and Drug Administration, have hampered any profitable promotion of the product; during 1962–1967, they required that FPC be made from cleaned and eviscerated fish. In 1967, after a committee of the National Academy of Sciences gave a favorable report for the use of the entire fish, the FDA certified FPC, but classed it as a food additive rather than a food, which means it comes under many restrictions that apply to potentially toxic additives. This means that children under 8 are not to have more than 20 grams of it per day because of the fluoride content of the fish bones. One of the most restricting regulations is that FPC can be sold only at the retail level and only in one pound or smaller packages, which thus prevents its use in manufactured food products, but it is said that this ruling was intended to be only temporary. Soya is cheaper to produce. There is also now some question as to whether the supply of fish needed for large scale production and use of FPC is adequate. There is still some interest in FPC among American food manufacturers, so this must be a continuing story.

The statement from "An AID Nutrition Research Rationale and Program for the 70's," published in February 1970, summarizes the present situation:

> Fish protein concentrate (FPC) properly made is an excellent source of protein and contains important amounts of calcium and phosphorus as well as trace elements. The market price for FPC, based on protein content, is almost three times the cost of protein in soy flour. This cost must be reduced before the use of FPC can be considered economically feasible.
>
> Fish protein can also be utilized in the form of sun-dried fish or as a protein hydrolsate, etc.
>
> In developing countries with large marine resources, the production of

edible processed fish proteins by a variety of methods should be encouraged in conjunction with the simultaneous development of a basic fisheries industry.

The excellent amino acid composition of fish proteins makes it especially suitable as a supplement in weaning foods and in foods for children. Consumer acceptance and performance characteristics must be established by evaluation of finished products. These trials should be made with products derived from the types of fish that will be available in a given region and produced by a practical efficient process intended for full commercial production.

Research needed, according to AID, is:

1. Improvement, simplification, and cost lowering of processing systems.
2. Improvement in color, flavor, and functional properties of FPC.
3. Exploration of alternate processes for utilizing fish proteins.
4. Extensive food formulation studies with consumer evaluations by indigenous populations of products containing fish protein.

Oilseed Protein

Approximately "8 million metric tons of fermented and cooked soybean products are consumed annually in the Far East" (U.N. Bulletin 1968) and "another 3 million metric tons of peanuts, coconuts, and other oilseeds are eaten in the world." It was also said that "no use is being made of the remaining 90 million metric tons of oilseeds" for human feeding. With proper processing of the meal left from soya, peanuts, cotton, seasame, sunflower, and other seeds in oil production, this meal which contains 40–50% of good quality protein could be used more effectively as another source of protein for human consumption. These meals are the world's cheapest sources of protein and probably will remain so.

Single-Cell Proteins Such as Yeast, Algae, and Bacteria

It is known that certain Single-Cell Proteins (SCP) are readily used by animals and man. The chief advantages of this source is their rapid growth and their ability to convert cheap energy and nitrogen into high-quality protein (U.N. Bulletin).

PAG Guidelines No. 12, February 1972, says,

Child eating mung-bean protein with rice and vegetables in a pilot nutrition center. (Courtesy FAO, Rome, Italy. Photo by P. Botts.)

Single-cell protein may be looked upon as a food, since it has a significant caloric and vitamin content in addition to protein. The nutritive value of the protein component is of particular importance if the product is to be used as a protein supplement. Although single-cell protein processes may be inherently closer to chemical than to microbiological technology, it is strongly suggested that the traditional concept of good manufacturing practice be applied in the sense that it is currently used in the food industry. Plants and equipment should be of sanitary design and special care should be exercised in all aspects of processing, including raw material selection, quality control, sanitation, handling and packaging.

The present methods of growth have thus far proved too expensive for use as a major component of the diet.

PAG Statement No. 4 on Single-Cell Proteins, June 1970, says that,

There is adequate evidence to indicate that some species of yeasts, algae, and bacteria can be safe and useful sources of proteins, vitamins, and minerals for animal and human feeding. However, the safety of such materials will depend on the organisms selected, the quality of the substrates utilized and the conditions of growth.

This publication also states that

Yeasts grown on molasses, sulfite liquors, and vegetable waste have established their safety and nutritional value when employed as a minor component of human diets. Since single-cell protein functions as a naturally concentrated source of protein and B-vitamins, it can be added to foods in small quantities for purposes of fortifying their protein value and vitamin content, [and] the number of potential food uses would seem to be limited only by imagination, safety, and economics.

The statement made by AID concerning single-cell proteins said that "There is a tendency to relegate single-cell proteins, particularly those derived from petroleum, to some distant future. This is probably a gross underestimate of the technological capabilities of the petroleum industry, and a hard look at properties of petroleum-derived proteins is warranted."

In Bulletin 13, 1971–72, of the Protein Advisory Group, it was reported that extensive research and development is now being done on the industrial production of microalgae and microfungi. Some of the research is on *Spirulina,* an algae which formed a part of the diet of certain tribes of Chad for a long time, as well as Aztecs living near Mexico City. The authors say more work is needed on these algae products, however, involving biological testing and acceptability by people, as well as on the economics of production.

Textured Vegetable Protein

The chief virtue of new textured vegetable proteins, says PAG, rests in their ability to supply "precisely reproducible balanced dietary inputs of essential amino acids with greatly enhanced agronomic efficiency and with high consumer acceptance." At present, these products are selling in the U.S. at one-fourth to one-fifth less than meats, which is, however, too expensive to interest developing countries. It is expected that simpler and cheaper methods of production will emerge in the future.

Green Leaves and Seaweed

Thus far, the use of green leaves and seaweed as a source of protein has proved too expensive to be practical. The 1968 U.N. report says "the efficiency of photosynthesis of conversion of nitrogen to protein is high and the possibility of a technical breakthrough should not be underestimated."

The Protein Advisory Group, June 1970, Statement No. 11, says

> With regard to the present interest in the development and use of various "unconventional" protein concentrates, though recognizing the limitations on them, the PAG did not feel it appropriate to give a simple recommendation for or against further work on leaf protein. It noted the good biological value and useful vitamin A content of leaf protein; the many sources from which it can be prepared; the several forms that the product can take; the possibility of integrating production with the preparation of other products as a means of reducing costs; and acknowledged the considerable volume of work on the subject by Mr. N. W. Pirie and many others over the last two or three decades.

The PAG drew attention to the disadvantages of color, flavor, and lack of stability in the less processed forms. They feel the bland stable form cannot compete in price with oilseed protein concentrates.

Other Protein Sources and Products

The Nutrition Division of AID is conducting extensive study and research along with other agencies interested in international nutrition. In the AID Nutrition Research Rationale and Program for the 70's, published in February 1970, the widespread distribution of the very simple of the cereal-based foods and beverages such as Incaparina and CMS is discussed. This report says that such more sophisticated products as "Goodles," a macaroni product containing corn, soy, and wheat flour, and such soy-based beverages as Puma and Saci are being tested. Some disadvantages are apparent, and changes must be effected in the processing of three seeds—soy, cottonseed, and peanut—which are produced world-wide in the largest tonnages. They also mention, see page 418–420, the need for "considerable improvement" of fish protein concentrate. Some promising protein sources which are abundant in localized regions include coconut, sesame, rape seed, and sunflower seed.

STUDY QUESTIONS

1. How does each of the following accomplish the purpose of selecting a project which the country being served most wants and involving this country in the entire program?
   a. UNICEF
   b. AID
   c. FAO

2. How and to what extent are the efforts of WHO, UNICEF, and FAO coordinated?

3. How did the original creation of CARE and other international agencies with nutrition programs differ? How has this affected their current programs?

4. How are the programs of UNICEF, FAO, and WHO changing to meet new needs?

5. What sources of high-protein foods look promising now to increase the world supply of protein? Defend your answer.

6. How are the programs of U.S. international nutrition agencies related to the programs of FAO, WHO, and UNICEF?

TOPICS FOR INDIVIDUAL INVESTIGATION

1. Evaluate the success and failures of international organizations and their program for improvement of food supply and nutrition of man. Compare the advantages and disadvantages of international efforts with group efforts or the people-to-people approach.

2. FAO made 1966 the International Rice year. Discuss the reasons for this and tell what the value of rice is to the world's population.

3. Select one UNICEF project in a particular country. If you can find the needed data, show how the planning and eventual take over by the government of that country followed the stated objectives of UNICEF. If you cannot find all of these data, write a possible plan which would fulfill all of these objectives.

4. Discuss whether it is possible for all people of the world to be adequately fed. Present figures on population and food production in support of your answer.

5. Choose one previously food-deficit developing country and trace as many as possible of the international nutrition programs which have helped them to attain independent status. Outline for one of these programs as many of the projects as you can which you believe have been significant in the country's development.

REFERENCES AND SUGGESTED READINGS

FAO (Food and Agriculture Organization)

*FAO. *What It Is, What It Does, How It Works.* FAO, Rome, Italy, 1965.

*FAO. *The McDougall Memoranda—Some Documents Relating to the Origins of FAO and the Contributions Made by Frank L. McDougall.* Rome, Italy, 1956.

Hambridge, G. *The Story of FAO.* Van Nostrand, New York, 1955.

Phillips, R. W. Food and Agriculture Organization Completes 15 Years. *Science,* 132: 871, 1960.

U.S. Dept. of State. United Nations' Conference on Food and Agriculture, Hot Springs, Virginia, May 18–June 3, 1943. Final Act and Section Repts. Pub. No. 1948, Conference Ser. 52, 1943.

Yates, P. L. *So Bold an Aim.* FAO, Rome, Italy, 1955.

UNICEF (United Nations International Children's Fund)

Facts about UNICEF. Leaflet, 1971, U.N., New York.

Heilroner, R. L. *Mankind's Children.* Public Affairs Pamphlet No. 279, New York, 1959.

Judd, W. H. Speech About the United Nations Children's Fund, Congressional Record, Proceedings and Debates of the 87th Congress (Second Session), U.S. Gov. Printing Office, Washington, D.C., 1962, p. 1.

News of the World's Children. Vol. 19, No. 5, Dec. 1971, U.N., New York.

Pate, Maurice. UNICEF Goals in Maternal and Child Health. *Amer. J. Pub. Health,* 50: (Part II), 8, Supplement to June 1960.

Sinclair, A. UNICEF and the African Mother. *J. Amer. Assoc. Univ. Women,* 54: 143, 1961.

*FAO publications are available in the United States at UNIPUB Inc., P.O. Box 443, New York, N.Y. 10016.

*All UNICEF publications from U.N. salesroom, New York.

Sinclair, A. The World's Deprived Children. *Children,* U.S. Children's Bureau, 9: (84), 1962.

Tomorrow's Too Late, 1971, U.N., New York.

*UNICEF. *What It Is, What It Does, and How It Works.* Pub. 6001.

*UNICEF. *Bulletin of the United Nations Children's Fund.* International Edition, 8: 2, 1960.

*UNICEF. UNICEF Compendium, Vol. VII, 2nd Ed., 1961.

*UNICEF. *Children of the Developing Countries.* World Publishing, New York, 1963.

*UNICEF. *Facts and Fallacies.* 1965.

*UNICEF. *What It Is and How It Works for a Better World for Children.* New York, 1965.

*UNICEF. *UNICEF and You and What You Can Do Together.* New York, 1966.

*UNICEF, FAO, and WHO. *Dry Skim Milk Distribution.* Report prepared with the help of G. Herlitz, A. Vergara, and A. Wallgren. United Nations, New York, 1959.

U.S. Committee for UNICEF. *The World's Children and UNICEF.* U.N., New York.

UNICEF at 25. Leaflet and Booklet, U.N., New York, 1971.

WHO (World Health Organization) and PAHO

Behar, M., W. Ascoli, and N. S. Scrimshaw. An Investigation Into the Causes of Death in Children in Four Rural Communities in Guatemala. *WHO Bull.,* 19: 1093, 1958.

Calder, Ritchie. *Ten Steps Forward.* World Health 1948–1958.

Deutsch, A. *The World Health Organization.* Public Affairs Pamphlet No. 265, 1958, New York.

National Research Council. Meeting Protein Needs of Infants and Children. *Nat. Acad. Sci.,* No. 843, 1961.

Programme Review-Nutrition Executive Board, 49th Session WHO, Dec. 1971.

Protein Malnutrition. Proceedings of a Conference in Jamaica (1953), Sponsored jointly by FAO, WHO, and the Josiah Macy, Jr., Foundation. Cambridge Univ. Press, London, 1955.

Ramos-Galvan, R., J. L. Perez Navarrette, and J. Cravioto. Various Aspects of Growth and Development of Mexican Children. *Bol. Med. Hosp. Infant (Mex.),* 17: 445, 1960.

Rogers, E. S. Program and Progress of the World Health Organization. *J. Amer. Diet. Assoc.,* 26: 15, 1950.

Scrimshaw, N. S. and M. Behar. World-Wide Occurrence of Protein Malnutrition. *Fed. Proc.,* 18: 82 (Supplement 3, Part 2), 1959.

World Health Magazine. WHO, Geneva, Switzerland, Feb. 1964, and in particular June–July 1966.

*WHO. *Epidemiological and Vital Statistics Report,* Vol. II, 1958; Vol. 13, 1960.

*WHO. *WHO Fact Sheets 1–5.* Jan.–Mar. 1958.

*WHO. *WHO Activities in Nutrition.* 1948–1964.

*WHO. *WHO Brochure.* 1965–66.

*WHO. *The First Ten Years of the World Health Organization.* 1958.

*WHO. *The Second Ten Years of the World Health Organization.* 1969.

*WHO. *What It Is, What It Does, and How It Works,* 4th Ed. Nov. 1950.

*All UNICEF publications from U.N. sales room, New York.

*WHO publications, Geneva, Switzerland.

International Cooperative Activites and Organizations

Berg, Alan and Robert Muscat. *Nutrition Program Planning*. International Conference on Nutrition, National Development and Planning, Cambridge, Mass., Oct. 1971.

FAO/WHO/UNICEF Protein Advisory Group. *Lives in Peril—Protein and the Child*. FAO publication—World Food Problems No. 12, Rome, Italy, 1970.

FAO/WHO/UNICEF Protein Advisory Group. PAG Bulletin No. 12, 1971, U.N., New York.

FAO/WHO/UNICEF Protein Advisory Group. PAG Bulletin 13, Vol. 2, No. 1, 1972, U.N., New York.

FAO/WHO/UNICEF Expert Committee on Nutrition, 8th Report, Nov. 1970, U.N., New York.

United Nations. *International Action to Avert the Impending Protein Crisis—Report to the Economics and Social Council of the Advisory Committee on the Application of Science and Technology to Development*. U.N., New York, 1968.

UNESCO (United Nations Education, Scientific and Cultural Organization). *The Milk Conservation Program—An Appraisal by UNICEF/FAO Assisted Milk Conservation Program*. Private Communication, 1948–60. U.N., New York.

PAG (Protein Advisory Group) FAO/WHO/UNICEF, United Nations, New York

PAG Statement No. 4. Single-Cell Proteins. Oct. 1969.

PAG Guidelines No. 6. *PAG Guidelines for Preclinical Testing of Novel Sources*. March 1972.

PAG No. 7. *PAG Recommendations on Prevention of Food Losses and Protein-Calorie Malnutrition*. Reissued April 1972.

PAG No. 7. *Human Testing Procedures*. Reissued, March 1972.

PAG Guidelines No. 8. *Protein-Rich Mixtures for Use as Weaning Foods*. February 1971.

PAG Statement No. 8. *On Plant Improvement by Genetic Means*. Sept. 1970.

PAG Statement No. 9. *Revised PAG Guidelines for Fish Protein Concentrates*. January 1971.

PAG Guidelines No. 10. Wickstrom, B. *Marketing of Protein-Rich Foods in Developing Countries*. No date given.

PAG Statement No. 11. *Leaf Protein Concentrates*. June 1970.

PAG Statement No. 13a. *International Action to Avert Impending Protein Crises*. Reissued, April 1972.

PAG Statement No. 16. *Potential of FPC*. August 1971.

Stakman, E. C., R. Bradfield and P. C. Mangelsdorf. *Campaigns against Hunger*. Belknap Press, Harvard University Press, Cambridge, Mass., 1967.

PAHO (Pan American Health Organization)

Horwitz, A. *Health and Progress in the Americas*. Pan American Sanitary Bureau, Misc. Pub. No. 80, 1966.

Horwitz, A. Health and Development. *Americas*, 17: 54–58, 1965.

INCAP. *The Institute of Nutrition of Central America and Panama*. Pub. V-13, Guatemala, 1962.

PAHO. *What It Is, What It Does, How It Works*. Pan American Sanitary Bureau, Misc. Pub. No. 77, Washington, D.C., 1964.

AID (Agency for International Development)

AID. *AID in Action.* General Foreign Policy Series 172, 1961.

AID. *AID . . . in Summary,* 1966.

AID. *AID . . . in Summary,* 1967.

AID. *Facts about the Foreign Aid Program for FY-1967.* March 1966.

AID. *New Initiatives in Economic Assistance.* 1966.

AID. *Food for Freedom.* Nov. 1966, p. 3.

AID. Office of War on Hunger and Bureau of Latin American Affairs. *Final Report.* The Sixth Conference on the Americas on Malnutrition as a Factor in Socio-Economic Development, Bal Harbour, Florida, May 1969.

AID. *Report of The In-Service Workshop On Nutrition and Child Feeding.* Easton, Maryland. May 26–29, 1969.

AID. *Food for Peace Annual Report on Public Law 480.* 1969.

AID. *Report Conference on Use of Growth Charts for Assessing Progress in Children and Teaching Parents.* May 1971, Columbia, Maryland.

AID and American School Food Service Assn. *Report on Nutrition Workshop "Reaching the Preschool Child."* July–Aug. 6, 1970.

AID. *The Protein Gap—AID's Role in Reducing Malnutrition in Developing Countries.* 1970.

AID. *Improving the Nutrient Quality of Cereals—Report of a Workshop on Breeding and Fortification.* June 1971. The workshop was held at Annapolis, Maryland, December 1970.

AID. *An AID Nutrition Research Rationale and Program For the 70's.* 1970.

AID. Cutting, William A. M. *Growth Charts—Experience and Emphasis in Asia.* Conference on Use of Growth Charts for Assessing Progress of Children and Teaching of Parents, May 1971, Columbia, Maryland.

AID. *The AID Research Program 1962–1971 Project Objectives and Results.* Reprinted June 1971.

AID. *Population Program Assistance Aid to Developing Countries by the United States, Other Nations and International Private Agencies.* December 1971.

AID. *Voluntary Foreign AID Programs.* (List of such programs with pertinent data), 1971.

Ilesha Health and Weight Chart. *Nutr. Rev.,* 26 (No. 9): 267–269, 1968.

CARE (Cooperative for American Relief Everywhere)

*CARE. *Food for Needy Peoples through CARE,* a report to the United States government on overseas use of farm commodities through *P.L. 480.* New York, 1962.

*CARE. *Facts about CARE.* New York, 1964.

*CARE. *Who Is CARE-Why-How-What ?* New York, 1966.

*CARE. *CARE Goes to School.* New York.

*CARE. *Fact Sheet—1966–67.* New York.

*CARE. *Food Crusade.* New York.

Church Service Organizations

Cantor, Sidney. Challenge: U.S. Food Industry and World Hunger. *Cereal Science II,* (6) 255, 1966.

*Publications on CARE from World CARE Headquarters, 660 First Avenue, New York, N.Y. 10016.

Dedicate Fresh-Water Distillery. *Christian Century*, 81: 1358, 1964.
Hutchens, Frank L. Japan Church World Service. *Christian Century*, 77: 1132, 1960.
Lauds Church Aid to the Hungry. *Christian Century*, 80: 262, 1963.
Myers, M. B. Church World Service Expands Its Nutrition Program. *Food for Freedom*, 36: 12, Feb. 1967.
Parker, E. C. Family Feeding in Taiwan. *Christian Century*, 78: 1293, 1961.
Share Your Surplus. *Christian Century*, 79: 1378, 1962.

Others

The Salvation Army Yearbook. London, England, 1967.
American National Red Cross. *Brief History of Nutrition Service*. Washington, D.C., 1947. Mimeograph, Nutrition Service, 1908–1954.
Interdepartmental Committee on Nutrition for National Defense. *Manual for Nutrition Surveys*. National Institutes of Health, Bethesda, Md., 1963.

General

Goodman, N. M. *International Health Organizations*. Blakiston Division, McGraw-Hill, New York, 1952.
Gortner, W. A. International Facets of USDA Research. *J. Amer. Diet. Assoc.*, 50: 279, 1967.
Jeliffe, D. B. *Child Nutrition in Developing Countries*. U.S. Dept. of H.E.W., P.H.S., U.S. Gov. Printing Office, Washington, D.C., 1968.
Natl. Inst. Allergy and Infectious Diseases. *The First Five Years of the United States-Japan Cooperative Medical Science Program 1965–1970*. U.S. Gov. Printing Office, Washington, D.C., 1971.
Pirie, N. W. Orthodox and Unorthodox Methods of Meeting World Food Needs. *Scientific Amer.*, 216: 27–34, 1967.

Protein-Rich Foods

Altschul, Aaron M. Food: Proteins for Humans. *Chem. & Eng. News*, 24: 68–81, Nov. 1969.
Bennett, I. L. Food and Population—An Overview. *World Review of Nutr. and Diet*, 11: 1–6, 1969.
Berg, Alan. Priority of Nutrition in National Development. *Nutr. Rev.*, 28: 109–204, 1970.
Berg, Alan and Robert Muscat. *Nutrition Program Planning—A Conceptual Approach*. International Conference On Nutrition, National Development and Planning, Oct. 1971. M.I.T., Cambridge, Mass.
Borlaug, Norman F. Evolve or Perish—The Challenge of Change. *War on Hunger—A Report from AID*, Vol. VI, No. 2, pp. 2–4, 17–18, Feb. 1972.
Borlaug, Norman F. Genetic Improvement of Crop Foods. *Nutr. Today*, Vol. 7, No. 1, pp. 20–21, 24–25, Jan./Feb. 1972.
Borlaug, Norman F. *The Green Revolution*. Peace and Humanity Lecture given by Dr. Borlaug on the occasion of his receiving the Nobel Peace Prize for 1970 and reprinted

by the kind permission of Dr. Borlaug and the Nobel Foundation 1970 in *Cajamus,* Newsletter of the Caribbean Food and Nutrition Institute, Vol. IV, No. 4, pp. 229–262, 1971.

Brown, Lester R. *Seeds of Change, the Green Revolution and Development in the 1970's.* Praeger Publishing Co., New York, 1970.

Boyko, H. Salt-Water Agriculture. *Scientific Amer.,* 216: 89–96, 1967.

Chalman, M. Nutritional Value of Fish Flour Supplement. *J. Amer. Diet. Assoc.,* 37: 234, 1960.

Commodities Fisheries Prospects for Developing Countries. *Ceres—FAO Review,* Vol. 4, No. 6, Nov.–Dec. 1971, p. 16.

Ethyl Corporation. *Food for America's Future.* McGraw-Hill, New York, 1960.

Fisheries Offer Wide Field For Campaign Projects. *Freedom From Hunger Campaign News.* July 1961, p. 4.

FAO. Fish—The Great Potential Food Supply. *World Food Problems,* No. 3, Rome, Italy, 1960.

FAO. *Report on an Expert Panel on Fish Meal and Fish Flour for Human Consumption.* Washington, D.C., Sept. 28–29, 1961, 1962.

Gray, W. D. *Microbial Protein of the Space Age-Developments in Industrial Microbiology,* Vol. 3. Plenium Press, New York, 1962.

Green Revolution Grows Greener—War On Hunger: A Report From AID. May 1972, pp. 10–11.

Holden, Constance. Fish Flour: Protein Supplement Has Yet to Fulfill Expectations. *Science,* 173: 410–412, 1971.

Howe, E. E., G. R. Jansen, and M. L. Anson. An Approach toward the Solution of the World Food Problem With Special Emphasis on Protein Supply. *Amer. J. Clin. Nutr.,* 20: 1134–1147, Oct. 1967.

Inter-Institutional Committee on Nutrition. *The Promises and Problems of the New Foods.* Report No. 3, 1971, University of Georgia, Athens, Ga.

Iowa State University Center for Agricultural and Economic Development. *Alternatives for Balancing World Food Production Needs.* Iowa State University Press, Ames, Iowa. 1967.

Jelliffe, D. B. and F. J. Bennett. *Cultural and Anthropological Factors in Infant and Maternal Nutrition.* Proceedings of Fifth International Congress of Nutrition, Fed. Proc. 20 (1, Part III): 185, 1961.

Sidwell, V. D., B. R. Stillings, and G. M. Knobl. The Fish Protein Concentrate Story. *Food Tech.,* 24: 880–882, 1970.

Stockwell, Edward G. *Population and People. Problems of American Society.* Quadrangle Press, Chicago, Ill., 1968.

United Nations Dept. of Economic and Social Affairs. *Strategy Statement on Action to Avert the Protein Crisis in Developing Countries.* UNIPUB, New York, 1971.

UNICEF News. *Improving A Miracle. Experts Study the Green Revolution.* UNICEF, New York, March, 1972.

U.S. Dept. of Interior. *Fish Protein Concentrate, Life Line of the Future.* Fish and Wild Life Service Bureau of Commercial Fisheries, Sept. 1962.

U.S. Office of Education. *A Study of Methods of Changing Food Habits of Rural Children in Dakota County, Minnesota.* Nutr. Educ. Ser. Pamphlet No. 5, 1944.

Appendices

Appendices

APPENDIX 1
Teaching Hints

In teaching a course such as *Food and Man,* the following have proved helpful;

1. The use of films showing people of different cultures using food in their own ways.

2. Encouraging students to read novels, biographies, and books on travel, as well as cookbooks, which describe foods of particular cultural groups.

3. Adapting ideas and theories borrowed from the behavioral sciences to interpret food behavior to lead students to appreciate the integration of disciplines.

4. Placing reference books and materials in a special reading room near the classroom where the teacher may help students.

5. Allowing students to share the teacher's library gathered from around the world and constantly growing. This encourages students to collect their own libraries. A book table, with contributions from students and resident faculty auditors, demonstrates the interest aroused.

6. Assigning projects suited to the students' present or projected needs. This has proven a good method of judging the student's understanding of the material he has handled.

APPENDIX 2
Glossary

Aflatoxin   One of a group of closely related, highly toxic compounds produced by fungi of the *Aspergillus flavus* group, which grow on peanuts, grains, or beans in storage or in the field, in the presence of moisture.

Basal metabolism   The metabolic activity required to maintain the life processes of the body at complete rest. The basal metabolic rate is measured in calories.

Biological value of protein   A value which represents the amount of protein (nitrogen) which is absorbed and retained in the body for growth and maintenance.

Buddha   Indian philosopher, founder of Buddhism, 563–483 B.C.

Calorie   A unit of heat or energy. Specifically, it equals the amount of heat required to raise the temperature of 1 kilogram of water 1° C at 1 atmosphere pressure.

Colter   Cutter on a plough to cut the turf.

Cretinism   A disease in which there is a deficiency of thyroid secretion.

Demographic   Pertaining to the statistics of birth, deaths, and diseases.

Folic acid   One of the B vitamin group, necessary to prevent a type of anemia which affects the blood cells.

Glume   Either of two empty bracts at the base of the spikelet in grasses.

Haft   The handle of a weapon or tool.

Hydrogenated fat   Fat which has been made solid at room temperature by forcing hydrogen to combine with the unsaturated fatty acids.

Hypoglycemia   An abnormally low level of blood sugar.

Littoral   A coastal region.

Malabar   A western coastal region of India.

Malthus   An English economist, 1766–1834, who held that the population

434

increases faster than the means of support unless checked by famine, pestilence, and war. He proposed social and moral restraints.

Megaloblastic macrocytic anemia   A type of anemia characterized by immature, oversized red blood cells.

Mesopotamia   The ancient country between the Tigris and Euphrates rivers.

Miso soup   Japanese soup often used for breakfast.

Mozambique   A district in Northern Portuguese East Africa.

Niacin   One of the B vitamins which is necessary for prevention of pellagra.

Osteoporosis   A bone disease characterized by increased porosity and softness of bone because of loss of calcium.

Phoenicians   Natives of an ancient Semitic country north of Palestine and East of Syria. The country flourished from the sixteenth to the second century B.C. Its chief cities were Tyre and Sidan.

Pliny   A Roman scholar and naturalist, 23–79 A.D.

Plutarch   A Greek philosopher and biographer, about 46–120 A.D.

Radiograph   An X-ray picture.

Saracen   A member of the nomadic people living in the Syrian-Arabian deserts—an Arab, or any Moslem especially in the time of the Crusades.

Sorghum   A cereal plant also called Indian millet and milo.

Solstice   One of the two times a year midway between the two equinoxes when the sun is farthest from the equator, about the 21st of June or the 22nd of December.

Thiamin   One of the B vitamins, essential for the prevention of beriberi.

Totem   An animal, plant, or other object which serves as an emblem of a family, clan, tribe, or group.

Totemism   Belief in totems or totemic relationships; the use of totems as a system of control of social, marriage, and religious customs.

Urolithiasis   A condition marked by presence of urinary calculi (stones).

Yaws   An infectious disease of the tropics characterized by eruptions on the skin.

YWD   Young World Development.

APPENDIX 3
Textbooks on Nutrition

The reader wishing to obtain more information on basic nutrition can find reliable information in the following books:

Arlin, M. T. *The Science of Nutrition*. Macmillan, New York, 1972.

Bogert, L. J., G. M. Briggs, and D. H. Calloway. *Nutrition and Physical Fitness*, 9th Ed. W. B. Saunders, Philadelphia, Pa., 1973.

Chaney, M. S. and M. L. Ross. *Nutrition*, 8th Ed. Houghton-Mifflin, New York, Boston, 1972.

Fleck, H. *Introduction to Nutrition*, 2nd Ed. Macmillan, New York, 1971.

Gift, H. H., M. B. Washburn, and G. G. Harrison. *Nutrition, Behavior, and Change*. Prentice-Hall, Inc., Englewood Cliffs, N.J., 1972.

Guthrie, H. *Introductory Nutrition*, 2nd Ed. C. V. Mosby, St. Louis, Mo., 1971.

Martin, E. A. *Nutrition in Action*, 3rd Ed. Holt, Rinehart and Winston, New York, 1971.

Robinson, C. H. *Fundamentals of Normal Nutrition*. Macmillan, New York, 1973.

Taylor, C. M. and O. F. Pye. *Foundations of Nutrition*, 6th Ed. Macmillan, New York, 1966.

Wilson, E. D., K. H. Fisher, and M. E. Fuqua. *Principles of Nutrition*, 3rd Ed. John Wiley, New York, 1974.

For the advanced student:

Pike, R. and M. Brown. *Nutrition, An Integrated Approach*. John Wiley, New York, 1967.

436

APPENDIX 4
Books for
General Reference

Ainsworth-Davis, J. R. *Cooking through the Centuries*. E. P. Dutton, New York, 1931.

Allen, Steve. *The Ground is our Table*. Doubleday, Garden City, New York, 1966.

American Heritage Magazine. *American Heritage Cook Book*. Simon and Schuster, New York, 1962.

Aresty, E. B. *The Delectable Past*. Simon and Schuster, New York, 1964.

Aykroyd, W. R. *The Story of Sugar*. Quadrangle Books, Chicago, 1967.

Balsdon, J. P. V. D. *Life and Leisure in Ancient Rome*. McGraw-Hill, New York, 1969.

Baumgartel, Elsie. *Cultures of Prehistoric Egypt*. Oxford University Press, London, 1955–60.

Beal, George M., Joe M. Bohlen, and J. Neil Raudabaugh. *Leadership and Dynamic Group Action*. Iowa State University Press, Ames, Iowa, 1971.

Beck, P. *Clementine in the Kitchen*. Hastings House, New York, 1943.

Birch, Herbert G. and Joan Dye Gussow. *Disadvantaged Children. Health, Nutrition, and School Failure*. Harcourt, Brace and World, New York, 1970.

Bjere, Jens. *The Kalhari*. Hill and Wang, New York, 1961.

Black, John D. *Food Enough*. Science Press, Lancaster, Pa., 1943.

Booth, Sally Smith. *Hung, Strung and Potted. A History of Eating in Colonial America*. Clarkson and Potter, New York, 1971.

Borgstrom, George. *The Hunger Planet*. Collier Books, New York, 1967.

Bowles, Cynthia. *At Home in India*. Harcourt, Brace and Co., New York, 1956.

Brown, Lester B. *Seeds of Change—The Green Revolution and Development in the 1970's*. Praeger, New York, 1970.

Brown, Lester R. and Gail W. Finsterbusch. *Man and His Environment: Food*. Harper and Row, 1972.

Burgess, Anne and Dean, R. F. A., Eds. *Malnutrition and Food Habits.* Macmillan, New York, 1962.

Calder, Nigel. *Eden was No Garden.* Holt, Rinehart and Winston, New York, 1967.

Calder, Lord Ritchie. *A Starving World.* Macmillan, New York. 1962.

Children of the Developing Countries. A Report by UNICEF. The World Publishing Co., Cleveland, 1963.

Clair, C. *Kitchen and Table—A Bedside History of Eating in the Western World.* Abelard Schuman, New York, 1964.

Clark, Ella E. *Indian Legends of the Pacific Northwest.* University of California Press, Berkeley, Calif., 1963.

Coffin, R. P. T. *Mainstays of Maine.* Macmillan, New York, 1945.

Collis, Robert. *African Encounter: A Doctor in Nigeria.* Scribner's, New York, 1961.

Contours of Change. The Yearbook of Agriculture, U.S.D.A., Washington, D.C., 1970.

Cochrane, Willard. *The World Food Problem.* Thomas Y. Crowell Co., New York, 1969.

Cousins, Norman. *Dr. Schweitzer of Lambarene.* Harper and Brothers, New York, 1958.

Cummings, R. O. *The American and His Food.* Univ. of Chicago Press, Chicago, Ill., 1940.

Cussler, Margaret and DeGive, Mary L. *Twixt the Cup and the Lip.* Twayne Publishers, New York, 1952.

Davis, Hassoldt. *World Without a Roof—An Autobiography.* Duell, Sloan and Pearce, New York, 1957.

Delderfield, R. F. *God is An Englishman.* Pocket Books, New York, 1971.

Derosier, Norman W. *Attack on Starvation.* The Avi Publishing Co., Westport, Conn., 1961.

Dineson, Isak. *Out of Africa.* Random House, New York, 1952.

Dutton, Joan Perry. *The Good Fare and Cheer of Old England.* Reynal and Co., New York, 1960.

Ellwanger, G. H. *The Pleasures of the Table.* Doubleday, New York, 1962.

Farmers and a Hungry World. Published under the auspices of the Agriculture Committee of the Greater Des Moines Chamber of Commerce with the Cooperation of the Iowa State University Center for Agricultural and Economic Development. The Iowa State University Press, Ames, Iowa, 1967.

The First Ten Years of the World Health Organization. WHO, Geneva, Switzerland, 1958.

Fitch, Florence Mary. *One God. The Ways We Worship Him.* Lothrop, Lee and Shepard, New York, 1954.

Fitch, Florence Mary. *Their Search for God. Ways of Worship in the Orient.* Lothrop, Lee and Shepard, New York, 1953.

Food. One Tool in International Economic Development. Assembled and published under the sponsorship of the Iowa State University Center for Agriculture and Economic Adjustment. Iowa State University Press, Ames, Iowa, 1965.

Food and Fiber for the Future. Report of the National Advisory Commission on Food and Fiber. Superintendent of Documents, U.S. Government Printing Office, Washington, D.C., 1967.

Freeman, Orville L. *World without Hunger.* Praeger, New York, 1968.

Galbraith, John Kenneth. *The Liberal Hour.* The New American Library, New York, 1960.

Gatti, Ellen and Atilio. *The New Africa. A World Background Book.* Scribner's, New York, 1960.

Gibney, Frank. *Five Gentlemen of Japan.* Farrar, Straus and Young, New York, 1953.

Glass, David C., Ed. *Environmental Influences.* The Rockefeller University Press and Russell Sage Foundation, New York, 1968.

A Good Life for More People. The Yearbook of Agriculture, U.S.D.A., Washington, D.C., 1971.

Guy, C. *An Illustrated History of French Cuisine.* Orion Press, New York, 1962.

Gyorgy, Paul and Burgess, Ann, Eds. *Protecting the Pre-School Child. Programmes in Practice.* Lippincott, Philadelphia, Pa., 1965.

Hackwood, F. W. *Good Cheer. The Romance of Food and Feasting.* Sturgis and Walton, New York, 1911.

Hambidge, Gove. *The Story of FAO.* Van Nostrand, New York, 1955.

Hamsun K. *Hunger.* Duckworth, 1949. Farrar, Straus & Giroux, New York, 1967.

Harwood, J. and E. Callahan. *Soul Food Cookbook.* Nitty Gritty Pub., San Francisco, Calif., 1970.

Heyerdahl, Thor. *Kon-Tiki. Across the Pacific by Raft.* Rand McNally, Chicago, 1950.

Hickernell, Marguerite R. and Ella W. Brewer. *Adam's Herbs.* Herb Lore, New York, 1947.

Hoffman, Paul G. *World without Want.* Harper and Row, New York, 1962.

Holland, John Ed. *The Way It Is.* Harcourt, Brace and World, New York, 1969.

Iowa State University. *Alternatives for Balancing World Food Production Needs.* Iowa State University Press, Ames, Iowa, 1967.

Irving, Washington. *Old Christmas in Merrie England.* Peter Pauper Press, Mount Vernon, New York. No date given. Was originally a chapter in Irving's *Sketch Book.*

Jelliffe, D. B. *Infant Nutrition in the Sub-tropics and Tropics.* Who, Geneva, Switzerland, 1955.

Jelliffe, D. B. *Infant Nutrition in the Sub-tropics and Tropics,* 2nd Ed. WHO, Geneva, Switzerland, 1968.

Jelliffe, Derrick B. *Child Nutrition in Developing Countries.* U.S. Dept. H.E.W., Washington, D.C., 1968.

Kawasaki, Ichiro. *The Japanese Are Like That.* Charles E. Tuttle Co., Rutland, Vermont, 1960.

Keith, A. N. *Bare Feet in the Palace.* Atlantic, Little, Brown, Boston, 1955.

Kent, N. L. *Technology of Cereals—With Special Reference to Wheat.* Pergamon Press, New York, 1966.

Kimball, M. *The Martha Washington Cookbook.* Coward-McCann, New York, 1940.

Kimball, M. *Thomas Jefferson's Cookbook.* Garrett and Massie, Richmond, Va., 1941.

Kluckhohn, Clyde. *Mirror for Man.* Fawcett Publications, Greenwich, Conn., 1964.

Kotz, Nick. *Let Them Eat Promises. The Politics of Hunger in America.* Prentice-Hall, Englewood Cliffs, New Jersey, 1969.

Laver, James. *The Age of Optimism. Manners and Morals 1848–1914.* Weidenfeld and Nicholson, London, 1966.

Lamprey, L. *The Story of Cookery.* F. A. Stokes, New York, 1940.

Lebner, E. and J. Lebner. *Folklore and Odysseys of Food and Medicinal Plants.* Tudor, New York, 1962.

Lin, Yu-Tang. *My Country and My People.* Reynal-Hitchcock, New York, 1937.

Lucas, J. M. *Fruits of the Earth.* Lippincott, Philadelphia, Pa., 1942.

Lutes, D. *The Country Kitchen.* Little, Brown, Boston, 1941.

Mariani, Fosco. *Meeting with Japan.* Viking Press, New York, 1960.

May, Jacque. *The Ecology of Malnutrition in the Far and Middle East.* Hafner Publishing Co., New York, 1963.

May, Jacque. *The Ecology of Malnutrition in the Five Countries of Eastern and Central Europe.* Hafner Publishing Co., New York, 1963.

May, Jacque. *The Ecology of Malnutrition in Middle Africa.* Hafner Publishing Co., 1965.

May, Jacque. *The Ecology of Malnutrition in Central and Southeast Europe.* Hafner Publishing Co., New York, 1966.

May, Jacque. *The Ecology of Malnutrition in West Africa and Madagascar.* Hafner Publishing Co., New York, 1968.

Mayer, Albert. *Pilot Project, India. The Story of Rural Development at Etawah, Uttar Pradesh.* University of California Press, Berkeley, Calif., 1958

McBride, M. M. *Harvest of American Cooking.* Putnam, New York, 1956.

Mead, Margaret, Ed. *Cultural Patterns and Technical Change.* A Manual prepared by the World Federation for Mental Health, United Nations, 1953.

Mellen, Kathleen Dickenson. *In a Hawaiian Valley.* Hastings House, New York, 1947.

Mendes, Helen. *The African Heritage Cookbook.* Macmillan, New York, 1971.

Michener, James A. *Hawaii.* Random House, New York, 1959, p 834.

Miller, J. *Camel Bells of Baghdad*. Houghton-Mifflin, Boston, Mass., 1934.

Montagu, Ashley. *Man: His First Two Million Years. A Brief Introduction to Anthropology*. Dell, New York, 1970, p 262.

Najafi, Najmeh and Helen Hickley. *Reveille for a Persian Village*. Harper and Bros., New York, 1958.

Nichols, N. B. *Good Home Cooking Across U.S.A.* Iowa State College Press, Ames, Iowa, 1952.

Norbu, T. and H. Heinrich. *Tibet Is My Country*. E. P. Dutton, New York, 1961.

O'Brien, M. M. *The Bible Cookbook*. Collier Books, New York, 1961.

Orr, John Boyd. *Food, Health and Income. Report on a Survey of Adequacy of Diet in Relation to Income*. Macmillan, London, England, 1936.

Orr, John Boyd and David Lubbock, *The White Man's Dilema*, Unwin Books, Allen and Unwin, London, and Noble Inc., New York, 1965.

Osborn, Fairfield. *Our Plundered Planet*. Little, Brown, Boston, Mass., 1948.

Paddleford, C. *How America Eats*. Scribner's, New York, 1960.

Paton, Alan. *The Land and People of South Africa*. Lippincott, Philadelphia, Pa., 1955.

Pike, Magnus. *Man and Food*. McGraw-Hill, New York, 1970

Pirie, N. W. *Food Resources Conventional and Novel*. Penguin Books, Baltimore, Md., 1969.

Power to Produce. The Yearbook of Agriculture, U.S. Department of Agriculture, 1960.

Prentice, E. Parmalee. *Hunger and History. The Influence of Hunger on Human History*. Caxton Printers, Caldwell, Idaho, 1951.

Pre-School Child Malnutrition. Primary Deterrent to Human Progress. National Academy of Sciences, National Research Council, Washington, D.C., 1966.

Progress in Meeting Protein Needs of Infants and Pre-School Children. Publication No. 843, National Academy of Sciences, National Research Council, Washington, D.C., 1961.

Repplier, A. *To Think of Tea*. Houghton-Mifflin, Boston, Mass., 1932.

Richards, Audrey I. *Hunger and Work in a Savage Tribe*. World, Cleveland, Ohio, 1964.

Sardi, V. and R. Gehman. *Sardi's—The Story of a Famous Restaurant*. Henry Holt, New York, 1953.

Schultz, Theodore W. *Food for the World*. University of Chicago, Chicago, Ill., 1945.

Schweitzer, Albert. *More from the Primeval Forest*. Fontana Books, Great Britain, 1958.

Scrimshaw, Nevin S. and John E. Gordon, Eds. *Malnutrition, Learning and Behavior*. M.I.T. Press, Cambridge, Mass., 1968.

Shotwell, Louisa R. *The Harvesters: The Story of the Migrant People*. Doubleday, Garden City, New York, 1961.

Simon, A. *Food—The History of Agriculture*. Horizon Press, New York, 1953.

Simoons, F. J. *Eat Not This Flesh*. Univ. of Wisconsin Press, Madison, Wisc., 1960.

Simpson, Colin. *Japan—An Intimate View*. A. S. Barnes, New York, 1959.

Smallzried, K. *The Everlasting Pleasure*. Appleton-Century-Crofts, New York, 1956.

So Bold an Aim. FAO, Quebec, Canada, 1945, Rome, Italy, 1955.

Spargo, John. *Bitter Cry of the Children*. Original Edition 1906. Reprinted by Quadrangle Press Paperbacks, Chicago, Ill., 1968.

Stakman, E. C., Richard Bradfield, and Paul C. Mangelsdorf. *Campaigns against Hunger*. The Belknap Press of Harvard University Press, Cambridge, Mass., 1967.

Stevens, James. *Paul Bunyan*. New York, 1925 and 1947.

Stockwell, Edward G. *Population and People*. Quadrangle Books, Chicago, Ill., 1968.

Swift, Louis F. *The Yankee of the Yards*. A. W. Shaw, Chicago, Ill., 1927.

Thomas, Gertrude I. *Food of Our Forefathers*. F. A. Davis, Philadelphia, Pa., 1941.

Trager, James. *Foodbook*. Grossman Publishers, New York, 1970.

Van der Post, Laurens. *The Lost World of the Kalahari*. William Morrow, New York, 1958.

Verrill, A. H. *Foods America Gave the World*. L. C. Page, Boston, Mass., 1937.

The Village People. *Anchorage Daily News*, 1966.

Von Tempski, Armine. *Born in Paradise*. Duell, Sloan and Pearce, New York, 1940.

Walden, Howard. *Native Inheritance. The Story of Corn in America*. Harper and Row, New York, 1966.

Ward, Barbara. *The Rich Nations and the Poor Nations*. Norton, New York, 1962.

Wason, B. *Cooks, Gluttons and Gourmets*. Doubleday, New York, 1962.

Wells, Evelyn. *Champagne Days of San Francisco*. Doubleday, New York, 1947.

Wells, Evelyn. *A City for Saint Francis*. Doubleday, New York, 1967.

Williams, Robert R. *Williams-Waterman Fund for the Combat of Dietary Diseases. A History of the Period 1935 through 1955*. Research Corporation, New York, 1956.

Wiser, William H. and Charlotte Viall Wiser. *Behind Mud Walls*. Agricultural Missions, New York, 1951.

Wittenberg, M., and E. C. Hamke. *The Lifeline of America-Development of the Food Industry*. McGraw-Hill, New York, 1964.

Wolf, L. *The Literary Gourmet*. Random House, New York, 1962.

Woodham-Smith, Cecil. *The Great Hunger*. Harper and Row, New York, 1962.

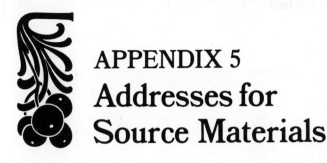

APPENDIX 5
Addresses for
Source Materials

Readers who wish further information on some of the programs for improvement of nutrition may write to the following:

AID Publications

1. Office of Nutrition
    Technical Assistance Bureau
    AID, U.S., State Dept.
    Washington, D.C. 20523

2. Periodicals and Special Publications
    Division, Office of Public Affairs
    AID, Room 4953
    State Dept. Building
    Washington, D.C. 20523

CARE
World CARE Headquarters
660 First Ave.
New York, N.Y. 10016

Food and Agriculture Organization of the U. N.
Liaison Office for North America
1325 C St. S.W.
Washington, D.C. 20437

Food and Nutrition Board
National Academy of Sciences/National Research Council

2101 Constitution Ave.
Washington, D.C. 20418

Freedom from Hunger Foundation
1917 H St. N.W.
Washington, D.C. 20006

League for International Food Education
1155 Sixteenth St. N.W.
Washington, D.C. 20036

UNICEF
UNIPUB Inc.
P.O. Box 443
New York, N.Y. 10016

Young World Development
1717 H St. N.W.
Washington, D.C. 20006

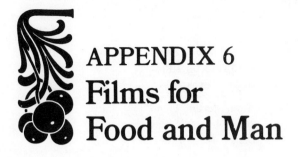

APPENDIX 6
Films for
Food and Man

Films for Food and Man arranged in order of times mentioned in the Survey.

Name of Film	Address	Year
Hungry Angels	Assn. Films 561 Hillgrove Avenue La Grange, Ill. 60525	1958
Hunger in America	A. V. Center Indiana University Bloomington, Ind.	1969
Four Families	McGraw-Hill	1960
Food for Life	Universities Film Libraries	
The Hunters	Contemporary Films 267 West 25th New York, N.Y. 10001	1958
People to People	Center for Disease Control Atlanta, Ga. 30333	1959
Puritan Family in *New England*	Coronet 65 E. South Water St. Chicago, Ill. 60601	1955
Food or Famine	FAO Shell Film Library 450 N. Meridian St. Indianapolis, Ind. 46204	1962

Name of Film	Address	Year
Children of the Sun	Assn. Sterling Films 8615 Director's Row Dallas, Texas 75247	1962
Child of Darkness, Child of Light	Assn. Sterling Films 8615 Director's Row Dallas, Texas 75247	
Nutrition Survey— Kingdom of Thailand	U.S. Govt. Film Services 245 West 55th St. New York, N.Y. 10019	
Tomorrow Food Feeding Billions	Contemporary Films 267 W. 25th St. New York, N.Y. 10001	
Kwashiorkor (made in Nigeria)	Penn State University University Park, Pa. 16802	1960
Invite the Far Eastern World into Your Kitchen	Corning Glass Works Corning, N.Y.	1968
The Food Crisis	New Production Univ. of Indiana Bloomington, Ind.	1966
Who Shall Reap	U.S.D.A. Washington, D.C.	1969–70
Tomorrow's Food Feeding Billions	Cont. Films, McGraw Hill 327 W. 41st St. New York, N.Y. 10036	
Global Struggle for Food	McGraw-Hill 327 W. 41st St. New York, N.Y. 10036	1960
A Simple Cup of Tea	AID Dept of State Washington, D.C. 20523	
The First Priorities	UN—Nat. Educ. TV & Radio 10 Columbus Circle, New York, N.Y.	
Three Times a Day	Sterling Films 600 Madison Ave. New York, N.Y. 10002	1970

Name of Film	Address	Year
Food for People	Ency. Brit. Educ. Corp. 1822 Pickwick Ave. Glenview, Ill.	
Remnants of A Race	Ency. Brit. Educ. Corp. 1822 Pickwick Ave. Glenview, Ill.	

UNITED NATIONS AND UNICEF FILMS

A NEW-FASHIONED HALLOWEEN. UNICEF. 20 mins.

ASSIGNMENT CHILDREN. UNICEF. 20 mins.

CHILDREN OF AFRICA. UNICEF. 14 mins.

CHILDREN OF ASIA. UNICEF. 15 mins.

CHILDREN OF THE SUN. UNICEF. 10 mins.

FOOD FOR THOUGHT. UNICEF. 17 mins.

KANTATISKIWA-DAWN OF A NEW DAY. UNICEF. 14 mins.

THE CHILDREN'S FOUNTAIN. UNICEF. 13½ mins.

UNICEF'S CHILDREN. UNICEF. 8½ mins.

WE ARE ONE. UNICEF. 15 mins.

WHEN A MAN HUNGERS. UNICEF. 28 mins.

A FEW NOTES ON OUR FOOD PROBLEM. U.S. Information Agency. Order from: Voters, 1730 M St. N.W., Washington, D.C.

THE LAND MUST PROVIDE. FAO. Order from: Shell Film Library, 450 N. Meridian St., Indianapolis, Ind.

Index

449

Index

459

Index
459

U.S. Dept. of Agriculture (continued)
Interagency Committee on Nutrition
Education, 398
Utensils for eating and drinking,
Early Americans, of, 96
first American fork, 86
Greek, 33
medieval Europe, 59
New England, 86
salt cellars, 86
trenchers, 86

Vavilov, 18, 19
Vayda, 8, 15
Vedder, E. B., 311
Villages, units of early agricultural
community, 23, 50, 51
Vitamins, discovery of, 183
A, 184
B, 184
B12, 185
C, 178, 184
D, 184, 303
E, 184
Voluntary agency programs, 405, 412
Von Stiegel, Baron, 86

Walden, H. T., 77
Walsh, J., 289
Wason, B., 53
Wasson, C. R., 254
Waterbalk, H. T., 23, 24
Wechsberg, J., 36
Western Hemisphere health programs,
385–411
Wharton, T., 316

Wheat, 13, 39
White, C., 251
White, L., 3
Wild emmers, 13
Wiley, Harvey, 98
Willerman, B., 128, 129
Williams, C., 322
Williams, R. R., 185, 311
Wines, of Greeks, 35
World Health Organization (WHO),
373–381
definition of health, 376
history, 373–379
nutrition program, 376–380
six regions of world, 373
WHO/FAO expert committee on nutrition,
377
Women in agriculture, 10
food preparation by Greek women, 33
at Roman meals, 43
Wood, Jethro, 85
Woodward, Henry, 83
World Food Program, 356
World Plan for Agricultural
Development, 357
Wyler, R., 15

Xeropthalmia, 191, 301

Yates, P. L., 356
Young, Charlotte, 123
Young World Appeal, 361
Young World Development (YWD), 361

Zeuner, F. E., 16

OI